BEAUTY IMAGINED

BEAUTY IMAGINED
A History of the Global Beauty Industry

GEOFFREY JONES

OXFORD
UNIVERSITY PRESS

OXFORD
UNIVERSITY PRESS

Great Clarendon Street, Oxford OX2 6DP

Oxford University Press is a department of the University of Oxford.
It furthers the University's objective of excellence in research, scholarship,
and education by publishing worldwide in

Oxford New York

Auckland Cape Town Dar es Salaam Hong Kong Karachi
Kuala Lumpur Madrid Melbourne Mexico City Nairobi
New Delhi Shanghai Taipei Toronto

With offices in

Argentina Austria Brazil Chile Czech Republic France Greece
Guatemala Hungary Italy Japan Poland Portugal Singapore
South Korea Switzerland Thailand Turkey Ukraine Vietnam

Oxford is a registered trade mark of Oxford University Press
in the UK and in certain other countries

Published in the United States
by Oxford University Press Inc., New York

© Geoffrey Jones 2010

The moral rights of the author have been asserted
Database right Oxford University Press (maker)

First published 2010

All rights reserved. No part of this publication may be reproduced,
stored in a retrieval system, or transmitted, in any form or by any means,
without the prior permission in writing of Oxford University Press,
or as expressly permitted by law, or under terms agreed with the appropriate
reprographics rights organization. Enquiries concerning reproduction
outside the scope of the above should be sent to the Rights Department,
Oxford University Press, at the address above

You must not circulate this book in any other binding or cover
and you must impose the same condition on any acquirer

British Library Cataloguing in Publication Data
Data available

Library of Congress Cataloging in Publication Data
Library of Congress Control Number 2009939945

Typeset by SPI Publisher Services, Pondicherry, India
Printed in Great Britain
on acid-free paper by
Clays Ltd., St Ives plc

ISBN 978-0-19-955649-6

Permission Acknowledgements

Grateful acknowledgement is made to the following individuals, firms and archives for permission to use the following illustrations:

Advertising Archive for Plates 11 and 25.

Baker Library Historical Collections, Harvard Business School, for Plate 10.

Beiersdorf for Figs 2.1, 2.2, and 4.5 and Plate 15.

Centre for Business History, Stockholm, and Henkel for Plate 9.

Club Cosmetics for Plate 12.

Coty for Figs 1.1, 1.2, and 7.1, and Plates 7, 8, and 29.

Yves de Chiris for Plate 2.

Bertrand Estrangin and Nicole Cherpitel for Plate 4.

Jo Freeman for Fig. 8.3.

Hagley Museum for Fig. 8.2 and Plates 19 and 24.

Henkel for Plate 5.

Hindustan Lever for Fig. 6.2.

Robert Isear's heirs, and the Schlesinger Library at the Radcliffe Institute, Harvard University for Fig. 5.1.

Jünger & Gebhardt for Plate 3.

London Institute of Fashion for Figs 4.6 and 5.4.

Natura for Fig. 9.2.

Miriam and Ira D. Wallach Division of Art, Prints and Photographs, New York Public Library, Astor, Lenox and Tilden Foundations for Plate 1.

Georg Oddner's and Knut Wulff's heirs, and Malmö Museer and Skånes Näringslivsarkiv for Plate 21.

L'Oréal for Figs 4.3, 5.2, 6.1, and 8.1 and Plates 6, 14, 20, 26, 27, and 32.

Pola Research Institute of Beauty and Culture for Fig. 2.3.

Procter & Gamble for Fig. 9.1 and Plates 13, 16, 17, 22, and 28.

Revlon for Plates 18 and 25.

Shiseido for Plates 23 and 31.

Sixten Sandgren for Fig. 5.3.

Stiftung Rheinisch-Westfälisches Wirtschaftsarchiv for Fig. 1.3.

Unilever plc for Figs 3.1, 4.1, 4.2, and 4.4, and Plate 30.

Preface

This book is about the history of the global beauty business. Beauty holds a fascination for all of us. Artists, philosophers, scientists, clerics, economists, and many others have long debated its nature and implications. It has been less studied as a business, and for good reason. Although the industry is now enormous, its origins lay in numerous small firms which have left a legacy of colorful myths but fewer records and hard facts. In part, this was intentional, for beauty is an industry built around mystique, whose secrets are closely guarded. Despite the imperfections in this study, I hope that it has made a contribution to highlighting the beauty industry's importance and significance in all our lives, as well as its fascinating history full of men and women larger than life.

In seeking to write a global history of the beauty industry, I have relied on the work and dedication of research associates based both at the Boston campus of the Harvard Business School and the School's Global Research Centers around the world. In Boston, Joyce Chi, Meghan Gallagher-Kernstine, and Lexy Lefort made important contributions to the research. I benefited greatly from working with David Kiron on HBS cases on L'Oréal and Coty, Akiko Kanno on Shiseido, and Ricardo Reisen de Pinho on Natura.

I would like to acknowledge in particular the remarkable contribution of Oona Ceder, the research associate on the project for the last three years. Oona drew on her own distinguished background in political science to join me in unraveling the history of the beauty industry. She undertook field research in France, Germany, Sweden, and the United Kingdom, as well as the United States. She assumed the responsibility of locating photographs and negotiating permissions. She read draft chapters and commented on them, selflessly and with deep insight. This book would not exist without her.

The research for this book was also greatly aided by the many companies who opened their archives, and whose executives agreed to be interviewed.

I would like to thank in particular Beiersdorf, Club Cosmetics, Coty, Gillette, Henkel, Korres, L'Oréal, Natura, Oriflame, Pola, Procter & Gamble, Shiseido, Unilever, and Wella. The list of people in these companies who assisted the research is too long to mention, but I would like to acknowledge in particular Jean-Paul Agon, Bernd Beetz, Wolfgang Bügel, Helge Burkhardt, Cysette Burset, Antonio Luiz da Cunha Seabra, Thorsten Finke, Beate Fischer, Daniela Giacchetti, Julie Handorff, Peter Harf, Stephanie Hélin, Christian Hillen, Kevin Janeczko, Robert af Jochnick, George Korres, Lena Philippou Korres, Guilherme Leal, Marie-Aude Torres Maguedano, Aaron Owen, Lesley Owen-Edwards, Ed Rider, Horst Rühle, Martine Smadja, Ruth Sutcliffe, Satoshi Suzuki, Noriyo Tsuda, the late Shu Uemura, and Thomas Wölk.

Many others, including academics, researchers, and librarians, have contributed to the book. I should especially like to thank Gunnar Ahlström, Katherine Baird, Maria Ines Barbero, Eugénie Briot, Lynn Catanese, Olivier Cottarel, Vincent Dessain, Lynn Eaton, Masako Egawa, Suzanne Fisher, Patrick Fridenson, Walter Friedman, Gelina Harlaftis, Gustavo Herrero, Christian Hillen, Arne Högberg, Alexander Husebye, Nancy Koehn, Manuela Kuhl, Jean Laudereau, Celeste Lee, Laura Linard, Andrea Lluch, Carol Lockman, Marjorie McNinch, Wolfgang Metternich, Walter Molsberger, Bernard Nicholson, Roger Nougaret, Susie Pak, Núria Puig, Margaret Rose, Sixten Sandgren, Satoshi Sasaki, Evridiki Sifneos, Christian Stadler, Richard S. Tedlow, Erwin Weishäupl, and Mayuka Yamazaki. I appreciated feedback from the participants of seminars at Copenhagen Business School, Harvard Business School, the Department of Economic Sciences, University of Athens, the Economic History Workshop at UCLA, and various annual meetings of the Association of Business Historians, the European Business History Association, and the Business History Conference.

I would like to give a special note of thanks to Tom McCraw, David Merrett, Tom Nicholas, and Véronique Pouillard. They read a draft of the manuscript at a critical stage in its development during the fall of 2008. In addition to pointing out many errors of fact and interpretation, they helped me to see the wood from the trees. They bear no responsibility for this final version of the book, but without their intervention it may never have been finished. The manuscript also benefited enormously from the superb editing of Jeff Strabone, and from the guidance and patience of my editors at Oxford University Press, Matthew Derbyshire and David Musson.

The research for this book was generously funded by the Division of Research at the Harvard Business School year after year, to whom I am extremely grateful. Many ideas were tested and honed in the School's classrooms, and I am grateful for successive MBA sections for engaging in debates on beauty.

Finally, I owe a big debt of thanks to Dylan and Rattana for their patience and support. They had to live with the writing of this book for far too long.

Geoffrey Jones
Harvard Business School

Contents

CONTENTS

List of Illustrations

List of Plates

Introduction

The Business of Beauty

Beauty, what a wonderful and dangerous word!
Luiz Seabra, founder of Natura, Brazil's largest beauty company[1]

The beauty business began modestly with the sale of products widely deemed an affront to public morality. Today, consumers around the world spend $330 billion a year on fragrances, cosmetics, and toiletries.[2] The industry's transformation from humble moral nuisance to a global brand-driven powerhouse offering products essential to daily life is one of the more intriguing stories in modern business history. The origins of beauty products lie primarily in local knowledge of the scents and healing properties of plants, flowers, and herbs, whose uses were bound by age-old religious and cultural beliefs. Yet somehow these delicate flora became the foundation of a global industry made strong by a century of virtually uninterrupted growth that not even economic meltdowns and world wars have been able to stop.

While the scale of the industry is impressive, its existence also raises many questions. What are consumers really buying when they buy a perfume, or face cream, or lipstick? Scents which last a few hours or face creams that can't be seen once applied are neither straightforwardly utilitarian products, like food or computers, nor status-symbol luxuries, like expensive watches or designer jeans. Why do consumers pay so much for products whose ingredients are well known to represent only a small proportion of the retail price? Beauty is certainly, as one recent study showed, one of America's most profitable industries, just behind pharmaceuticals and software, and far above the average of all industries.[3]

Many apparent paradoxes add to the puzzle posed by the industry. While rarely considered fundamentally "bad," such as the trade in narcotics or tobacco, the beauty industry has attracted a legion of both critics and cynics over the years. The importance of women as consumers, in particular, has led to a long-standing critique of the industry as an instrument for the oppression of women by men (and their corporations). Feminist writers have regularly blamed its advertising campaigns for encouraging an obsession with physical perfection that traps women in an endless spiral of hope, self-consciousness, and self-hatred.[4] Yet beauty is also an industry in which women have been unusually prominent as entrepreneurs and business leaders. The list of triumphant women is striking in view of their under-representation in so much of business.

The paradoxes do not end here. The beauty industry has always been obsessed with the latest fashions. The coolest celebrities feature as spokes-people to the world for the leading brands. Advertisements proudly highlight the latest technological breakthroughs designed to firm, uplift, and hydrate skin, reverse the signs of aging, and make hair shine as never before. Yet the hype surrounding the newest fashions and technologies co-exists with profound respect for the past. Leading brands carry the names of people who lived one hundred or even two hundred years ago. Some iconic brands first made their appearance a century ago.

There are puzzles, too, concerning the geography of beauty. Many of the world's leading brands identify themselves with two cities, Paris and New York, and two countries, France and the United States. Even brands owned by companies which are neither French nor American lay claim to these countries and cities. The most expensive skin cream line sold by Shiseido, the largest Japanese maker of cosmetics, is called Clé de Peau Beauté. A one-ounce jar of Clé de Peau Beauté La Crème, a night cream, will cost an American consumer at least $500. What has made Paris and New York such symbols of beauty? What makes their inhabitants and streets acclaimed as beautiful so much more often that those of Milan or London, Shanghai or Los Angeles, Rio de Janeiro or Buenos Aires?

The globalization of today's beauty industry itself is not without its para-doxes either. It is both astonishing in its scale, and puzzling in its apparent limitations. It is remarkable how an industry which had its roots in people making creams in their kitchens, or small pharmacies making concoctions for their customers, could become so international. Today the ten biggest companies collectively account for over one-half of sales throughout the world. The two biggest companies, L'Oréal and Procter & Gamble (P & G), now account for over one-fifth of total world sales alone. They own mega-brands which span the globe. Avon, the world's biggest beauty brand, was worth $11.3 billion in 2008. Unilever's Dove and P & G's Pantene, in second and third place, had sales of $5.3 billion and $4.5 billion respectively.[5]

The global spread of such mega-brands provides compelling evidence about how fast brands, fashions, and trends cross borders in the twenty-first century. A mere three decades ago there were virtually no cosmetics in China. The Communist regime of Mao Zedong regarded their use as abhorrent symbols of "bourgeois decadence." Today China is the world's fourth largest market for beauty products. The consumers in the $17.7 billion Chinese beauty market are as interested in the latest trends, such as the use of minerals in make-up, as their Western peers.

Yet in other ways it is the persistence of local differences, not the homogenization of global preferences, which is most striking. While absolute spending on beauty products almost invariably rises with a country's wealth, countries differ markedly in their propensity to buy beauty products. Among the world's richest countries, consumers in France and Japan spend over $230 per capita annually on beauty products, whilst Americans and the Germans spent $173 and $164 respectively. Among the largest emerging markets, Brazilian per capita spending was almost $100, whilst Indian spending was less than $4.[6]

Equally striking are the wide variations between countries in types of products consumed. Europeans spend, proportionately, far more on fragrances and skin care than Americans, who in turn spend far more on color cosmetics than Europeans. The Asia-Pacific region is a modest market for fragrance, accounting for only 6 per cent of the world fragrance market, but represents an impressive 40 per cent share of the skin care market. While in the United States the make-up market is twice the size of the skin care market, in China the skin care market is four times the size of the make-up market. The huge Asian skin care market is unique, moreover, because skin-lightening products form a significant proportion of the sales of the more expensive skin care brands.

Moreover, although leading brands might be global, their appeal is not. In fragrances, every market's list of its top 20 brands is unique. The top-selling fragrance in Germany, for instance, does not even appear on the lists for France and the United States.[7] Only one brand, Chanel N°5, now over 80 years old, holds strong market positions across the world. People in different

3

countries like quite different scents. In the words of one executive, "American women tend to prefer fresh, clean perfumes, whereas European women tend to prefer heavier, more complex scents, both of which contrast with the Asian preference for light scents."[8] For an industry which looks global, it has some decidedly local characteristics.

Principal themes

This book recovers the history of a business that we typically take for granted but whose global growth tells us a lot about the modern world. Based on unprecedented access to the historical archives of companies, and interviews with leading figures in the industry today, it describes the people and the firms that have built the industry since the nineteenth century. It explores how they have contributed to what today we consider to be beautiful.

The book approaches the history of the industry through three lenses. The first lens is that of the entrepreneurs who built the industry. The fact that our story gets under way in the nineteenth century is not meant to imply that these entrepreneurs were the creators of cosmetics and fragrances as such. On the contrary, the ancient Egyptians, Greeks and Romans, the medieval Chinese, Arabs and Europeans, and virtually every other pre-industrial society used products designed to help people look attractive and alter their scent. Few, if any, of the products marketed by today's industry can be regarded as truly new conceptually, even if their composition and presentation are of more recent origin.[9]

The age-old usage of beauty products is known to have been intimately associated with both prevailing medical knowledge and religious devotion. Both sensuous and mysterious, fragrances have long been central to religious ceremonies, as well as to healing and well-being. Many have also argued that, on a deeper level, human use of cosmetic artifices has rested on biological imperatives to attract and to reproduce. The argument that the search for ways to seem beautiful is based on the need to reproduce goes back to the theory of sexual selection first proposed by Charles Darwin, who included a section on "Beauty" in The Descent of Man, first published in 1871.[10] The biological significance of appearance and smell has since found support in scientific experiments. Certain features often considered attractive in women, such as clear skin and lustrous hair, signal fecundity.[11] The sense of smell has been shown to affect partner selection, especially by providing signals about immune systems, moods, and general health.[12] Debates continue in multiple disciplines as to how strong a role such biological signs play in romance and reproduction.[13]

The entrepreneurs featured in this book, then, were less responsible for creating humans' desire to use artificial means to enhance their attractiveness than they were for translating such perennial desires into brands, factory production, and ultimately, multinational enterprises. The following chapters will explore their origins and motivations, and will explain how they made their local products global. This book represents, then, a contribution to the history of entrepreneurship. Since the time of Joseph Schumpeter, the importance of entrepreneurs in driving change within industries and markets, and generating the "creative destruction" which Schumpeter saw as central to capitalism, has been recognized.[14] However, the search for generalizations concerning the "inherently subtle and elusive character" of entrepreneurship, as one economist described it, has also proved challenging.[15] Entrepreneurial cognition, or how entrepreneurs perceive opportunities, remains poorly understood.[16] This book will explore, in particular, whether common characteristics can be discerned in the entrepreneurs who succeeded in this industry, and how they identified opportunities.

In contrast to the subject of entrepreneurship, the growth of big business, the drivers of corporate performance, and the expansion of firms over borders to become multinationals are the staples of modern business history, as developed by Alfred D. Chandler. Chandler explored how firms which were prepared to build their "organizational capabilities" by making a three-pronged investment in production, distribution, and management could become first-movers in their industries, and retain that position provided they regularly refreshed their capabilities.[17] One limitation of this approach, for our purposes, is its focus on capital-intensive, mass marketing and mass production industries, leaving it with little to say about the peculiarities of industries like fashion and beauty, in which there were large numbers of small and medium-sized entrepreneurial firms, and creativity, rather than managerial hierarchies and administrative routines, was at a premium. This book, at its most general level, hopes to bridge the gap between more traditional business history methodologies and the non-traditional features of such creative industries. These industries have also not featured widely in the literature on the history of multinationals, although the work of Mira

Wilkins and others provides the essential background for understanding how global business has evolved.[18]

The second lens employed in this book concerns the construction of the market for beauty. The chapters which follow will seek to establish how beauty was conceived, and translated into brands, by these firms. This question is a major one, for whatever the evidence that certain geometric features of a face appear to be regarded as attractive in all cultures,[19] it is demonstrably the case that, over the broad sweep of history, ideals of beauty and hygiene have been highly variable. Societies have differed enormously concerning their ideals of beauty. This variation reflects humanity's inherited differences in skin tone and hair textures, fashions and clothes, and religious and behavioral norms, as well as the effect of different diets, climates, and availability of natural ingredients. Preferences for hairstyles (or no hair at all), facial appearance, scent, and washing with water have all fluctuated over the ages. In the West, at least, male conceptions of the ideal female body size have also varied considerably over the centuries, although in China a persistent emphasis on thinness is apparent.[20]

Gender makes a difference, too. While the woman became the major consumer of beauty products as we know them today, this was not the case in many past societies. The paradigms of beauty in ancient Greece were primarily male. Both genders in that society used perfumes, even though women applied perfume oils to their skin and hair, whilst men preferred bathing in perfume oil.[21] Both the men and women of ancient Rome dyed their hair extensively.[22] The use of the same fragrances by both sexes was common in Islamic, Indian, and European history as well.

It was evident to observers in the nineteenth century, as improvements in transport and communications made cultural contacts more frequent, that ideals of beauty varied enormously between cultures and geographies. An article in the leading scientific journal *Scientific American*, entitled "Facts for the Curious—Female Beauty," published in 1851, observed:

> The ladies of Arabia stain their fingers and toes red, their eye-brows black and their lips blue...The Japanese women gild their teeth, and those of the Indies paint them red...Hindoo females, when they wish to appear particularly lovely, smear themselves with a mixture of saffron, turmeric and grease.... The modern Persians have a strong aversion to red hair; the Turks, on the

contrary, are warm admirers of it. In China small round eyes are liked; and the girls are continuously plucking their eye brows, that they may be thin and long.[23]

Two decades later Charles Darwin confidently asserted in *The Descent of Man*, "it is certainly not true that there is in the mind of man any universal standard of beauty with respect to the human body."[24]

Thus there was nothing "inevitable" about the beauty ideals conceived by the nineteenth-century pioneers of the modern industry. The fact that beauty came to be associated with Paris and New York was also a matter of historical contingency, not necessity. This book, by exploring how beauty ideals have been chosen and encapsulated in brands, contributes to an emergent literature which has drawn on both business and fashion history. In particular, Regina Blaszczyk has shown how, in the American mass consumer market for household furnishings, many small producers relied upon what she termed "fashion intermediaries" such as magazine editors and retail buyers to understand what consumers wanted to buy. In this model, businesses did not so much impose their wishes on consumers as try to understand what consumers wanted.[25] These insights have implications for the beauty industry, but the industry is also rather different from glassware or pottery because it is concerned with the beauty of the consumer herself, not the objects in her house.

The industry's construction and dissemination of particular, Western ideals of beauty provides important insights about the social and cultural impact of globalization. This book will explore the extent to which, as beauty expanded internationally, it suppressed local identities, contributing to the wider story of the imposition of Western, and white, values and perceptions on much of the rest of the world. It provides, as a result, new historical evidence that contributes to the ongoing debates about the extent to which globalization contributes to the homogenization of cultures.[26]

The book's third lens will focus on the issue of legitimacy. Insofar as the beauty industry has shaped perceptions of what it means to be attractive, those perceptions play an important as well as controversial role in shaping broader constructions of gender, age, and ethnicity. Recent research by economists and others has highlighted just how important being considered "beautiful" is for both individuals and societies. Although the advantages and challenges of being attractive have long been a staple of literature and theatre, in recent years economists and others have gone beyond amusing or tragic anecdotes to show, by way of experiments and other means, the very real consequences of being considered attractive. It appears that workers of above-average attractiveness get paid more than those considered less attractive, at least in the United States, suggesting that there is a "beauty premium" comparable to the race and gender premiums that also shape the American labor market.[27] Attractive professors appear to be judged as more effective instructors by students, and being perceived as attractive may even reduce a young adult's propensity for criminal activity.[28] Insofar, then, as the beauty industry's products and pitches influence perceptions of being attractive, their use offers real opportunities for people to access the "beauty premium," and real penalties if they are not deemed attractive.

In approaching the beauty industry through these three lenses, the heterogeneity of the industry presents an obvious challenge. What, after all, do perfume and toothpaste have in common? What unites a bar of soap sold in a rural African village and a lipstick on display in the Bergdorf Goodman store on Fifth Avenue in Manhattan? This book will argue that these products do indeed share many common characteristics, but it is readily conceded that the industry contains two distinct spectrums. A first spectrum has health and hygiene at one end and artifice at the other. A second spectrum extends from luxury or premium products to the mass market.[29] In the remainder of the book, care will be taken to map out the separate momentums and distinctive characteristics of the different ends of each of these two spectrums.

Outline

The chapters that follow are grouped into three parts. Part 1, "Beauty Imagined," is concerned with the origins of the modern beauty industry. Part 2, "Beauty Diffused," explores the geographical and social spread of the industry during the twentieth century, and explores the implications of that spread. The final part, "Beauty Reimagined," takes the story up to the present day and shows how the traditional characteristics of the industry, which took hold in the nineteenth century and persisted for most of the twentieth, are now in the process of being radically changed. The book ends with three appendices which provide historical estimates of the size of the beauty industry, of its largest firms, and of the most significant mergers and acquisitions.

Beauty has become a huge industry which affects the daily lives of almost everyone. It is remarkable that so little has yet been written about the extraordinary people who made beauty a business. This book is a start in filling this void. It is my hope also that a history of the globalization of such an industry as beauty, which carries such profound consequences for individuals and societies, can provide a new way of looking at issues which are fundamental to understanding the forces shaping our world in the twenty-first century.

Notes

1. Quoted in Geoffrey Jones and Ricardo Reisen de Pinho, "Natura: Global Beauty Made in Brazil," Harvard Business School Case no. 9-806-200 (August 29, 2007), p. 7.

2. This is the estimated size of the retail market in 2008. The beauty industry is defined here to include fragrances; hair and skin care products; sun care; color cosmetics, including make-up and other products for the face, eyes, lips, and nails; men's grooming products, including shaving creams; bath and shower products, including toilet soap; deodorants; oral care; and baby care. This definition conforms to that used by Euromonitor, a major source of contemporary data on the industry, but differs from the leading trade journal *Women's Wear Daily*, whose annual lists of the largest beauty firms exclude toiletries such as toilet soap and dental products. The beauty industry, as defined here, overlaps with many others, including fashion, professional services such as beauty salons and hairdressers, and medical products and services such as Botox and plastic surgery.

3. Michael E. Porter, "The Five Competitive Forces that Shape Strategy," *Harvard Business Review* 86:1 (January 2008), pp. 79–93.

4. Naomi Wolf, *The Beauty Myth: How Images of Beauty are Used against Women* (New York: Harper Perennial, 1992).

5. The data on market share of brands and market size in this chapter are drawn from Euromonitor and its Global Market Information Database.

6. These figures are for 2006.

7. Chandler Burr, *The Perfect Scent: A Year Inside the Perfume Industry in Paris and New York* (New York: Henry Holt and Company, 2008), pp. 141–8.

8. Geoffrey Jones and David Kiron, "Bernd Beetz: Creating the New Coty," Harvard Business School Case no. 9-808-133 (December 8, 2008), p. 12.

9. The literature on the historical use of beauty products is enormous. For an arbitrary selection, see Feliciano Blanco-Davila, "Beauty and the Body: The Origins of Cosmetics," *Plastic and Cosmetic Surgery* 105 (2000), pp. 1196–204; Fenja Gunn, *The Artificial Face: A History of Cosmetics* (New York: Hippocene Books, 1973); Edward H. Schafer, "The Development of Bathing Customs in Ancient and Medieval China and

the History of the Florate Clear Palace," *Journal of the Oriental Society* 76 (1956), pp. 57–82; B. V. Subbarayappa, "The Tradition of Cosmetics and Perfumery," in B. V. Subbarayappa (ed.), *Chemistry and Chemical Techniques in India* (New Delhi: Munshiram Monoharlal Publishers, 1999).

10. Charles Darwin, *The Descent of Man, and Selection in Relation to Sex* (1871; repr. Princeton: Princeton University Press, 1981), pp. 343–54.

11. Nancy Etcoff, *Survival of the Prettiest* (New York: Anchor Books, 2000); Geoffrey Miller, *The Mating Mind: How Sexual Choice Shaped the Evolution of Human Nature* (New York: Anchor Books, 2001).

12. Rachel Herz, *The Scent of Desire* (New York: William Morrow, 2007); "The Scent of a Man," *The Economist*, December 20, 2008.

13. Roger Scruton, *Beauty* (Oxford: Oxford University Press, 2009) provides a philosophical critique of the work of evolutionary psychologists on beauty and sexual selection.

14. Joseph Schumpeter, *Capitalism, Socialism, and Democracy* (New York: Harper, 1943).

15. William J. Baumol, *Entrepreneurship, Management, and the Structure of Payoffs* (Cambridge, Mass.: MIT Press, 1988). For a review of the business history literature on entrepreneurship, see Geoffrey Jones and R. Daniel Wadhwani, "Entrepreneurship," in Geoffrey Jones and Jonathan Zeitlin (eds), *The Oxford Handbook of Business History* (Oxford: Oxford University Press, 2007).

16. Norris Krueger, "The Cognitive Psychology of Entrepreneurship," in I. J. Zoltan Acs and David B. Audretsch (eds), *Handbook of Entrepreneurship Research* (Boston: Kluwer, 2003).

17. Alfred D. Chandler, especially *Strategy and Structure* (Cambridge, Mass.: MIT Press, 1962); *The Visible Hand* (Cambridge, Mass.: Harvard University Press, 1977); and *Scale and Scope* (Cambridge, Mass.: Harvard University Press, 1990).

18. The foundational studies are Mira Wilkins, *The Emergence of Multinational Enterprise* (Cambridge, Mass.: Harvard University Press, 1970) and *The Maturing of Multinational Enterprise* (Cambridge, Mass.: Harvard University Press, 1974). A recent survey is provided by Geoffrey Jones, *Multinationals and Global Capitalism* (Oxford: Oxford University Press, 2005).

19. Etcoff, *Survival*, pp. 137–43.

20. Freedom Leung, Sharon Lam, and Sherrien Sze, "Cultural Expectations of Thinness in Chinese Women," *Eating Disorders* 9 (2001), pp. 339–50. The emphasis on females having slim bodies and tiny waists was encouraged by waist- and foot-binding between the thirteenth and nineteenth centuries. See Ping Wang, *Aching for Beauty: Footbinding in China* (Minneapolis: University of Minnesota Press, 2000).

21. F. T. Walton, "My Lady's Toilet," *Greece & Rome* 15:44 (May 1946), pp. 68–73.

22. Ortha L. Wilner, "Roman Beauty Culture," *Classical Journal* 27:1 (October 1931), pp. 26–38.

23. "Facts for the Curious—Female Beauty," *Scientific American*, August 30, 1851.

24. Darwin, *Descent*, p. 353.

25. Regina Lee Blaszczyk, *Imagining Consumers: Design and Innovation from Wedgwood to Corning* (Baltimore: Johns Hopkins University Press, 2000); Regina Lee Blaszczyk (ed.), *Producing Fashion: Commerce, Culture and Consumers* (Philadelphia: University of Pennsylvania Press, 2009).

26. M. E. Guillen, "Is Globalisation Civilizing, Destructive or Feeble? A Critique of Five Key Debates in the Social Science Literature," *Annual Review of Sociology* 27 (2001), pp. 235–60.

27. Daniel S. Hamermesh and Jeff E. Biddle, "Beauty and the Labor Market," *American Economic Review* 84 (1994), pp. 1174–94.

28. Markus M. Mobius and Tanya S. Rosenblat, "Why Beauty Matters," *American Economic Review* 96 (2006), pp. 222–35; J. M. Ritter, R. J. Casey, and J. H. Langlois, "Adults' Responses to Infants Varying in Appearance of Age and Attractiveness," *Child Development* 62 (1991), pp. 68–82; D. S. Hamermesh and A. M. Parker, "Beauty in the Classroom: Professors' Pulchritude and Putative Pedagogical Productivity," *American Economist* 44 (2003), pp. 17–29; Naci Mocan and Erdal Tekin, "Ugly Criminals," NBER Working Paper no. 12019 (January 2006).

29. Traditionally, the beauty industry has been sharply differentiated between premium or prestige brands, sold through department stores and other exclusive distribution channels, and mass-market brands, sold through supermarkets or drugstores. The terms "premium" and "luxury" are often used interchangeably, although some writers assert that "luxury" is conceptually different from prestige. See J. N. Kapferer and V. Bastien, *The Luxury Strategy* (London: Kogan Page, 2009), ch. 1.

Part 1

Beauty Imagined

1

Scent and Paris

My desire is to give all women the ability to be beautiful.
François Coty, founder of the Coty beauty company, 1905[1]

From ancient craft to capitalist industry

Many of the most distinctive features of today's beauty industry made their first appearance in fragrances. The craft of making perfume was reinvented during the course of the nineteenth century into a capitalist industry. The craft itself has an ancient and global heritage. Roman emperors were said to have slept and bathed in a world of scent. While much of the extensive knowledge of fragrances in ancient Rome was lost in Europe after the fall of Rome, it survived in the Islamic civilizations which flourished during the European Middle Ages as centers of science and culture.

Arab and Persian pharmacists and perfumers used new "essential oils"—the compounds containing the distinctive scents of plants or animals used to make fragrances—from the aromatic plants found on the Indian peninsula. They also developed the technique of distillation and the suspension of essences in alcohol, which enabled smaller amounts of raw materials to be used to create perfume than in the ancient processes involving the extraction of scent from flower petals by placing them between trays of purified fat or by soaking them in warm oil.[2] In the era of the Crusades, this knowledge about perfumes was carried back to medieval Europe, where monasteries manufactured and sold alcohol-based scented waters.[3]

The uses of fragrances, and the creams, oils, and powders which were major carriers of fragrant oils, were intimately associated with healing. Pharmacy and perfumery were not discrete professions. Scented and aromatic alcohol waters were often ingested as well as used externally, a practice which continued into the nineteenth century.[4] Continuing the older traditions of using fragrances to purify the air both spiritually and in other ways, four-teenth-century doctors believed that the bubonic plague, or the Black Death as it was much later termed, was an odor which could be countered by inhaling other odors such as cinnamon, rose, and musk. As the Black Death also resulted in a long-term European aversion to using water for washing, per-fumes were also used as cleaning agents. Herbal knowledge was widely used for healing purposes, sometimes by people thought to be witches but who today might be seen as healers who understand the antibody properties of essential oils. Alleged witches, chemists, apothecaries, and artisans formed part of the diverse pre-industrial world of beauty.[5]

When the craft of perfumery re-entered Europe from the Islamic world, its initial center was the Italian city-state of Venice, both because of its access to Mediterranean trade routes and its position as a center for glassmaking, then crucial for the distillation of essential oils from plants. Perfume was in time diffused elsewhere, and during the second half of the seventeenth century the trade in perfumery developed strongly in France. This growth benefited from the reign of Louis XIV, the so-called Sun King, whose policies stimulated luxury trades through patronage, protectionism, and infrastructure improve-ments, including the development of street lighting using lanterns throughout Paris.[6] Perfume was widely applied to the linens, clothes, and food of the aristocrats at court.[7]

The perfumery trade in France was the preserve of glovemakers, or "gantiers-parfumeurs," who were organized into a guild association of craftsmen. The link with glove production arose because the toxic and putrid substances needed to tan hides meant that leather gloves had to be scented before they were worn. The glove- and perfume-makers' guild had been chartered by a French king as early as 1190. It developed strict regulations for who could produce and trade in both gloves and perfumery. To gain entrance, the guild required seven years of formal training under one of its recognized master perfumers, providing future per-fumers (or, as they would colloquially come to be called, "noses") with the required technical skills to create scents.[8] By the middle of the eighteenth century, there were an estimated 250 master perfumers in France.[9]

These master perfumers also included some based in Grasse, a town in Provence in the south of France, which had a well-established leather industry, and which started expanding the cultivation of flowers and plants for use as essential oils during the seventeenth century. Grasse's altitude gave it a fresh climate which, together with extensive sunshine, made the area ideal for flower growing.[10] A Grasse guild of *gantiers-parfumeurs* was granted its own separate status in 1729. Even as the fashion for scented gloves waned, Grasse's production of the raw materials increased as demand for other types of perfumery grew.[11]

The patronage of the French court reinforced the aspirational status of perfume. At the "perfumed court" of Louis XV in the eighteenth century, a different perfume was used every day of the week.[12] The eight Parisian master perfumers who supplied the court depended heavily on royal patronage, and some became the forebears of enduring perfume dynasties, including Houbigant.[13] By then, perfume formed only one component of Parisian beauty culture. The *gantiers-parfumeurs* not only sold scented oils and other forms of perfumery but were also active making soaps, powders, white face paints, rouges, and hair dyes.[14] Elite perfumers co-existed with businesses which supplied products to the less wealthy. The guilds of mercers, spicers, and wigmakers also sold cosmetics, as did vinegar-makers. Shopkeepers, often women, sold their own perfumery and cosmetic preparations, as did artisans and craftsmen, advertising their wares using posters.[15]

There were also additions to the product range during the eighteenth century. In Cologne, then an independent city-state, an Italian expatriate, Johann Maria Farina, commercialized a new, light scent based on fruits and herbs, which was named after his hometown. Eau de Cologne found an enthusiastic market among those who disliked the heavier scents associated with the French aristocracy. By the middle of the century, it was also used by soldiers for washing, in preference to scarce or dirty water.[16]

The commercialization of perfumery, which was mirrored in neighboring Britain where Europe's most flourishing consumer society had developed, provided the backdrop for the subsequent emergence of a more modern capitalist industry.[17] The outbreak of the French Revolution in 1789, although initially disruptive for the perfume trade because of its association with the court and the aristocracy, ended up facilitating this transition to an increasingly commercialized industry whose members began to seek broader retail markets at home and, through exports, abroad. An already weakened guild system was finally abolished in 1791. By the end of the 1790s new high-end perfumery shops were opening in Paris.[18]

The rise to power of Napoleon, crowned emperor in 1804, also helped lay the foundations for the recovery of the French industry. While Napoleon himself consumed huge quantities of eau de Cologne, Houbigant made traditional heavier perfumes for his first wife, Josephine. A Napoleonic ordinance in 1810, which required declaration of ingredients for products marketed for internal consumption, also served to clarify the status of fragrances. As most manufacturers did not wish to reveal their ingredients, they gave up the market for internal uses of scented waters, although some medicinal uses persisted. The spheres of perfumery and health increasingly diverged.

As Europe emerged from war in 1815, a new generation of perfumers started to appear. They combined a continuing focus on prestige with a new commercial awareness. Among the most creative figures was Eugène Rimmel, the son of a French perfumer of the same name who had opened a shop and laboratory in London in 1834. London, home to a large court as well as the British aristocracy and an affluent mercantile middle class, had developed a substantial perfumery business during the eighteenth century. The subsequent long period of war between Britain and France, during which the latter's ports were blockaded, enabled London perfumers to dominate world markets until at least the 1820s.[19] Even before those wars, a number of firms, including the predecessor to the House of Yardley, had experimented with branding scented toilet soaps and lavender scents. Although trademarks had a long history, they had limited significance when products were mostly made and consumed locally. Brands as such became significant as conveyors of information, and as sources of value for firms, as markets widened during the nineteenth century, and products once sold as commodities were differentiated.[20]

The younger Rimmel, like a surprising number of subsequent entrepreneurs in this industry, was an outsider, only becoming naturalized as a British citizen in 1857. This proved no handicap to his business, and may indeed have played some role in his recognition of opportunities which others did not see. Although his perfume was expensive, Rimmel envisaged, as the spread of railroads opened up possibilities of reaching wider markets, new ways to reach potential customers beyond the clients who visited his London shop.

Rimmel focused on building a brand which could convey the attributes of prestige and quality. He became one of the first to publish illustrated mail-order catalogues, and to place advertisements in theatre programs. He saw that design could enhance the value of his product, arranging for the labels

1.1 Eugène Rimmel, founder of
the perfume and cosmetics firm
Rimmel, circa 1870.

of his perfume bottles to be designed by the French lithographer Jules Chéret, whose patron he became. A series of product innovations ranged from perfumed cushions to the first factory-made, non-toxic mascara.[21] At home in the world of art and literature, Rimmel wrote an illustrated history of the making of perfumes and cosmetics, *The Book of Perfumes*, printed on scented paper. By then he was well advanced in collecting warrants for supplying ten different European royal families.[22]

Among other members of this generation of perfumers who combined creativity with a new awareness of the need to market products was Pierre-François-Pascal Guerlain. Born in Picardy, a fraught relationship with his father led him to seek his fortune beyond France. He worked in a small soap firm in England, and undertook medical and chemical studies. He returned to France as a sales representative, initially importing fashionable cosmetic products from Britain. He then opened a small shop in Paris in 1828, first selling scented toilet waters, soaps, and creams.[23] Guerlain began to sell his own fragrances, creating original and personalized fragrances for women, although these continued to be used to scent gloves, handkerchiefs, linen closets, and other objects rather than being applied directly to the skin. By 1841 he was able to move his shop to the fashionable Rue de la

Paix, and his prestige was confirmed when he was appointed supplier to Empress Eugénie, the wife of Emperor Napoleon III, from the time of their wedding in 1853.[24]

Guerlain and similar exclusive perfume houses, whose customers were drawn primarily from the wealthy elite, co-existed with other firms whose client base was anchored in the middle class. The market for luxury goods as a whole in France and elsewhere remained modest, even if it widened steadily during the first half of the century.[25] While in 1810 the production of perfume and other beauty products was worth less than 2 million francs, by 1856 it reached 18 million francs ($3.5 million).[26] The number of perfumeries making and selling their products in Paris increased from 139 in 1807 to 280 in 1867.[27] By 1867, there were an estimated 151 wholesale perfumers in London, and 849 of London's retail perfumers were engaged in production.[28]

The associations with fashion and social prestige meant that luxury fragrances were strongly clustered in Europe's two most affluent capital cities. Rimmel described London and Paris as "the headquarters of perfumery," while dismissing perfumers elsewhere as largely engaged in "counterfeiting."[29] Whether or not they sold knock-offs of London and Paris brands, perfumers elsewhere generally supplied the cheaper spectrum of their local markets.

The perfume industry which emerged in the United States, especially around the port city of New York, where the importers of French essential oils were clustered around the docks, fell into this category.[30] Many of the American firms were founded by emigrants. These included Colgate, a New York soap manufacturing business started by the English emigrant and Baptist deacon William Colgate in 1806. In the 1860s, the company started to develop a substantial business in perfumery, and came to advertise itself increasingly as a "perfumer." A successful line of products using the Cashmere Bouquet brand was launched in 1872, and by the early twentieth century the firm offered no less than 625 varieties of perfume.[31]

Fragrances transformed
During the second half of the nineteenth century there was a sudden growth in the French fragrance industry. Sales increased dramatically: production of perfume and other beauty products soared from 45 million francs in 1878 to

100 million francs ($19 million) in 1912.[32] This growth demonstrated the power of entrepreneurial agency in expanding the market for beauty.

Perfumers fueled this growth by finding ways to offer a wider range of scents at prices that increasing numbers of people could afford. As fragrances have a direct impact on the scent of the consumer, the basic product—the scent of the "juice"—has always mattered in the value of a perfume. Although an aspirant consumer might be persuaded to buy a perfume made by Rimmel because he sold to European royalty, if the resulting scent was not pleasing to the consumer's taste, the wearer was unlikely to repeat the purchase. There was not, however, a great variety in the "juices" available until the late nineteenth century. Perfume firms were largely limited to purchasing the same scent ingredients from suppliers of raw and intermediate materials. For consumers, this meant that the majority of fragrances for sale were made with the same perfume base or semi-finished mixture of essences. The perfume recipes used by different firms did not vary a great deal, resulting in a duplication of products from brand to brand.

The perfume houses employed other strategies to differentiate themselves from each other. These ranged from establishing close relationships with one particular raw material supplier, who might favor them with a unique mix of essences for a perfume base, to investing in attractive packaging and other brand-building measures.[33] The fact that nineteenth-century France had stronger legal protection for trademarks than either Britain or the United States might have encouraged such investment in brand-building.[34]

During the second half of the century, a number of firms moved to widen the range of raw materials available to perfumers. The town of Grasse emerged as a vibrant cluster of innovative firms, stimulated by the building of an irrigation system during the 1850s which facilitated large-scale planting of flowers, and the construction of a railroad between Grasse and Paris, which made it much quicker and easier to sell essential oils to the Parisian firms. As the number of perfume-makers in Grasse and the surrounding region increased from 58 in 1846 to 79 in 1866, a cluster of related crafts, including glassmaking and printing, also emerged.[35]

New methods of solvent extraction, developed during the 1830s, provided a new means of extracting essential oils from flowers too delicate to withstand the traditional method of steam distillation. The Grasse firms employed the new technology to reduce progressively the volume of flowers which were required to extract scented essences. Roure-Bertrand Fils in particular became a powerhouse of technological innovations. By the 1870s this firm had developed a new form of solvent extraction called concrete essence extraction, which provided perfumery with concentrated substances entirely soluble in alcohol.[36]

The firm of Chiris had an even greater impact on the industry's growth. Chiris had been founded in 1768 by Antoine Chiris, who had learned the craft of perfumery in Paris. In a pattern typical of Grasse firms, successive patriarchs of this family single-handedly made all of the major decisions, while training their sons in the skills needed to succeed in due course. Antoine's son Anselme developed the firm's activities in Austria and Germany, and he also studied in England. Anselme's son Léopold, in turn, expanded the business into Russia, where he set up that country's first factory for extracting essential oils from raw materials shipped from France. By 1850, Chiris was the largest firm in Grasse's essential oils industry, with sales of over half a million francs and over 500 employees.[37]

Most remarkably, Chiris undertook a global search for new natural ingredients, acquiring land in Algeria as early as 1836, only two years after the French had annexed the country as a colony. By 1865, Chiris was growing geraniums, orange trees, cassia trees, and eucalyptus at the Algerian site, and had built a large factory there. Algeria was only the beginning of the creation of supply channels, plantations, and factories elsewhere in Africa, including Madagascar, and in Asia, including China, Vietnam, and the Philippines. Léon Chiris, the founder's great-grandson, who took over the business with his brother Edmond in 1862, became a celebrated innovator in the extraction and creation of both natural and synthetic essences, and went on to found a perfumery school which became a training ground for a new generation of perfumers.[38]

Chiris was instrumental, then, in providing French perfumers with a new range of exotic raw materials by building supply chains which enabled a flow of natural essences from all corners of the world. It was ironic that the growing vitality of the Parisian fragrance industry, and to some extent the beauty industry in the West as a whole, rested on the role of colonialism in making available new raw materials. The resources and labor of Africans and Asians were put to service in an industry which would progressively assert the supposedly superior beauty of Western features and fashion.

However, science as well as colonialism was put to the service of beauty. As nineteenth-century organic chemists identified the chemical patterns underlying natural scents, they acquired a deeper understanding of the chemistry of scent which in turn allowed them to produce the synthetic equivalents of natural scents that could not be captured from natural sources and, perhaps more impressively, scents which did not exist in nature. Synthetic vanilla and rose scents were two of the first to be created. The availability of new chemicals, and improved methods of extracting familiar fragrances, resulted in an explosion in the range of scents that a perfumer could utilize, beginning in the late 1890s.[39]

A number of entrepreneurs and creative geniuses—sometimes the same person, sometimes in partnership—took advantage of scientific advances to create entirely new and original fragrances, reinventing the concept of French perfume as such. In 1880 the perfumer Paul Parquet became a joint owner of Houbigant. Two years later he created Fougère royale, a scent containing synthetic coumarin, the smell of newly mown hay. The new fragrance, based on the interplay between lavender, coumarin, and oak moss, was used both as a soap perfume and as a perfume in its own right. In 1889 Guerlain launched the equally novel Jicky. With the death of Pierre-François-Pascal in 1864, the Guerlain business had been left to his two sons, Aimé and Gabriel, who divided the roles of perfumer and manager between them. While Gabriel managed the firm, Aimé became the master perfumer. Jicky employed synthetic scents and the new processes of solvent extraction to obtain floral essences in pure, unadulterated form.

These new, commercially sold synthetic perfumes were revolutionary in their design. Previously, perfumes were reminiscent of one individual "note"— to use the musical metaphor employed to describe perfume—which tried to replicate nature. The new perfumes were more abstract, and their ambition was not merely to duplicate nature, but to offer scents not found in nature. They marked the end of single-note perfumes. Jicky offered three notes, beginning with a fresh blend of citrus and lavender, enhanced with herbs; a middle note of spices magnified by sandalwood; and finally base notes of the animal scents of amber, musk, and civet. Some have drawn connections between the creations of these perfumers and modernism in painting and music.[40] The impact of the new fragrances was all the greater because Guerlain and Houbigant were at the top of the hierarchy of prestige of France's perfume houses.[41] The new fragrances led to gender confusion in the marketplace. Paul Parquet had conceived Fougère royale as a female fragrance, but it was men, not women, who favored the scent. Fougère (fern) became the basis for the leading male fragrance family. Jicky was conceived as a unisex fragrance, perhaps the original such fragrance of the modern era, but women initially rejected its provocative and non-traditional combination of unfamiliar notes, and it too found its main market amongst men until shortly before World War I.[42]

This confusion reflected shifting patterns in the gender composition of the fragrance market. Historically, in Europe and elsewhere, perfumes were used by both men and women, and both sexes used the same scents. During the nineteenth century, as people began to wash more, many Western men started to use little or no perfume, instead using toilet soap, eau de Cologne, and scented oils for the hair. Men and women also started to favor different scents. Sweet floral blends, notably involving the scent of violet, came to be regarded as the exclusive preserve of women.[43] Insofar as men used scents, these were increasingly expected to be different and sharper than those of women.

This trend reflected the contemporary norms of a new and more emphasized femininity that arose over the course of the nineteenth century.[44] Women were to emerge as the primary consumers of the more complex and abstract fragrances, whilst men remained far more modest users of simpler scents such as eau de Cologne. These developments were related to the emergence of sharper gender differentiation in Western clothing, or at least the clothing of the affluent, as Victorian men increasingly abandoned decoration in favor of dark clothing, whilst their female counterparts turned to frilly and colorful dresses.[45] In fragrances, however, such gender differentiation was neither immediate nor clear-cut. As the evidence of Fougère royale and Jicky shows, the transition took time even for the most expert perfumers to understand. Although initially synthetics were extremely expensive, over time technological advances enabled firms to reduce costs. Good profit margins could be made on perfumes which remained expensive but which could still become more accessible as incomes rose.[46] However, for more perfume to be sold, bigger factories were needed. Firms began moving their manufacturing out of central Paris to larger and cheaper sites in surrounding towns. L. T. Piver was the pioneer, building a factory for the production of toilet soap in the Parisian suburb of La Villette as early as 1840. Piver had previously followed the standard practice of making toilet soaps by remelting ready-made soap from the long-established industry in Marseilles, but realized he could produce soaps and other scented toiletries of a higher quality, and in greater quantities, with his own modern soap factory. Marseilles soaps often emitted unpleasant odors which could not always be masked by perfume.[47] Beginning in the 1860s an exodus from Paris started in earnest, although firms retained their exclusive retail outlets and head offices in the capital.

The transformation of the industry included growing sophistication in the use of distribution channels. The late nineteenth century saw a divergence between perfumers who resolved to maintain the highest prices and an image of great exclusivity, and those whose prices were lower.[48] While the former sold in their own shops, the latter sold at the department stores which had emerged in Paris in the 1850s, such as Le Bon Marché, Les Grands Magasins du Louvre, and Les Grands Magasins du Printemps. These stores, like their equivalents in New York and Chicago, such as Lord and Taylor, Macy's, and Marshall Field's, sold a wide selection of different products in "departments" all under one roof.[49] The same perfume might be sold at a higher price in a perfumer's own shop than in a department store, reflecting the personalized service and exclusive atmosphere in a boutique.[50]

Perfume houses also sometimes combined developing their own brands with supplying the private-label businesses of department stores. This was one of the strategies of Roger et Gallet, founded in 1862 by Charles Armand Roger and Charles Martial Gallet, a merchant and a banker respectively. These men were not creative "noses" but entrepreneurs who perceived that the perfume market was an attractive commercial proposition. They began by buying the eau de Cologne business which a member of the Farina family had opened in Paris in 1806. A long and drawn-out legal battle with the Cologne firm Muehlens over who owned the legal right to use the trade name Farina, which had become the household name for this product category, resulted in victory in 1880 for Roger and Gallet. These savvy entrepreneurs fully exploited the value of their acquired franchise, developing a prestige perfumery business that specialized in perfumed toilet soaps. They integrated vertically also, building a large modern factory outside Paris. At the end of the century, they also secured exclusive French rights to use the newly invented synthetic form of violet scent, one of the most popular at that time.[51]

Firms which sought to achieve maximum exclusivity placed less emphasis on perfumed soaps, and emphasized their position at the artifice end of the beauty spectrum. They drew inspiration from Paris's position as the apex of luxury and placed their perfumes within that setting. France's status as the world capital of fashion and luxury grew during the middle decades of the century. Charles Frederick Worth, an Englishman who moved to Paris, broke away from the tradition of dressmaking to become a "dress artist," establishing the art of "haute couture" (French for high dressmaking, and a term for the creation of exclusive fashions). In time, the House of Worth was joined by other fashion houses[52] and by other luxury firms, such as Louis-François Cartier, who opened his first jewelry store in Paris in 1853. Perfumery, jewelry and other crafts, such as chocolate and champagne, all expanded at this time as French entrepreneurs seized opportunities to employ new technologies to make handmade luxuries in greater quantities, whilst retaining exclusivity and craftsmanship as central to the marketing proposition.[53]

Paris grew too as a global center for luxury retailing, which added to the city's allure for the wealthy and fashionable of the world. Beginning in the 1820s, the creation of enclosed, fashionable shopping arcades provided a location for exclusive shops selling luxury goods. Later, much of Paris was demolished under the direction of Georges Eugène Haussmann, and replaced by a monumental city of public buildings and broad boulevards which became the site for many of the city's most exclusive shops.[54] In 1855 Paris hosted the third Universal Exhibition—the first such international exposition of products had been held in the Crystal Palace in London in 1851—featuring dazzling displays of French fashion, as well as perfumes, soaps, and cosmetics. Parisian haute couture would set the dominant fashion standards for many decades to come.[55] The most luxurious American department store, created by John Wanamaker in Philadelphia, opened its own Paris bureau in 1880, which identified the latest fashions to be taken across the Atlantic.[56]

Perfumers moved to associate their brands with Paris's burgeoning status as the capital of fashion. Scents were named after Parisian neighborhoods, such as Guerlain's Parfum des Champs-Élysées (1904) and Lenthéric's Cœur de Paris (1912). The connections between the Parisian worlds of fashion and fragrance also grew closer as designer houses themselves began selling perfumes. The trend was begun by Paul Poiret, a designer who established his own fashion house in 1904, creating a new fashion style using vibrant primary colors. In 1911 he created an affiliate to produce fragrances to match his fashions.[57]

The creation of strong brand identities was facilitated by advances in design and packaging. During the 1890s the Art Nouveau style, characterized by sensuous lines, beautiful women with flowing hair, and floral motifs, had emerged in France. The perfumery houses were soon exploiting this fashion in their package designs. Distinctive designs were further enhanced by the Western fascination with "Oriental" images, focused on the romantic and exotic associations of an imagined Asia and an imagined view of Asian women, which became strongly represented in perfume names and packaging beginning in the late nineteenth century. French perfumery advertising reflected in particular the contemporary artistic craze for "Japonisme," or traditional Japanese arts.[58]

The stunning pace of technological, manufacturing, and marketing advances in France put its perfume industry far ahead of others in size and, especially, stature. London firms still carried social cachet, however. Although Rimmel lost its dynamism after Eugène's death in 1887, houses such as Atkinson's and Penhaligon's prospered by serving a socially exclusive clientele. Yardley held an international reputation for scented toilet soap and lavender water, but mostly sold unbranded products to pharmacies. Only after the firm's sales fell sharply at the turn of the century, and a new generation of the family took control, was there a sustained push into perfumery, along with a more prominent use of Yardley as a brand name.[59]

Overall, the British industry was now dwarfed by its French counterpart. Its reputation rested on niche products such as lavender water and male toiletries. The London houses may have been handicapped by Britain's climatic conditions, which could not match the south of France for the manufacture of a wide range of essences, nor for access to the grape-based alcohols which lent a distinct scent to perfume.[60] Moreover, while London was associated with social prestige and affluence, it could not match the wider reputation of Paris for haute couture and luxury. London's own reputation lay in male fashion, symbolized by the tailors of Savile Row, which became less of an asset for perfumers as the gendered consumption of beauty products took hold, with women as the major consumers.

There was a powerful new entrant on the other side of the continent. Russia had begun to modernize its extremely backward economy after the abolition of serfdom in 1861. There was a heavy French presence in many of Russia's new industries, ranging from petroleum to steel, and including perfume. In 1864 Henri Brocard, the son of a small Parisian perfumer, opened a soap and perfume business in Moscow with his Belgian wife, who had been educated in Russia. Importing ingredients from Roure Bertrand Fils in Grasse, Brocard expanded a business which sold in the major cities in Russia, and its factory in Moscow made perfumes, soaps, powders, cosmetics, and even dental care products. Highly attuned to the aspirational status of fragrance, Brocard supplied the courts of both Russia and Spain.[61]

Another Moscow house, A. Rallet, founded in 1847, also had links to Grasse. The French perfumer Edouard Beaux was one of the first directors. Ernest Beaux, his son, joined the business in 1898, and became a creative genius in fragrances. He was responsible for a series of successful fragrance launches, beginning with Bouquet de Napoleon, an eau de Cologne that celebrated Napoleon's last victory in Russia. In 1898, the year that the company was bought by Chiris, it employed over 2,000 people and owned 12 branches in Russia, the Balkans, and Asia. Beaux himself returned to France after the Communist revolution, and went on to create the iconic Chanel N°5.[62]

The Russian market for perfume and other beauty products was evidently growing fast during these decades, although the fact that a large percentage of the population was rural and poor was a major constraint. Nevertheless, there is evidence that the leading Russian houses may have been amongst the world's largest perfume companies by the 1900s. Brocard had sales of $500,000 in 1904.[63] Rallet, which sold in the Balkans as well as in Asian countries surrounding Russia, achieved sales of 50 million francs, or nearly $10 million, by 1914.[64] In contrast, at the turn of the century the sales of Houbigant—one of the few French firms for whom figures exist, and probably one of the largest—were equivalent to $200,000.[65] A study in 1896 identified 114 perfume houses in Paris with more than five workers: of these, only 14 firms had more than 50 employees, and only one had more than 500.[66] The House of Yardley, probably the largest London perfume house, had sales of $73,000 in 1906.[67]

In the United States, there were also many firms selling perfume by the new century. Like Colgate, they were primarily focused on the cheaper end of the market. Among them was the California Perfume Company (which would take the name Avon in 1939), which originated as a door-to-door bookselling company which offered perfume samples to prospective customers who were mostly female. David McConnell, the owner, found his perfumes were more popular than his books, which within a few years were phased out to enable a focus on perfume as well as soaps and toiletries.[68]

The one American perfumer in this era who pursued an ambition to build a more expensive brand was Richard Hudnut, the son of a New York druggist. Following a visit to Paris, he transformed his father's store into a luxury shop selling high-priced perfumes. In 1880 he registered his trademark, Hudnut, in both France and the United States. Over the following decades he was responsible for creating at least 90 different fragrances. The "father of American cosmetics," as he came to be called, also launched several brands of cosmetics of his own, including DuBarry in 1903.

Hudnut's strategy for building a prestige business was to forge a strong French identity for his brand. His bottles carried the legend "Richard Hudnut, New York and Paris." This was matched by a relentless pursuit of quality standards. The firm emphasized its "supreme governing principle" of quality, in the words of a "Beauty Book" it published in 1915. These tactics succeeded. Hudnut's finer perfumes were accepted for sale in American department stores. Meanwhile, he also pursued a larger business selling cheaper products for sale "on approval."[69] Timing was crucial for Hudnut's success. He was able to exploit a real window of opportunity. While the prestige of Parisian fashion and perfumes was strongly established in the American market, the major Parisian companies still limited their business strategies to exporting through local agents. Hudnut could therefore combine the marketing advantage of being "French" with the cost advantage of manufacturing locally.[70]

Hudnut's advantage was transitory. By the time he sold his business in 1916, Parisian firms had entered the American market more aggressively. The lead was taken by a remarkable newcomer to the French industry.

François Coty and accessible luxury

As the new century began, the French fragrance industry was further transformed by one of the beauty industry's most creative figures, François Coty. Born Joseph Marie François Spoturno on the Mediterranean island of Corsica, which was also the birthplace of Napoleon, he had arrived in Paris in 1898. Through Corsican connections, he was introduced both to the Parisian artistic world, where he met the woman he married in 1900, and to the Chiris

1.2 François Coty, founder of the perfume and cosmetics firm Coty, circa 1915.
He assumed an adapted version of his
mother's maiden name as he strove to
create a perfume brand which symbolized
style and elegance.

family. His interest in perfume seems to have been inspired by visiting
the Universal Exposition held in Paris in 1900, which included an extraordinary celebration of French fashion and perfumery, which attracted 50
million visitors, a number not to be reached again at an international fair
until the Montreal Expo in 1967.[71]

Coty launched his own perfumery business with his grandmother, who had
raised him after his mother died when he was very young and his father had
left the family. She served as an angel investor by providing a small loan.
The business failed within a year. As an outsider to the industry and to Paris,
he faced hostility and skepticism: one immediate response, and perhaps a sign
of his marketing genius, was to take his mother's maiden name of Coti, and
modify it to Coty. In 1903 he spent time at the perfumery school run by Chiris
in Grasse, and the following year he employed two of the synthetics he had
studied in Grasse to create La Rose Jacqueminot, his first perfume. He finally
secured an order of 12 bottles of this creation from a prominent Parisian
department store, after smashing a bottle on the floor in a successful gambit
to get customers to smell it.[72]

Coty's business grew quickly, and he set about breaking the traditional business models of the perfume industry with as much gusto as his initial bottle-smashing. He was a highly talented "nose," and was able to combine his olfactory sensitivity and creativity with a great gift for marketing. He benefited from a close relationship with Chiris, who served as his main supplier of essential oils, and its affiliate, Rallet, provided the vehicle for his early sales in Russia.[73] While his short course in Grasse may have given him only limited technical knowledge of perfume, this very lack of accumulated experience and craftsmanship freed him to experiment. Coty became noted for using new synthetic ingredients which others had declined.[74] He created two entirely new classes of perfume, soft sweet floral and chypre. L'Origan (1905) was the first floral-oriental scent and the first four-note scent, and was destined to exercise a long-lasting influence on perfumery. Later, in 1917—at the height of World War I—he also launched Chypre de Coty, a spicy and powdery fragrance using oakmoss from the island of Cyprus to which he added jasmine, giving rise to the modern definition of the chypre family of scents.[75]

It was above all Coty's determination to expand the market for perfume which set him apart. He still regarded perfume as a luxury, but he wanted to sell it to more people. Following the example of established houses, he opened his own store in the fashionable Place Vendôme in Paris in 1905, next to the luxurious hotel opened by César Ritz seven years previously. There he displayed his perfume alongside scented powders, creams, and even stationery, becoming a pioneer of the idea of a branded line of scented products.

Coty, in a way atypical in the French industry at the time, sought to build a national, and later international, market using professional salesmen. By the late nineteenth century American and British manufacturers of mass-produced consumer goods such as soap and processed foods employed their own sales forces to sell to retailers.[76] However, the use of such salesmen was not common in France and did not suit such an exclusive industry as perfumery. Nevertheless, by 1907 Coty had seven salesmen selling his products in France. Their mission was to carefully select retailers who were required to sell at the price he fixed. He also actively followed the emergent trend of moving his products into a growing number of department stores.[77]

The shape and design of perfume bottles became central to Coty's strategy. Perfume was still typically sold in pharmaceutical-style bottles, albeit with attractive labels. Coty commissioned René Lalique, a master jeweler, to design elegant new bottles for his new ranges. Their novel "dragonfly" flaçon design was launched in 1909. A perfume, Coty said, "needs to attract the eye as much as the nose."[78] This attention to the elegance and design of the bottle was to become, and remain, a key component of fragrance marketing. As a result, the bottle came to cost more than the juice contained within it. Coty was able to combine such elegance with the pursuit of wider markets by following the example pioneered by a handful of other firms—selling perfumes in smaller bottles.

Coty was also determined to achieve greater scale. He built his own glass factory, which could make 100,000 bottles per day by 1914, and he started making cosmetics, including face powder and lipstick. He worked hard to erode the sharp social distinctions which had previously marked perfume consumption. For most of the nineteenth century, the upper-class women who consumed primarily fine, floral perfumes applied them to their clothes and handkerchiefs rather than to their skins. In contrast, the application of stronger, animal-scent-based fragrances to bodies and hair was primarily associated with women who were not considered respectable by middle-class society, such as actresses and the consorts of wealthy men. By steadily introducing perfumes that were popular with all women, Coty strove to democratize perfume consumption.[79]

Coty was the most colorful of a number of new entrepreneurial actors in the French perfume industry. These included the Wertheimers, a Jewish family from the province of Alsace in France. When Alsace was lost to Germany as a result of the Franco–Prussian war in 1870–1, the parents and their oldest son took German citizenship, while their two younger sons, including Ernest, retained their French citizenship and moved to Paris. Continuing in the path for which he had been trained at his father's necktie firm, Ernest established his own successful necktie business in 1892. Six years later, he became a partner of Emile Orosdi, originally a food trader, who owned the firm of Bourjois, which had originated as a maker of theatrical make-up.

The company, now named E. Wertheimer & Cie, began selling the Bourjois brand in the department stores in France and elsewhere in a chain of stores owned by members of the Orosdi family. The fragrance business was expanded, and Ernest Wertheimer turned out to possess a "nose" for creating perfumes. He also had an excellent network of business connections from his native Alsace, including the families who had founded the Parisian department store Galeries Lafayette. In 1909 Wertheimer and Orosdi provided a loan for them to enlarge their department store with a new majestic building, providing a convenient way to expand further the by then rapidly growing market for Bourjois products.[80]

Coty and the Wertheimers, then, worked to take perfume, if not to the masses, then to many more people than had previously used it. Coty in particular was a disruptive innovator, and his style of disruption was not appreciated in Paris. In 1890 Aimé Guerlain and Charles Gallet had organized a perfumer's association, Le Syndicat National de la Parfumerie Française. It grew from 30 members at its inception to 70 in 1900 and was composed primarily of prestigious Paris perfume houses such as L.T. Piver, Guerlain, and Houbigant. Coty was repeatedly refused membership, both before and after World War I.[81]

Global markets

As the nineteenth century progressed, several developments occurred that stimulated commerce between countries: radical improvements in transport associated with the coming of the railroads and steamships; a transformation in communications with the spread of the telegraph; the adoption for a time of free trade; and the expansion of Western colonial possessions. International travel was suddenly much easier than ever before. In an era without passports, visas, and work permits, millions of people moved from one country to another, especially from Europe to the United States. By the end of the century, international trade was also growing at unprecedented levels. At mid-century, Western manufacturing companies began to open factories in foreign countries. By 1914 these multinational enterprises could be found across a swathe of industries, usually those characterized either by brands or proprietary technology. This era of growing integration of the world's markets has been called the "first global economy."[82]

In volume terms, the international trade in perfumery was a modest element in this wider story of globalization. However, the aspirational nature of expensive perfumes and toilet soaps meant that perfumery assumed its position amongst other emergent luxury products, such as fashion and jewelry, consumed by the emergent social elite living in the affluent cities of Europe, the United States, and Latin America.

By mid-century, both France and Britain had achieved significant export volumes. While French perfumery was exported mainly to other nations in Europe and the Americas, the British exported to India, China, and Australia.[83] In 1860 more than half of French perfumers sold products abroad, and 40 years later the percentage was closer to three-quarters.[84] The volume of French exports of perfumery soared from around 200 tonnes in the mid-1870s to 360 in 1900, and exports of essences over the same period went from 150 to 350 tonnes.[85] There were also growing sales to foreigners who came to Paris to shop. From the end of the American Civil War (1861–5), socially prominent New Yorkers began crossing the Atlantic to buy the latest Paris fashions, including fragrances. American perfumes were also exported to Europe to supply the cheaper end of the market. Colgate perfumes were among the small number of foreign brands sold in late nineteenth-century France, alongside exclusive British brands such as Atkinson's.[86]

The typical pattern was for exports to be sold abroad through local import agents. A handful of firms sought deeper engagement with foreign markets. A number of perfume houses opened shops outside their home countries. By 1865 Piver had six Parisian boutiques, as well as shops in London and Brussels. Rimmel had eight stores by the 1870s. Shops in London, Paris, and Nice—where he also purchased flower gardens—were joined by stores in fashionable cities in the Netherlands, Belgium, and Italy.[87]

By then the house of Muehlens was also energetically selling its distinctive eau de Cologne in foreign markets. In 1792, the Cologne banker Wilhelm Muehlens had secured a license to use the name Farina, and the popularity of the light scent encouraged the firm to experiment with branding a product which was at that time still regularly drunk in addition to being used as a refreshing alcohol-based toilet water. The brand 4711 Original Eau de Cologne, named after the street number where the business was located, was created in 1807, and was soon being sold in wider markets. Cologne was occupied by France between 1792 and 1814, but when this large domestic market was suddenly lost, the firm immediately began appointing agents in cities in other German principalities. The founder's son, Peter Josef, had strong artistic talents, and he encouraged the design of a distinctive bottle by the glass blower Molanus in 1820, and an iconic blue-gold label two decades

1.3 Muehlens invoked a universal ideal of female beauty targeting women everywhere in the world in this advertisement for perfumed soap for the United States, 1897.

later, which became enduring symbols of brand identity. By mid-century Muehlens was selling its products in Asia as well as Europe. The firm's reputation was enhanced when 4711 Original Eau de Cologne won great praise at the 1867 Paris Universal Exposition.[88] In the same year, Muehlens began investing in Bertrand Fils in Grasse.[89]

It was Ferdinand Muehlens, a member of the family's third generation, who took the firm's internationalization to a new level. Ferdinand was trained as a perfumer and praised as a talented nose.[90] Before taking over from his father in 1873, he was sent to tour the world for almost two years to gain greater understanding of global markets. While in the United States, he became impressed with American marketing methods, and soon afterwards the firm began an assault on the American market. It first exported 4711 products through an exclusive agent, and in 1878 opened its own office and subsidiary in New York. The branch began to make scents in a rented basement in the following year. This was probably a response to rising tariffs in the United States, which made it difficult to build volume by exporting. A factory for manufacture, warehousing, and distribution was built in Jersey City in 1899.[91]

Growing sales in France provoked the dispute with Roger et Gallet over the Farina trademark, and although Muehlens lost the case this had limited impact on the firm's international expansion.[92] In 1880 Ferdinand opened a small factory in Riga in Latvia, then part of Russia, again allowing access to a large market with growing trade barriers.[93] In Sweden, a local entrepreneur began selling the products of the firm in 1880, and this turned into a manufacturing business whose products were distributed by the Swedish partners.[94] By 1900, at which time the firm was also selling toilet soaps and cosmetics, the firm possessed its own sales branches in multiple European cities and in almost 20 countries.[95]

Although data on the level and geographical breakdown of Muehlens' sales have been lost, it does emerge as a pioneer of the international marketing of fragrances. Ferdinand, who ran the company until his own son took over in 1900, closely supervised exporting strategy, requiring regular market reports from the international sales agents, many of whom were employees dispatched from Cologne. Royal warranties were also actively pursued and obtained, even from the Shah of Iran.[96] It was also understood that brands might require different expressions in different countries. While the firm's advertising and raw material purchases were centralized in Cologne, the American market was approached with specific products including an extended range of soaps, bath salts, eau de Cologne, and perfume.[97]

The French perfume houses mostly took a more passive approach to foreign markets until the turn of the century. But the size of the American market, and its thirst for all things French, eventually caught their attention. Among the Parisian houses opening offices in New York between 1905 and 1914 were Guerlain, Roger et Gallet, and Houbigant.[98] A number of French houses also established offices and warehouses in other European cities to facilitate sales.

The new entrants to the industry were the ones who paid the most attention to the potential of foreign markets. Parfums Caron was founded in 1903 following an earlier failure by Ernest Daltroff, the French-born son of Jews who, like many others, had emigrated to France and elsewhere to escape the anti-Semitism in Russia at this time. Daltroff was a highly creative perfumer who had a strong international perspective from the start. Fluent in five languages, he traveled extensively, taking long trips on ocean liners where he was surrounded by socialites. Daltroff became particularly keen on learning to use the exotic scents of the rainforests of South America. Facing numerous incumbents in the domestic market, his travels also convinced him that there was a large demand for French luxury in the world's cosmopolitan cities. He used agents to begin selling in Latin American markets, and by 1913 he had begun selling in the United States. Noting that the champagne industry exported 65 per cent of its production, Daltroff explicitly focused his attention on the international market.[99]

It was Coty, however, that made the greatest impact on the American market. In 1905, knowing nothing about that market, he sent his energetic mother-in-law Virginie to investigate. She recognized that not only perfume, but also cosmetics had major growth potential. A business was started, and, following the earlier strategy of Muehlens, was adjusted to the perceived needs of the American market. It proved so successful that by 1912 Coty was ready to open a New York branch in a Fifth Avenue building, furnished with stained glass windows by Lalique. By 1914 Coty's brand of face powder was selling at 30,000 items a day in the United States alone.[100]

Summing up

The scale of François Coty's business was not typical, but it certainly high-lighted the extent of the changes that had taken place since the early nineteenth century. By 1914 the range of scents that perfumers could use had been greatly expanded. An increasingly globalized world, dominated by the West, had been scoured for exotic ingredients. Production had shifted to factories. Firms sold brands with discrete pricing and distribution strategies. Beautiful bottles, exquisite packaging, and associations with the romance of Paris had become as essential to prestigious brands as the quality of the scent itself.

A succession of entrepreneurs had transformed an ancient craft into a modern industry. Whether it was the Chiris family embarking on its search for a wide range of natural materials, or Coty's pursuit of a widened market for fragrance, these entrepreneurs imagined a different industry from the one they inherited, and they implemented the strategy and the organization to realize their vision. Frequently these men were noses, and it was striking how such innate understanding of scent seems to have been passed from generation to generation. Yet it was also striking how many of the formative figures were "outsiders" of one sort or another, frequently with cosmopolitan or immigrant backgrounds. This was an age of unprecedented mobility, enabling people both to seek new opportunities beyond their home countries, and to flee from anti-Semitism and other restrictive policies. It mattered less where an entre-preneur came from than where he ended up working. Paris, and to a much lesser extent other cities such as New York, London, and Moscow, were where the latest fashions could be seen, where young creative talent in perfumery and design flocked, and where affluent consumers lived and visited.

The nature of the market for fragrance had been transformed. Although the association with luxury was long established, at the start of the nineteenth century fragrance was also still being used for hygienic purposes, drunk for reasons of health, and rarely applied to the skin. A hundred years later perfumes were part of the world of fashion. Developments in perfumery had also further etched the period's sharper gender divisions and roles into society. Scents now reminded men and women of their roles in the world.

Notes

1. Cited in Elizabeth Coty and Roulhac Toledano, "François Coty: Emperor of Perfume, France's First Billionaire," unpubl. MS.

2. Edwin T. Morris, *Fragrance: The Story of Perfume from Cleopatra to Chanel* (New York: Charles Scribner, 1984), pp. 3–34, 83–93.

3. Edward Sagarin, *The Science and Art of Perfumery* (New York: McGraw-Hill, 1945), p. 10.

4. Ghislaine Pillivuyt, *Histoire du parfum. De l'Égypte au XIXe siècle: Collection de la parfumerie Fragonard* (Paris: Éditions Denoël, 1988), p. 149.

5. Annick Le Guérer, *Le parfum: Des origines à nos jours* (Paris: Éditions Odile Jacob, 2005), p. 88.

6. Joan DeJean, *The Essence of Style: How the French Invented High Fashion, Fine Food, Chic Cafes, Style, Sophistication and Glamour* (New York: Free Press, 2005).

7. DeJean, *Essence*, pp. 251–2.

8. Elisabeth de Feydeau, "De l'hygiène au rêve: L'industrie française du parfum (1830–1939)," unpubl. doctoral diss., University of Lille, 1997, pp. 12–14.

9. Richard Stamelman, *Perfume: Joy, Obsession, Scandal, Sin. A Cultural History of Fragrance from 1750 to the Present* (New York: Rizzoli, 2006), pp. 57–8.

10. Morris, *Fragrance*, chs 6 and 7.

11. Feydeau, "De l'hygiène," p. 17.

12. Constance Classen, David Howes, and Anthony Synnott, *Aroma: The Cultural History of Smell* (New York: Routledge, 1994), p. 73.

13. Stamelman, *Perfume*, p. 56; Feydeau, "De l'hygiène," pp. 16–17.

14. Catherine Lanoë, *La poudre et le fard: Une histoire des cosmétiques de la renaissance aux lumières* (Seyssel, France: Éditions Champ Vallon, 2008), ch. 6.

15. Morag Sarah Martin, "Consuming Beauty: The Commerce of Cosmetics in France 1750–1800," unpubl. doctoral diss., University of California, Irvine, 1999, chs 1 and 2.

16. Pillivuyt, *Histoire*, pp. 167–8.

17. Neville Williams, *Powder and Paint: A History of the Englishwoman's Toilet Elizabeth I–Elizabeth II* (Longmans: London, 1957), ch. 3; Maxine Berg, "New Commodities, Luxuries and Their Consumers in Eighteenth-century England," in Maxine Berg and Helen Clifford (eds), *Consumers and Luxury: Consumer Culture in Europe 1650–1850* (Manchester: Manchester University Press, 1999).

18. Martin, "Consuming Beauty," pp. 56–61.

19. Feydeau, "De l'hygiène," pp. 9–10; Lucien Toussaint Piver, *Exposition universelle internationale de 1900 à Paris: Rapports du jury international. Groupe XIV: Industrie chimique, troisième partie, classe 90—parfumerie* (Paris: Imprimerie nationale, 1902), p. 381.

20. E. Wynne Thomas, *The House of Yardley 1770–1953* (London: Sylvan Press, 1953), pp. 31–7. On the history of branding, see Mira Wilkins, "When and Why Brand Names in Food and Drink?," in Geoffrey Jones and Nicholas J. Morgan (eds), *Adding Value: Brands and Marketing in Food and Drink* (London: Routledge, 1994); Paul Duguid, "Developing the Brand: The Case of Alcohol, 1800–1880," *Enterprise & Society* 4 (2003), pp. 405–41; and Nancy F. Koehn, *Brand New* (Boston, Mass.: Harvard Business School Press, 2001).

21. Anne Pimlott Baker, "Rimmel, Eugène (1820–1887)," *Oxford Dictionary of National Biography*, online edition, <www.oxforddnb.com/view/article/92475>, May 2005, accessed January 8, 2009.

22. Eugène Rimmel, *The Book of Perfumes* (London: Chapman and Hall, 1865; repr. Chestnut Hill, Mass.: Elibron Classics, 2004); Baker, "Rimmel;" Feydeau, "De l'hygiène," p. 188.

23. Feydeau, "De l'hygiène," pp. 45–9.

24. Colette Fellous, *Guerlain* (Paris: Éditions Denoël, 1987), pp. 16–21.

25. Louis Bergeron, *Les industries du luxe en France* (Paris: Éditions Odile Jacob, 1998).

26. Eugénie Briot, "La chimie des élégances: La parfumerie parisienne au XIXe siècle, naissance d'une industrie du luxe," unpubl. doctoral diss., Conservatoire National des Arts et Métiers, Centre d'Histoire des Techniques et de l'Environnement, 2008, pp. 102–3.

27. Piver, *Exposition*, p. 383; Eugénie Briot, "César Birotteau et ses pairs: Poétiques et mercatique des parfumeurs dans le Paris du XIXe siècle," in Bruno Blondé, Eugénie Briot, Natacha Coquery, and Laura Van Aert (eds) *Retailers and Consumer Changes in Early Modern Europe: England, France, Italy and the Low Countries* (Tours: Presses Universitaires François-Rabelais, 2005), p. 74.

28. *Catalogue of the British Section, Paris Universal Exhibition of 1867* (London: Spottiswoode, 1867), p. 68.

29. Rimmel, *Book*, p. 233.

30. Morris, *Fragrance*, p. 217.

31. David R. Foster, *The Story of Colgate-Palmolive* (New York: Newcomen Society, 1975), p. 10.

32. Briot, "La chimie," pp. 102-3.

33. Briot, "La chimie," pp. 265-8.

34. Paul Duguid, "French Connections: The International Propagation of Trademarks in the Nineteenth Century," *Enterprise & Society* 10 (2009), pp. 3-37.

35. Marie-Christine Grasse, "The History of the Grasse Perfume Industry," *Business Briefing Global Cosmetics Manufacturing 2004*, available at <www.touchbriefings.com/pdf/846/grasse_WEB.pdf>, accessed January 17, 2008.

36. Stamelman, *Perfume*, pp. 95-6; Morris, *Fragrance*, p. 183; "Roure Bertrand," <www.perfumeprojects.com/museum/marketers/Roure>, accessed January 9, 2008.

37. Feydeau, "De l'hygiène," pp. 33-6.

38. Feydeau, "De l'hygiène," pp. 36-9.

39. Morris, *Fragrance*, pp. 185-7; Stamelman, *Perfume*, p. 96; Briot, "La chimie," pp. 114-271, 464-6.

40. Stamelman, *Perfume*, p. 97.

41. Ghislaine Sicard-Picchiottino, *François Coty: Un industriel corse sous la IIIe République* (Ajaccio: Albiana, 2006), pp. 46-7.

42. Fellous, *Guerlain*, pp. 39-52.

43. Briot, "La chimie," pp. 323-6.

44. Classen *et al.*, *Aroma*, pp. 82-4.

45. Joanne Entwistle, *The Fashioned Body* (Cambridge: Polity Press, 2000), pp. 156-68.

46. For example, the price of a kilo of synthetic vanillin fell from 8,800 francs in 1876 to 45 francs in 1913 (Stamelman, *Perfume*, pp. 97, 151).

47. Feydeau, "De l'hygiène," pp. 96-8.

48. Briot, "La chimie," pp. 394-5.

49. Michael B. Miller, *The Bon Marché: Bourgeois Culture and the Department Store, 1869-1920* (Princeton: Princeton University Press, 1981); Michael S. Smith, *The Emergence of Modern Business Enterprise in France, 1800-1939* (Cambridge, Mass.: Harvard University Press, 2006), pp. 121-3; Feydeau, "De l'hygiène," pp. 344-9.

50. Briot, "La chimie," p. 395.

51. Feydeau, "De l'hygiène," pp. 51-3; Briot, "La chimie," pp. 240, 324-5.

52. François-Marie Grau, *La haute couture* (Paris: Presses Universitaires de France, 2000).

53. Smith, *Emergence*, p. 294.

54. Valerie Steele, *Paris Fashion: A Cultural History* (Oxford: Berg, 1998), pp. 135-50.

55. Marco Belfanti and Fabio Giusberti, "Global Dress: Clothing as a Means of Integration (17th–20th Centuries)," *Proceedings of the XIIIth International Economic History Congress,* January 22–26, 2006.

56. Regina Lee Blaszczyk, *American Consumer Society 1865–2005* (Wheeling, Ill.: Harlan Davidson, 2009), pp. 77–8.

57. Morris, *Fragrance*, p. 194.

58. Robert Opie, *Packaging Source Book: A Visual Guide to a Century of Packaging Design* (London: Macdonald, 1989), pp. 54–65; Stamelman, *Perfume*, p. 167; Edward W. Said, *Orientalism* (New York: Vintage Books, 1979).

59. Thomas, *House*, pp. 45–52; Rheinisch Westfälisches Wirtschafts Archiv (hereafter RWWA), Abteilung 162 Muehlens, 162–199–4, Yardley, Customer correspondence, 1915–32.

60. Williams, *Powder*, pp. 99–100.

61. Crédit Lyonnais Archives (hereafter CL), DEEF 13601, Brocard et Cie, "Études Financières," April 20, 1905; Société par parts de Parfumerie Brocard et Cie à Moscou, June 1921.

62. Le Guérer, *Le parfum*, pp. 203–4.

63. CL, DEEF 13601, Brocard et Cie, April 20, 1905; Société par parts, June 1921.

64. Lehman Brothers, *Coty Inc.* (New York: Lehman Brothers, 1929).

65. Feydeau, "De l'hygiène," p. 33.

66. Piver, *Exposition*, p. 462.

67. RWWA, 162-198-4, Yardley, Real Ledger, 1845–1909.

68. Katina Lee Manko, "'Ding Dong! Avon Calling!': Gender, Business and Door-to-Door Selling, 1890–1955," unpubl. doctoral diss., University of Delaware, 2001.

69. Morris, *Fragrance*, pp. 218–19; Richard Hudnut, *Beauty Book, Containing Some Account of Marvelous Cold Cream and Other Complexion Specialties* (New York: Richard Hudnut, 1915); <www.perfumeprojects.com/museum/marketers/Hudnut.php>, accessed January 15, 2009.

70. After selling his business, Hudnut moved to live permanently in Paris, where he opened a new prestige perfume business based around a luxury salon in the prestigious rue de la Paix.

71. Sicard-Picchiottino, *Coty*, ch. 1.

72. Sicard-Picchiottino, *Coty*, pp. 63–8.

73. Orla Healy, *Coty: The Brand of Visionary* (New York: Assouline, 2004); Elizabeth Barille and Keiichi Tahara, *Coty: Parfumeur and Visionary* (Paris: Éditions Assouline, 1995).

74. Barille and Tahara, *Coty*, pp. 71–5.

75. Sicard-Picchiottino, *Coty*, pp. 89–90.

76. Walter A. Friedman, *Birth of a Salesman* (Cambridge, Mass.: Harvard University Press, 2004), pp. 97–105.

77. Sicard-Picchiottino, *Coty*, pp. 76–8.

78. Healy, *Coty*, p. 15.

79. Sicard-Picchiottino, *Coty*, pp. 50–1.

80. Stamelman, *Perfume*, p. 247; Bruno Abescat and Yves Stavridès, "Derrière l'empire Chanel...La fabuleuse histoire des Wertheimer," <www.lexpress.fr/actualite/economie/la-fabuleuse-histoire-des-wertheimer_485301.htm>, accessed April 4, 2007.

81. Sicard-Picchiottino, *Coty*, pp. 45, 82.

82. Geoffrey Jones, *Multinationals and Global Capitalism* (Oxford: Oxford University Press, 2005), ch. 2.

83. Rimmel, *Book,* pp. 234–5.

84. Sicard-Picchiottino, *Coty*, p. 49.

85. Feydeau, "De l'hygiène," p. 179; Piver, *Exposition*, pp. 387–8.

86. Eugénie Briot, personal communication, December 15, 2008.

87. Feydeau, "De l'hygiène," pp. 187–8.

88. RWWA, 162-125-1, untitled history of "the 4711 Enterprise," n.d., pp. 8–9.

89. *160 Jahre no. 4711* (Cologne: the company, 1952). Two years later, Muehlens acquired further shares in this firm (RWWA, 162-617-1, "Bemerkungen zur Urkundensammlung 2. Generation," p. 2).

90. *160 Jahre no. 4711.*

91. RWWA, 162-83-8, Materialsammlung 4711 Archiv IV, "Fragebogen," April 15, 1985, and "Geschichte des 4711-Geschäfts in den USA," letter from Walter Leuschner to Ferdinand Muehlens, March 17, 1978.

92. RWWA, 162-136-3, Geschichtliche Forschungen zu Kölnisch Wasser und seinen Produzenten, Herr Schreiber, "4711" Rechtsabteilung, to Ernst Rosenbohm and Dietrich Taubert, Historisches Archiv der Firma Muehlens, December 23, 1959; and Historisches Archiv, Hamburg, to Fräulein Latz re: Herr Schreiber's inquiry about activities in France, 1794–1931, January 8, 1960.

93. RWWA, 162-125-1, "the 4711 enterprise."

94. RWWA, 162-125-1, Nils Ternberg to Walter Leuschner, February 20, 1984.

95. RWWA, 162-125-1, "the 4711 enterprise," pp. 8–11.

96. *160 Jahre no. 4711.*

98. RWWA, 162-83-8, Materialsammlung 4711 Archiv IV, "Fragebogen," April 15, 1985.

98. Florence E. Wall, "Historical Development of the Cosmetics Industry," in M. S. Balsam and Edward Sagarin (eds), *Cosmetics: Science and Technology*, 2nd edn, vol. 3 (New York: John Wiley, 1974), pp. 101, 103, 118.

99. Jean-Marie Martin-Hattemberg, *Caron* (Toulouse: Éditions Milan, 2000), pp. 19–21, 41; Grégoire Colard, *Le charme secret d'une maison parfumée* (Paris: Éditions J. C. Lattès, 1984).

100. Sicard-Picchiottino, *Coty*, pp. 83–4; Healy, *Coty*, pp. 17–18; Stamelman, *Perfume*, p. 179.

2

How Do I Look?

The circle of customers is international.
Paul Beiersdorf, founder of Beiersdorf, 1890[1]

The rise of visual self-awareness

Perfumery was not the only aspect of beauty to evolve from domestic knowledge and local crafts into a modern industry. After all, what good is it to smell
nice if you look like a wreck, particularly in an age when new technologies
focused unprecedented attention on appearance? New commercial products
and services emerged in the modern era to help beautify one's hair, skin, and
face. As with perfumery, the cultivation of physical beauty can be traced back
for millennia, but for the most part the work of caring for one's appearance
was done in the home. As flickering candlelight gave way to gas and electricity, and as the quality of mirrors improved, people had unprecedented
opportunities to look at themselves. Narcissus, Ovid tells us in the *Meta-
morphoses*, saw his reflection for the first time in a pool. With the spread of
commercial photography in the late nineteenth century, one could study,
preserve, and distribute one's own image anywhere.[2] The reflecting pool
was now in one's pocket. Visual self-awareness was intensified in a way that
had never happened before, and new industries rose alongside that awareness
to cater to it.

When it came to moving the work of beauty from the home to the market,
the perfumers were matched in imagination by a new set of entrepreneurial
actors whose expertise lay in hairdressing and salons, pharmacy and theatrical
make-up, and who had no hesitation about using health claims, enticing
advertising, and other devices to pitch their new beauty products. Indeed, in
the case of certain products, like toothpastes, claims of health and beauty were

inseparable. These products created distinct opportunities for women, who were almost entirely absent from perfumery, to emerge as entrepreneurs.

The history of hair

The origins of some of today's most important beauty companies lay in the creation of brands and products designed to shape, clean, and change the color of hair. This may not seem surprising given that hair plays such an important role in appearance. The graying of hair, or its loss altogether, provides a potent signal of aging. The display of hair, especially female hair, has carried emotional and sexual connotations around the world. Historically, married women in many Western and Eastern cultures covered their hair, while Islamic women covered their hair regardless of their marital state. As a result, even as perfumery became a public trade, caring for hair was a more private matter, at least for women.

In Europe, while barbers—the ancestors of today's surgeon's—had shaved men and cut their hair for centuries, there were no equivalent public venues for women of any social class. Women had their hair dressed within the private sphere, by other women. It was, once more, the court of Louis XIV that provided an exception. A new profession of celebrity hairdresser emerged when Monsieur Champagne was employed to create fashionable styles for the aristocratic elite that frequented the court. Even two centuries later, however, the overwhelming majority of women still had their hair dressed privately by other women, usually by friends or relatives or, for the wealthier, a female maid.[3]

During the middle of the nineteenth century, the fashion for more elaborate and longer hair for women returned to Europe. As in the case of perfume, the demand for fashionable hairstyles began to widen to affluent middle-class women, who looked to well-known aristocratic women as fashion trendsetters.[4] The beautiful Spanish countess Eugénie de Montijo, who married France's Napoleon III in 1853 at the age of 26, became one of the first global fashion celebrities, when the royal court's hairdresser arranged her bleached reddish-blonde hair in a novel style for her wedding ceremony. Dyed with a secret tincture exclusively created by a Spanish coiffeur for Eugénie, her hair displayed blonde highlights that became highly fashionable.[5]

The new fashions helped to stimulate a demand for luxury hairdressers. The service was pure artifice, as a single shampooing would wash out the style, but by the 1870s Paris boasted a small number of "haute coiffure" hairdressers who used "false" hair—actually human hair collected at salons—to assemble hair-pieces and wigs which were blended with a customer's own hair at salons. Paris also had a small set of male hairdressers whose customers belonged to the women on the fringes of respectable society.

François Marcel, whose given name was Marcel Grateau, began his career as a barely respectable hairdresser serving lower-class customers in Montmartre, one of the poorest neighborhoods in Paris. He mastered the art of waving, or "ondulation," by hot scissors, which was used by many women at home, but he was not satisfied with the results. The procedure took too long, making it unprofitable for salons, whilst hair was easily damaged by burning. According to the later legend surrounding Marcel, he also judged that the result could not match the blonde, naturally wavy hair of his mother, which he believed should be attainable for every woman. In 1872, after years of experimentation, he found a solution which consisted of wrapping the strands of hair around the straight, cutting edge of the burning scissors instead of around the rounded loops. The result was quicker and more predictable and produced natural-looking waves.[6]

Marcel turned a technical innovation into a successful business. In 1885 Marcel, perceiving the power of celebrity endorsement, contacted a famous French actress, Jane Hading, asking her to let him wave her hair using the new technique. She agreed, and when she performed her next play sporting Marcel's waves, it was an immediate sensation.[7] Within 25 years Marcel earned a million francs, and retired from the business to a castle in Nor-mandy.[8]

The "Marcel wave," however, had the problem that it did not last well. This provided an opportunity for another entrepreneurial hairdresser, Karl Nessler. Nessler was born in a small German town in the Black Forest in 1872. He started his apprenticeship in a male barbershop, but like Marcel he was later said to have been inspired by his female family members to figure out a means to help all women achieve wavy hair, as only some of Nessler's sisters had naturally wavy hair, while the others struggled to achieve it. He eventually sought more opportunities in Switzerland, where he learned the art of wig-making as well as more advanced hairstyling. As part of the process of setting the wig hair into lasting waves, the hair was rolled tightly around wooden blocks, smeared with bread dough, and baked. This method gave Nessler the idea that living hair could also be permanently waved through a chemical process, and not just temporarily set with heat.

As Nessler's reputation grew, he was able to get a job at a fashionable salon in the city of Geneva. Next, now fluent in French, he moved to Paris. He also adopted the more French-sounding name Nestle, apparently thereafter using the two names somewhat interchangeably, although professionally he called himself Charles Nestle. In Paris, he continued to work with different substances and formulas for waving hair permanently, experimenting on a young German woman from his home region who worked in a Paris salon and whom he eventually married. After a decade, in 1906, Nessler perfected his perming machine.[9]

By then, Nessler had moved to a fashionable salon in London. Losing his job after experimenting on a customer, he had to offer his new perm for free in the new salon he set up, as few customers who were willing to take the risk wanted to pay for it. After meeting much skepticism from other hairdressers and customers alike, in 1908 he registered a patent for the machine and opened a larger salon. The real breakthrough came in 1910, when it became possible to switch to the use of electricity to heat the heating rods, significantly shortening the procedure. In 1911, Nessler expanded his business by building a factory and opening a salon, where he and his staff were soon performing 3,000 perms a year.[10]

Marcel and Nessler, then, were drivers of a change which made fashionable styles far more accessible to women than previously, and made going to salons a socially aspirant experience rather than a morally dubious one. The wider impact was a transformation in the market for female hairdressing. In 1896 there were 47,640 hairdressers in Paris, nine-tenths of whom were male, mostly working alone.[11] By 1909 Paris had 300 female hairdressing salons, and another 1,800 serving both men and women.[12] Paris stood, as in fragrances, at the apex of prestige for female hairdressing.

The growth of the salon business created a new distribution channel for beauty entrepreneurs. Among the new entrepreneurs who sought to exploit the opportunity offered by the rise of hair fashion was Franz Ströher, who was to become the founder of the German company later named Wella. Ströher learned the craft of tatting lace in his parental home in Saxony, where he and his four siblings helped their family survive financially after their father died when Ströher was 3. He apprenticed to a hairdresser and became one in

1872 at the age of 18, and then traveled widely in Europe, learning the latest hair fashions in Paris and elsewhere.[13]

In 1880 Ströher started a company making handmade hair tulle. This material had been used as a base for wigs for some time, but a new use arose with the arrival of the hair "transformations," as hairdressers and women liked to place a nearly undetectable hair net, called "invisible," around the expensive finished coiffure to protect it.[14] Capitalizing on his lacemaking skills, he soon also started manufacturing wigs and hairpieces, which he sold to salons. In 1900 he invented the waterproof Tüllemoid. This artificial tulle kept wigs securely in place by allowing the scalp to breathe through it, reducing the build-up of perspiration that threatened to make a wig slip. It was an immediate sensation and became Ströher's first best-selling product.[15]

Meanwhile Hans Schwarzkopf, another German entrepreneur, created a product which revolutionized the hygiene of natural hair. Throughout the nineteenth century washing hair remained both unusual and unfashionable. During the 1890s some French hairdressers began offering a "dry shampoo," using chemicals, but it remained a small part of the salon business, whilst washing with water was unusual because of the lack of indoor plumbing and water heaters.[16] Although drugstores and pharmacies sometimes retailed shampoos, some were dangerous.[17]

Schwarzkopf, a qualified chemist, opened a small drugstore in Berlin in 1898. In 1903 he launched a pioneering powder shampoo, initially in response to a customer who had asked for a special mixture for her hair, which she felt was lacking in luster. The customer was so pleased that news spread by word of mouth, and soon requests came in also from other stores that wanted to sell his shampoo, a name Schwarzkopf coined himself from the Hindi word *chāmpo*, to massage. He sold the shampoo in individual paper packets, intended for single use, but they were often used by an entire family at the weekly Saturday bath typical in Germany at the time. He developed the product into a trademark, choosing the silhouette of the black head still used today. The business grew quickly.[18]

The location of the business in Berlin, the cosmopolitan capital of Germany, added to the appeal of Schwarzkopf's new brand. In 1905 a Dutch entrepreneur approached Schwarzkopf to buy a dozen bags of shampoos as samples, leading to an arrangement which gave Schwarzkopf distribution rights in the Netherlands. Soon afterwards the company started selling to Russia and elsewhere in Europe. In 1911, the first foreign branch office was founded in Austria-Hungary, and a local firm was retained as distribution and sales partner.[19]

However, the most radical innovation occurred in hair dyeing. During the nineteenth century dyeing hair was primarily a concern for men and female actresses. The use of commercial products to change hair color was widely regarded as inappropriate for respectable women, whilst most of the products on offer were rightly regarded as hazardous.[20] Towards the end of the century, the practice of dyeing and bleaching hair began to spread to middle-class and aristocratic women. Highly alkaline soaps were applied to the hair, and women would follow the long-established practice of sitting in the sun for hours to bleach it. An easier, though less effective, way was to powder the hair with pollen and crushed yellow flower petals.

It was within this context of a growing consumer interest in changing hair color, amid enduring concerns about both the health hazards and the perceived morality of the process, that Eugène Schueller invented the first safe synthetic hair-color formula in 1907. His parents, who had moved to Paris from Alsace, owned a bakery and pastry shop. In 1890, when Eugène was 9, they lost everything on a bad investment. Eugène, who had attended a private school, had to be moved to a state school as the family could not afford the tuition. Later, he was able to attend a local college in return for goods furnished by his parents' bakery to the school canteen. Further difficulties, and another loss of much of the family business, meant that he had to leave this school as well. Finally, in 1901, he entered the Sorbonne, where he studied for three years and earned a degree in chemistry.[21]

Schueller's path towards the salon business was fortuitous. A Paris hairdresser who realized the lack in the market of a satisfactory colorant, and who had tried but failed to make one, paid a visit to Schueller's chemistry teacher at the Sorbonne, asking for help. Schueller was chosen to work on the project. The results, tested on elderly men and women at the hairdresser's salon, were not successful, and in 1904 Schueller took a job at a pharmacy, where he remained until 1908. While in this position, he started experiments with hair colorants in his own kitchen. There were numerous small explosions as the work progressed, with the police being called on several occasions. However, he saw a real opportunity in the market, despite the fact that hair-coloring services made up only a minimal part of all hairdressing services at that time.[22]

In December 1907 Schueller registered two trademarks for hair colorants, Noir et Or and L'Auréale. The first one was never used, while L'Auréale was only used for a few months as Schueller found the process of applying it too long. But he liked the association between the name, which means "halo," and the then-fashionable, henna-treated, shining bright red- or gold-colored hair that was meant to be radiant like a "halo." He settled on the name L'Oréal, which evoked both the "halo" and the gold (*or*). Launched in 1908, the first L'Oréal colors came in three shades. Certain that he had a promising product with the right name, Schueller found a partner, with whom he invested 125,000 francs (around $24,000), and founded a company in 1909.[23]

Schueller's major achievement was to communicate the potential of the new product to initially skeptical hairdressers, to whom his products were exclusively supplied. In October 1909 he started regular publication of a newsletter for hairdressers, which laid the foundation for what he called his communication strategy. In the same year, he also published a book in which he presented his views on the aim of hair coloration, along with his technique for its safe use, providing as a result a user's manual on the product for hairdressers. In 1910 Schueller established a school, and in 1913 a demonstration hall, for hairdressers.[24] These steps laid the foundation for L'Oréal's close relationship with French hairdressers, which was key to the growth of the business, for effectively he co-opted them as the marketers of his brand.

As in the case of Schwarzkopf, the first tentative steps were taken to sell beyond France. By 1914 Schueller's products had reached the Netherlands, Austria and Italy. These new, safe products for changing the color of hair, as well as washing it, met needs which were not confined to France and Germany, and their "universal" nature was immediately apparent. This did not mean that internationalization was easy. Both hair texture and strength vary considerably across the planet, but such variation was small between neighboring Western European countries, where initial marketing efforts were focused. The greater challenge for a small firm lay in gaining access to hairdressers and consumers in other countries, and in responding to different societal attitudes towards changing hair color.

It was hardly surprising, given the circumstances of the time, let alone the fledgling nature of their own businesses, that these creators of hair products paid no attention to non-European hair, even though both France and Germany had extensive colonies in Africa and elsewhere. The poor inhabitants of these colonies were in no position to purchase branded consumer goods, but the emergent world of fashion and beauty was also a Western world in which Europeans and their descendants were regarded as beautiful. These underlying assumptions were most strikingly seen in the United States, where African-Americans represented over one-tenth of the population before World War I, but where the commercial beauty industry made no provision for their distinctive hair texture or skin tones.

The treatment of African-American hair, which is often tightly coiled, became the basis for a large ethnic beauty industry. Whether because of a desire to look more like white people or because of a desire to make their hair more "manageable," products to "straighten" African hair became a fertile area for African-American entrepreneurs.

Two women, Annie Turnbo Malone and Madam C. J. Walker, were among the most successful entrepreneurs, building businesses considerably larger than Schwarzkopf's or Schueller's before 1914. Turnbo Malone, orphaned as a child and raised in poverty, began experimenting with hair care preparations during the 1890s. By the following decade she was selling hair products containing sage and egg to African-Americans. Moving to St. Louis in 1902, she built a regional and then a national market, registering the trade name "Poro," an African term for a devotional society. Madam C. J. Walker, born to former slaves in Louisiana, also developed a hair care business after inventing a remedy for hair loss in response to the thinning of her own hair. Walker's improvement on the existing technologies using heating combs to straighten African hair, which became known as the Walker System, provided the foundation of her success.[25]

Both Turnbo Malone and Walker got started by selling their own products from door to door, focusing on developing a large mass market for their products. As African-Americans lived in segregated areas, this strategy was particularly effective in reaching their target markets. Moreover, it not only much reduced the initial need to advertise, but explicitly associated products with ethnic communities.[26] As Turnbo Malone's business grew, she continued to hire representatives and she also franchised beauty schools. Walker used both direct selling and mail order. Walker's second husband, whom she married in 1906, had not only provided her with a new name, but helped her with advertising and promotion, as he was a newspaperman. The Walker Manufacturing Company had sales of over $1 million by World War I. While this meant it was significantly smaller than Rallet in Russia, it was much larger than most if not all Parisian perfume houses at that time. Both Turnbo Malone and Walker were probably millionaires by 1914 and, as a result, were among the first American self-made female millionaires.[27]

By 1914, then, the creation of products and services designed to manage and style hair had become a significant component of the beauty industry. The growth of hairdressing salons for women had started to commercialize services and products long restricted largely to homes. A range of practices considered dangerous or illegitimate or both, from washing hair to changing its color, had begun to be legitimized, at least in affluent, big cities. This development provided a new retail space for people to buy products and an important mechanism for diffusing fashion. The salons and the hairdressing profession, meanwhile, became a new market for entrepreneurs which, if cultivated carefully, provided the basis for commercial success. Moreover, these services and products had demonstrated the potential both to serve as the basis for large ethnic home-market businesses and, at the other extreme, for successful internationalization.

Second skin: the rise of skin care outside the home

The use of creams for the skin was another age-old beauty ritual. As in hairdressing, there was a small luxury trade for most of the nineteenth century. This market consisted largely of two types of products sold mainly by perfumers: "milks," or emulsions intended to freshen and clean the face, made by crushing the seeds of plants, such as roses, and mixing with water; and "cold creams," made from mixing fats and water, and used to smooth skin.[28] The sale of such fashionable scented creams co-existed with the much older and wider use of handmade creams and lotions whose ingredients were passed down from generation to generation like kitchen recipes.[29]

The commercial development of mass-marketed skin creams built on both these traditions. The first widely sold commercial creams heavily emphasized their health benefits and were often created by pharmacists and chemists. Among the earliest entrepreneurs in this tradition was Theron T. Pond, a pharmacist in New York state and a partner in a saddle business, who in 1846 developed a product derived from the bark of witch hazel designed to relieve cuts and burns. Although he died shortly afterwards, his partners continued the business of selling Pond's Extract. By the 1870s Pond's was also employing witch hazel, which had long been used by Native Americans to soothe sores and swelling, in a range of creams, soaps, and lip balms.[30]

Another skin care product emerged from the activities of Robert Chesebrough. Chesebrough started out by refining and selling kerosene for use in lamps in the 1850s. Born in Britain but working in New York, he became interested in the supposed healing qualities of petroleum derivatives after seeing a worker who was cleaning an oil rig collect residue to be used for healing cuts and bruises. After years of research, Chesebrough created the first "petroleum jelly" which was pure, odorless, and safe. He patented the name Vaseline to describe it, derived from the Saxon word *wasser* (water) and the Greek word *oleon* (oil). He began selling the product from the back of a wagon, and the business grew quickly, not least because of his success in getting medical endorsements, including that of the leading British medical journal *The Lancet* in 1876. Three years earlier he had persuaded Colgate to distribute the product, an arrangement that would continue until the 1950s. In 1880 the company incorporated, only to be taken over in the following year by John D. Rockefeller's Standard Oil Company, which was on its way to becoming one of the biggest companies in the United States, where it remained until it was broken up by a historic antitrust ruling in 1911.[31]

The growth of a mass market for these and other creams, like the cold creams which grew in popularity at the turn of the century, was facilitated by major new developments in media and advertising which drove the creation of a mass market for consumer goods. Advertising for brand-name goods proliferated in newspapers, billboards, and colorful trade cards given away by retailers. The American market, where local advertising gave way to national advertising, drove many of these changes, although they were echoed in prosperous Western European countries such as Britain.[32] The sellers of creams placed their advertisements in mass-circulation female fashion magazines, which had started appearing in the late eighteenth century and were widespread by the late nineteenth.[33]

Pond's and other companies were also able to use the services of advertising agencies which, with the growth of mass-circulation print media, were transformed from buyers of space in newspapers to creators of advertising copy. J. Walter Thompson pioneered the placing of advertisements in women's magazines. This agency, like many others in the emergent American advertising and media industry, was based in New York. During the 1890s the electrification of that city led to the construction of massive illuminated advertising signs, beginning on Broadway. By the turn of the century some 25 advertising agencies were active in the city. It was also America's largest center for women's magazine publishing. It was the home of the magazine publisher Condé Nast, who purchased *Vogue* magazine in 1909 and launched the predecessor to *Vanity Fair* in 1913.[34]

In 1886 Pond's launched its first national advertising campaign for Pond's Extract with J. Walter Thompson.[35] Advertising drove Pond's sales, although the growing professionalization of the media had its downsides also. Pond's Extract's wide-ranging claims to cure multiple illnesses were being met with growing skepticism. In response, the company launched Pond's Cold Cream and Vanishing Cream, based on mineral oils, in 1907, but by then there were so many face creams on the American market that right through to 1914 the firm struggled to expand the new brand.[36]

The Hamburg firm of Beiersdorf, founded by pharmacist Paul Beiersdorf in 1882, perhaps came closest to perceiving that the key to developing a mass market in a skin cream brand lay in combining health claims with artifice. By the time Beiersdorf launched what became the iconic skin care brand Nivea, the firm already had considerable experience in marketing toiletries. Initially a manufacturer of medical plasters, Beiersdorf expanded to making a lip pomade in stick form and medicinal soaps. Paul Beiersdorf maintained contacts with university researchers and exported his products to clinics and apothecaries, especially in large European university cities. In 1890 a family tragedy forced the sale of his firm to a young pharmacist, 27-year-old Oscar Troplowitz, whose uncle Gustav Mankiewicz, another pharmacist, provided the capital.[37] Troplowitz subsequently married Gustav's daughter, and in 1906 his brother-in law Oscar Mankiewicz became a partner, initially with 10 per cent of the business.

Troplowitz was scientifically gifted and also possessed marketing savvy. After researching the plasters market in America, where products had better adhesive properties than Beiersdorf's plasters but were often irritating to the skin, he invented Leukoplast ("the white plaster"), which offered durable as well as non-irritating adhesion along with skin-healing properties.[38] Troplowitz also invented Germany's first toothpaste, mixing his own dentist's tooth-cleaning powder with paste and storing it in a metal tube for better preservation. His dentist also came up with a medicinal prescription powder designed to treat mouth disease with the paste. Troplowitz recognized the

2.1 Oscar Troplowitz, the second proprietor of Beiersdorf in Germany, 1906.

potential of a product with both cleaning and medicinal properties, and
devised an innovative advertising campaign. He launched the toothpaste,
and a decade later, in 1903, it received the brand name Pebeco, named after
the initials of the company's founder, Paul Beiersdorf.

The Pebeco brand was sold using the network of pharmacists and wholesalers who sold the firm's plasters. An in-house sales force was also used to
visit retailers. The brand's advertising emphasized the functional benefits—
that it both cleaned teeth and prevented disease. Pebeco soon built a leading
position in the German market.[39] Like Coty, the company also pursued a
global vision. Before becoming a partner, Mankiewicz had worked for Lehn &
Fink, an American firm which sold the disinfectant Lysol. In 1893 Lehn & Fink
began selling Beiersdorf's plasters and salves in the United States, and in 1903
was given the license to manufacture Pebeco. Pebeco was one of the largest
toothpaste brands in the United States by 1914.[40]

Elsewhere, Beiersdorf created wholly-owned distribution companies in
Britain and Austria, appointed exclusive distributors in other markets, and
in some cases provided machinery to help local manufacture. In Asia and
elsewhere, where volumes were low, merchant firms sold Beiersdorf's products.[41] By 1914 two-fifths of Beiersdorf's sales, which had grown twelve-fold
over the previous 14 years, were made outside Germany.[42]

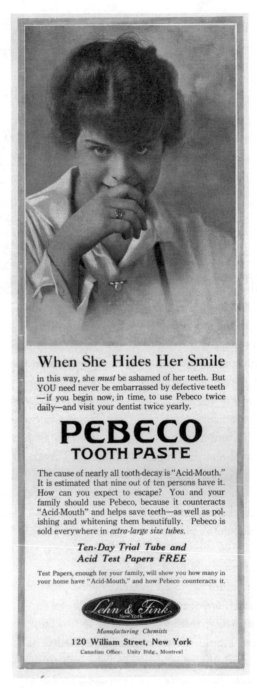

2.2 Consumers are urged to start the practice of good dental hygiene at a young age with the regular use of Pebeco in this 1916 advertisement for the American market.

The success of Pebeco encouraged expansion into other toiletries. In 1904, Troplowitz purchased a soap factory, adding to its portfolio of medicinal soaps a finely milled, but inexpensive, toilet soap. The new toilet soap, named Nivea (Latin for "snow white") in 1906, was joined by other toiletries. In 1911 Troplowitz acquired the German patent for a durable and smooth ointment base called Eucerit which was derived from lanolin as an emulsifier, along with the Bremen-based factory which produced it. Giving it the same name as that of his toilet soap, since it also shared the white color of fresh snow, he launched Nivea Creme, initially sold in green and yellow jars designed in the modern Art Nouveau style.[43] After the cream was launched in 1912, the Nivea product line was extended to a powder and a hair lotion.[44]

Troplowitz was amongst the first to understand the potential for increasing the emotional component of the claims made for a skin care brand. While the functional claims of creams using witch hazel or petroleum jelly to soothe or heal skin could be verified, or falsified, by the individuals who used them, the non-medical benefits of skin creams were harder to demonstrate. Even if scented, creams did not have the direct impact on the sense of smell that perfumes did, which could be exploited by advertising to build emotional associations of romance or desire. While skin creams could, and increasingly did, claim to make skin softer and less wrinkled, the visible impact of using them was far less transformational than that of hair dye or rouge. The application of cream to bare skin certainly affected the sense of touch, but that experience was an intimate and personal one.

Troplowitz's solution to this marketing challenge was to emphasize the feminine nature of the new brand, suggesting to consumers that they could make themselves feel more feminine as well as healthy by using the cream. He asked the well-known poster artist Hans Rudi Erdt to design a new Nivea woman, an elegant lady described as a "vulnerable 'femme fragile'." Posters had come into widespread use in the last quarter of the nineteenth century as one of the most important forms of publicly displayed advertising, and Troplowitz, artistically inclined himself, was personally acquainted with many of the German painters and graphic artists who made them. This was the origin of a beauty ideal that invoked health and the practicality of a simple routine, yet also suggested refined living and classical femininity. During one of his trips to Paris, Troplowitz also met another German artist who designed the sphinx series of Nivea advertisements, employing a juxtaposition of the "femme fragile" with the "femme fatale" by rendering a domesticated sphinx "with the body of a beast of prey...patterned with flowers" and wearing a pretty hat. Reflecting the taste of the elite in Germany, this first Nivea campaign thus flirted with the emerging theme of independence for women without subverting traditional standards of submissive femininity.[45]

It was apparent to Troplowitz that the market for his new skin cream, like his toothpaste, was far from limited to Germany. Both Pond's and Chesebrough had exported from early in their corporate lives, demonstrating a demand in Europe for good-quality creams with medicinal claims. By the 1870s Chesebrough was selling Vaseline in Britain, France, and Spain, and it opened a factory in Canada in 1910. Pond's also opened its own sales office in London during the 1870s, which handled sales in the rest of Europe.[46] Troplowitz resolved to follow the successful Pebeco model, and in 1914 signed a contract with Lehn & Fink granting the US firm exclusive rights to use the Nivea trademark and to manufacture Nivea products.[47] However, the subsequent outbreak of World War I severely curtailed the company's ambitions.

The potential for marketing skin creams by building their emotional and aspirational associations was also apparent to an emergent cohort of female entrepreneurs. Among the pioneers were Harriet Hubbard Ayer, who bought a recipe for a face cream while in Paris in 1886, and then marketed it using a fraudulent testimonial from Juliette Récamier, a French fashion icon during the first half of the nineteenth century.[48] However, Ayer also built sales by seeking celebrity endorsements, including that of the opera singer Adelina Patti and the famous English beauty Lillie Langtry, and by advertising in fashion magazines. Her involvement in the business came to an end in 1893, however, after relations with her male business partner deteriorated to such an extent that he got her committed to an insane asylum.[49]

Beauty salons in fashionable cities were a frequent entry point for women. Many female businesses, and not only in beauty, began with products made in the owners' own kitchens, which could, if successful, form the basis of a business. Homemade creams were the starting point of most of the female beauty salons of the era.[50] The pioneers included Irish-born Frances Denney, who was unusually well educated in science, being the first woman to graduate with a degree in chemistry from Trinity College in Dublin. She opened a beauty salon in Philadelphia in 1897, where she sold her own creams and cosmetics and introduced the first regimen for skin care, "Cleanse, Freshen and Lubricate." In 1910 she opened the first beauty salon in an American department store, no less than John Wanamaker's in Philadelphia.[51]

However, it was to be Helena Rubinstein and Elizabeth Arden who used the salon route to create brands destined long to outlive them. The former, born as Chaja Rubinstein into an orthodox Jewish family in Cracow, Poland (then part of Russia), emigrated to Australia in 1896, allegedly carrying a pot of cold cream. In 1903 she opened a salon in the city of Melbourne, over which she lived and where she sold a cream called Valaze, which she claimed to have imported from a European skin specialist. In practice she most likely made the cream in the salon, packing it into glass jars and adding attractive labels by hand. She incorporated European artisanal traditions of adding scents such as rose and lavender to her creams, and she soon also had local actresses endorsing her products.[52]

Although Rubinstein became an Australian citizen, her ambitions were wider. In 1905 she toured Europe, including Paris and London, visiting beauty salons and seeking exposure to European beauty culture. She opened another salon in Sydney in 1907, where she met her future husband, an American whose family was also Polish and Jewish. She opened another salon in New Zealand, in the following year, but the major advance came with a salon in the fashionable Mayfair district of London, launched by providing free treatment for aristocrats. In 1909 she acquired another small salon in Paris, along with the skin creams of the salon's former Russian owner. She and her family moved to Paris in 1912. By 1914 Helena Rubinstein had established a substantial business, with five beauty salons in four countries and a range of skin creams.[53]

The North American equivalent to Rubinstein was Elizabeth Arden. She had been born Florence Nightingale Graham on a farm in Canada, the youngest of five children of British immigrants. She left school before she was 18 and entered training as a nurse, but tired of it rapidly, eventually moving to New York City in 1907 aged around 30. Despite her namesake and her early training, Arden was less interested in nursing the body back to health than in using health claims to sell products that made the body beautiful on the outside. She began her career as a cashier in an exclusive Fifth Avenue beauty salon owned by Eleanor Adair, the proprietor of a London salon business which also operated in Paris.[54] After starting and then leaving her own beauty salon partnership with one Elizabeth Hubbard, who made beauty creams, she borrowed the name Elizabeth and adopted the surname Arden. The source of the latter is unknown. While it was later rumored that it came from the poem

"Enoch Arden" by Tennyson, it has been more plausibly explained by her reading about the death of a prominent Californian rail baron and horse owner, who owned a large estate called "Arden" in Orange County.[55] The overall purpose was evident—to promote a high-class and Anglophile association for her own business, which was launched in 1910. From then on, Arden focused on luxury. She launched her first line of creams, called Venetian, with exquisite packaging that matched her salon's décor, and by 1914 this brand was being stocked by fashionable New York department stores.[56]

The affluent consumers of these creams reflected the significant shifts in attitudes towards age which had occurred over the previous decades. In the early nineteenth century older women, typically defined as women over 35, whilst sometimes praised as saintly grandmothers, had generally also been dismissed as highly unattractive. By the early twentieth century women beyond the age of 35 were no longer dismissed as totally uninteresting, at least by men; rather, the commercial beauty industry had begun to focus on selling products which promised to make them look younger by applying creams, visiting salons, or dyeing their hair.[57] The promise to women either to preserve or restore their youth was to become central in skin care brands.

The demand for skin creams also extended beyond the Western world. The greatest non-Western market at the time was Japan. While India and many other Asian countries had fallen under European colonial control by the middle of the nineteenth century, and the once great empire of China suffered growing humiliation at the hands of the Western powers, Japan's development had taken another course after American gunboats arrived in its ports in 1853, demanding the end of the country's self-imposed 200-year policy of seclusion from the world economy. A period of civil war ended, in 1868, with the coming to power of a government which sought to modernize the country at speed in order to avoid the fate of other Asian countries.

Japan's immediate focus was on building the institutions needed to create a modern economy. The new, post-1868 Japanese government's far-ranging vision also included modernizing—and, at least partly, Westernizing—the appearance of a society whose long-established cosmetic practices included tooth blackening and shaving eyebrows; and, for elite men and women, wearing white make-up. Concerned to implement Western gender distinctions in beauty practices, it banned the whitening of male faces and encouraged white painted faces for women as a way to retain traditional values. The Emperor's

2.3 "Western Code of Etiquette" (1887) and "Beauty Culture and Toilet Dainties" (1908), two beauty advice manuals from the late nineteenth and early twentieth centuries. The manuals instruct Japanese women in how to use new, Western-style beauty products.

© Pola Research Institute of Beauty and Culture

"face" was Westernized to encourage this trend. By 1914 the government had also managed virtually to eliminate female eyebrow shaving and tooth blackening, at least in urban areas.[58] The concept of a beautiful Japanese face changed over the space of half a century from having narrow eyes, thin eyebrows and long faces to having rounder eyes and faces with thick eyebrows.[59]

It was from the pharmacy that entrepreneurs emerged to make the products to facilitate the new, Westernized beauty ideals. Among the most important was Arinobu Fukuhara. In 1872 he left his position as head pharmacist of the Japanese navy to open the Shiseido Pharmacy in the Ginza district of central Tokyo. At a time when medicine in Japan meant traditional Chinese herbal medicine, he created Japan's first Western-style pharmacy. Following the path of Beiersdorf, Fukuhara began by making pharmaceutical products and launched into toothpaste in 1888. Hair oils to help women maintain Western-style buns or chignons followed.

It was the launch of an expensive skin lotion named Eudermine in 1897 that marked Shiseido's emergence as a fledgling beauty company. The formula for the lotion originated with a Japanese scientist who had studied in Germany. Fukuhara realized, as did Troplowitz a few years later, that creating attractive emotional associations was the way to build a skin care brand. Unlike competitor brands which did not possess such emotional appeal, the brand name chosen was foreign, derived from classical Greek terms for "good" and "skin." It was sold in a striking red glass bottle decorated with a red ribbon tied around its neck. The brand proved so successful that it continues to be sold by Shiseido even today.[60] While Shiseido did not seek at this time to sell outside Japan, other Japanese companies were more ambitious. Club Cosmetics, the maker of a successful soap and, from 1911, a "British-style" moisturizing cream, began exporting to China in that year using the Two Gorgeous Girls brand name.[61]

Thus by 1914, a commercial market for face creams, both expensive and cheap, was growing throughout the West and even in Japan and China. Skin creams, as a product, were more difficult to market than perfume or even hair dye, as the results were not immediately perceptible. The marketing solution was found in crafting brand images which built associations to fashion and celebrity through brand names, packaging, and exclusive salons, which in turn supported promises of staying youthful. The following decades were destined to see these as yet embryonic ideas worked out on a scale which few in 1914 could have imagined.

Face painting

The smallest, and most controversial, category of products which affected appearance was color cosmetics. This was surprising, given that before the nineteenth century face powders, rouges, lipsticks, and similar products made at home or by artisans were widely used. However, as the toxicity of many of these decorative cosmetic products became better understood in the nineteenth century, demand understandably fell off.[62] A pale and clear skin, blushing cheeks, and a natural appearance became the norms of female beauty in the West.[63] The use of "face painting" and other cosmetic devices became associated with prostitutes or, at best, actresses.[64] Male use of cosmetics, which had been extensive in the pre-industrial era, came to be associated, prejudicially, with effeminate or homosexual men.[65] The marketing challenge for color cosmetics, then, was the opposite of that for skin creams, for the results of use were visible, and widely regarded as morally illegitimate.

The entrepreneurs who strove to build demand for color cosmetics needed to address both the health and the ethical objections to their use. The former was met by seeking to improve the quality of the products. Innovations such as Philadelphia-based Henry Tetlow's discovery in 1866 that zinc oxide made both a good and harmless face powder, for example, were important in enhancing the demand for face powders. Tetlow's Gossamer Face Powder developed a considerable following in the United States.[66] However, dangerous ingredients frequently found their way into products and caused scandals when consumers were poisoned or disfigured. There was no requirement for companies to disclose ingredients, and exaggerated advertising was the norm rather than the exception in a product category which most believed to verge on the immoral. The first significant piece of federal consumer legislation in the United States, the 1906 Pure Food and Drugs Act, was silent on cosmetics, which were not regulated until 1938.[67]

The ethical objections to wearing cosmetics, based on wider societal values slow to give way, were most susceptible to change for more cosmopolitan and fashion-driven women. By the late nineteenth century, sales of cosmetics by prestigious fragrance houses such as Guerlain, Rimmel, and Hudnut encouraged the association of cosmetics with fashion. The makers of theatrical make-up, such as Bourjois and Leichner, also became significant forces behind the building of socially acceptable cosmetics through their creation of fashionable brands which in time could be diffused to the wider population. Leichner was founded by the German opera singer and chemist Ludwig Leichner, who had already distinguished himself for two noteworthy achievements: he pioneered grease paints in stick form, inventing the proprietary name "greasepaint," and, following the formation of his company in 1873, he created the first lead-free make-up for stage actors, and a face powder that did not contain glycerin.[68] Theatrical make-up was also the path for what became one of the best-known figures in the American industry, Max Factor.

Max Faktorowicz, the son of a Polish rabbi, apprenticed with a leading wigmaker before being hired by a prominent coiffeur in Berlin. From this salon, he secured a position in Moscow, at the age of 14, with the wigmaker and cosmetician for the Imperial Russian Grand Opera. He traveled with the troupe as its make-up artist, developing a reputation for his ability to work extremely fast as well as expertly. At 22, after completing his military service, he moved to Moscow, where he opened a shop in which he sold his handmade color cosmetics and other toiletries as well as wigs. Faktorowicz's products also came to the attention of the members of the Tsar's court. However, the anti-Semitic atmosphere of Russia and the repressive life of the Tsarist court led him to emigrate. On arrival in the United States in 1904, he took the name given to him at the Ellis Island immigrant station: Max Factor.

Factor moved to St. Louis, Missouri, where he opened a small perfume, make-up, and hair goods business at the St. Louis World's Fair in 1904. Four years later, he moved to Los Angeles, where he opened a store in the city's theatrical district. He sold his own creations, and also served as the West Coast distributor for manufacturers of stick greasepaint and other theatrical items made by Leichner.

As the early pioneers of the American film industry began to assemble around Hollywood, then a small village just outside Los Angeles, actors began to visit the Factor shop with their make-up problems, and occasionally some members of the general public made purchases. In 1914, just as the first feature films were being made in Hollywood, Max Factor perfected the first make-up specifically created for motion picture use—thinner greasepaint in cream form, packaged in a jar and created in 12 precisely graduated shades. Unlike theatrical make-up, it did not crack or cake.[69]

By 1914 the market for commercial color cosmetics remained small compared to that for skin creams, and demand was found primarily in fashionable American and European cities. In the United States, leading department stores such as Macy's had begun selling color cosmetics, as did mail order companies such as Sears.[70] In Paris, where younger middle-class women had begun using color cosmetics more frequently since the 1880s, both pharmacies and department stores sold this type of cosmetics.[71] It is unlikely that sales of color cosmetics even in fashionable cities were very large, and while some products such as face powders had become respectable, others like lipstick, eye shadow, and nail varnish remained barely respectable.

In countries more removed from the world of fashion, the market for color cosmetics remained constrained. In Sweden, for example, the moral condemnation of cosmetics remained strong.[72] Before World War I, hardly any Swedish women used color cosmetics, or "smink" as they were known, although some long-established soap firms, such as Grumme, launched a rouge as early as 1911 which was advertised as a safe product that "does not, as is customary, destroy the skin." By 1914, a small but steady domestic manufacture of some cosmetics, such as eyebrow color, tinted lip pomades, and rouges, had become a part of the Swedish beauty industry. Both established firms like Barnängen and smaller, entrepreneurial firms would enter the category in increasing numbers starting in 1918.[73]

As the market size was so modest, it was not surprising that there was little globalization in color cosmetics before World War I. For the most part it was the preserve of perfumers, such as Coty and Muehlens, who could translate the prestige of their fragrances to cosmetic products, and hence sell in fashionable markets. On a smaller scale, Helena Rubinstein had also managed to build a multinational salon business. However, these efforts were but small indicators of what was to come.

Summing up

The growth of commercial products and services designed to make people, especially women, look more attractive paralleled the growth of the market in fragrances. Entrepreneurs did not so much invent the use of many of these services and products as encourage consumers to buy them rather than make them at home. Far more so than in the case of fragrances, this involved establishing their legitimacy. Products such as hair dyes and face powders had to appear safe, and this safety had to be communicated to consumers through advertising or, as in the case of Schueller, by co-opting hairdressers in marketing the product.

A greater challenge was to overcome ethical objections to the use of products. This remained a work in progress in 1914. Societal objections to cosmetics for the hair proved easier to overcome than for the face, and face powders were considered more respectable than eye shadow and lipstick. Creating fashionable and enticing brands was key. For hairdressers, beauty salon entrepreneurs, and sellers of skin creams alike, imagining the association with fashion and celebrity in one form or other was a prerequisite for a luxury brand, and increasingly essential for mass brands also. The contemporary emergence of fashion and aesthetically oriented media targeted at women, such as women's magazines, was important in enabling this shift in marketing position to take place.

It was more challenging to establish aspirational brands in hair and decorative cosmetics than in fragrances. Although Paris held a special status in fashionable hairdressing, and leading French fragrance houses sold creams and some color cosmetics, the makers of hair dyes, shampoos, creams, and lipstick could draw only a less immediate benefit from building associations with Paris. They were, as yet, product categories in the making. It was not surprising that among the hairdressers, pharmacists, make-up artists, and beauty salon owners who built them, "outsiders"—immigrants, Jews, provincials, children of slaves, women—featured greatly. For an industry focused on reinventing people at a surface level, it is fitting that so many of the formative entrepreneurial figures were born under other names.

The borders of the new industry had also become clear in these decades. The consumers of expensive hair styles and beauty salons, skin creams and color cosmetics were female. The brands were advertised in women's magazines. The beauty of a woman was identified with youth, which was certainly not a new idea, but more novel were the claims of the industry to preserve this youth even as the years passed. Western cities, celebrities, and fashions set the benchmark for aspirations. White faces, skins, and blonde hair were the focus of the beauty norms that were disseminated worldwide. These borders of beauty did not exclude others from profitable opportunities, but it certainly framed the nature of the opportunities taken. Japanese entrepreneurs seized the opportunity to introduce Japanese women to Western cosmetics, but the perception of the ideal Japanese face was changed in the process.

Everyone within reach of the cosmetics markets, regardless of geography and ethnicity, experienced the transformative effects of living in an age of global trade and modern visuality, a world where technologies of electricity and photography circulated throughout the industrialized portions of the world and gave people new opportunities to ask themselves, How do I look? The beauty industries legitimized themselves by creating the standards that framed the answer to that question: if you buy our products, you will look beautiful.

Notes

1. Beiersdorf AG, *100 Jahre Beiersdorf, 1882–1982* (Hamburg: Beiersdorf AG, 1982), p. 24.

2. Teresa Riordan, *Inventing Beauty: A History of the Innovations That Have Made Us Beautiful* (New York: Broadway Books, 2004), pp. 4–5.

3. Karen Stevenson, "Hairy Business: Organizing the Gendered Self," in Ruth Holliday and John Hassard (eds), *Contested Bodies* (London: Routledge, 2001), pp. 138–9.

4. Caroline Cox, *Good Hair Days: A History of British Hairstyling* (London: Quartet, 1999), p. 17.

5. Erich Körner, *Zauber der Frisur: 5000 Jahre Haarkosmetik und Mode* (Darmstadt: Wella AG, 1964), pp. 175–7.

6. Körner, *Zauber*, p. 187.

7. Stevenson, "Hairy Business," pp. 138–9.

8. Körner, *Zauber*, p. 191.

9. Körner, *Zauber*, pp. 196–9; <www.nessler-todtnau.de>, accessed September 25, 2007.

10. Körner, *Zauber*, pp. 198–200.

11. Steve Zdatny, *Fashion, Work, and Politics in Modern France* (New York: Palgrave Macmillan, 2006), pp. 2–3, 11, 25.

12. Zdatny, *Fashion*, p. 11.

13. Wella AG, *Wella History* (Darmstadt: Wella, n.d.), pp. 3–4; Wella AG, *60 Jahre Dienst am Friseurhandwerk* (Darmstadt: Wella, n.d.).

14. Körner, *Zauber*, p. 184.

15. Wella AG, *Wella History*, pp. 3–4; Wella AG, *60 Jahre Dienst*.

16. Steven Zdatny (ed.), *Hairstyles and Fashion* (New York: Berg, 1999), pp. 18–20.

17. Neville Williams, *Powder and Paint: A History of the Englishwoman's Toilet Elizabeth I–Elizabeth II* (Longmans: London, 1957), pp. 127–8.

18. By 1909 the firm had sales of over 470,000 RM ($112,000) (Henkel Archives (hereafter HA), D440 Schwarzkopf Dokumentations Forschungsgeschichte, "Schwarzkopf—Firmengeschichte," n.d.).

19. HA, D440, "Schwarzkopf—Firmengeschichte."

20. Kate Mulvey and Melissa Richards, *Decades of Beauty: The Changing Image of Women 1890s–1990s* (New York: Octopus, 1998), p. 18.

21. Jean Laudereau, "Mémoire de L'Oréal 1907–1992," unpubl. MS, pp. 16–18. Laudereau is L'Oréal's in-house company historian and a retired company executive.

22. Laudereau, "Mémoire," pp. 16–18.

23. Laudereau, "Mémoire," pp. 12, 20. The new company was called Schueller et Spery. The name L'Oréal was adopted in 1939.

24. Laudereau, "Mémoire," pp. 22, 24–5; L'Oréal Archives (hereafter L'Oréal), Historique du Group L'Oréal, internal company document, March 20, 2008, p. 1; and Publithèque Oréal, *Chronologie de la coloration. Volume II, 1930–1945*, unpubl. internal company archival series put together by François Clauteaux, November 1992, p. 9.

25. Kathy Peiss, *Hope in a Jar* (New York: Henry Holt, 1998), pp. 67–70.

26. Robert Mark Silverman, *Doing Business in Minority Markets* (New York: Garland, 2000), pp. 52–3.

27. Juliet E. K. Walker, *The History of Black Business in America* (New York: Macmillan, 1998), pp. 208–11.

28. G. W. Septimus Piesse, *The Art of Perfumery*, US edn (Philadelphia: Lindsay and Blakiston, 1867), pp. 289–300.

29. Peiss, *Hope*, ch. 1.

30. Peiss, *Hope*, p. 23.

31. Unilever Archives London (hereafter UAL), Chesebrough-Pond's Inc., 100th Anniversary 1888–1988, C P Box.

32. For an introduction to the large literature on this subject, see Susan Strasser, *Satisfaction Guaranteed: The Making of the American Mass Market* (New York: Pantheon, 1989); Pamela Walker Laird, *Advertising Progress: American Business and the Rise of Consumer Marketing* (Baltimore: Johns Hopkins University Press, 1998); Walter A. Friedman, *Birth of a Salesman* (Cambridge, Mass.: Harvard University Press, 2004); and Regina Lee Blaszczyk, *American Consumer Society, 1865–2005* (Wheeling, Ill.: Harlan Davidson, 2009).

33. Christopher Breward, "Femininity and Consumption: The Problem of the Late Nineteenth-Century Fashion Journal," *Journal of Design History* 7 (1994), pp. 71–89.

34. "Advertising," in Kenneth T. Jackson (ed.), *The Encyclopedia of New York* (New Haven: Yale University Press, 1995).

35. J. Walter Thompson Archives, John W. Hartman Center, Duke University (hereafter JWT), Account Files, Chesebrough-Pond's Inc., Account Histories 1955–1959, "Pond's Chronology," Box 3.

36. JWT, Account Files, Chesebrough-Pond's Inc., Account Histories 1955–1959, "Pond's Case History," May 5, 1959, Box 3.

37. Hans Gradenwitz, *Die Entwicklung der Firma Beiersdorf & Co., Hamburg, bis zum 1. Oktober 1915* (Hamburg: Beiersdorf AG, 1915), pp. 5–13; Ekkehard Kaum, *Oscar Troplowitz: Forscher, Unternehmer, Bürger* (Hamburg: Verlag Günther Wesche, 1982), pp. 13–27; Hellmut Kruse, *Wagen und Winnen: Ein hanseatisches Kaufmannsleben im 20. Jahrhundert* (Hamburg: Die Hanse, 2006), p. 86.

38. Gradenwitz, *Die Entwicklung*, pp. 18–20, 27; Kaum, *Troplowitz*, pp. 39–41.

39. Gradenwitz, *Die Entwicklung*, pp. 13–17; Kaum, *Troplowitz*, pp. 35–7, 59–61; *100 Jahre Beiersdorf*, pp. 24–5.

40. Beiersdorf Archive (hereafter BA), Entwicklung 1919–1945, Lehn & Fink-Komplex, Verträge 1893–1924, "Vertrag betreffend: 'Pebeco'/Translation of the Agreement of 4th/16th Dec. 1903," JWT, Account Files, Lehn & Fink 1926–1967, Account Histories, "Lehn & Fink," January 28, 1926, Box 12.

41. *100 Jahre Beiersdor* p. 26; Kaum, *Troplowitz*, pp. 61–3.

42. *100 Jahre Beiersdorf*, pp. 26–8.

43. Gradenwitz, *Die Entwicklung*, pp. 25–7; Kaum, *Troplowitz*, pp. 41–59; *100 Jahre Beiersdorf*, pp. 20–4.

44. Gradenwitz, *Die Entwicklung*, p. 27; see also Beiersdorf AG, *Nivea: Evolution of a World-famous Brand* (Hamburg: Beiersdorf AG, 2001). Later the company discovered that Guerlain had registered the name Nivea in the nineteenth century and briefly made a skin cream sold in France under that name (Kruse, *Wagen und Winnen*, pp. 126–7).

45. Beiersdorf *Nivea: Evolution*, pp. 28–31.

46. JWT, Howard Henderson papers—Special Projects—Case History Projects. Clients: Chesebrough-Pond's 1959, "A Brief History of Pond's Creams," March 17, 1944, Box 4; Peiss, *Hope*, p. 99.

47. BA, Entwicklung 1919–1945, Lehn & Fink-Komplex, Verträge 1893–1924, "Agreement of February 5th 1914 re: 'Nivea-Preparations'."

48. Mulvey and Richards, *Decades*, p. 20.

49. Linda Scott, *Fresh Lipstick* (New York: Palgrave Macmillan, 2005), pp. 79–81.

50. Angel Kwolek-Folland, *Incorporating Women: A History of Women and Business in the United States* (New York: Twayne, 1996), p. 131.

51. <http://francesdenney.co/history>, accessed January 22, 2007.

52. Lindy Woodhead, *War Paint* (Hoboken, NJ: John Wiley and Sons, 2004), pp. 36–54.

53. Woodhead, *War Paint*, pp. 69–91, 103–4. Rubinstein's annual turnover was £30,000 in 1914, or nearly $3 million today.

54. "The Big Business of Beauty," *News Front* (May 1964), pp. 18–21.

55. Woodhead, *War Paint*, p. 94.

56. Woodhead, *War Paint*, pp. 92–102.

57. Lois W. Banner, *American Beauty* (Chicago: University of Chicago Press, 1983), p. 225.

58. Mikiko Ashikari, "The Memory of the Women's White Faces: Japaneseness and the Ideal Image of Women," *Japan Forum* 15 (2003), pp. 55–79.

59. Interview by author with Noriyo Tsuda, Pola Culture Research Center, Tokyo, March 23, 2007.

60. *The Shiseido Story. A History of Shiseido: 1872–1972* (Tokyo: Shiseido, 2003).

61. *Club Cosmetics Hachijyunenshi* (Club Cosmetics: 80 Years of History) (Osaka: August 1983, Club); *Hyakkaryoran—Club Cosmetics Hyakunenshi* (Club Cosmetics—100 Years of History—Profusion of Flowers) (Osaka: December 2003 Club).

62. Gilbert Vail, *A History of Cosmetics in America* (New York: Toilet Goods Association, 1947), ch. 3.

63. Mulvey and Richards, *Decades*, pp. 21, 39, 56–7.

64. Peiss, *Hope*, p. 39.

65. Peiss, *Hope*, pp. 23–4.

66. Vail, *History*, pp. 100–1.

67. Richard Corson, *Fashions in Makeup, From Ancient to Modern Times* (London: Peter Owen, 2003), pp. 427–31; Gwen Kay, *Dying to be Beautiful: The Fight for Safe Cosmetics* (Columbus, Oh.: Ohio State University Press, 2005), ch. 1.

68. Martin Harrison, *The Language of Theatre* (London: Routledge, 1998), p. 140; <www.britannica.com/eb/topic-242817/greasepaint>, accessed February 6, 2009.

69. Peiss, *Hope*, pp. 58–9; Fred E. Basten, *Max Factor* (New York: Arcade, 2008), chs 1–3.

70. Peiss, *Hope*, pp. 50–60.

71. Mary Lynn Stewart, *For Health and Beauty: Physical Culture for Frenchwomen, 1880s–1930s* (Baltimore: Johns Hopkins University Press, 2001), pp. 13–14, 96.

72. Johan Söderberg, *Röda Läppar och shinglat hår: Konsumtionen av kosmetika i Sverige, 1900–1960* (Stockholm: Ekonomisk-historiska institutionen, 2001), pp. 11, 169–72.

73. Centre for Business History/Centrum för Näringslivshistoria (hereafter CfN), CfN 1093.79, firm data sheet for A/B Grumme & Son (inkl. Hylin & Co.), collected by Erik Dahmén between 1919 and 1946; <www.shenet.se/recept/sminktrad.html> and <www.shenet.se/recept/rougetrad.html>, accessed March 13, 2009; and CfN, Henkel Norden AB, Accession 7307, Barnängens Tekniska Fabrikers AB, Serie F 11: 8.

3

Cleanliness and Civilization

Cleaning up the West

The transformation of a handful of soap manufacturers into the world's largest beauty companies would have seemed an unlikely scenario in the middle of the nineteenth century. The craft of making soap, like perfume, was ancient, but so was people's refusal to use it. At least until the 1860s there was limited demand for soap. The Romans made soap by boiling fats and oils with an alkali, but they regarded it as a novelty. They preferred to clean themselves by scraping the dirt off in hot baths scented with perfumes.[2] Likewise, the ancient Chinese made soaps from vegetables and herbs but were far more likely to use creams and ointments for personal hygiene.[3]

Hygiene in Europe was driven for centuries after the Black Death by a fear of washing with water. Instead, Europeans cleaned themselves—to the extent they did at all—by dry washing and wiping, using water only sparingly for the hands and face, and wearing hygienic, clean linen. Although soap was sometimes used for washing clothes, there was little demand for washing the body with it. Only the daintiest members of the aristocracy used soaps, and only the scented soaps made by perfumers.[4] When people of other cultures first encountered Europeans, the historical record shows that they noticed their powerful stench.[5] Despite this unpromising history, a mass market for branded soaps emerged, supported by advertising which tried to persuade the world that the use of soap was evidence of the superiority of Western civilization. The dirtiest people in the world had reinvented themselves as the cleanest and, with the zeal typical of recent converts, preached the gospel of cleanliness across the world to all their colonized, unwashed masses.

In Europe, the craft of making soap, if not the practice of using it for personal washing, had persisted for centuries in clusters around the Mediterranean in Marseilles, France; Savona, Italy; and Castille, Spain, where olive oil could be combined with a plant called barilla which provided alkali.[6] Like perfumery, the craft was extensively regulated. During the second half of the seventeenth century, the French government laid out specific rules regarding the use of the "savon de Marseilles" trademark, which specified that only natural ingredients, excluding animal products, could be used in its manufacture.[7]

Elsewhere soap-makers often used rendered animal fat and, later, imported oils.[8] In early nineteenth-century Britain small soap firms were located around the ports of London, Merseyside, Bristol, and Newcastle, where they could use imported animal fats from Australia and the Americas, vegetable oils from West Africa, and copra from the Pacific.[9] In America, soap was manufactured by makers of candles or starch clustered near sources of raw material supply, especially the port of New York and the town of Cincinnati, whose meat-packing industry provided lard and tallow.[10]

The soap made by these firms was sold in large unbranded cakes. People also made soaps in their own kitchens. There was little recognition that soap was a useful product. In Britain, an excise tax that was levied on soap as a luxury in 1712 was only repealed in 1853.[11] By then changing attitudes towards smell and hygiene suggested that soap might one day find a wider market. A new interest in describing and classifying smells, and in making efforts to eradicate bad smells rather than masking them with perfume, emerged during the eighteenth century.[12] As doctors reached a new under-standing of the role of skin in removing body wastes, they began to understand better the case for washing in warm water.[13]

New societal concerns about hygiene were stimulated by rising urban populations and inadequate public infrastructure. As their populations expanded, London, Paris, New York City, Boston, and other large Western cities began to develop squalid slums whose inhabitants had no access to clean water. Even the richest urban inhabitants walked on roads where horses regularly deposited large amounts of manure. At best, most people relieved themselves in outdoor privies built over shallow pits, using leaves and sticks, cobs of corn, linen, or newspaper to clean themselves.

As Britain was at the forefront of urbanization in the Western world, it was among the first countries to see the results of poor hygiene in large cities. Massive waves of contagious diseases, including influenza, typhus, typhoid fever, and cholera, swept through British towns during the 1830s and 1840s. In response, Britain was one of the first countries to invest in networks of pipes to supply water to cities.[14] In the United States, where there were also major epidemics, urban water systems also began to be constructed, though primarily for drinking water and sewage removal rather than washing water. In France, the public provision of piped water even in Paris only began in the 1860s, and then only to affluent homes.[15]

Even if the expansion of public water supplies stimulated the demand for soap, the technical constraints on making more of it were only slowly eased. A scarcity of alkali limited production until the French chemist Nicholas Leblanc laid the basis for the industrial manufacture of soap by inventing the process of obtaining alkali from common salt at the end of the eighteenth century. Three decades later Michel Eugène Chevreul, also French, discovered that the oils and fats from animals were glycerides, and that boiling with caustic soda or caustic potash formed the salts of fatty acids, or soaps, liberating the glycerin. As a result, the vast quantities of inedible fats and oil by-products from meat-packing eventually made large-scale soap production possible.[16]

It took a series of major military conflicts to raise awareness of hygiene's importance. During the Crimean War (1853–6), which pitted Britain and France against Russia, the British army nurse Florence Nightingale achieved great success in saving lives simply by washing patients and attending to their hygiene. The lessons about the benefits of hygiene had a major impact on the United States during the Civil War (1861–5), when the Union government established a Sanitary Commission which launched a successful hygiene-promoting campaign to prevent the illness and death of soldiers by encouraging extensive washing with soap.[17] War may be a dirty business, but it was good for the soap business.

Creating a mass market for the unwashed masses

In the aftermath of these wars, there was growing interest in using water for purposes of personal hygiene. The soap industry was a clear beneficiary of this trend, but not its primary creator. After 1865, as both soldiers and the women who had volunteered for nursing duties and cleaning returned home to American cities and farms, the success of the Sanitary Commission resulted in a renewed drive to raise standards of hygiene in the United States.[18] Doctors and other interest groups became campaigners for cleanliness. "Sanitarians," often women's organizations, encouraged habits of hygiene and washing.[19] Being dirty and smelling bad began to be regarded as clear evidence of social and ethnic inferiority. In the United States, dirtiness became associated in particular with the millions of immigrants who began arriving from southern and eastern Europe.[20] In France, the discourse was different. Less concerned with markers of social status, French elites and policy-makers, driven by the national obsession about the declining French birthrate, were intensely preoccupied with the perceived need to encourage women's reproductive health.[21]

The expanding provision of clean water began to make posssible the wider use of soap for washing. Bathtubs appeared in middle-class American households, and the first water heaters appeared in the 1870s, although the majority of Americans still lacked their own built-in bathtubs, toilets, and sinks before 1914.[22] It was far from automatic, however, that the new enthusiasm for hygiene would translate into a large market for branded soaps per se. When people did buy soap they were accustomed to buying it in large generic blocks from retailers. There appeared no reason, especially if consumption was growing, why consumers could not simply buy larger quantities of a low-cost and undifferentiated commodity.[23]

Consequently, it was in imagining how soap could be sold as a differentiated branded product that entrepreneurs shaped the emergent market. The task required creating brand identities that would provide reasons, beyond the purely functional ones, to purchase soap in this fashion. To this end, successful entrepreneurs employed advances in scientific knowledge, manufacturing, and packaging technology to assure consumers of the quality of their products and to make them attractive. Above all, they created high-quality but affordable, even cheap, products, making them accessible to growing numbers of people.

The first attempts, however modest, to develop brands other than perfumery toilet soaps suggested a number of possible directions. During the 1830s Benjamin Talbot Babbitt, a New York entrepreneur, began wrapping small cakes of soap under the brand name B. T. Babbitt's Best Soap. During the early 1850s he devised one of the first known instances of premium marketing when he began offering free color plates of pictures in return for 25 saved wrappers of his soap.[24]

The company that transformed the American market for branded soap, however, was Procter & Gamble (hereafter P & G). Founded by a pair of immigrants, one British and one Irish, the firm had begun in Cincinnati in 1837 selling candles and unbranded soap cakes. After the end of the American Civil War, during which its sales of soap had greatly expanded, the emergence of oil lamps seemed to doom its core candle business. The solution was found in Ivory Soap, launched in 1879. Although the creation of Ivory went down in popular mythology as being the result of an accidental discovery of a process which made the soap float in water, it was in reality the result of a deliberate strategy to transform soap from a commodity into a mass-market brand. This required using vegetable oils, as animal fats were too perishable. Furthermore, the vegetable oils had to be cheaper than the pure olive oil used in so-called "castile" soaps imported from Britain. The solution was found in the use of cheaper palm and coconut oils to create a white, perfumed soap that could be wrapped individually, promoted as mild enough to be sold for both laundry and personal use, and sold on the basis of its purity.

The marketing strategy was devised by Harley Procter, the youngest member of the second generation of owners, who proceeded to grow the brand through advertising. Before the 1880s American magazines still carried limited advertising, and these were mostly for patent medicines claiming to cure diseases. In 1882 Procter placed a half-page advertisement in a religious weekly for Ivory, and in the following year placed an expanded version of the ad in *The Century Magazine,* the best-selling general monthly magazine of the day. The advertisements, which broke from tradition by emphasizing the brand rather than the company, included testimonials from professors concerning the soap's purity and quality. As sales increased, a major fire at the company's plant was used in 1884 as an opportunity to build a much larger new plant on the outskirts of Cincinnati with a much increased capacity to make two million boxes of soap annually.[25]

The growth of P & G was repeated in many branded packaged goods, but by the early twentieth century the soap industry had emerged as one of the largest advertisers in the United States.[26] The companies which were first movers in these investments were often able, as Chandler has shown, to establish long-lasting market leadership in their industries. By 1890 sales of P & G's Ivory had made the firm the largest soap-maker in the United States.[27] The other companies that followed the path of mass production and mass marketing, including Colgate, Palmolive, Babbitt, and J. D Larkin, also grew rapidly, although without catching up with P & G, and in some cases came up with novel strategies. Larkin, for example, sold soap, and later other products, exclusively through the mail to women in co-operative buying clubs. Soap was a much larger business than perfumery and cosmetics. Larkin's sales were over $15 million in 1906, most of which were soap.[28]

As these firms grew their sales through advertising, they drew on, and sometimes reinforced, prevailing social values and prejudices. Cleanliness was associated in advertising with the supposed virtues of white people, and more especially those from northwestern Europe who originally settled the United States.[29] African-Americans and other persons of color were characterized as dirty. African-Americans were regularly promised that they could lighten their skins if they washed with soap.[30] Within such an ideological framework, some activists who aspired to raise the status of African-Americans became prominent in educational campaigns which emphasized washing and tooth-cleaning as ways of social advancement.[31]

The British counterpart of the American mass-marketers was created by William Lever. Born in 1851 in the northern English county of Lancashire, Lever went into the family grocery business and remained a grocer until his mid-thirties. During the mid-1880s he decided to enter the manufacture of soap and acquired a soap works. He made a soap containing copra, or pine kernel oil, which helped it lather more easily than traditional soaps made of animal fats. He imprinted a brand name on a bar of soap and wrapped it, launching the Sunlight Soap brand in 1885. Two years later he bought the site on which he would build Port Sunlight, a huge factory on the banks of the Mersey opposite Liverpool, with a purpose-built village for its workers providing a high standard of housing and leisure facilities. In 1896 he went into seed-crushing to produce oil for his soap works. New brands followed. Lifebuoy, containing a percentage of carbolic acid, was launched as an antiseptic soap in 1895. Five years later on Lever launched soap flakes under the brand Lux.

Lever was a marketing genius who understood how to persuade consumers to buy brands rather than a commodity. His advertising campaigns, heavily influenced by developments in the United States, where he began selling in the

1890s, convinced millions of wives of British blue-collar workers to buy his soap for washing clothes. High levels of advertising expenditure were accompanied by selling strategies such as the exchange of soap wrappers for gifts. The traditional British soap-makers were initially outraged by his branding of a product that had always been sold by its quality and not differentiated by brand, but outrage rapidly turned to alarm as the new techniques destroyed their markets.[32] Lever's company went public in 1895, was the largest British soap firm by 1900, and by 1914 sold half the soap used in Britain.[33]

The growth of mass-marketing soap companies was led by American and British firms. Although late nineteenth-century Germany saw the precipitous growth of manufacturing industries such as chemicals and engineering, it was slower to develop branded consumer goods. Certainly the country's soap industry was less developed in comparison to Britain's, although chemical firms, especially Henkel, developed advanced methods of making soap powders for laundry by mixing soap with crushed soda and bleaching agents.[34] The expanded market for toilet soap was therefore left to many enterprising medium-sized, family-owned firms, which made toilet soaps, perfumes, toiletries, and cosmetic products. The more substantial of these firms, such as Mouson and Georg Dralle, evolved from craft to factory production, and built export markets. By the turn of the century, Mouson's exports amounted to about half, and Dralle's to a quarter, of total sales.[35]

In some ways it was most surprising that the long-established soap industry of France was unable to make the transition into selling brands. The Marseilles soap-making firms, or *savonneries,* increased their production substantially, from 50,000 tons in 1842 to 90,000 tons in 1890, but primarily by new firm creation rather than by increasing scale. There were almost 100 companies by the 1890s, although consolidation had reduced their number to around 40 by 1914. They continued to make large cakes of soap intended for either household or personal use; retailers would then cut and wrap these smaller cakes for their customers. They competed against each other on the basis of fragrance and shape, but remained focused on preserving the industry's collective reputation for quality.[36] There was, however, sufficient technological innovation—for example, artificial soda and tropical oilseeds were added to olive oil in making soap during the century—for the other traditional olive oil soap-making industries of the Mediterranean to look towards Marseilles as a source of technological expertise.[37]

The building of the French toilet-soap market was primarily left to other types of firms. Paris perfumers sold expensive scented soaps in small volumes and progressively made their own soaps rather than remelting soap from Marseilles. Shortly before World War I there were also moves to create a mass-produced toilet-soap market. In 1911 an American chemical entrepreneur and a French chemist launched the firm of Cadum. Following the American and British model, it engaged in brand-building by employing new advertising and marketing strategies, and using what became a famous image of a baby—the "Bébé Cadum"—launched in 1912. The new company sold toilet soap in pharmacies as a fine and luxurious, but mass-produced, product.[38]

The emergence of soap, and the practice of washing with water, as a symbol of social status and of the moral superiority of Western civilization would have seemed implausible at the start of the nineteenth century. By 1914 it was an article of faith. The soap industry had not originated this massive change—it had, after all, co-existed well enough with Western stench. The rise of the use of soap could not have happened without the growth of the public provision of water supplies. However, once societal attitudes towards hygiene had begun to shift, the soap companies drove the growth of demand both through advertising and the creation of mass-production facilities. More fundamentally, they had shaped the nature of the market. There was no obvious reason why soap could not have continued to be provided as a cheap, homogenous commodity which cleaned bodies. Instead, it became a differentiated, packaged, and heavily advertised branded product whose sale could be sufficiently profitable to make entrepreneurial fortunes and help lay the basis for giant business enterprises.

Toiletries

As the nineteenth century progressed, a succession of toiletry products were commercialized. The manufacture of shaving products, an unusual case of a category focused on the male consumer, expanded alongside shifting fashions for wearing beards. While being clean-shaven fell out of fashion during the middle decades of the nineteenth century, the trend was sharply reversed later in the century. While men had traditionally been shaved by barbers who used straight razors, the 1901 invention of an effective safety razor by the Gillette Company, a Boston-based metal fabricator, drove the demand for shaving creams that could be used at home.[39] Women did not use razors for removing facial or other hair; female leg shaving was virtually unknown, at least in the United States, before 1914. During World War I, however, Gillette launched a special razor to assist women with shaving under their arms.[40]

Among the pioneers of commercial shaving creams was the Connecticut firm created by James Baker Williams, who began experimenting during the 1840s to determine the best soaps for shaving. The result was Williams' Genuine Yankee Soap, the first manufactured soap for use in shaving mugs. The J. B. Williams Company developed a national market in the United States for shaving creams.[41] By the end of the century, soap companies included a shaving cream line amongst their products, and packaging innovations served to increase its use. In 1912 the Mennen Company, founded in New Jersey 34 years earlier by the German immigrant Gerhard Heinrich Mennen and originally a talcum powder maker, launched a pioneering shaving cream tube.

Toothpaste was an even larger category. During most of the nineteenth century, only affluent Europeans and Americans cleaned their teeth, primarily using powders and mouthwashes, although an Englishman had invented a modern-style toothbrush as early as 1780, with a handle carved from cattle bone and the brush portion made from swine bristles. The habit of tooth cleaning became increasingly common towards the end of the century, as tooth decay spread in Western cities alongside growing sugar consumption and the introduction of new technologies in flour milling and refining. There were many homemade tooth-cleaning products, but during the 1850s a new toothpaste in a jar called Crème Dentifrice was developed.[42]

In 1873 Colgate added a new toothpaste, packaged in a jar and available as a powder or a paste, to its growing portfolio of perfumes and soaps. Selling toothpaste in jars was expensive; the cost of one jar was equivalent to half a day's wage for a manual worker in the United States in 1890. In 1896, however, Colgate launched the collapsible toothpaste tube, which led to a sharp fall in prices and facilitated mass production.[43] Demand was driven by advertising. Toothpaste became one of the most heavily advertised consumer products in the United States. Colgate also sought to improve the flavors of Colgate Dental Cream to make it more palatable. In 1911 and 1912 Colgate distributed two million free tubes of toothpaste to schools in America, and gave out brushes and sent hygienists into classrooms to teach brushing techniques. The emphasis given to the merits of brushing reflected the fact that, although toothpaste was marketed as a health care product, the lack of scientific understanding at this time about the causes of tooth decay meant that the pastes themselves had no practical effect.[44]

The lack of functional effect did nothing to slow the growth of the toothpaste market. The commercial potential of the new product attracted new entrepreneurial entrants. Companies which had their origins in pharmacy, such as Beiersdorf, perceived dental hygiene as a natural extension of their business. In the United States, Bristol-Myers, a drugs firm that had achieved great success with a laxative mineral salt, launched the highly successful Ipana toothpaste brand in 1916. Entrepreneurial dentists sometimes created their own brands. This was the origin of one of Sweden's first dental care firms, which created the brand Stomatol, giving rise to the expression "a Stomatol-smile," still used in Sweden to describe pearly white healthy teeth.[45]

The expanding toothpaste market in particular revealed the interconnected nature of the emergent system of consumer capitalism. The mass production of heavily advertised processed foods and confectionery created an epidemic of tooth decay. The toiletry companies employed the same marketing and branding strategies as the food companies to build a market for the solution in the form of toothpaste. By the interwar years, and perhaps earlier, flashing one's white-toothed smile and fresh breath had become an important element of the American beauty aesthetic. Toothpaste brands boosted their sales by promising everyone the chance to make this brand-new face their own.[46]

Soap and beauty

During the last decades of the century, entrepreneurs began to imagine soap and other toiletries more explicitly as aids to beauty, progressively moving these products along a spectrum from hygiene to cosmetics. This positioning built on the much longer tradition of toilet soaps sold by perfumers, and was quite easily transferred to luxury toiletry companies. In London, firms such as Vinolia developed a range of luxury toilet soaps, perfumes, and creams marketed using testimonials from celebrities.[47]

While the market for soap was not initially gendered, the more the product was focused as a beauty aid, the more advertising shifted to female consumers. William Lever was not unaware of the potential of this market: even his advertising campaigns for Sunlight Soap suggested that washing clothes made a woman "look older" than her husband, and that using his soap could improve the situation by alleviating the chore of washing clothes. During the 1900s Lever took further steps in this direction when he formally entered the toilet-soap market with new brands, including Plantol, a soap made entirely from vegetable oils. Later he acquired luxury toilet-soap companies, beginning with Vinolia in 1906.[48]

However, it was left to others to develop fully the potential of selling soap as a beauty product. Thomas J. Barratt, another British entrepreneur, became a key figure in these developments. In 1864 the 23-year-old Barratt joined the small firm of A. & F. Pears, which had originated in 1789, as a bookkeeper. Pears was already noted for an expensive transparent soap, perfumed with the scent of English garden flowers and sold primarily to the wealthy.[49] Barratt, who married the owner's daughter in 1865 and was made a partner, transformed the business into a leading manufacturer of an effective yet beautifying mass-produced branded soap. While Pears had spent a grand total of £500 on advertising from its foundation until the mid-1860s, Barratt raised advertising spending to £126,000 per annum (over $600,000) by 1907. He expanded advertising beyond the usual small newspaper items and crude posters to national campaigns and full-page color spreads.

The most significant aspect of Barratt's advertising was its content. The Pears brand was promoted as an aid to health and beauty, primarily for women. Barratt employed both expert testimonials and celebrities to build the brand. He secured endorsements from leading medical professors and doctors for his soap. In 1882, some years before Harriet Hubbard Ayer did so, he recruited the noted actress Lillie Langtry to promote Pears with a testimonial. Barratt repeated this successful strategy, emulated by many more advertisers in the late nineteenth century, with other famous and beautiful actresses and opera singers.[50]

Barratt was optimistic about the potential market for his brand. He launched a successful advertising campaign in the United States during the 1880s by persuading Henry Ward Beecher, a prominent American Congregationalist clergyman, social reformer, and abolitionist, to provide a testimonial. Beecher appeared in an advertisement saying, "If Cleanliness is next to Godliness Soap must be considered as a Means of Grace and a Clergyman who recommends moral things should be willing to recommend Soap."[51] Barratt proceeded to buy the whole front page of the *New York Herald* to display this testimonial.[52] Among Barratt's most famous marketing gambits was the creation of the world's most instantly recognizable advertising icons. He paid £2,200 ($10,000) for the use of a painting by Sir John Everett Millais, among the most popular contemporary painters, of a curly-headed young boy called "Bubbles" for use in Pears advertisements.[53]

Barratt employed every means available to bring the name of his brand to the public's attention. His advertising posters were displayed on train stations and buses. In 1891 he launched the *Pears Annual*, a large-format publication which contained not only Pears advertisements, but also quality fiction, color plate illustrations, and large, separately packaged prints of original art for framing. It sold millions of copies before ceasing publication in 1920. Barratt's claim that the *Pears Annual* would bring original works of art to the attention of a wider public reflected his own strong artistic interests, which included building his own private art collection and writing a three-volume history of the upscale London suburb where he lived.[54]

In the United States, too, there was a growing view that soap might be sold to women as a beauty product. In 1898 the B. J. Johnson Soap Co. launched a "floating soap" made of palm and olive oils, called Palmolive. Over the years the company sought to reposition this brand from being a skin cleanser to a premium brand that would significantly enhance a woman's beauty, but sales remained low until the Lord & Thomas advertising agency was hired in 1910. The agency launched a national advertising campaign which included coupons for free samples, and featured ancient beauties using oils in luxurious baths. The campaign succeeded in categorizing Palmolive as a premium beauty brand.[55]

The transformation of the Woodbury's Facial Soap brand was even more noteworthy. This brand had been created as a quasi-patent medicine by Dr. John Woodbury, a New York dermatologist, who claimed it could cure medical problems extending from skin defects to constipation. After the sale of the business to the Cincinnati soap company Andrew Jergens in 1901, the new owners sought to retain the health claims of Woodbury Facial Soap whilst framing it as a beauty aid by, for example, using attractive women in advertisements. Sales, however, stagnated, despite high advertising expenditures.[56]

The turning point came when Jergens decided to use the services of the advertising agency J. Walter Thompson. The agency launched a systematic examination of the American toilet-soap market, establishing that it was primarily composed of middle- and upper-class women aged between 16 and 60, and then allocated the account to the agency's women's department, headed by Helen Landsdowne Resor. A highly enterprising woman, Resor had worked briefly as an auditor for P & G, and was then hired as the copywriter for the newly opened Cincinnati branch of the agency in 1908. She was promoted to the New York office four years later and proceeded to build her reputation by exploring how consumer products could be sold to women. An ardent feminist, she hired professional women into the agency, creating separate editorial departments for men and women in order to enhance women's careers.[57]

Resor and her colleagues relaunched the marketing campaign for Woodbury's Facial Soap with advertising focused on the leading national women's magazines, such as *Ladies' Home Journal*. The new campaign combined education about skin and skin problems with some explicit, if muted, claims concerning the soap's ability to enhance sex appeal. In 1911 Resor came up with the slogan "A skin you love to touch," which was used in advertisements that featured, in a radical step for the time, a man and woman embracing. The promise to women that the right soap could not only transform their complexions, but also their entire lives, proved hugely successful. By 1916 Resor's campaign had secured a six-fold growth in sales of the brand.[58] In the words of one historian, a mundane convenience product had been turned into a tool for "self-transformation."[59]

Making the world smell good

The lower prices of soap and other toiletries offered a much better opportunity than skin creams or perfumery to develop international markets. Consequently, it was not surprising that ambitious entrepreneurs rapidly turned their attention to export markets. Typically firms would begin by using local distributors, and would in time open their own sales branches if volumes justified. Export strategies became more difficult, however, as many countries imposed tariffs later in the century. As in many other industries, firms responded by jumping over such barriers, building their own factories in attractive markets.

In building his large American market for Pears' Soap, Barratt relied upon a New York distribution agency. However, in the years before World War I a rise in the American tariff on soap to 50 per cent led to plans to open his own factory, though the plans were suspended when the tariff was reduced again in 1913.[60] Lever, who sold much larger volumes of household soap, had already taken that route. Tariffs and transport costs posed a direct challenge to the firm's mass-production and marketing strategies. As a result, beginning in the 1880s, Lever started building or acquiring factories in the developed markets of the United States and elsewhere, creating one of the world's first largest multinational enterprises at that time.

The creation of factories in foreign markets carried advantages other than cost. As his export business grew quickly, Lever was quick to understand that markets might differ in their enthusiasm for colors and scents. His attempts to grow Lifebuoy soap in the United States, for example, were handicapped by American consumers' dislike of the scent. Differences in preferences for soap, shaped by local factors and local competitors, were probably sharper than those in the preferences for luxury fragrances, whose consumers might have more international experience leading them actively to seek genuine Parisian scents. Consequently, opening a foreign factory raised the possibility of adjusting products for local preferences.[61]

Whilst British soap firms were especially active internationally, they were joined by many others. In Sweden, the ink and toiletries firm Barnängen developed a substantial international business in toothpaste, a category it had entered in 1898 when it acquired the formula and rights to the Vademecum dental rinse brand, invented the year before by a medical student, and subsequently used for a toothpaste. It had foreign factories in St. Petersburg, Russia and in Norway, and by the 1910s, Vademecum was being sold using local agents throughout Europe, the United States, Asia, Africa, and South America, becoming the major vehicle of the firm's international business. The brand proved particularly popular in tropical climates, where its antiseptic properties led some to treat it as a universal health remedy in addition to its dental uses.[62] American firms primarily focused on their vast domestic market, but also exported to Canada, to Latin America, and to some Asian markets. Unlike Colgate's sales of perfumes, soap was rarely exported to Europe, although by 1913 Palmolive soap was sold in Britain through the large pharmacy chain owned by Boots, a prominent pharmacy retailer.[63]

As companies marketed their products internationally, their advertisements made the same association between cleanliness and "whiteness" as they did domestically. This was reflected in crude racial stereotypes used to advertise soap and other toiletries, which were presented as components of the Western contribution to "civilizing" colonized peoples. In colonial southern Africa, for example, the alleged lack of hygienic habits among Africans became a central component of the colonial view of indigenous Africans. This view dismissed the extensive traditional practices involving the regular use of soil mixed with oil or fat for cleaning purposes, which seem likely to have been much more hygienic than those followed by Europeans, at least before the late nineteenth century.[64]

The advertising campaigns for Pears' Soap were particularly vivid in their use of such ethnic stereotypes about cleanliness. Between the 1890s and the 1920s advertisements regularly claimed that washing with Pears' Soap would whiten the skin of people of color, thereby "civilizing" them. One infamous advertisement from 1899 showed the American Admiral George Dewey using Pears' Soap in the Philippines and was entitled "The White Man's Burden." The soap was claimed to be "a potent factor in brightening the dark corners of the earth as civilization advances."[65] The advertisements of leading American soap firms were even more offensive in their depictions of non-Western races.[66] The advertisements of traditional Marseilles and Greek soap firms likewise proclaimed that they were capable of "turning even a negro white."[67]

It was not surprising that the association between modern civilization and washing with soap was quickly seized upon in Japan. Although soap had been introduced to Japan by European merchants in the sixteenth century, it was used mainly for medicinal purposes. People used a mixture of rice bran, pumice, and loofah for cleaning purposes, while hand and hair washing remained uncommon. After 1868, and mirroring government-imposed changes in cosmetic practices, Japan's urgent drive to modernize included the rapid adoption of Western hygienic practices.

This provided Western firms with a promising market, albeit one limited by the overall low income of the country. By the end of the century sales of P & G's Ivory Soap were widespread among upper-class customers in Japan.[68] As in skin care and cosmetics, local entrepreneurs also seized the new opportunities to manufacture and sell such products. Business was challenging not only because of the novelty of Western toiletries and the country's low income levels, but also because of the nature of pre-existing sales and distribution channels. Centered on large-scale wholesalers called *toiya*, these channels

3.1 Pears' toilet soap advertized as taking "civilization" to Africa, 1884.

offered a way for entrepreneurs to sell their products, but they also provided a formidable obstacle to the development of sales of branded goods.[69]

The pioneering entrepreneurs who attempted to overcome these challenges emerged from quite diverse origins. In 1877 Tomijiro Kobayashi, the young son of a liquor manufacturer, joined a newly formed soap-maker in Tokyo, initially as a factory worker. Fourteen years later his growing interest in Western products led him to establish his own firm, T. Kobayashi & Co. Tokyo, initially to trade in the raw materials for soap and matches. The firm launched its own brand of soap in 1893, followed by its first toothpaste product, Lion Toothpowder, in 1896. This name was chosen in keeping with contemporary usage of bold animals as motifs for toothpastes, and Tomijiro chose lions because of their strong fangs.

Tomijiro's choice of industry was influenced by his conversion to Christianity and his strong exposure to prevailing Western values. He became enthusiastic about toothpaste through his involvement with the YMCA and with Christian missionaries, through whom he also learned of American manufacturing techniques. In 1909 the company launched its first toothbrush, and two years later and just after Tomijiro's death, it began selling its first toothpaste in a tube, Lion Dental Cream, designed to compete with imported American products. In 1913 Kodomo Toothpaste, designed especially for children, was launched.

Tomijiro, like his Western counterparts, understood the importance of marketing, testimonials, and product quality in persuading consumers to buy toiletries. Following the launch of Lion Toothpowder, the brand was exhibited at both national and international expositions and trade fairs. The company sought quality verification from research institutions outside Japan. Marching bands were used to promote brands, attracting crowds to whom samples would be distributed along with fliers containing product information. There were dental health awareness lectures, visits to schools, and campaigns to promote "brushing days." Lion's products were distributed through specialty stores, whose number had reached 170 by 1902, and which also sold soaps, fragrances, and face powders made by other firms.

Tomijiro and his son, who took over after his father's death in 1910, also pursued international ambitions. He first set up an office in Tianjin, China in 1906, and sent three people there to build a business selling Lion toothpaste and cosmetics, as well as other Japanese brands including Seiko watches and

Yamaha musical instruments. As other branches were opened in China and southeast Asia, the company customized products for each market, using favorable Chinese names for Chinese markets.[70]

Lion formed one of the more successful of a cluster of Japanese entrepreneurial ventures which sought to create new businesses selling hygiene. Nagase Tomiro, who formed Kao in 1887, was a *toiya* wholesale merchant who diversified into manufacturing, using his existing merchant networks to enable Kao to expand rapidly the geographical spread of its sales. He launched a branded soap in 1890, and toothpaste in the following year. Within two decades, Kao marketing campaigns, which emphasized both hygienic efficacy and modern stylishness, had created a successful business.[71]

Summing up

In 1914 beauty was still a small business. The size of the American beauty industry, excluding toilet soap, was $17 million, whilst that of France, including toilet soap as well as its large exports of perfumery, was $19 million.[72] These were small amounts compared to later decades, and they were small amounts at the time. Only one-fifth of Americans may have used any toiletry or cosmetics in 1916.[73]

Nonetheless, the foundations of a new industry had been laid. Ancient crafts and household-based production of creams and other products had been turned into manufactured and branded products. The emergence of a market for these products was made possible by the sweeping economic and social changes resulting from the industrialization of the West. Rising incomes enabled growing numbers of people to earn the money and the leisure to spend more on products that might help them attract partners or buy the signs of social aspiration. Urbanization and travel allowed people to come together to observe, and smell, each other on unprecedented scales. Electricity enabled people to see themselves more clearly. Scientific advances removed constraints on raw material supply. New manufacturing technologies permitted production on a larger scale. Improvements in transportation permitted regional, national, and international markets to be built.

The founding entrepreneurs of the industry responded to these conditions by building brands which sought to define aspirations and claimed to satisfy them. The right soap promised to signal social respectability, and even to transform one's romantic life. The market for beauty products had also become gendered. The right skin cream promised to make a woman more feminine. The right fragrance promised to make one a part of the world of fashion and style of Paris. Concerns about the industry's legitimacy were already apparent as well. The brands' marketers provided assurances of quality and framed the products' emotional associations, which resonated with many consumers and promised them the opportunity to improve their self-confidence by buying beauty products. Yet the fact that these promises were made with increasing amounts of artifice—whether the beautiful bottles and packaging of luxury perfumes, or the wrappers and promotion schemes of mass-produced soap—raised questions about the legitimacy of the entire endeavor.

Europeans and their descendants had come to represent the universal ideal of beauty, and had disseminated that ideal across the globe. A small number of cosmopolitan Western cities, most notably Paris, had become the arbiters of style and fashion. Western countries came to regard themselves—and to convince others to regard them—as embodying the world's highest standards of hygiene, and to regard much of the rest of humanity as dirty. As hygiene and beauty became symbols of Western modernity, consumption of the new industry's products began to be diffused throughout the world, beginning with the social elites of large cities. Charles Darwin had observed in 1871 that there was no universal standard of beauty. But Darwin had studied biology, not marketing. By 1914, he might have changed his mind.

Notes

1. Baker Library, Harvard Business School, Advertising Ephemera, Trade Cards, Series 1:624, Box 8.

2. Luis Spitz, "The History of Soaps and Detergents," in Luis Spitz (ed.), *Sodeopec: Soaps, Detergents, Oleochemicals and Personal Care Products* (Champaign, Ill.: AOCS Press, 2004), pp. 1–2.

3. Edward H. Schafer, "The Development of Bathing Customs in Ancient and Medieval China and the History of the Florate Clear Palace," *Journal of the Oriental Society* 76 (1956), pp. 57–82.

4. G. Vigarello, *Concepts of Cleanliness: Changing Attitudes in France since the Middle Ages* (Cambridge: Cambridge University Press, 1988).

5. Katherine Ashenburg, *The Dirt on Clean: An Unsanitized History* (New York: North Point Press, 2007).

6. Spitz, "History," p. 3.

7. Patrick Boulanger, *Mémoires du Savon de Marseille* (Marguerittes, France: Éditions de l'Équinox, 1994).

8. Spitz, "History," pp. 1–3.

9. Charles Wilson, *The History of Unilever*, vol. 1 (London: Cassell, 1954), pp. 10–20.

10. Davis Dyer, Frederick Dalzell, and Rowena Olegario, *Rising Tide* (Boston, Mass.: Harvard Business School Press, 2004).

11. Richard L. Bushman and Claudia L. Bushman, "The Early History of Cleanliness in America," *Journal of American History* 74 (1988), pp. 1213–38.

12. Alain Corbin, *The Foul and the Fragrant: Odor and the French Social Imagination* (Cambridge, Mass.: Harvard University Press, 1986); Robert Jütte, *A History of the Senses* (Cambridge: Polity Press), pp. 207–11.

13. Morag Sarah Martin, "Consuming Beauty: The Commerce of Cosmetics in France 1750–1800," unpubl. doctoral diss., University of California, Irvine, 1999, ch. 4.

14. Vigarello, *Concepts*, pp. 180–1.

15. Ashenburg, *Dirt*, pp. 183–97.

16. Spitz, "History," p. 3.

17. Dyer *et al.*, *Rising Tide*, p. 18.

18. Suellen Hoy, *Chasing Dirt: The American Pursuit of Cleanliness* (New York and Oxford: Oxford University Press, 1995), ch. 2.

19. Hoy, *Chasing Dirt*, ch. 3; Ashenburg, *Dirt*, pp. 213–27.

20. Ashenburg, *Dirt*, pp. 213–14.

21. Mary Lynn Stewart, *For Health and Beauty: Physical Culture for Frenchwomen, 1880s–1930s* (Baltimore: Johns Hopkins University Press, 2001), p. 66.

22. Juliann Sivulka, *Stronger than Dirt* (New York: Humanity Books, 2001), pp. 66–71.

23. Pamela Walker Laird, *Advertising Progress: American Business and the Rise of Consumer Marketing* (Baltimore: Johns Hopkins University Press, 1998), p. 54.

24. Sivulka, *Stronger*, pp. 52–4.

25. Dyer *et al.*, *Rising Tide*, ch. 2.

26. James D. Norris, *Advertising and the Transformation of American Society, 1865–1920* (New York: Greenwood Press, 1990), ch. 3.

27. Dyer *et al.*, *Rising Tide*, ch. 3.

28. Howard R. Stranger, "From Factory to Family: The Creation of a Corporate Culture in the Larkin Company of Buffalo, New York," *Business History Review* 74:3 (Autumn 2000), p. 416.

29. Sivulka, *Stronger*, pp. 100–5.

30. Sivulka, *Stronger*, pp. 98–100, 257–62.

31. Sivulka, *Stronger*, pp. 262–5; Hoy, *Chasing Dirt*, pp. 89–92.

32. Wilson, *Unilever*, vol. 1, pp. 38–41.

33. Wilson, *Unilever*, vol. 1, p. 210.

34. Alfred D. Chandler, *Scale and Scope* (Cambridge, Mass.: Harvard University Press, 1990), pp. 431–2; Wilfried Feldenkirchen and Susanne Hilger, *Menschen und Marken: 125 Jahre Henkel 1876–2001* (Düsseldorf: Henkel KGaA, 2001), pp. 22–36.

35. Institut für Stadtgeschichte, Karmeliterkloster, Frankfurt: Abteilung. 3.7.1, J. G. Mouson & Co. (W1/17); Henkel Archive (hereafter HA) 455/21, Gründung Kosmetik 1962–1969, Georg Dralle, company history, September 5, 1967.

36. Michael S. Smith, *The Emergence of Modern Business Enterprise in France, 1800–1939* (Cambridge, Mass.: Harvard University Press, 2006), pp. 281–2; Patrick Boulanger, *Mémoires*, pp. 33–57; Spitz, "History," pp. 3–4.

37. Evridiki Sifneos, *Soap Making in Lesvos* (Athens: Livani, 2002).

38. Marie-Emmanuelle Chessel, "Une méthode publicitaire américaine? Cadum dans la France de l'entre-deux-guerres," *Entreprises et Histoire* 11 (1996), pp. 61–76.

39. Dwight E. Robinson, "Fashion in Shaving and Trimming of the Beard: The Men of the *Illustrated London News*, 1842–1972," *American Journal of Sociology* 81 (1976), pp. 1133–41; Gordon McKibben, *Cutting Edge: Gillette's Journey to Global Leadership* (Boston, Mass.: Harvard Business School Press, 1998).

40. Teresa Riordan, *Inventing Beauty: A History of the Innovations That Have Made Us Beautiful* (New York: Broadway Books, 2004), pp. 136–43.

41. J. B. Williams Collection, University of Connecticut, "A Brief History of the J. B. Williams Company of Glastonbury, Conn.," n.d., Box 2, folder 28.

42. Peter Miskell, "Cavity Protection or Cosmetic Perfection?," *Business History Review* 78 (2004), pp. 33–6; <www.colgate.com/app/Colgate/US/Corp/History>, accessed January 20, 2009.

43. David R. Foster, *The Story of Colgate-Palmolive* (New York: Newcomen Society, 1975), p. 10.

44. Susan Strasser, *Satisfaction Guaranteed: The Making of the American Mass Market* (New York: Pantheon, 1989), pp. 95–7; Miskell, "Cavity Protection," pp. 32–5.

45. This company was acquired by the soap and toiletry company Grumme in 1911: Centre for Business History/Centrum för Näringslivshistoria (hereafter CfN), 1093.79, Erik Dahmén, firm data sheet for Grumme A/B; *Svenskt Biografiskt Lexikon* (*SBL*), Band 22 (Stockholm, 1977–79), Lenhardtson, J Albin M, 1861–1934, p. 541.

46. Fred E. H. Schroeder, "Say Cheese! The Revolution in the Aesthetics of Smiles," *Journal of Popular Culture* 32:2 (Fall 1998), pp. 123–35.

47. Wilson, *History*, vol. 1, pp. 56–7, 78, 119, 121–2; Andrew M. Knox, *Coming Clean: A Postscript after Retirement from Unilever* (London: Heinemann, 1976), pp. 155–6.

48. Wilson, *History*, pp. 41, 57.

49. <http://bubbles.org/html/history/bubhistory.htm>, accessed February 5, 2008.

50. Marlis Schweitzer, "Uplifting Makeup: Actresses' Testimonials and the Cosmetics Industry, 1910–1918," *Business and Economic History On-Line* (2003) available at <www.h-net.org/~business/bhcweb/publications/BEHonline/2003/Schweitzer.pdf>, accessed October 22, 2009; Norris, *Advertising*, pp. 48, 56; John A. Hunt, "A Short History of Soap," *Pharmaceutical Journal* 263, 7076 (December 18/25, 1999), pp. 985–9.

51. Bushman and Bushman, "Early History," p. 1218.

52. Mike Dempsey, *Bubbles: Early Advertising Art from A & F Pears Ltd.* (London: Fontana, 1978), p. 3.

53. Dempsey, *Bubbles*, p. 4.

54. Terry Nevett, "Thomas James Barratt," in David Jeremy (ed.), *Dictionary of Business Biography*, vol. 1 (London: Butterworth-Heinemann, 1984).

55. Sivulka, *Stronger*, pp. 143–7.

56. Barry Horstman, "Soapmaker Built Cosmetics Giant," *Cincinnati Post*, September 7, 1999; Sivulka, *Stronger*, p. 75.

57. Laird, *Advertising*, pp. 286–7; Linda Scott, *Fresh Lipstick: Redressing Fashion and Feminism* (New York: Palgrave Macmillan, 2005), pp. 149–50. Helen Landsdowne married Stanley Resor in 1917 and took his surname.

58. Laird, *Advertising*, pp. 297–8; Scott, *Fresh Lipstick*, pp. 179–83; Norris, *Advertising*, pp. 52, 59–60; J. Walter Thompson Archives, John W. Hartman Center, Duke University (hereafter JWT), Account Files, A. Jergens Co., Account Histories 1916–1926, Memorandum on Andrew Jergens Company, "Woodbury's Facial Soap," April 19, 1916, Box 1; and Excerpt from Account History: "Woodbury's Facial Soap," 1926, Box 1; JWT, Account Files, A. Jergens Co., Howard Henderson files, 1930–1959, Memorandum from Howard Henderson to Stanley Resor, December 21, 1939, Box 1; JWT, Account Files, A. Jergens Co., Memoranda re: Woodbury Slogan, 1946–50, "Woodbury's Facial Soap," n.d., Box 1.

59. Regina Lee Blaszczyk, *American Consumer Society, 1865–2005* (Wheeling, Ill.: Harlan Davidson, 2009), pp. 120–3.

60. Mira Wilkins, *The History of Foreign Investment in the United States to 1914* (Cambridge, Mass.: Harvard University Press, 1989), p. 344.

61. Wilson, *Unilever*, vol. 1, pp. 99–100, 104–5, 109, 188–91.

62. CfN, Henkel Norden AB, accession 7307, Barnängens Tekniska Fabrikers AB, Serie F 11:6, "PM över utländska företag inom Barnängen;" *Det började med Bläck: Barnängen 1868–1943* (Stockholm: Esselte, 1943), pp. 42, 53, 74–5.

63. JWT, Corporate Vertical Files, Colgate-Palmolive 1969–1974, 20/2, "The History of Colgate-Palmolive," Box 5.

64. Timothy Burke, *Lifebuoy Men, Lux Women* (Durham, NC: Duke University Press, 1996), pp. 17–34.

65. Anne McClintock, *Imperial Leather. Race, Gender and Sexuality in the Colonial Context* (New York: Routledge, 1995), pp. 207–31.

66. Sivulka, *Stronger*, pp. 98–106; Baker Library, Harvard Business School, Advertising Ephemera, P & G Ivory Soap advertisements.

67. Sifneos, *Soap Making*, p. 71.

68. Gennifer Weisenfeld, "'From Baby's First Bath': Kao Soap and Modern Japanese Commercial Design," *Art Bulletin* 86 (September 2004), pp. 573–98.

69. Louisa Daria Rubinfien, "Commodity to National Brand: Manufacturers, Merchants, and the Development of the Consumer Market in Interwar Japan," unpubl. doctoral diss., Harvard University, 1995.

70. Lion Company, *Lion 100 Year History* (Tokyo: Lion Co, 1992; in Japanese).

71. Rubinfien, "Commodity," pp. 34–45; Tsunehiko Yui, Akira Kudo, and Haruhito Takeda, in association with Eisuke Daito and Satoshi Sasaki, *Kaoshi Hyakunen (1890–1990) (Hundred-year History of Kao (1890–1990))* (Tokyo: Kao Corporation, 1993; in Japanese), pp. 33–5.

72. See Appendix 1.

73. Kathy Peiss, *Hope in a Jar* (New York: Henry Holt, 1998), p. 50.

Part 2

Beauty Diffused

4

Beauty Amid War and Depression

Grow young along with me, the best is yet to be
Elizabeth Arden advertisement, 1936[1]

War and peace

Beauty fades under normal circumstances. In wartime, it fades a lot faster. The outbreak of World War I in August 1914 brought a sudden halt to the flows of capital, trade, and people which had characterized the preceding decades. The prospects for the commercial beauty industry were far from auspicious. As the major European nations mobilized their people and industries for the ugly business of war, who had time for frivolous things like beauty? Paris, the capital of beauty, was almost lost to the German army during the first months of the war. No perfumes or soaps, no matter how exquisite, could conceal the loss of one-tenth of France's population by the war's end in 1918.

As peace returned to Europe, so did the beauty industry, but it was a new peace and a changed industry with new centers of power. Many countries in the decade after the war set aside traditional restrictions on behavior and mobility that had limited the growth of markets. The new postwar order ushered in conditions which fundamentally reshaped the industry. During the nineteenth century much of the creativity, and most of the exclusivity, of the industry had come from Europe. The emergence of the United States as the world's largest market for beauty products, and the rise of American brands to an aspirational status which matched those of France in global appeal, changed the rules of the game.

A new world beauty order

The growth of the American population, which had reached over 100 million by 1920, combined with its higher per capita income compared to Europe, would have given the American market a unique status regardless of the war. Even so, American neutrality until 1917, and the lack of any conflict on its own territory afterwards, permitted a continued expansion of its market even as those in Europe were disrupted. American entrepreneurs could continue to expand their sales and invent new products, while their European counterparts were obliged to switch their factories to war-related products, or close down. By 1919 US production of cosmetics and toiletries had reached $60 million, whilst retail sales in the following year were nearly $130 million.[2]

The war also resulted in an accelerated flow of creative talent into the United States, primarily New York, reinforcing that city's status as a hub of talent, fashion, and retailing to match Paris. Helena Rubinstein took advantage of the American citizenship of her husband and fled from Paris to New York in October 1914. She opened her first salon the following year.[3] The celebrity hairdresser Charles Nessler, interned as an enemy alien in Britain, also escaped to New York under a false identity, and built a new business.[4] The 1917 Communist revolution in Russia produced another influx of refugees. This cohort included Prince Georges Matchabelli, the son of nobility in Georgia and an amateur chemist. He began blending perfumes for his friends at an antique shop in New York before founding his own perfume company in 1926.[5]

As America entered the 1920s, the manufacturers of beauty products could take advantage of the proliferation of nationally distributed printed media for promoting their brands. Women's magazines provided a major venue for companies to advertise. *Vogue, Harper's Bazaar,* and similar magazines popularized styles and fashions and provided venues in which beauty companies could advertise. The leading advertising agencies, including J. Walter Thompson, N. W. Ayer, and many others, were clustered in midtown Manhattan and had by now become collectively known as Madison Avenue.[6]

The advertising professionals on Madison Avenue spoke to a society of consumers with unprecedented income, leisure, and incentives to invest in their own physical appearance. European and American surgeons alike developed skills in plastic surgery in response to horrific wartime injuries, but there was an important difference in the States. There, after the war, the previously sharp distinctions between reconstructive and cosmetic surgery faded away. American plastic surgeons convinced themselves and others that they were performing a worthwhile mission by making people—not just injured soldiers but their increasingly female clientele—more attractive and confident. A disproportionate number of customers during the 1920s were also Jews seeking to have their noses reshaped in a more "Anglo-Saxon" fashion.[7]

The interest in physical appearance was evident as summer beach resorts began organizing pageants involving women wearing swimsuits. In 1921 the first Miss America contest was held in Atlantic City, designed by hoteliers to keep tourists at the resort at the traditional end of the American summer, Labor Day.[8] Taking control of one's body, and making it appear more attractive, received growing emphasis in the United States and elsewhere, as the view spread that human beings could shape and improve their bodies by exercise, diet, and surgery.[9] In Western societies there was a growth in the numbers of people taking exercise, and the concern for appearance manifested itself in different ways in different countries. In the United States, the growth of slimming practices from the 1920s, for example, was primarily focused on women, but in Britain slimming was primarily focused on middle-aged men, whose fat stomachs were regarded as a threat to health and even national efficiency.[10]

During the 1920s the American beauty market boomed. The social importance of smelling and looking "clean" was by now firmly established in the American cultural psyche. The war served further to diffuse hygienic habits, as the need to keep millions of soldiers free of disease resulted in soap, razors, and other toiletries becoming required elements of soldiers' equipment.[11] Soap companies continued to make the case for hygiene. In 1927 they joined together to form the Cleanliness Institute, whose primary function was co-operative sales promotion to teach the American public the importance of keeping clean.[12] The use of the term "institute" emphasized the seriousness, indeed national importance, now awarded to cleanliness. The advertising campaign for Lever Brothers' Lifebuoy Soap, launched in 1926, warned of the grave personal and business consequences caused by "body odor," a concept which Lever invented and its products prevented.[13] Hygiene was increasingly associated with beauty. The Camay perfumed beauty bar, launched by P & G in 1926, became advertised as "The Soap of the

Beautiful Woman." Just as soap was transformed from being about hygiene to being about beauty, so toothpaste brands increasingly emphasized their ability to make their users more attractive with whiter teeth and fresher breath.[14] These qualities had never been explicit priorities for most people.

Toiletries were now mass-market products in the United States. The owners of the leading brands were the largest firms active in the beauty industry, though household soap rather than personal cleanliness was their mainstay. P & G's total sales reached $189 million in 1919.[15] Mergers created more large enterprises. Between 1926 and 1928 Colgate, Palmolive, and Peet, a third soap company, merged. Lever Brothers merged with the largest Dutch manufacturer of margarine in 1929 to create Unilever, the largest company in Europe.[16]

The well-established mass market for skin creams also continued to grow. Helen Landsdowne Resor, who together with her husband Stanley Resor had bought the J. Walter Thompson agency from its aging founder in 1916, was an influential force. In 1916 her agency was hired to devise a new marketing strategy for Pond's Vanishing Cream and Pond's Cold Cream, whose sales had remained disappointing since their launch. Resor's new campaign sought to persuade women to incorporate both creams into a daily beauty regimen. The message was driven home by reviving the use of actresses' testimonials, a practice that had fallen out of favor since the era of the Pears' Soap campaigns, and departed from the norm by employing celebrity endorsements not only in fashion magazines but also in large-circulation middle-class journals. The campaign was targeted at building the middle-class market for the cream, which was positioned as a more respectable means of looking beautiful than using more explicit cosmetics. The sales of Pond's two creams rose from $307,000 in 1916 to $1.6 million in 1923, making them the largest-selling creams in the United States.[17]

Resor recognized and responded to women's rising social and economic independence, which encouraged and increasingly permitted women to make their own choices about what to buy and how to appear. In both the United States and Europe, growing numbers of young women entered retail and clerical work. Political emancipation had accompanied these changes. In 1920, for instance, women won the right to vote throughout the United States.

The new campaign that Resor launched in the early 1920s broke new ground and provided the cultural foundation for subsequent beauty advertising right

4.1 The advertising campaign for Pond's creams in the United States employed this picture of the Queen of Romania, along with testimonials of prominent professional women, leisured socialites, and two other European queens, 1925.

up to the present day. By this time, sales of Pond's creams were starting to fall in the face of competition from more exclusive brands. Resor persuaded Mrs. O. H. P. Belmont, a prominent socialite who was active in the women's movement, to endorse the brand. Later, less politically active but still recognizable women—famous actresses, typically—were chosen to represent the brand. The brand's pitch was clear: it offered to make women attractive and lovable, just like the celebrities, and the beauty of it all was that any woman could become beautiful if she used the brand. The underlying message was that every woman had a responsibility to herself, as well as to those around her, to take control of her appearance and be her beautiful, successful best.[18]

The American color cosmetics market also expanded during these years. Still barely acceptable in 1914, product innovations made their use both more accessible and desirable. The first metal lipstick container was invented by Maurice Levy in Connecticut in 1915. The first screw-up lipstick appeared six years later.[19] In 1916 Northam Warren created the first commercial liquid nail polish when he launched the Cutex brand of manicure preparations. A new form of mascara was invented by an Illinois chemist, T. L. Williams, whose Maybelline Cake Mascara, launched in 1917, became the first modern eye cosmetic to be manufactured for everyday use.[20] As usual, early adapters were young. In 1925 the concept of a "generation gap" was invented to describe the difference between mothers and daughters regarding the use of lipstick in America.[21] By the end of the 1920s, three thousand different face powders and several hundred rouges alone were being sold on the American market.[22]

Hollywood also played a pivotal role. During World War I the American industry was able to pull ahead of the French firms which initially dominated the cinema industry. By the 1920s the industry, now concentrated in southern California, was able to benefit from the size of its home market and its control of distribution networks to dominate both the American and international markets.[23] Movie theatres reached almost every American town, diffusing new lifestyles and creating a new celebrity culture around movie stars that exercised a powerful influence on how beauty, especially female beauty, was defined.[24] Max Factor forged the direct link between cosmetics and Hollywood. His work for actors resulted in the principle of "Color Harmony," which established for the first time that certain combinations of a woman's complexion, hair, and eye coloring were most effectively complemented by specific make-up shades. As he grew in fame alongside the movies, he also played a significant role in legitimizing the use of cosmetics. In particular, he began referring to his cosmetics as make-up, a word long used by actors but not widely used more generally because of the disreputable image of actors.[25] Now, for perhaps the first time in Western culture, actors could be thought not just beautiful on the outside but beautiful and respectable on the inside, too. That was a big change for people until recently regarded as barely above prostitutes.

Max Factor's store in Los Angeles also began to make wider sales. In 1916 he introduced Eye Shadow and Eyebrow Pencil for public sale, the first time such products had been available beyond the theatrical make-up line. Advertisements prominently featured screen stars, whose studios required them to endorse Max Factor products.[26] A distribution company was contracted to penetrate the drugstore market, and in 1927 nationwide distribution of Max Factor cosmetics began. The date coincided with the premiere of the first talking movie, *The Jazz Singer,* at which Max Factor and his family were in attendance.[27]

It was not just Max Factor who benefited from Hollywood. In 1925 Lever Brothers launched the perfumed Lux bar toilet soap specifically for the American market. This brand was a pioneer of the concept of accessible luxury, for it was presented as similar in quality to a fine French toilet soap, but far cheaper. Initially the advertising did everything possible to build associations with France. Then in 1928 J. Walter Thompson launched a national campaign for Lux based on the claim that nearly 100 per cent of Hollywood screen stars used the brand. The association with the celebrities of the expanding film industry was reinforced by testimonials from actresses and directors, and proved hugely successful. By 1930 Lux had become the largest-selling toilet-soap brand in the United States.[28]

The beauty business flourished outside Hollywood as well. By the 1920s, Elizabeth Arden and her competitors had succeeded in creating a successful business at the luxury end of the market. Elizabeth Arden's early pre-eminence in salons was challenged by Helena Rubinstein, who began manufacturing her own products in 1917, a move followed by Elizabeth Arden a year later, as well as by other women, including Dorothy Gray, who opened a New York beauty salon in 1916. These heavily advertised brands were taken across the nation over the following decade. By 1925 Elizabeth Arden was manufacturing 75 individual products, owned salons in nine cities, and distributed in the most

4.2 Advertisement for the Lux "Soap of the Stars" campaign, featuring famous Hollywood actress Ginger Rogers, 1935.

prestigious department stores in the United States. As their products were premium-priced, they emphasized how they helped maturing women stay young as they got older. Arden in particular promised women they could join high society if they used her products. Rubinstein also emphasized the association between her products and opulence, taking the opportunity to wear lavish jewelry on public occasions, whilst also regularly being photographed wearing a white laboratory coat to emphasize her commitment to the "science of beauty."[29]

These were profitable businesses which allowed many of their founders to exit by selling their brands to larger companies. In 1926 Dorothy Gray sold her business to Lehn & Fink, which distributed Pebeco toothpaste in the

4.3 Helena Rubinstein in her laboratory, 1920s.

© L'Oréal DR/Archives Helena Rubinstein

United States and acquired in the same year the A. S. Hinds cosmetics business, makers of the well-known Hinds Honey & Almond Cream. In 1928 Helena Rubinstein sold her American business to the investment bankers Lehman Brothers for a reported $7.3 million (or over $90 million in 2008), although she retained her European and Australian businesses, which represented around one-quarter of her total turnover.[30]

The American market for expensive fragrances also expanded, but remained the preserve of European, primarily French, brands. The war was, as in the case of color cosmetics, an important driver of growth, since familiarity with French perfumes increased as American servicemen brought them back home from Europe.[31] The popularity of French perfumes was part of the wider pre-eminence of haute couture fashion, which achieved new heights as new designers refreshed and renewed the allure of Paris. The designs of Coco Chanel, the most dramatic new arrival into the world of Parisian fashion, became symbolic of the era's New Woman, who enjoyed more freedom of choice than the narrow range of tight corsets and long skirts which had dominated women's wear for much of the Victorian era.[32] In New York, style consultants and department store buyers diffused these latest Parisian fashions to the American market.[33]

The growing sales of French fragrances were not simply a reflection of the aura of French fashion. The 1920s saw another wave of creativity in the French industry. New scents, and ever more exquisite bottle designs and packaging, proliferated.[34] The worlds of fashion and beauty became increasingly connected as more Parisian couture houses added perfumes to their business.[35] In 1921 Chanel launched her famous N°5, the first scent to be marketed by a fashion designer under her own name. Its creator was Ernest Beaux, another refugee from Russia, who created a rich floral scent which combined sharp synthetic aldehydes with expensive natural oils such as jasmine. Chanel departed from elaborate perfume bottles to sell her product in a clear glass bottle with elegant black and white graphics. The combination of the scent and the coherence between the perfume and Chanel's designer image, which led some to regard Chanel N°5 as the first lifestyle fragrance, created a perfume which was destined to become an industry leader for the remainder of the century.[36]

The creativity of the Parisian industry was supported by new business strategies to grow in scale and to build sales in the United States. Chanel N°5 was originally sold in Chanel's own shops, where she gave out samples to high-society clients. In 1924 Ernest Wertheimer suggested that her perfume could be sold on a larger scale. Parfums Chanel, a separate company from Chanel's fashion enterprise, was established and controlled by the Wertheimers, who soon moved production to the Bourjois factory.[37] The Wertheimers were able to reduce costs while building businesses in both the premium and mass segments. In quick succession, Bourjois opened offices around Europe, beginning with London in 1919, as well as in Sydney and Buenos Aires. By the end of the decade it was claimed that it was the third-largest perfume company in the world.[38] In 1928 Bourjois, which formed a separate American company, launched the perfume Evening in Paris specifically for the American market. It was a commercial success, selling at a higher price than the French equivalent, launched later.[39]

The strategy of Bourjois was echoed by other companies. The importance of the American market encouraged the creation of American affiliates, while the high level of tariffs led some to begin local production. These new firms spent heavily on advertising and some created brands uniquely for the market.[40]

Guerlain opened an American office in 1927, and its Shalimar perfume swept the American market.[41] Ernest Daltroff's Caron, which confined its small domestic business to exclusive Parisian department stores, was among those which created customized powders and scents for the American market. In 1923 a New York affiliate, the Caron Corporation, was founded, with a store on Fifth Avenue and a factory outside the city. By 1925, three-quarters of Caron's total business was in the United States.[42]

François Coty took his commitment to the American market even further. By the 1920s Coty was a towering figure in the beauty industry. His vertically integrated business manufactured its own packaging and bottles in a large "Cité des Parfums" outside Paris and owned multiple research laboratories. Coty's huge facility at Suresnes attracted other perfumers, including Guerlain, Worth, and Hudnut, becoming a large manufacturing cluster as a result.[43-] After failing to persuade Houbigant to merge their production facilities, although not their brands, the main source of growth became diversification into creams and make-up.[44] By the end of the 1920s Coty claimed to hold 60 per cent of the French perfume market, a position supported by the operation of retail stores in a number of French cities. Distribution companies were also established in Britain and Romania, and in 1926 Coty also purchased Rallet, whose Russian business had been destroyed in 1917, and re-established in France as a private-label business supplying perfumes to couturiers and perfumers.[45]

The American market became the focus of particular attention. In 1922 a separate company, Coty Inc., was formed in New York to avoid tariffs on finished goods by using some American ingredients. While the essential oils and artful packaging were shipped to New York, the perfumes were assembled with American alcohol. This enabled Coty to sell a perfume such as L'Origan for the same price as in France. Retail showrooms were also opened in cities, including Chicago, San Francisco, and Memphis.[46] Coty Inc. became publicly traded in 1925. Net profits of the American venture rose from $1 to $4 million between 1923 and 1928. Coty's US sales reportedly reached $50 million by the following year (or half a billion in 2008 dollars).[47] This made it the largest seller of cosmetics and perfumes, though not toiletries, in the United States.

The rapid expansion of the American business led, in 1929, to Coty Inc. acquiring the majority interest in Coty's European companies, creating a giant beauty business legally domiciled in the United States.[48] This may not have been Coty's initial intention, but an attempt to persuade the leading French bank Crédit Lyonnais to invest in the capital of Coty SA, which owned the rights to the brand outside the United States (and Cuba) and Britain, in order to retain control in France, was unsuccessful. This may have also reflected Coty's "outsider" status in the French industry, and perhaps suspicion of his apparent admiration of the Italian fascist dictator Mussolini.[49] While the 1920s witnessed a large flow of European companies investing in the American market, Coty was one of only a handful of cases where a shift of domicile occurred.[50] The move provided a test of how far the national heritage of brands and businesses could be relaxed in pursuit of foreign markets. In its public pronouncements, the company was careful to insist that its American products were identical to those sold in France and that there was strict monitoring from France of the American production.[51]

It is highly unlikely that any other country matched the scale and dynamism of the American market, both because discretionary incomes were lower, and because social inhibitions were stronger. Nonetheless qualitative evidence suggests a similar trend of rising consumption in response to changing social attitudes, rising employment opportunities for young women, the impact of Hollywood, and increasingly powerful corporate advertising strategies. In Britain a discernable wearing down of social and geographical barriers to wearing cosmetics was observed, as wearing lipstick and rouge became "class-less."[52] In Sweden, the use of color cosmetics also began to become more acceptable during World War I, especially in the capital city of Stockholm, although it was only in the 1930s that the use of color make-up was widely accepted.[53]

The same upward trend in consumption of beauty products appeared beyond the Western world, albeit from lower bases. The Japanese market appears to have experienced similar growth, as does that in Thailand.[54] In Latin America, there was a growing market in Argentina which, with its cosmopolitan capital city of Buenos Aires, boasted living standards equal to those in much of Western Europe and was one of the world's largest markets for Hollywood films.[55] While before the 1920s the market was primarily supplied by imports, by 1935 Argentina had 105 factories making beauty products, with 1,800 employees.[56]

The 1920s, then, saw a widespread expansion of the boundaries of the commercial market for beauty. Retail sales of cosmetics and toiletries in the

American market reached $378 million in 1929. New York had become a close rival to Paris as a hub in the global industry. Hollywood celebrities had joined Paris as symbols of aspiration. The fast-growing American market became the driver of a new transnationalism in the beauty industry, of which the Americanization of Coty formed only one component. Bourjois did not merely launch American-specific perfumes. In January 1929 it also acquired Woodworth, a cosmetics company founded in New York in 1854.[57] American companies likewise began acquiring their own French perfume brands. In 1928 E. R. Squibb, a leading American pharmaceutical company which sold toiletries such as toothpaste, bought Lenthéric. This Parisian firm, founded in 1885, had begun selling in America in 1902, and had become a well-known brand in the market. In 1929 Lehn & Fink bought the Lesquendieu perfume business, which included the Tussey brand of lipstick.[58] Corporations were, it seemed, orchestrating the merger of the world's two largest beauty markets into one.

The Great Depression: leadership matters

Events soon took another turn when the stock market crash in October 1929 heralded a period of extraordinary crisis. The resulting flight of capital back to America and the imposition of high American tariffs rapidly diffused the economic crisis worldwide. There were major crises in most European countries and near-catastrophe in Latin America, Australia, and elsewhere as the price of primary commodities tumbled, but the impact on the United States remained among the most severe. Within four years the American economy had shrunk by one-third, and one-quarter of the American labor force was out of work. For the beauty industry, the crisis provided both a test of the legitimacy of the entire industry and of the capabilities and strategies of individual firms.

The beauty industry went into shock. American production of cosmetics and toiletries fell from $193 million in 1929 to $97 million in 1933, while retail sales fell from $378 million to $300 million. The number of companies in the American beauty industry fell from 815 to 490 in only four years.[59] As market conditions deteriorated, weak strategies were cruelly exposed. Among the major companies most adversely affected were those who had cheapened and extended premium brands, and who now found themselves exposed as consumers emphasized quality and the mass market stumbled.

Helena Rubinstein was amongst the companies which experienced severe difficulties arising from this brand-cheapening strategy. After Lehman Brothers' acquisition, the bankers had taken the company public and sought to extend the brand into the mass market. This strategy, and the loss of Rubinstein's creative genius, proved catastrophic in the new market conditions. There was such a sharp fall in sales that, in 1931, Rubinstein was able to buy back a majority of the stock in her American company for a mere $1.5 million. The volume strategy was reversed, and Rubinstein refocused on the prestige market. By 1937 she was able to open a flagship salon on Fifth Avenue in New York with luxurious baths, facial and manicure services, exercise facilities, and a restaurant.[60]

There were bigger problems still at Coty, where the strategy of moving into the mass market turned out to have been poorly executed. As the Great Depression took hold, Coty's sales fell and the company responded by cutting prices. This contributed to a catastrophic fall in sales in America from $50 million to $3.5 million by 1933.[61] Coty himself, who had been vilified in the French press for tax evasion after creating Swiss holding companies, largely withdrew from managing the company. Meanwhile management of the company was left in the hands of Vincent Roubert, a nose who was trained in Rallet's laboratory in Grasse.[62] Following Coty's death in 1934, when he left a personal fortune of $250 million, there was a (successful) fight for majority control of the firm by his ex-wife, Yvonne Cotnaréanu, who was owed alimony.[63] The Coty business empire shrank. In 1939 the company was split into a US-registered company and a Panama-based Coty International which controlled all the non-US business. They had identical boards and remained largely owned by Yvonne Cotnaréanu. Both were shadows of their former selves. In 1939 Coty Inc.'s domestic sales were $6.6 million, while those of its French affiliate were a modest $1.7 million.[64]

The unwinding of Coty's business can be explained on several levels. While the cheapening of the brand had clearly been excessive, the business as a whole had also depended too much on its founder, even as the growth in scale required more depth in management. During the 1920s François had remained obsessively in control of every aspect of his expanding business, and although this was quite characteristic of the cosmetics business, he might have carried it to excess.[65] The relocation of the ownership to New York and the huge focus on the American market might also have been a step too far.

It suggested that beauty brands, especially those originating in luxury, risked losing legitimacy if they departed too radically from their historical and cultural roots.[66]

Among other casualties of the era were many African-American companies. The ethnic beauty market had continued to flourish during the 1920s amid high levels of segregation. The Miss America pageant excluded African-Americans from the start.[67] As the numbers of beauty parlors expanded during the 1920s, they too were racially segregated.[68] As long as the majority white population remained unable to appreciate beauty in black people, the field was wide open to black entrepreneurs.[69]Although Madame C. J. Walker had died in 1919 and Turnbo Malone's business was devastated when she and her husband divorced and fought for control of the business in 1927, other ethnic entrepreneurs had flourished. These included Anthony Overton, who built a substantial business in Chicago, which developed as the African-American equivalent of New York City for the ethnic beauty market. The Great Depression, which resulted in a high rate of unemployment for African-Americans, devastated their businesses, too. By 1933, for instance, little remained of Overton's once-large empire.[70]

Despite great difficulties for individual firms, by the mid-1930s sales in the American beauty industry in general were again moving upwards, although during that decade the number of establishments and employment did not regain the levels seen in 1929.[71] There were no further cross-border acquisitions or shifts of domicile. As the industry slowly recovered from the crisis, a new wave of product and marketing innovation drove sales, but the focus was domestic rather than cross-border. In 1935, when color films began to be made in Hollywood, Max Factor developed a new Pan-Cake Make-up to prevent actors' faces from appearing in red or blue tones. Its launch to the public marked the first time Max Factor used color in advertisements.[72] Advertising also became more daring. In 1936 Woodbury's Facial Soap became the first advertiser in America, in any industry, to use full female nude images in advertisements placed in mainstream publications.[73]

The advent of commercial advertising on radio provided a hugely important new medium for American beauty companies.[74] Bristol-Myers' Ipana toothpaste, launched in 1916, was among the pioneers, starting radio advertising in 1925. Colgate-Palmolive began regularly advertising Palmolive soap on the radio from 1927. P & G became one of the largest spenders on the

American airwaves after it invented and developed "soap operas" on the radio, which became a central feature of its marketing campaigns.[75] The cosmetics brands followed a little later than toiletries, but Bourjois began sponsoring radio programs in 1928, Dorothy Gray in 1929, and Coty in 1930.[76] In 1931 Jergens Lotion began advertising on radio. Pond's started sponsoring radio programs after 1937.[77]

Despite the difficulties faced by some sellers of mass-marketed products, many suffered little impact from the crisis. The Depression destroyed some companies and provided new opportunities to others. Advertising campaigns for Lifebuoy Soap emphasized how bad breath or body odor could be a handicap when trying to find a job.[78] Pond's increased its share of the American face cream market from 12 per cent to 15 per cent between 1929

4.4 Advertisement for Unilever's Lifebuoy soap admonishes men to prevent "B.O"—"body odor," or run the risk of serious personal and professional failure, 1931.

and 1933.[79] Pond's Face Powder, launched in 1932, took it into the make-up market. Lipstick and rouge followed in the early 1940s.[80]

The luxury market also proved resilient. In response to the crisis, for example, perfume companies sold smaller bottles, offered colognes and toilet water as well as perfume, and, in some cases, pursued mass-market sales through drugstores.[81] American firms also edged into prestige fragrances, although they still often resorted to claiming French associations. When Jergens launched a perfume line in 1931, they adopted the brand name Henri Rocheau et Cie, incorporated in Paris and New York. This was against the strict advice of J. Walter Thompson that it was "misleading to the public" to use this address without an actual company in Paris manufacturing the perfume.[82] Elizabeth Arden also introduced her first perfume, Blue Grass in 1936 following a visit to Grasse, where she encountered a floral perfume which reminded her of the bluegrass of Kentucky.[83]

During the late 1920s many entrepreneurs even perceived opportunities to expand the small male market. There were successful male hair products on the market, including Wildroot Cream Oil, the American equivalent of the British brand Brylcreem, launched in 1928,[84] while Bristol-Myers had success with Vitalis, a clear, alcohol-based tonic. In 1928 Carl Weeks' Armand launched the Florian line of men's toiletries, which included skin lotions, moisturizers, and a face powder. To combat perceptions of effeminacy, the line was advertised as a "real, he-man, Mascu-line of toilet needs, scented, blended, made for men."[85]In the following year Helena Rubinstein opined that men would soon be buying lipstick and rouge in substantial quantities.[86]

The downturn in economic conditions quickly ended hopes for a boom in the male market.[87] Instead, growth was more modest. A cluster of small firms, led by Seaforth, innovated in packaging and marketing to create a gift market for male toiletries. It was estimated that 90 per cent of such sales were made to women, primarily before Father's Day and Christmas.[88] William Lightfoot Schultz also found a market niche. In 1937 he created the Early American Old Spice line of soap and toiletries, designed for female consumers, but in the following year he launched Old Spice for men, a spice-cologne shaving lotion which would become established as a leading brand for decades.[89]

The aftermath of the Great Depression did see a discernible shift in public attitudes which had an impact on the regulatory environment faced by the industry. There was growing skepticism during the 1930s about the waste and deceptiveness of the advertising industry.[90] Early in the decade the practice of not revealing that the endorsements used in cosmetics advertising were paid for came under criticism by regulators. A number of cases of cosmetic poisoning provoked growing calls for a regulatory response, especially concerning the medical claims made for products. As criticism of the industry mounted, by 1936 Pond's had already begun to have all its advertising approved by its attorneys as well as by dermatologists. In 1937 the Federal Trade Commission (FTC) filed malpractice suits against a number of prominent firms. In the following year the Food, Drug, and Cosmetic Act was passed, which created stricter codes about what claims could be made for cosmetics sold in the United States.[91] Beauty had finally risen to the level of government regulation.

The scope of the new legislation was circumscribed by successful lobbying by the industry. Neither the ingredients in hair dyes nor warnings about possible long-term health risks needed to be declared or printed on product labels, provided they carried a warning about possible irritation. Yet some firms found their freedom to make claims restricted. Elizabeth Arden was obliged to change the name of her Orange Skin Food to Orange Skin Cream because it was not a nutrient.[92] The closer regulatory scrutiny, which had few parallels elsewhere at the time,[93] may have facilitated the American industry's continued growth by assuaging some concerns about the industry's practices and the validity of product claims.

The Great Depression may have halted in its tracks the emergent trend towards transnational mergers focused on the American market but it provided only a temporary jolt to the growth of the beauty market. By 1938 retail sales in the United States had climbed back to $400 million. In the absence of comparable data, it is unclear whether the beauty industry in Europe fared better or worse than its American counterpart during the 1930s. Anecdotal evidence from advertising, brand launches, and new firm creation suggests that it was also quite resilient in the face of economic difficulties. In France, for example, it was not the makers of branded perfumes and cosmetics but the traditional Marseilles soap industry that showed the most vulnerability to the loss of export markets during the 1930s.[94]

The large domestic market also enabled American firms to grow. By the late 1930s the leading American firms were larger than their European equivalents.

However, the trying times of the Depression decade had also revealed the fragility of competitive advantages held by firms in the industry. A wide divergence in the reported financial performances of even the largest firms in the United States suggested how, in an industry which was still fragmented as well as highly competitive, individual corporate strategies, creativity, and capability influenced performance.[95]

Reaching consumers: from the elites to the streets

As beauty companies strove to build markets in the United States and elsewhere, they worked hard not only to build brand equity but also to ensure reliable distribution so that consumers could find their products easily. As firms grew in scale, becoming national and sometimes international, the challenges of reaching consumers grew. It was not simply a matter of securing access to distribution channels, but also learning from them. Department store buyers and hairdressers were close to final consumers and, consequently, provided important information about their desires.[96]

There were now thousands of retail outlets where beauty products could be purchased in the United States and Western Europe. Luxury fragrance, skin care, and cosmetics brands were sold in department stores and exclusive salons. The key problem for companies was to gain access, and a good location, for their brands in such stores. The difference between a well-located counter and one in a corner might be 100 feet, but those feet could translate into thousands of dollars a day. Not surprisingly, stores became the location for the highly aggressive sales techniques which became a distinctive feature of the American retail environment. These included "hidden" demonstrators, hired by the cosmetics companies, who pretended to be normal sales staff, whilst in practice pushing their own firm's brands.[97]

There was also a much smaller, but strategically important, channel for luxury brands: the exclusive chains of beauty salons and flagship stores, primarily in Paris, New York, and other capital cities. Flagship stores and salons were important signals of exclusivity and status. This is where tastes were made and disseminated. In France, the prestigious fragrance houses owned such stores in Paris, as they had since the nineteenth century, and in which they presented their products in a setting of luxury and elegance. Each salon projected its own distinctive image through architecture and decoration. While Guerlain's salon was "classical," for example, others such as Coty and

Roger et Gallet used Art Deco architecture. In 1938 Guerlain also opened a "beauty institute," above its shop on the Champs Élysées.[98]

At the other end of the distribution chain there were chain stores and drugstores which sold mass toiletries and cosmetics brands. There were wide national differences in the relative importance of particular outlets. In the United States, drugstores were the main outlet for such products, and relatively few were sold in grocery stores. In many European countries, specialty pharmacies were major channels, and sometimes the source of new entrepreneurial ventures. The British pharmacy retail chain Boots developed, unusually, its own private-label business. The company became involved in toiletry manufacturing towards the end of its brief ownership by United Drug between 1920 and 1933, when it began making some of the US company's brands, including Mum deodorant and Ingram's shaving cream. When the American parent, in financial difficulties, sold the firm back into British ownership, this manufacturing continued for some years and provided the basis for further expansion. In 1935 Boots launched its own skin care brand, No 7.[99]

For hair care and some other companies, access to salons was critical to reaching consumers. In France, the number of hair salons had reached, according to one estimate, 40,000 by 1929, many of them now serving women and increasingly staffed by female hairdressers.[100] In 1920 there were 5,000 beauty parlors in the United States. Ten years later there were 40,000. While skin treatments and the use of cosmetics had formerly been a major component of the services provided by salons, during the interwar years the fashion shift towards shorter hair and permanent waves turned the salons primarily into locations for hairstyling. The feminization of hairdressing provided a further example of how women interacted with one another on both sides of the industry—as sellers and buyers—as the beauty industry evolved.[101]

The salon trade provided the major distribution channel for many hair care companies. In France, for example, relations with the salons were central to the rapidly growing L'Oréal business. Eugène Schueller volunteered for military service on the outbreak of World War I and served in the French army throughout the war, leaving his wife and his mother-in-law to run the company.[102] Afterwards, Schueller turned his hand to many entrepreneurial ventures, becoming a manager and co-owner of a plastics company, part-owner of a company which made paint for automobiles, and founder of a company which made film.[103]

Hair dyes, however, remained Schueller's primary interest. There were continued innovations, including Imédia, the first fast-acting coloration process, launched in 1929. Schueller's hair dyes were initially advertised for both men and women as a means to make them look younger, but as female hairdressing rose in importance, the emphasis changed. By the mid-1930s the emphasis on combating aging and grey hair had firmly shifted towards enhancing and achieving feminine beauty. Among the steps taken to appeal to female consumers, Schueller launched a women's magazine, *Votre Beauté*, and commissioned leading artists to design product posters for distribution to the salons.[104]

Schueller sold his hair dyes exclusively to salons, for whom hair dyeing was increasingly important as a source of income. He targeted celebrity hairdressers, such as the famous Antoine, to enhance the value of his products, and he continued to build close relationships with the professional trade.[105] In 1923, a second professional trade journal for the salons was launched, the *L'Oréal Bulletin*, designed as a technical review of how to administer the growing L'Oréal product range. Retail markets, meanwhile, were next on the agenda. In 1928 Schueller created his first shampoo, and six years later he launched a mass-market shampoo, Dop. The Monsavon toilet-soap business was also acquired in 1928.[106]

Although hair care was at the heart of Schueller's business, his close observation of fashion directed his attention to the spread of sunbathing. In both Europe and America the fashion for suntanning had spread during the 1920s, encouraged by medical opinion that sunlight had healing qualities. In retrospect, this was an oversimplification on both health and beauty grounds. Subsequent scientific research would indeed show the importance of exposure to sunlight to combat Vitamin D deficiency. However it has also revealed suntanning's potential to increase the risk of skin cancer, and demonstrated that extended exposure to sunlight can create molecules called free radicals which damage skin by attacking the collagen which keeps skin supple and youthful. The immediate effect of increased suntanning was an epidemic of sunburn, and for that result the industry was well prepared. Many creams were created in response, although their effectiveness seems to have been doubtful.[107]

Schueller was ahead of the game, launching Ambre Solaire, the first filtered tanning oil, in 1935. L'Oréal's technical director had the idea for the product, but it had taken the company's small scientific staff months to locate an active ingredient that promised to block the sun's rays. By April they had a product, which was then tested on five people who were sent to the Côte d'Azur. The new brand was launched in time for the French summer vacations, beginning in June, and advertised as a lotion that enabled one to tan naturally without burning. Schueller sold his new product in both hair salons and perfumeries.[108]

In Germany, Wella matched L'Oréal's intimacy with salons. As the fashion for short hair took hold and the demand for wigs melted away, the firm diversified into hairdressing accessories such as face towels and shop window mannequins. Then in 1924 Wella acquired a license to make a new generation of permanent wave machines that were easier to use by salons than their predecessors. The launch of the new machine three years later was accompanied by a new range of products, including the perming agent Wellin and a hair care product, Kolestral. During the 1930s Wella's business grew as curls and perms became *en vogue*. A "full-service philosophy" was offered to professional salon customers with "Wella Courses," and a dedicated magazine for hairdressers was launched in 1930.[109]

Schwarzkopf, which had initially sold its shampoos in retail outlets, also turned to the salon trade. After the death of the founder Hans in 1921, the business was managed by his widow Martha, who energetically pursued opportunities to build markets. The firm launched poster advertising in public places such as train stations. In 1927 the Schwarzkopf Institut für Haarhygiene, which researched new hair treatment methods for hairdressers, was founded, and a hairdressers' academy was added in 1936. In 1930 Schwarzkopf launched its first brand for professional hair salons, Haarglanz, whose rollout was supported by "demonstrators" sent around the country to salons to talk about the new brand. In 1932, the world's first branded hair conditioner was launched.[110]

The beauty salons were also the key distribution channel through which many American hair care brands were launched. Hair care was still a small category.[111] But new brands served to entice more consumers to use products. Breck launched the first pH-balanced shampoo and later included shampoos differentiated between oily and dry hair as well as Lanolin Crème Shampoo, a detergent-based formula for hair washing created in the early 1930s by the predecessor to Helene Curtis.[112]

Clairol, another brand launched through salons, was especially influential in growing an American market for hair dyes. This brand originated when Lawrence M. Gelb, an entrepreneurial chemist from New York, and his fashionable wife Joan discovered a "shampoo tint" hair color on a trip to Paris in 1931. First importing the formula from the firm which had created it and later licensing it before the French firm failed in 1935, the couple demonstrated the new product to hairdressers at salons upon their return to the United States. Joan adopted the alias Joan Clair for her sales pitch to the salons. The new product, Instant Clairol Oil Shampoo Tint, produced a natural color and was a commercial success.[113]

Charles Revson, perhaps the most important new entrant to the American beauty industry in the middle decades of the century, also started his business in beauty salons. Revson had been born in the Jewish quarter of Montreal before his family emigrated to the United States. In 1931, aged 25, he went to work as a salesman for a small New Jersey company which made an opaque nail varnish that contrasted with the transparent nail varnish typically sold at that time. When the company failed to promote him, he persuaded his brother and a chemist to establish their own company, called Revlon Nail Enamel. Focusing his sales on the salons, where women could have a manicure whilst getting their hair waved, his sales grew. In 1937 Revson began retailing his nail polish in department stores and some drugstores, though carefully maintaining premium prices and not selling to discounters. Despite competition from many smaller brands, Revlon secured at least 80 per cent of the American nail polish market before Elizabeth Arden entered the category in 1940. In that year, Revlon also started selling lipstick.[114]

There were many country-specific geographical and institutional challenges to reaching consumers. The large rural population of the United States was one such challenge: sales of cosmetics and toiletries were clustered in larger towns. The direct sales model used by the California Perfume Company (renamed Avon in 1939 after a brand of its products) provided the breakthrough in reaching rural customers with no access to retail chains or department stores. The company's sales grew from $2.9 million in 1929 to $6.5 million in 1939, despite the ravages of the Great Depression. Four-fifths of these sales were made in towns with fewer than 2,500 people. Although sales continued to be primarily in toiletries and skin care, the Avon brand of color cosmetics was created in 1929.[115]

The overwhelming majority of Avon's direct sellers, who amounted to 30,000 in all by 1933, were women, most of whom were married. Avon appealed to women who felt bored or trapped and wanted to take more initiative. In order to manage such a workforce, which had a high turnover rate, the company invested extensively in "motivational" literature designed to encourage women to take responsibility for themselves, their families, and their neighborhoods by entering business.[116]

While direct selling was primarily an American phenomenon before 1945, there were smaller examples elsewhere, including Japan. In 1929 the 27-year-old Shinobu Suzuki, an ambitious young man with a gift for languages, left his jobs working in a tea trading company and selling ball bearings in order to launch a venture in his home city of Shizuoka with 80 yen he had borrowed from relatives. His company became known as Pola Cosmetics and sold a new skin cream he had tried on his wife. Suzuki at first tried to sell in beauty parlors, but when this failed he turned to direct sales, which he saw as a way to educate women about how to apply make-up. Unlike Avon, however, Suzuki employed men as his representatives, dressing them in suits and ties to take his products around affluent districts first of his own city, and then to other cities as he expanded nationally. The 200 salespeople hired by 1937 included only one woman.[117]

In Japan, the major challenges faced by beauty companies in reaching consumers were institutional. Firms had continued to expand markets through educational and marketing campaigns. Kao and Lion, for example, gave away samples of their Western-style toiletries in girls' schools and built markets in remote rural areas through educational campaigns pitched to women's groups. Marketing strategies continued to build associations between brands and modernity. In 1927, when Kao introduced one of the first shampoo products on the Japanese market, it was named Modan (modern brand).[118] Shiseido's magazines for regular customers, who were organized into the formal Camellia Club in 1937, provided news about the latest Parisian fashions and trends.[119]

The problem was the traditional Japanese distribution system. During the 1920s a product might reach consumers through five or six intermediary agents, wholesalers, and the retailer.[120] Especially after a major financial crisis in 1927, there was rampant price-cutting and discounting as all levels of the distribution system came under competitive pressures. The numerous small, family-owned retailers, facing market saturation as well as competition from department stores, sold many different products and often used branded cosmetics as loss leaders to draw customers into their shops. By the early 1930s the Tokyo market had become notorious for price-cutting and bankruptcies.[121]

From the late 1920s both Kao and Lion implemented strategies to gain more control over the distribution system, counter discounting by the *toiya* wholesalers, and educate retailers about their brands.[122] However, it was Shiseido which adopted the most radical approach. The company introduced Japan's first voluntary chain store system following the Tokyo earthquake in 1923 as a radical step to curb price discounting. The chain stores which joined the system were required to provide an exclusive retail space for Shiseido and uphold Shiseido prices, and were in turn guaranteed a 20 per cent profit rate. There was no franchise fee, and stores were free to join or leave at any time. By 1928 Shiseido had put in place a nationwide network of 7,000 chain stores.[123] Shiseido also became directly involved in wholesaling. In 1927 it acquired the Osaka merchant which had sold its products in western Japan, and then began creating new wholesale companies dedicated solely to company products, all while trying to keep *toiya* investing in them so as to retain their expertise.[124]

The strategies of the Japanese companies to gain greater control over distribution channels—like Avon's army of female direct sellers in rural America and L'Oréal's efforts to build close relationships with hairdressers—were part of the wide range of efforts by beauty companies to reach consumers across class, geography, and custom. Collectively they contributed to the erosion of the geographical and institutional barriers which had previously restricted the markets for branded beauty products.

The world becomes more complex

In the aftermath of World War I a new, and more complex, stage in the globalization of the beauty industry was ushered in. In the broadest terms, the story of the nineteenth century had been one of firms growing from their original cities to serving wider regions, then building national markets, and finally seeking foreign markets. This was the path of many consumer goods, and the beauty industry followed the example of larger industries such as household soap and sewing machines. The speed of this process also varied between product categories and individual firms, and in only a few cases was it far advanced by 1914. Nevertheless, the process of internationalization seemed to be set on a linear course.

The war delivered a rude shock to any belief that globalization was inevitable and linear. Governments expropriated the physical assets and trademarks of firms based in enemy countries. Restrictions on profit remittances and trade proliferated. They did not go away when peace returned in 1918. During the 1930s tariffs reached such high levels that there was a meltdown in international trade.[125]

The owners of even the most successful businesses and fashionable brands learned that there was nowhere to hide from political shifts. The Russian industry was nationalized as a result of the Communist revolution in 1917. Two decades later the international expansion of the Spanish perfumery industry, which had developed export markets in Latin America in particular, was derailed by the outbreak of the Spanish Civil War in 1936. In the wake of the war and the autarkic policies of the Fascist victors that followed, the principal companies (Perfumeria Gal, Myrurgia, and Antonio Puig), retreated to their protected if impoverished home market, where they sold cheaper products, such as toilet soap and eau de Cologne, which could be made with domestically grown raw materials.[126]

German-owned companies found their nascent international businesses totally disrupted. Germany lost World War I, and its firms lost their foreign assets, including expropriated trademarks.[127] Muehlens had its extensive American business expropriated, and it was left with little beyond a subsidiary in neutral Sweden. It spent the interwar years rebuilding an international business, primarily through exports.[128]

Schwarzkopf also had to rebuild an export business. A factory was built in neighboring Czechoslovakia in 1930, followed by a sales branch in Austria a few years later.[129] Wella also created distribution companies elsewhere in Europe during the late 1920s, followed by a selling and production affiliate in New York City in the early 1930s. By 1938 production had also started in Britain and Argentina.[130] The outbreak of World War II, however, resulted once more in the German companies losing most of their foreign assets.

Beiersdorf provides a case study of just how challenging this era was for firms based in Germany. During World War I the firm's flourishing American toothpaste business withered. Its licensee Lehn & Fink continued to manufacture its products, but the US government expropriated the trademark Pebeco in 1919, and sold it to Lehn & Fink. Nivea was spared this fate, as its internationalization had not yet begun. The situation was only partially alleviated by the successive deaths of Oscar Troplowitz and Otto Hanns Mankiewicz in the previous year. Mankiewicz, who became the sole owner, had been born in Silesia, which in the postwar settlement became part of the newly established state of Poland. Poland was not treated as an enemy state by the United States. After a decade of litigation, American courts formally restored Beiersdorf's property.[131]

By the early 1920s, Lehn & Fink had resumed selling Pebeco, but the brand never regained its strong market position, perhaps because of its German associations, not to mention a medicinal taste which handicapped the brand as toothpastes became increasingly cosmetic.[132] Beiersdorf's relationship with Lehn & Fink never recovered. By the 1930s the sale of Nivea products in America had been transferred to a firm owned by a German chemist and former employee of Hoechst.[133]

Beiersdorf's business itself was rebuilt after the loss of foreign markets and the deaths of the founders. Its ownership stabilized when the Warburg Bank, long linked to the family, took an equity stake. Willy Jacobsohn, a pharmacist who was not a family member but who had successfully run the firm's Austrian affiliate, became chief executive in 1921. He proved to be a creative and dynamic entrepreneur who tripled domestic sales by 1930.[134] Seventy new or improved products were launched between 1919 and 1933, half of them in beauty.[135]

Building on the firm's emphasis on associating beauty with health, Jacobsohn relaunched the Nivea brand in 1925 with what became its classic blue tin and the white Nivea logo. While previously the brand had been advertised using an elegant woman in her boudoir at home, this female ideal was now replaced by "Nivea girls" shown in the open air and sun. The advertisements demonstrated beauty ideals of bronzed skin and healthy bodies which the consumer was encouraged to believe could be obtained by using Nivea cream. The emphasis on athletic bodies made the cream appeal to men as well as women, helping the brand to strengthen its hold on the German skin cream market.[136]

It was more challenging to rebuild international business. The company's strategy became driven by the desire to protect trademarks from future expropriation. Subsidiaries were founded in the neutral countries of Switzerland and the Netherlands in 1919 and 1921 respectively to serve as the legal owners of Beiersdorf's international trademarks.[137] Initially the company relied upon exports and contracts with exclusive distribution agents, but from the late 1920s foreign manufacturing affiliates, known as "ring firms," were established, which were not formally owned but held in trust by foreign citizens. By 1933 there were 13 such "ring" firms.[138]

The coming of Adolf Hitler and the Nazis to power in March 1933 provided new and potentially disastrous challenges. As German exchange controls tightened, Beiersdorf supplied capital to the ring firms through affiliates in London and, especially, New York. A complicated web of ownership and relationships led back to the parent firm in the form of trustee arrangements and options to repurchase shares. In 1940 it became too risky to rely even on these trustee arrangements. Beiersdorf sold the majority of its foreign assets for a token sum to a Swiss citizen, who was the owner of Beiersdorf's distribution and manufacturing partner in Basle.[139]

Beiersdorf's domestic business was also now under threat. Some members of the Nazi Party opposed female use of cosmetics for moral reasons, emphasizing that women should be healthy, sporty, and fertile rather than engaging in face painting.[140] In practice, Nazi ideology towards the use of cosmetics, as in many other matters, was contradictory. Insofar as there was an official policy, it was not to suppress cosmetics use, but rather to employ them to promote Nazi fantasies about the "natural beauty" of the allegedly superior German race.[141] The greater problem for the company was the Nazis' anti-Jewish policies, which were consistent and enforced with growing lawlessness. The Jewish members of Beiersdorf's management, who were in the majority, resigned soon after Hitler took power, some, like Jacobsohn, fleeing abroad to the company affiliate in Amsterdam in recognition of the threatening nature of the new regime.[142]

Beiersdorf as a company remained in business. Nazi interference with the parent company in Hamburg was kept at bay by timely action. As the Jewish members of the management departed, Carl Claussen, who had married a member of the Troplowitz family but was not Jewish, left his own Hamburg-based business to join Beiersdorf as chief executive. All shares held by Jewish owners were transferred to the non-Jewish members of the management, including the equity held by Warburg Bank. With its ownership and management structure secured, Beiersdorf's sales continued apace. Less expensive than the competitor creams of Mouson and Pond's, Nivea's sales even rose during the 1930s.[143]

Elly Heuss-Knapp, a talented female marketing manager, was responsible for powerful new Nivea advertising campaigns. These centered on what became an iconic slogan about "Nivea in Sonne und Wind" ("Nivea in sun and wind"). The brand had been identified as early as the 1920s with ideals fashionable in Germany and elsewhere for youth and for leisure in the sun and outdoors. Starting in 1933, Heuss-Knapp deployed the themes of light and sun to position the brand as a protective, as well as beautifying, product for use in all seasons by men, women, and children.[144] Facing anti-Semitic attacks from competitors, Heuss-Knapp's Nivea campaign was a delicate balancing act. As a result, her advertisements might be interpreted as aligned with Nazi ideology about the superiority of blonde and blue-eyed Nordic natural beauty, but they also built on the long-established brand identity, which emphasized health and athleticism for the liberated modern woman.[145]

Global fashions and local expressions

It was a paradox that such an era of political turbulence and virulent nationalism co-existed with a continuing diffusion of fashions and styles. The latter lurched forward towards a nascent international consumer culture, albeit one still confined primarily to wealthier countries and urban dwellers. This culture reflected growing travel and tourism. By the middle of the 1920s, 350,000 Americans visited Paris annually.[146] Fashion magazines also diffused the latest trends. And Hollywood provided a new momentum to this emergent culture, and one which was more accessible than Parisian haute couture.

The celebrity culture which emerged from Hollywood had wide appeal. By the 1930s Hollywood movies were available almost worldwide and served as a powerful diffuser of beauty ideals whose impact was strong even in countries far removed from Western cultural values.[147] Contemporaries noticed that beauty ideals seemed to be converging. In February 1929, when contestants from 17 countries assembled in Paris for a Miss Europe beauty pageant, a *New York Times* reporter was struck how "Parisian styles or clothing and the universal vogue of hair-dressing and the use of cosmetics and facial creams have succeeded in standardizing European beauty." Noting that the "modern eye demands slimness and petiteness above everything else," a convergence in the ideals for the body shapes of the women considered beautiful also appeared evident. The winner of the contest, Miss Hungary, was described as representing an "amalgamation of all that the Continent regards as lovely."[148]

The Hollywood film studios and the beauty industry shared a common interest in the globalization of consumer markets, which offered profitable opportunities if only the right strategies to exploit them could be found. The winning strategy required finding the right balance between emerging global consumer values and local expressions of them. International consumer culture was attractive around the world but, despite the kind of convergence reported in the Miss Europe contest, successful businesses needed to be relevant to individual national markets.

Hollywood sought to meet this challenge, during the 1930s, by displaying a wider range of female beauty types than earlier. The studios recruited actors and actresses from Europe and Latin America in particular, not only to make their firms more exotic, but also to enhance their international appeal. The arrival of Technicolor in that decade also encouraged filmmakers to display a wider range of hair color and skin tone for white female actresses, including dark-haired Austrian Hedy Lamarr and Portuguese-born Carmen Miranda. Max Factor, Richard Hudnut, and other companies matched this trend with the launch of cosmetics products, such as facial powders and rouges, designed to fit a wider range of skin tones and complexions.[149] While Hollywood imported foreign actors, Max Factor exported products to foreign markets. The firm began to export during the early 1920s, and formally established an export division in 1930. In 1935 a retail branch was opened in Bond Street, London. In 1940 branches were established in Manila, the Philippines and Canada, and the following year in Cuba.[150]

The emergent international consumer culture had several dimensions, but in view of the preponderance of female consumers in the beauty industry, the diffusion of common fashions and trends among younger women was especially relevant for firms. Variously known as the flapper in America and la garçonne in France, these characters personified a set of younger women, across a range of countries, who expressed desires for greater freedom, whether political, economic, or sexual, through specific visual styles and items of consumption. They wore sexy clothing, had bobbed hair, smoked cigarettes, and used lipstick, nail polish, and other cosmetics. This demographic has been identified as the "modern girl" in one recent study, and she might be regarded as the consumer equivalent of the New Woman. In each country, the more universal features of "modern girls" interacted with local traditions to produce distinct, country-specific versions of women's revised role.[151]

Amidst the political turbulence of these years, then, the emergent international consumer culture provided new opportunities to the beauty industry. This was evident in luxury brands, whose consumers traveled, read fashion magazines, and could pay for expensive, often imported, products. In order to reach these consumers, Guerlain, Roger et Gallet, and many other Parisian firms opened affiliates in other major European countries and occasionally Latin America, as well as New York, during the 1920s.[152] France remained as the major exporter of perfumery and related products throughout the period.[153]

Upscale American brands crossed the Atlantic in the other direction. Helena Rubinstein opened salons in Berlin, Vienna, and Cannes, supplied by small factories in France, Britain, and Austria.[154] Elizabeth Arden opened a London salon in 1922, and other salons followed in Paris, Berlin, Rome, Madrid, and Monte Carlo. By 1937 her business in Britain alone had annual sales of $1 million.[155] It was evidence of how far a global consumer culture had developed that Arden could pursue similar marketing approaches in quite different contexts. The company used broadly the same advertising copy in Nazi Germany as in the United States. Similar claims were made that the use of her cosmetics, and especially regular visits to her salons, would enhance the natural, healthy, and youthful look of liberated modern women.[156]

The extent to which a global luxury brand needed to, and could, be locally relevant was challenging for entrepreneurs. This was an important theme in the creation of Lancôme by Belgian-born Armand Petitjean in 1935. In the first decade of the twentieth century he and his two brothers had built a trading business in Latin America which included an agency for selling Coty's products. Coty himself was so impressed that he hired Petitjean to run Coty Inc. in 1932, though he resigned two years later, apparently disagreeing with the mass-distribution strategy. In 1935 Petitjean persuaded Jean-Baptiste and

Guillaume D'Ornano, also associates of Coty and fellow Corsicans, to join him in a new venture.[157]

Petitjean later claimed that he created Lancôme when he realized that a number of American firms were taking control of the domain of prestige beauty, and that a new French house was needed to combat them. Coty, he felt, had cheapened his brand too far, and he proposed a more subtle approach to giving a global brand some local relevance. In 1935 he launched five fragrances sold in bottles created by the renowned artist Georges Delhomme, formerly director of production at Coty. The defining idea was to create a separate scent for women from each of the five continents by building an association between each scent and the flowers, spices, and cultural identity of each part of the world. A true beauty brand, Petitjean argued, had to be relevant to women everywhere.[158] Within six months of the launch of the perfumes, Petitjean had opened over 30 foreign markets via exports and local agents, and foreign sales surpassed sales in France by a wide margin.[159]

The makers of mass-market brands were also well positioned to exploit the ongoing modernization of women's roles. Pond's was among the most internationalized of such brands. In 1923 almost one-third of Pond's annual revenues of $2.5 million was earned abroad; two-thirds of these international sales were in Europe. By 1941 Pond's total sales had grown to $9.8 million, of which 12 per cent was in Europe and 18 per cent elsewhere. Pond's opened its first foreign factory, in Canada, in 1927, followed by one in Britain in 1933. The company sub-contracted manufacturing in a further 12 countries during the 1930s and was selling in 96 countries overall by the end of that decade.[160] This level of internationalization was unusual in the beauty industry but was found in other branded and packaged goods by the 1930s.[161]

If the expansion of Pond's demonstrated the potential of global markets, as firms took their brands international the challenges also became more apparent. If consumer cultures combined elements of the international and the local, the problem was finding the exact proportions of that mix in each market. Even the British, who were especially exposed to American beauty culture through Hollywood and a shared language, made noticeably less use of soap and toothpaste than Americans.[162] Beyond Western countries, there were wider differences in ethnicity and culture, whilst income levels provided a constraint on the product categories which could be sold. The vast income inequality in Asian countries such as India and China, for example, greatly limited markets. The rich elites had a long tradition of using handicraft beauty products, whilst most of the rest of the population lived in such grinding poverty that they could not afford any consumer product. For the most part, sales were limited to toiletries, which consumer products companies such as Unilever and Colgate-Palmolive could sell to middle-class consumers in affluent cities, such as Shanghai.[163]

Latin America posed similar market challenges, albeit with variations across the region. During the 1940s J. Walter Thompson, investigating the market potential for dental products in Mexico, Cuba, and Argentina, concluded that 60 per cent of the Mexican population were so poor that they could not afford any dental product. In contrast, in the other two countries the entire populations were estimated to be affluent enough to buy commercial products to clean their teeth.[164] There was extensive use of fragrances in the entire region, by both men and women, which created a substantial market for French, Spanish, and British brands, but sellers of mass-market skin creams and cosmetics faced a stiffer challenge. Pond's used the same marketing techniques as in the United States, such as advertising in women's magazines, but found that the market was limited to rich urban elites, who often had sufficient money to buy more prestigious French brands.[165]

The extent to which marketing and products needed to be customized for each market was more pressing for cheaper brands than for their luxury counterparts, as most of their consumers were not likely to be regular international travelers, even if they were increasingly exposed to Hollywood and other diffusers of fashions. There was little disagreement among US and European firms that Western fashion and ethnicity set the global standard. Marketing campaigns in Latin America and elsewhere focused on offering local women the opportunity to emulate the latest fashions in the West.[166] However, there was considerable variation among firms as to how such ideas should be communicated in different markets.

The basic instinct at the J. Walter Thompson advertising agency, which worked for Pond's, Unilever, and many other beauty companies, was that of a worldwide convergence in consumer markets. This view was articulated by Samuel Weeks, the agency's Vice-President and Director of International Operations. In a memorandum written in 1930, he observed:

Motion pictures, wireless broadcasting, travel, the distribution of books and magazines, the exchange of plays and players, not to mention professional and amateur photography—all have brought the countries of the civilized world closer together...even the superficial differences between peoples are disappearing. More than ever, selling methods or advertising appeals that are sound for one country are found to be equally sound for another.[167]

The actual execution of such a view in marketing campaigns varied between firms, product categories, regions, and countries. In Mexico, Pond's, Max Factor, and other US cosmetics companies working with J. Walter Thompson typically used endorsements by white American celebrities to sell their products, with little concession to the local context.[168] The toiletry companies, which sold at lower prices, were more inclined towards localizing their advertising images. Palmolive used local celebrities in its Mexican marketing.[169] As Unilever rolled out Lux Toilet Soap in Latin America and elsewhere, it always used promotions by film celebrities, but it used local celebrities, not Hollywood stars. In Argentina advertising used local film stars who endorsed the brand and made personal appearances to promote it.[170]

In China and some other Asian markets, even Pond's sought to make advertisements and their appeal more local, using local models and containing other local cultural allusions.[171] Unilever's advertisements for Lux Toilet Soap employed the most famous Chinese film stars of the day, even though Hollywood film stars were well known in the country.[172] Advertising for Nivea typically portrayed a carefully balanced picture of Chinese and Western men and women. The former would wear both Chinese and Western clothing—typically, in the case of the women, Chinese dresses for daily and formal wear, but Western swimwear and sportswear for outdoor activities.[173]

The extent of local adaptation of brands, then, was a major marketing challenge, but there were other major differences between countries which made reaching consumers in different markets a complex affair even if fashions had converged. The availability and reach of specific media varied widely. In Europe, for example, American companies could not use their expertise in radio advertising, as almost no commercial advertising was permitted. While Unilever was used to advertising brands such as Lux in the printed media, it discovered that in Brazil women seldom read newspapers. Instead advertising had to be switched to the more popular medium of radio.[174]

4.5 A Nivea Creme advertisement for China features a local woman in Western dress along with a smaller image of women in traditional Chinese dress, 1937.

Access to local distribution channels was always difficult. In small markets, it never made economic sense for a firm to establish its own affiliate to sell or manufacture. Merchant intermediaries were used by firms such as Beiersdorf to sell small quantities of branded goods in Asian and Latin American markets.[175] In some smaller European markets, local distributors were used. In Sweden, the firm of Barlach developed from a small business sharpening haircutting scissors into an importer and distributor of foreign beauty products. The company imported and sold foreign brands, working closely with the foreign companies to advise what could be sold in Sweden. The use of such local distributors tended to encourage marketing towards local adaptation, as they were very aware of the specific preferences in their own local markets.[176]

Tariff barriers, meanwhile, obliged companies to consider manufacturing locally, as it did in all industries. This was a large investment which many smaller firms could not afford, and thus provided a further challenge in reaching foreign markets. The sellers of mass toiletries established many foreign factories. Unilever's factories spanned five continents by the 1930s, giving it the widest geographical spread of any company in any industry.[177] Bristol-Myers opened several factories in Latin America, where the Ipana toothpaste brand was sold widely.[178] Colgate-Palmolive, J. B. Williams, and Lehn & Fink were among the companies which responded to tariffs by contracting local firms to manufacture for them in Argentina and elsewhere in Latin America.[179]

A final challenge was the strength of local competition in many markets. While luxury French and American brands could sell at premium prices because of the importance of the country of origin in brand equity, in the mass market there were local brands in most countries which could, and did, successfully compete with foreign brands. Beauty was still a fragmented industry with many small firms. In 1938 there were 1,181 firms in the French industry alone, with just 28 of them accounting for 30 per cent of total sales.[180]

The formation of new firms in local markets was facilitated by tariffs, which provided protection against foreign brands, as did wars and economic crises. During both World War I and the Great Depression, for example, Swedish firms captured share in cosmetics from imports. A lot of new companies were formed during the war, and after a lull, the number of firms in the Swedish industry increased again from 72 in 1929 to reach nearly 100 by 1938.[181] In the larger British market, although the leading American and French brands held substantial market shares, they co-existed with numerous local brands.[182]

Among the larger firms was Yardley, which by the mid-1930s was selling a full range of fragrances, cosmetics, skin creams, and hair products. There were new ventures in color cosmetics, such as Gala and Goya, which in time built successful local brands.[183]

In many countries women were active sources of new entrepreneurial creativity. In this regard, the industry not only offered female consumers choices about what to buy and how to appear, but also provided fertile opportunities to make money and establish financial independence from men. In Europe, beauty institutes, many started by women, began to spread from Paris and London to less fashionable cities. In Germany the Marbert brand originated in 1936 in the regional industrial city of Düsseldorf as an institute started by two female entrepreneurs, Margarethe Ingrid Sendler and Berta Röber, which soon expanded to encompass the manufacture of cosmetics.[184]

In Sweden, at least one tenth of the 64 entrepreneurial beauty start-ups in the interwar decades were founded or co-founded by women, a greater number than before the war. Stockholm-based Annie Frissén was among many women who used her own capital and loans from friends to found a cosmetics firm in 1936, and soon after, the beauty institute Anita, making about 40 different cosmetic products for sale within three years.[185]

Even the formerly male-dominated world of Parisian perfumery could not keep out female entrepreneurs. Blanche Arvoy created two perfume houses in the early 1920s. These were Jovoy, whose fine perfumes in bottles briefly featured whimsical animals, and Parfums Corday, which proved a more permanent creation.[186] At the house of Caron, the former dressmaker Félicie Vanpouille joined Ernest Daltroff as joint owner in 1920. They had met in 1905, and she soon became Daltroff's creative collaborator as well as lover. Vanpouille transferred her knowledge of couture design to creating innovative bottles, including one shaped like the skirt of a Parisian cancan dancer developed particularly for the American market in 1936. Although their romantic relationship eventually ended, she continued to play a major creative and management role in the company, of which she became sole owner after Daltroff's death in 1941 in New York, where he had fled after the German occupation of France.[187]

There were also many new firms in Asia and Latin America. In Japanese-occupied Korea, Jung Suk Jung, the wife of the founder of the Doosan business group, created the first Korean-made branded cosmetic product in 1920.[188] In China, pharmacies and merchants began selling their own brands. The

China Chemical Industry Company, founded in 1912, grew in response to the boycott movement against foreign-made, especially Japanese, goods. In 1923, it produced China's first domestically made toothpaste, Three Star Tooth Paste, which was soon being exported to Southeast Asia.[189] Local firms also appeared in Latin America, often beginning as contract manufacturers for foreign firms, before also launching their own brands. Ylang Laboratories, founded in Buenos Aires in 1939, later built the large color cosmetics brand Miss Ylang after 1945.

The risks and challenges of international markets were sufficient, however, to deter many firms from venturing too far from home. Many large US cosmetics firms, including Avon and Noxell, confined their foreign ambitions to Canada. P & G also limited its foreign manufacturing to Canada until the 1930s, when it acquired a British company and built a large British laundry soap business.[190] Most firms which did grow abroad, other than some large toiletry firms, concentrated on the major Western markets and a few cosmopolitan cities elsewhere. United States firms were largely focused on Canada, Western Europe, and parts of Latin America. The French fragrance firms had most of their sales either in Western Europe or the United States. Most other European companies focused on neighboring countries. L'Oréal largely sold elsewhere in Western Europe.[191] While some Japanese companies built large international businesses—Club had 30 per cent of its sales outside Japan in the late 1930s—they were largely in China, as well as in Japanese-occupied Korea and Taiwan.[192]

World War II: greater challenges but a more established industry

During World War II, perhaps even more than during World War I, the beauty market proved highly resilient. Total retail sales in the United States reached $805 million in 1945. By 1948 perhaps 90 per cent of American women used lipstick, and two-thirds used rouge.[193] The war stimulated further innovation. In wartime Britain, there were lipsticks equipped with accessories such as emergency flashlights in case of blackout. Max Factor developed a long-lasting lipstick. Gala of London offered a refillable lipstick. Enterprising local pharmacies made their own cosmetics from simple ingredients. There was frequent resort to substitutes, such as boot polish instead of mascara, beetroot juice in place of lipstick, and machine grease instead of hand cream.[194]

The war inevitably disrupted the industry, although once more to different extents in different countries. In Germany and Japan, the ruling dictatorships

4.6 A wartime Gala advertisement in Great Britain showing a woman dressed for active military duty applying lipstick. The norm of near-universal use of lipstick had taken hold among women over the course of only a few decades, 1941.

forced firms to switch to war-related production. Following the occupation of France by Germany in 1940, the French industry also lost its export markets. An even bigger challenge loomed immediately after occupation, as the initial German plan was to move the entire Parisian fashion industry to Berlin or Vienna. This strategy was eventually abandoned, and the French industry continued to be able to produce and sell.[195] Survival, however, came at a cost, as the worlds of fashion and beauty contained many leading figures who would later be criticized for collaboration with the Nazi occupiers. These included Eugène Schueller, who had become closely associated with an extreme right-wing political party in France during the late 1930s. Towards the end of the war he switched his financial backing to the anti-Nazi resistance, and although he was later charged with collaboration, he was acquitted of all charges by the French courts.[196] Jewish executives had to flee the country. The Wertheimers went to the United States, via Brazil. As Bourjois had a factory in Hoboken, New Jersey, they were able to stay in business, and even launched a major new perfume, Courage, in 1942. They also created a Chanel facility and began making Chanel N°5, managing to continue to import jasmine essence from Grasse even during the war. In France itself, Coco Chanel moved into a prominent Parisian hotel with a Nazi lover and actively sought to take over the Wertheimer business interests, an effort which failed and left her reputation damaged.[197]

In the Western democracies, the story was different. Even in the United States some firms shifted entirely to wartime production, yet the war also provided new opportunities. In the United States perfume sales increased from $45 million in 1940 to $86 million in 1946, as working women had more income to spend, and partly as wartime rationing limited spending possibilities on other consumer goods such as clothes and cars. As French companies could not export perfumes into the American market, American firms developed their own brands. Helena Rubinstein introduced Heaven Scent in 1942, floating samples of the scent on pink and blue balloons on Fifth Avenue in New York.[198] In Britain, the industry was strengthened. It had exported $4 million of beauty products in 1939, and by 1947 the figure had risen to $13 million. The war years saw an increase in the domestic manufacture of formerly imported materials such as fatty alcohols and emulsifying agents, as well as the growth of research facilities and laboratory equipment.[199]

Perhaps the most striking feature of the war years was the official recognition given to the industry. Following the American entry into the war in 1941, the US government declared the production of lipstick a wartime necessity.[200] Initially the British government saw beauty as a luxury good whose production needed to be highly restricted, but a huge surge in illegal "black market" sales led, in 1943, to a new system of regulating production designed to curb these potentially hazardous products.[201] The industry had become too important in sustaining civilian morale to suppress it. Indeed wartime austerity, particularly clothes rationing, had the effect of increasing the demand for make-up and hairstyles to counterbalance the limitations of the wardrobe.[202] By 1944 a British government committee concluded that beauty products could "not be considered as luxuries enjoyed by the privileged few, but must be considered in the same category as cigarettes, sweets and beer and similar accepted necessities of a modern standard of living for the mass of people."[203] Beauty had once and for all emerged out from under the suspicions, moral and otherwise, that had traditionally marked it. It was now a necessary part of the war effort.

Summing up

Neither two major world wars nor the Great Depression proved able to halt the growth of the beauty market for more than a few years. In 1914 the legitimacy of categories such as hair dyes and color cosmetics was still barely established. By 1945 the governments of the major Western democracies had deemed their production a strategic necessity. In the United States, at least, even direct intervention by cosmetic surgery to modify appearance became acceptable. The market continued to expand as previous income and leisure constraints on consumption relaxed, both as more young women entered the workforce, and as brands gave consumers inexpensive access to the world of Hollywood celebrities. An emergent international beauty consumer culture became accessible to the middle classes throughout the West and to elites in cosmopolitan cities of Asia and Latin America.

The beauty industry aligned its strategies with shifting societal attitudes and fashions. Copywriters such as Helen Resor spoke to the changing economic and political status of women; Max Factor helped shape the association of cosmetic beauty with Hollywood celebrities; Schueller and the Gelbs built the association between feminine beauty and hair dyeing through working with hairdressers. Female direct sellers in rural America and cosmetics chain stores in Japan opened up new avenues to reach broader swathes of consumers. Entrepreneurs continued to build the legitimacy of their industry by founding institutes, whether for cleanliness or for beauty, which emphasized the seriousness of their endeavor, its scientific knowledge-base, and role in education, particularly women's education. Most of all, beauty companies used the new medium of radio and cinema to reach ever wider audiences. None of these developments, however, fundamentally modified the ethnic and gender borders of beauty which had been formed when the industry emerged.

World War I was the first in a series of events which tested the industry's faith in, and enthusiasm for, globalization. Assets and brands in foreign lands had been seized. Globalization was on hold until the 1920s. Hollywood grew as a powerful force behind the further diffusion of an international consumer culture. Its glamor gave American brands a widespread aspirational appeal. The lure of the American market prompted French companies to invest in it, while French and American firms experimented with buying each other's brands. Finding the right balance between the international appeal of such brands and their local relevance, however, presented a major challenge for the industry, and one in which no consensus emerged on its solution.

The Great Depression temporarily reversed the growth of the beauty market, but that was not the major effect. Rather, the cosmopolitanism of the 1920s now encountered an environment of tariffs, nationalism, fascism, and war. The brief era of cross-border mergers ended. The political activities of Coty and Schueller, and the flight of Willy Jacobsohn, the Wertheimers, Ernest Daltroff, and many others from persecution, were symbolic of the scale of the era's deglobalization. Throughout these miserable years, a recognizable international consumer culture remained stubbornly in place, but by 1945 Samuel Weeks' hopes expressed 15 years earlier, that "even the superficial differences between peoples are disappearing," looked distinctly forlorn.

Notes

1. Penny Dade, *All Made Up* (London: Middlesex University Press, 2007), p. 20.

2. US Department of Commerce, Bureau of the Census, *Fourteenth Census of the United States Manufactures: 1919. United States by Industries and Geographic Divisions and States* (Washington, DC: Government Printing Office, 1922); "Perfume, Cosmetic and Toilet Preparations Sales at Retail, 1914–1960," *Advertising Age* 32:42, October 16, 1961, p. 88.

3. Lindy Woodhead, *War Paint* (Hoboken, NJ: John Wiley and Sons, 2004), pp. 103–6.

4. Erich Körner, *Zauber der Frisur: 5000 Jahre Haarkosmetik und Mode* (Darmstadt: Wella AG, 1964), pp. 197, 199–201.

5. Helen Marie Caldwell, "The Development and Democratization of the American Perfume Market 1920–1975," unpubl. doctoral diss., University of Connecticut, 1995, p. 155.

6. Roland Marchand, *Advertising the American Dream: Making Way for Modernity, 1920–1940* (Berkeley: University of California Press, 1985); Regina Lee Blaszczyk, *American Consumer Society, 1865–2005* (Wheeling, Ill.: Harlan Davidson, 2009), ch. 4.

7. Elizabeth Haiken, *Venus Envy: A History of Cosmetic Surgery* (Baltimore: John Hopkins University Press, 1997), chs 1–3 and pp. 182–5.

8. Lois Banner, *American Beauty* (Chicago: University of Chicago Press, 1983), p. 16.

9. Marylène Delbourg-Delphis, *Le chic et le look: Histoire de la mode féminine et des mœurs de 1850 à nos jours* (Paris: Hachette, 1981).

10. Ina Zweiniger-Bargielowska, "The Culture of the Abdomen: Obesity and Reducing in Britain, circa 1900–1939," *Journal of British Studies* 44 (2005), pp. 239–73.

11. Juliann Sivulka, *Stronger than Dirt* (New York: Humanity Books, 2001), pp. 157–8.

12. Sivulka, *Stronger*, pp. 229–47.

13. Sivulka, *Stronger*, pp. 185–6.

14. Peter Miskell, "Cavity Protection or Cosmetic Perfection?," *Business History Review* 78 (2004), pp. 29–60; Fred E. H. Schroeder, "Say Cheese! The Revolution in the Aesthetics of Smiles," *Journal of Popular Culture* 32:2 (Fall 1998), pp. 123–35.

15. Davis Dyer, Frederick Dalzell, and Rowena Olegario, *Rising Tide* (Boston, Mass.: Harvard Business School Press, 2004), p. 57.

16. Charles Wilson, *The History of Unilever*, vol. 2 (London: Cassell, 1954), pp. 301–8; "Colgate and Palmolive to Combine Interests," *Wall Street Journal*, July 13, 1928, p. 3.

17. Kathy Peiss, *Hope in a Jar* (New York: Henry Holt, 1998), pp. 121–2; J. Walter Thompson Archives, John W. Hartman Center, Duke University (hereafter JWT), Account Files, Chesebrough-Pond's Inc., Account Histories 1955–1959, "Pond's Case History," May 5, 1959, Box 3; Marlis Schweitzer, "Uplifting Makeup: Actresses' Testimonials and the Cosmetics Industry, 1910–1918," *Business and Economic History On-Line* (2003), available at <www.h-net.org/~business/bhcweb/publications/BEHonline/2003/Schweitzer.pdf>, accessed October 22, 2009.

18. Linda Scott, *Fresh Lipstick: Redressing Fashion and Feminism* (New York: Palgrave Macmillan, 2005), pp. 149–53.

19. Jessica Pallingston, *Lipstick: A Celebration of the World's Favorite Cosmetic* (New York: St. Martin's Press), p. 70.

20. <www.maybelline.co.uk/about_us>, accessed April 15, 2007.

21. Pallingston, *Lipstick*, p. 164.

22. Peiss, *Hope*, p. 103.

23. Gerben Bakker, *Entertainment Industrialised: The Emergence of the International Film Industry, 1890–1940* (Cambridge: Cambridge University Press, 2008).

24. Banner, *American Beauty*, p. 283.

25. Fred E. Basten, *Max Factor: The Man who Changed the Faces of the World* (New York: Arcade, 2008), p. 46.

26. Peiss, *Hope*, p. 126.

27. Basten, *Max Factor*, pp. 59–61.

28. Tom Reichert, *The Erotic History of Advertising* (New York: Prometheus Books, 2003), pp. 118–19; Scott, *Fresh Lipstick*, pp. 184–6.

29. Woodhead, *War Paint*, pp. 115, 140, 145–8, 153–4; Peiss, *Hope*, pp. 87–9; Scott, *Fresh Lipstick*, pp. 137–9.

30. Woodhead, *War Paint*, p. 155, 163; Peiss, *Hope*, p. 107.

31. Between 1915 and 1925 imports of French fragrances and cosmetics into the United States increased from $2.4 million to $6 million. See Caldwell, "Development," pp. 72–112.

32. Valerie Steele, *Paris Fashion* (Oxford: Berg, 1998), pp. 247–9.

33. Véronique Pouillard, "Federating the Couture Business? Exchanges between the French, Belgian, and American Couturiers during the 1930s," paper presented to the Business History Conference, Cleveland, Ohio, May 31–June 2, 2007.

34. Ghislaine Sicard-Picchiottino, *François Coty: Un industriel corse sous la IIIe République* (Ajaccio: Albiana, 2006), p. 118.

35. Elisabeth de Feydeau, "De l'hygiène au rêve: l'industrie française du parfum (1830–1939)," unpubl. doctoral diss., University of Lille, 1997, pp. 386–8.

36. Richard Stamelman, *Perfume: Joy, Obsession, Scandal, Sin* (New York: Rizzoli, 2006), pp. 245–6; Edwin T. Morris, *Fragrance: The Story of Perfume from Cleopatra to Chanel* (New York: Charles Scribner, 1984), pp. 202–3; Yves de Chiris, personal communication, January 15, 2009.

37. Coco Chanel was given 10 per cent of the profits of Chanel: Feydeau, "De l'hygiène," pp. 389–92, 417.

38. "Mergers, Acquisitions," *Time*, January 21, 1929.

39. Caldwell, "Development," pp. 150–3; Sicard-Picchiottino, *Coty*, p. 118.

40. Caldwell, "Development," pp. 72–112.

41. Jean-Paul Guerlain, "The House of Guerlain—Evolution of a Parfumerie," *Perfumer and Flavorist* 4 (June/July 1979), p. 10.

42. Jean-Marie Martin-Hattemberg, *Caron* (Toulouse: Éditions Milan, 2000), pp. 48–67; Grégoire Colard, *Le charme secret d'une maison parfumée* (Paris: Éditions J. C. Lattès, 1984).

43. Elizabeth Coty and Roulhac Toledano, "François Coty: Emperor of Perfume, France's First Billionaire," unpubl. MS, pp. 231–2.

44. Sicard-Picchiottino, *Coty*, pp. 95–102, 127–9, 134; Feydeau, "De l'hygiène," pp. 417–21; "Coty Balance Improves," *Drug Markets* 25:4 (October 1929), p. 358.

45. Lehman Brothers, *Coty Inc.* (New York: Lehman Brothers, 1929); "François Coty Resigns from French Firm," *Women's Wear Daily*, May 21, 1930.

46. Morris, *Fragrance*, p. 204.

47. "Personality: He Has Young Ideas in Old Line," *New York Times*, September 2, 1962.

48. Lehman Brothers, *Coty*; Robert Halasz, "Coty Inc.," in Jay P. Pederson (ed.), *International Directory of Company Histories*, vol. 38 (Farmington Hills, Mich.: St. James Press, 2001), p. 140.

49. Crédit Lyonnais archives (hereafter CL), CL 98 AH Société Anonyme Coty, August 1929, M. G. de Watteville, "Société Anonyme Coty, Visite de Monsieur Alphonse Morhange, August 13, 1929," transcript of meeting at the arbitrage house Sauphar Morhange & Co, August 16, 1929. Coty bought several major French

newspapers, including *Le Figaro*, to disseminate his political ideas. See Sicard-Picchiottino, *Coty*, pp. 138–9 and ch. 5; Coty and Toledano, "François Coty," chs 9 and 12.

50. Mira Wilkins, *The History of Foreign Investment in the United States 1914–1945* (Cambridge, Mass.: Harvard University Press, 2004), pp. 227, 229.

51. Lehman, *Coty*.

52. Selina Todd, "Young Women, Work, and Leisure in Interwar England," *Historical Journal* 48 (2005), pp. 789–809; Neville Williams, *Powder and Paint* (Longmans, Green and Co.: London, 1957), p. 130.

53. Johan Söderberg, "Controversial Consumption in Sweden, 1914–1945," *Scandinavian Economic History Review* 48 (2000), pp. 5–6.

54. Louisa Daria Rubinfien, "Commodity to National Brand: Manufacturers, Merchants, and the Development of the Consumer Market in Interwar Japan," unpubl. doctoral diss., Harvard University, 1995, p. 133. See also Appendix 1.1. For Thailand, see Villa Vilaithong, "A Cultural History of Hygiene Advertising in Thailand, 1940s–early 1980s," unpubl. doctoral diss., Australian National University, 2006, ch. 2.

55. Fernando Rocchi, *Chimneys in the Desert* (Stanford: Stanford University Press, 2006); Mildred Anna Phoebus, *Argentine Markets for United States Goods* (Washington, DC: United States Department of Commerce, Latin American Division, 1926), p. 36.

56. Juan Pablo Dicovskiy and María Josefina Grosso, *El Sector de Artículos de Tocador, Cosmética, y Perfumería en Argentina: Síntesis de la Economía Real*, Centro de Estudios para la Producción, vol. 37, available at <www.industria.gov.ar/cep/sintesis/ser%202da%20epoca/S%EDntesis%2047_octubre04/sintesis47.pdf>, pp. 52–3.

57. "Mergers, Acquisitions," *Time*.

58. "Lenthéric Marks 75th Anniversary with its First Year Round Ad Drive," *Advertising Age*, June 13, 1960, p. 50; "Adapting a French Line," *Drug Markets* 28:3 (March 1931), p. 234.

59. Marshall Raines, "Status and Structure of the Cosmetics Industry," in M. S. Balsam and Edward Sagarin (eds), *Cosmetics: Science and Technology*, 2nd edn, vol. 3 (New York: John Wiley, 1974), pp. 28–9.

60. Woodhead, *War Paint*, pp. 162–77, 234–8.

61. "Personality," *New York Times*.

62. Sicard-Picchiottino, *Coty*, pp. 135–9.

63. Stamelman, *Perfume*, p. 263.

64. "Coty Details Plan of Reorganization," *New York Times*, March 17, 1939. For the size of the French affiliate, see CL, DEEF 57198/1, "Monographie—Parfumerie" (October 1945), pp. 12–13.

65. Sicard-Picchiottino, *Coty*, pp. 122–3.

66. J. N. Kapferer and V. Bastien, *The Luxury Strategy* (London: Kogan Page, 2009), p. 14.

67. Valerie Felita Kinloch, "The Rhetoric of Black Bodies: Race, Beauty and Representation," in Elwood Watson and Darcy Martin (eds), *"There She Is, Miss America": The Politics of Sex, Beauty, and Race in America's Most Famous Pageant* (New York: Palgrave Macmillan, 2004), pp. 93–109; Sarah Banet-Weiser, *The Most Beautiful Girl in the World* (Berkeley: University of California Press, 1999), ch. 4.

68. Julie A. Willett, *Permanent Waves* (New York: New York University Press, 2000), ch. 1; Tiffany M. Gill, "Civic Beauty: Beauty Culturists and the Politics of African American Female Entrepreneurship, 1900–1965," *Enterprise & Society* 5 (2004), pp. 583–93.

69. Susannah Walker, *Style and Status. Selling Beauty to African American Women, 1920–1975* (Lexington, Ky: University Press of Kentucky, 2007), ch. 2.

70. Juliet E. K. Walker, *The History of Black Business in America: Capitalism, Race, Entrepreneurship* (New York: Twayne, 1998), pp. 208–11; Robert Mark Silverman, "The Effects of Racism and Racial Discrimination on Minority Business Development: The Case of Black Manufacturers in Chicago's Ethnic Beauty Aids Industry," *Journal of Social History* 31 (1998), pp. 579–81.

71. Raines, "Status," p. 20. The number of establishments was 539 in 1939 compared to 815 ten years previously; employment was 192,000 in 1929 and 156,000 in 1939.

72. P & G Corporate Archives (hereafter P & G), Max Factor—Historical Events; Margaret Allen, *Selling Dreams* (New York: Simon and Schuster, 1981), pp. 41–2.

73. Reichert, *Erotic History*, p. 97.

74. Peiss, *Hope*, p. 105.

75. Dyer *et al.*, *Rising Tide*, pp. 62–3.

76. National Broadcasting Company, "A Study of the Network Broadcast Advertising of the Drug and Toilet Goods Industry," December 2, 1931, SPR: 6243 N 277s, Baker Library Historical Collections.

77. JWT, Information Center Records, Case Studies. Radio Case Histories, November 4, 1939, Box 1.

78. Constance Classen, David Howes, and Anthony Synnott, *Aroma: The Cultural History of Smell* (London: Routledge, 1994), p. 184.

79. JWT, Market Surveys, "Census Figures of Face Cream Industry," 1934, Microfilm Reel 712.

80. JWT, Account Files, Chesebrough-Pond's Inc., Account Histories 1955–1959, "Pond's Case History," May 5, 1959, Box 3.

81. Caldwell, "Development," pp. 137–9.

82. JWT, Account Files, A. Jergens Co., Howard Henderson Files 1930–1959, Howard Henderson to Stanley Resor, January 15, 1931, Box 1.

83. Woodhead, *War Paint*, p. 213; Caldwell, "Development," pp. 155–7.

84. Brylcreem was created by a small company in Birmingham. Designed to keep combed hair in place, it was among the first mass-marketed men's hair care products. It became a best-seller on both sides of the Atlantic. See H. G. Lazell, *From Pills to Penicillin. The Beecham Story* (London: Heinemann, 1976), p. 84.

85. "Carl Weeks Introduces a MASCU-line of Toilet Needs," *Drug Markets* 24:4 (April 1929), pp. 333–5.

86. "Rouge and Lipsticks for Men: Latest Beauty Shop Idea," *Chicago Daily Tribune*, August 28, 1929, p. 31.

87. Peiss, *Hope*, pp. 164–6.

88. Frazer V. Sinclair, "What is in the Future for Men's Toiletries?" *Drug and Cosmetic Industry* 59:5 (November 1946), pp. 632–3, 718–19.

89. The success of the male version was not immediate. The men's line only accounted for 20 per cent of Shulton's sales of $3 million in 1939: "The Story of Shulton, Inc.," *Soap and Chemical Specialities*, May 1957, pp. 53–6, 255.

90. Reichert, *Erotic History*, p. 101.

91. Peiss, *Hope*, pp. 196–8; Woodhead, *War Paint*, p. 205.

92. Allen, *Selling*, pp. 42–3.

93. There was also consumer protection legislation in Europe. In Britain the Pharmacy and Poison Act of 1933 made warnings on packaging and a patch test a legal requirement for any hair dye used in a salon: Caroline Cox, *Good Hair Days* (London: Quartet, 1999), p. 158.

94. Louis Pierrein, *Industries traditionnelles du port de Marseille* (Marseilles: Institut Historique de Provence, 1975), pp. 284–9.

95. In 1939 a Federal Trade Commission report on nine of the largest US cosmetic and perfume companies, with combined sales of nearly $39 million, showed that in aggregate they made a return on capital of 15.7 per cent in that year. Five companies were above the average, with rates from 20.3 to 40.8 per cent, while four had rates from 0.6 to 2.9 per cent: US Federal Trade Commission, *Perfume and Cosmetic Manufacturing Corporations* (Washington, DC: US Federal Trade Commission, May 20, 1941).

96. They were akin to the "fashion intermediaries" discussed by Blaszczyk for household furnishings. See Chapter 1.

97. Peiss, *Hope*, pp. 131–3.

98. Feydeau, "De l'hygiène," pp. 398, 500.

99. Stanley Chapman, *Jesse Boot of Boots the Chemists* (London: Mulvey and Richards, 1974), pp. 153–4, 199–200; Paul Whysall, "Interwar Retail Internationalization: Boots under American Ownership," *International Review of Retail, Distribution and Consumer Research* 7:2 (April 1997), pp. 157–69. In 1928 United Drug merged with

Bristol-Myers, Sterling Products, and others to create the giant Drug Inc. This was dissolved in 1933.

100. Steve Zdatny, *Fashion, Work, and Politics in Modern France* (New York: Palgrave Macmillan, 2006), pp. 56–7, 110.

101. Banner, *American Beauty*, p. 271.

102. Jean Laudereau, "Mémoire de L'Oréal 1907–1992," unpubl. MS, p. 27.

103. Sophie Boutillier, "L'économie des entrepreneurs: Changement économique et trajectories individuelles," Document de Travail, Lab. RII, Université du Littoral Côte d'Opale, 65 (June 2003), pp. 8–10.

104. L'Oréal Archives (hereafter L'Oréal), Historique du Group L'Oréal, internal company document, March 20, 2008; Publithèque Oréal, "Chronologie de la Coloration, Volume II, 1930–1945," unpubl. internal archival series put together by François Clauteaux, November 1992; Bruno Abescat, *La saga des Bettencourt* (Paris: Plon, 2002), p. 73.

105. For Antoine, see Zdatny, *Fashion*, pp. 4–5, 120.

106. *Eugène Schueller 1881–1957* (L'Oréal: Paris, 1982), p. 91. Monsavon had been founded in 1920 and, like Cadum, had built a mass-market toilet-soap business.

107. Kerry Segrave, *Sun Tanning in 20th Century America* (Jefferson, NC: McFarland, 2005), pp. 27–31, 74–5; Pallingston, *Lipstick*, p. 21.

108. "Chronologie Ambre Solaire, 1935–1992," 2nd edn (Publithèque Oréal, March 1993), unpubl. internal archival series.

109. Wella AG, *Wella History* (Darmstadt: Wella, n.d.), pp. 6–9.

110. Henkel Corporate Archive (hereafter HA), D440 Schwarzkopf Dokumentations Forschungsgeschichte, "Schwarzkopf—Chronologie/Schwarzkopf Heute (in Stichworten)," September 1976.

111. In 1935 total production in the United States of hair care products was $15 million: shampoo was $4 million and hair dye $2 million, with the remainder being hair tonics: JWT, Market Surveys, "Market in the United States for Hair Tonics and Kindred Preparations," August 1937, Microfilm Reel.

112. "Helene Curtis Enters a New Era of Innovation," *Drug and Cosmetic Industry* (August 1996), pp. 34–7.

113. P & G, *50 Colorful Years: The Clairol Story* (1982).

114. JWT, Market Surveys, "Nationwide Nail Survey among Beauty Shops," October 21, 1937, Microfilm Reel 257; Allen, *Selling*, pp. 38–40; Woodhead, *War Paint*, pp. 257–8.

115. Katina Lee Manko, " 'Ding Dong! Avon Calling!' Gender, Business and Door-to-Door Selling, 1890–1955," unpubl. doctoral diss., University of Delaware, 2001, ch. 4.

116. Katina Lee Manko, "A Depression-Proof Business Strategy: The Californian Perfume Company's Motivational Literature," in Philip Scranton (ed.), *Beauty and Business* (Routledge: New York, 2001), pp. 142–68.

117. *Eien No Bi Wo Motomete—POLA Monogatari* (*A Quest for Everlasting Beauty: POLA Corporation's History of 50 Years*) (Tokyo: Pola, 1980; in Japanese).

118. Rubinfien, "Commodity," pp. 12–13, 135–6, 381–7.

119. *The Shiseido Story: A History of Shiseido: 1872–1972* (Tokyo: Shiseido, 2003); Barbara Sato, *The New Japanese Woman* (Durham, NC: Duke University Press, 2003).

120. Rubinfien, "Commodity," p. 210.

121. Rubinfien, "Commodity," pp. 150–89.

122. Tsunehiko Yui, Akira Kudo, and Haruhito Takeda, in association with Eisuke Daito and Satoshi Sasaki *Kaoshi Hyakunen (1890–1990)* (*Hundred-year History of Kao (1890–1990)*) (Tokyo: Kao Corporation, 1993; in Japanese), pp. 88–9; Rubinfien, "Commodity," ch. 4; Satoshi Sasaki, "Rationalization of Distribution at Lion Dentrifice and Lion Soap Co in Pre-War Japan," *Keiei Ronshu* 51 (2004), pp. 111–38.

123. Rubinfien, "Commodity," pp. 238–48.

124. Satoshi Sasaki, "The Establishment of Shiseido Sales Co Ltd and the Management," *Keiei Ronshu* 501 (2002), pp. 123–45; Rubinfien, "Commodity," pp. 248–54.

125. Geoffrey Jones, *Multinationals and Global Capitalism* (Oxford: Oxford University Press, 2005), p. 28; Mira Wilkins, *The Maturing of Multinational Enterprise* (Cambridge, Mass.: Harvard University Press, 1974), ch. 8.

126. Núria Puig, "The Search for Identity: Spanish Perfume in the International Market," *Business History* 45 (2003), pp. 96–9.

127. Jones, *Multinationals*, p. 203.

128. Rheinisch-Westfälisches Wirtschaftsarchiv zu Köln (hereafter RWWA), Accession Abteilung 162, Muehlens KG, 162-125-1, Geschichte der Auslandsniederlagen, -repräsentanzen und des Stammhauses; *160 Jahre no. 4711* (Cologne: Muehlens, 1952).

129. HA D440, Schwarzkopf Dokumentations Forschungsgeschichte, "Schwarzkopf-Firmengeschichte," n.d.

130. Wella AG, *Wella History*, pp. 6–9.

131. Beiersdorf AG, *100 Jahre Beiersdorf, 1882–1982* (Hamburg: Beiersdorf, 1982), pp. 48–50.

132. JWT, Account Files, Lehn & Fink 1926–1967, Account Histories, "Lehn & Fink," January 28, 1926, Box 12.

133. Beiersdorf Archive (hereafter BA) Entwicklung 1919–1945, Lehn & Fink-Komplex, Verträge 1893–1924, "Auseinandersetzung mit Lehn & Fink," n.d., and "Plan for Compromise between P. Beiersdorf & Co. G.m.b.H. and Lehn & Fink, Inc.," 1922; Hellmut Kruse, *Wagen und Winnen: Ein hanseatisches Kaufmannsleben im 20. Jahrhundert* (Hamburg: Die Hanse, 2006), pp. 105, 138.

134. BA, Helge Burkhardt, "Eigentümer und Vorstände Beiersdorf," November 21, 2006; BA, Vertriebe Umsätze 1901–1970, "Aufstellung der Jahresumsätze (Netto)"; Kruse, *Wagen und Winnen*, pp. 93–4.

135. Beiersdorf, *Nivea: Evolution of a World Famous Brand* (Hamburg: Beiersdorf, 2001), pp. 34–47.

136. Uta G. Poiger, "Beauty, Business and German International Relations," *Werkstatt Geschichte* 45 (2007), pp. 56–7.

137. Beiersdorf AG, *100 Jahre*, pp. 46–51.

138. BA, Ausland Allgemein, Aufstellungen, "Übersichten, 1908–1989—Tochterfirmen, Vertreter, Lizenzpartner," May 25, 1934; "Übersicht über die finanzielle Verknüpfungen der P. Beiersdorf & Co. A.G., Hamburg, und ihre ausländischen Gesellschaften," c. 1934 or 1935.

139. The sale was to Richard Doetsch for 30,000 Swiss francs. In 1919, Beiersdorf established a company in Basle for the purpose of repurchasing and protecting Beiersdorf's international trademarks. Doetsch became its trustee shareholder in 1923. The partnership with Doetsch was extended until 1940, when he bought 100 per cent of the shares, thereby acquiring most of Beiersdorf's foreign business: BA, Ausland Allgemein, Aufstellungen,"Formelle Besitzverhältnisse per 31. März 1942," a chart describing Richard Doetsch's legal ownership of Beiersdorf's foreign subsidiaries, dated January 4, 1944.

140. Yvonne Barbara Houy, " 'Of Course the German Woman should be Modern': The Modernization of Women's Appearance during National Socialism," unpubl. doctoral diss., Cornell University, 2002, pp. 189–93.

141. Irene Guenther, *Nazi Chic? Fashioning Women in the Third Reich* (Oxford: Berg, 2004), pp. 99–106.

142. BA Grossbritannien, Geschäftsleitungs-Korrespondens, Willy Jacobsohn to F. A. Meyer, 1932–1933; Jacobsohn to Meyer, July 29, 1932; Meyer to Jacobsohn, October 19, 1932.

143. Nivea's domestic sales rose from RM 14 million to RM 26 million between 1934 and 1939: Beiersdorf, *Nivea*, p. 48; Poiger, "Beauty," p. 57.

144. Beiersdorf, *Nivea*, pp. 42–3, 48; Poiger, "Beauty," p. 57.

145. Poiger, "Beauty," pp. 57–64.

146. Steele, *Paris*, p. 258.

147. Camron Michael Amin, "Importing 'Beauty Culture' into Iran in the 1920s and 1930s: Mass Marketing Individualism in an Age of Anti-Imperialist Sacrifice," *Comparative Studies of South Asia, Africa and the Middle East* 24 (2004), pp. 79–95.

148. Lansing Warren, "Beauty in Europe Now is Standardized: Contest Queens of 17 Nations Look Alike," *New York Times*, February 17, 1929, p. 53.

149. Sarah Berry, "Hollywood Exoticism: Cosmetics and Color in the 1930s," in David Dresser and Garth S. Jowett (eds), *Hollywood Goes Shopping* (Minneapolis: University of Minnesota Press, 2000), pp. 108–35.

1. Late eighteenth-century aristocratic Japanese woman painting her lips (woodcut from print series "*Scenes of everyday life,*" by Kitagawa Utamaro, *c.* 1794-95).

2. (*below*) Map of the African business holdings of the Grasse-based perfume supplier firm Antoine Chiris (*c.* 1850).

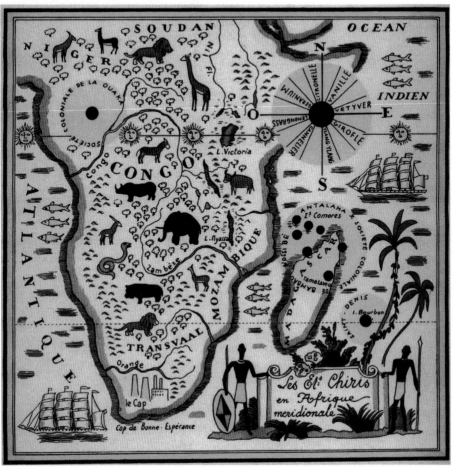

3. Fragrance advertisement by Muehlens, featuring an African woman and the exoticized product name "Bouquet Sudan: Parfumerie 4711–Cologne-Londres-Paris" (*c.* 1900).

4. Tooth powder advertisement for the large Russian perfume house Brocard. The caption reads: "Thanks to Brocard and its excellent tooth powder the elephant's teeth will be white and strong" (*c.* 1900).

5. Shampoon shampoo, the first non-soap based hair cleanser, was invented by Hans Schwarzkopf (1905).

6. L'Oréal's first product, L'Aureole hair-dye, was launched in 1909 and appears here in an advertisement by the poster artist Raoul Vion (1910).

© L'Oréal/DR and Raoul Vion.

7. "La Rose Jacqueminot," launched in 1904 by François Coty, was the perfume maker's first commercially sold fragrance.

8. Coty's exclusive shop in the Place Vendôme, Paris (*c.* 1914; drawing made in 1945).

PARFUMEUR · PLACE VENDOME · PARIS

9. Advertisement for Barnängens' toothpaste Vademecum that emphasized its appeal to people from all cultures (the caption reads "Men around the world use Vademecum") (*c.* 1914).

© Henkel. Courtesy of the Centre for Business History, Stockholm, Sweden.

10. Cover of price catalogue and beauty instruction manual produced by the American fragrance and cosmetics firm Richard Hudnut (1915).

11. Advertising campaign for Woodbury's Facial Soap, which was considered sexually provocative for its depiction of a couple in the act of embracing (1915).

12. Advertisement for leading Japanese cosmetics firm Club Cosmetics, using the Two Gorgeous Girls brand, created for the Chinese market (1920s).

13. Poster advertisement for the permanent waving products of Wella (1930).

14. L'Oréal's sunscreen cream Ambre Solaire was launched in 1935 and is advertised here with the famous 'pin-up girl' campaign (1935).

© Archives L'Oréal and Harry Meerson.

15. Advertisement for Nivea Creme using imagery of a healthy outdoor lifestyle designed by the advertising director Elly Heuss-Knapp (1935).

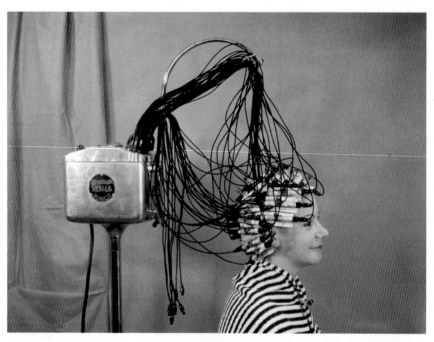

16. Wella's Junior perming apparatus, the first portable permanent wave machine for use in salons (1932).

150. P & G, Max Factor—Historical Events.

151. The Modern Girl Around the World Research Group (eds), *The Modern Girl Around the World: Consumption, Modernity, and Globalization* (Durham, NC: Duke University Press, 2008), especially ch. 1 for a statement of the overall hypothesis.

152. Feydeau, "De l'hygiène," pp. 511–12.

153. Total French beauty exports (including soap) grew from 244 million francs in 1919 to 713 million in 1929. They were still at 425 million francs in 1938. Raw materials represented about one-quarter of this amount: Feydeau, "De l'hygiène," p. 507; CL, DEEF 57198/1, "Monographie—Parfumerie," (October 1945), pp. 12–13.

154. Woodhead, *War Paint*, p. 148.

155. Woodhead, *War Paint*, pp. 124–5, 139, 192, 249.

156. Houy, "Of Course," ch. 4.

157. Laudereau, "Mémoire," pp. 261–3.

158. Jacqueline Demornex, *Lancôme, Paris* (Paris: Éditions Assouline, 2000), pp. 6–8.

159. L'Oréal, "60 ans de Lancôme: Le roman de la rose," *En Direct* 145 (March 1995), p. 4. The main source of the firm's initial growth was Nutrix, the first nourishing skin cream based on natural proteins.

160. In 1948 the 40 per cent of Pond's sales outside the United States earned 65 per cent of world profit: JWT, Account Files, Chesebrough-Pond's Inc., Account Histories 1955–1959, "Pond's Case History," May 5, 1959, Box 3.

161. Jones, *Multinationals*, pp. 84–6.

162. History of Advertising Trust, JWT Archives (hereafter HAT), JWT, "Data on the Market for Toothpaste in Great Britain, Lever Brothers 1931," Box 693.

163. Eugenia Lean, "Lux Soap in Republican China: The Commodification of Beauty and Selling Consumer Desire," workshop paper for Conference on Affect, Emotion, and Public Life in Modern China and Japan, Harvard University, May 6–7, 2005.

164. JWT, Market Surveys, "Market for Dentrifices, Mexico, Buenos Aires and Havana," July 1947, Microfilm Reel 713.

165. Kathy Peiss, "Educating the Eye of the Beholder: American Cosmetics Abroad," *Daedalus* 131 (Fall 2002), p. 3.

166. James P. Woodward, "Marketing Modernity: The J. Walter Thompson Company and North American Advertising in Brazil, 1929–1939," *Hispanic American Historical Review* 82 (2002), p. 276.

167. JWT, Samuel W. Meek Papers, International Development, Advertising, "Why Kodak Chose JWT," June 2, 1930, Box 4.

168. Julio Moreno, *Yankee Don't Go Home! Mexican Nationalism, American Business Culture, and the Shaping of Modern Mexico, 1920–1950* (Chapel Hill, NC: University of North Carolina Press, 2003), p. 139.

169. Moreno, *Yankee Don't Go Home!*, pp. 141–2.

170. Rory Miller, "Latin American Consumers, British Multinationals, and the Merchant Houses, 1930–1960," in Rory Miller and Colin Lewis (eds), *Consumers, Trade, and Markets in Latin America, 1750–1950* (London: Institute of Latin American Studies, forthcoming).

171. The Modern Girl Around the World Research Group, "The Modern Girl Around the World: Cosmetics Advertising and the Politics of Race and Style," in The Modern Girl (eds), *The Modern Girl*, pp. 28–31. The authors argue that Pond's and JWT always sought to market the facial creams "by appealing to existing standards of beauty among local elites, while at times stressing the global reach of its products." Their visual examples, however, are from China and India only, where Pond's seems to have made a special concession to local adaptation.

172. Lean, "Lux Soap."

173. BA, Nivea Advertising in China, 1920s–1930s.

174. Miller, "Latin American Consumers."

175. BA, Helge Burkhardt, "China Kurzdokumentation," August 24, 2006, and Ekkehard Kaum, "China Kurzdokumentation," July 7, 1988; BA, China, Gesamtschrift, 1932, China Export-Import-Bank AB (Ceibco), Johann Grodtmann, "Streng vertraulich! Ausreise von Herrn Erich Schild, des China Attaches," November 18, 1933.

176. By 1940 the firm had sales of $1 million (3 million Kronor): Björn and Curt Barlach, *De Första Åren: Tryckt i Samband med Företagets 100-årsjubileum 1896–1996* (Stockholm: Björntryck 1996).

177. Miller, "Latin American Consumers;" Geoffrey Jones, *Renewing Unilever* (Oxford: Oxford University Press, 2005), p. 8.

178. "Good Record of Bristol-Myers," *Barrons*, October 9, 1933.

179. Phoebus, *Argentine*; Dudley Maynard Phelps, *Migration of Industry to South America* (Westport, Conn.: Greenwood Press, 1939), pp. 6–9.

180. CL, DEEF 57198/1, "Monographie—Parfumerie," pp. 12–13.

181. Johan Söderberg, *Röda läppar och shinglat hår: Konsumtionen av kosmetika i Sverige 1900–1960* (Stockholm: Ekonomisk-historiska institutionen, 2001), pp. 151–73; Erik Dahmén, *Entrepreneurial Activity and the Development of Swedish Industry, 1919–1939* (Homewood, Ill.: Richard D. Irwin, 1970), p. 307; Centre for Business History/ Centrum för Näringslivshistoria (hereafter CfN), Stockholm, CfN 1093.79 and CfN 1093.80, 81, 82, firm data sheets for 1919 to 1946, collected by Erik Dahmén and used in

his *Svensk Industriell Företagsverksamhet* (Stockholm: Industriens Utredningsinstitut, 1950).

182. There were about 600 firms in the industry in the late 1930s, of which around 30 had a significant turnover, while 70 employed 70 per cent of the workforce: Meeting at the Board of Trade, November 6, 1945, BT 64/1739, British National Archives.

183. Ernest Morgan, *Yardley 1770–1935* (London: William Clowes, 1935), pp. 36–41; Maggie Angeloglou, *A History of Make-up* (New York: Macmillan, 1970), pp. 129–31; Myram Picker, *My Story* (London: Fanfare Press, 1965).

184. HistoCom, Frankfurt, IW 1201 Marbert GmbH, Düsseldorf, fact sheet, June 6, 1972.

185. CfN 1093.80, 81, 82, Dahmén study data sheet, A/B Firma Facta and beauty institute Anita AB.

186. <www.perfumeprojects.com/museum/marketers/Corday>, accessed April 16, 2007.

187. Jean-Marie Martin-Hattemberg, *Caron* (Toulouse: Éditions Milan, 2000), pp. 84–5.

188. <www.eherstory.kr/eng/pavilion/englisho3.jsp>, accessed March 6, 2009.

189. Fang Wenhui, *Keshouhinkogyou No Hikakukeieishi* (Tokyo: Nihon Keizai Hyouron-sha, 1999); Lean, "Lux Soap."

190. Dyer *et al.*, *Rising Tide*, p. 101.

191. By the early 1940s L'Oréal's largest affiliates were in Belgium, the Netherlands, Sweden, and Germany, as well as French North Africa: CL, DEEF 59853, Memorandum on L'Oréal, April 8, 1943.

192. *Club Cosmetics Hachijyunenshi* (*Club Cosmetics: Eighty Years of History*) (Osaka: Club Cosmetics, August 1983); *Hyakkaryoran—Club Cosmetics Hyakunenshi* (*Club Cosmetics, 100 Years of History—Profusion of Flowers*) (Osaka: Club Cosmetics, December 2003); Yui *et al.*, *Kaoshi*, pp. 156–7.

193. Peiss, *Hope*, p. 101.

194. Pallingston, *Lipstick*, p. 115; Meg Cohen Ragas and Karen Kozlowski, *Read My Lips: A Cultural History of Lipstick* (San Francisco: Chronicle Books, 1998), p. 27.

195. CL, DEEF 57198/1, "Monographie—Parfumerie," pp. 12–13.

196. Zdatny, *Fashion*, p. 288 n. 1 provides a guide to the extensive literature on Schueller's political activities; Boutillier, "L'économie," p. 10.

197. Bruno Abescat and Yves Stavridès, "Derrière l'empire Chanel...La fabuleuse histoire des Wertheimer," *L'Express*, April 7–August 8, 2005, available at <www.lexpress.fr/actualite/economie/la-fabuleuse-histoire-des-wertheimer_485301.html>, accessed February 2, 2007.

198. Caldwell, "Development," pp. 190–9.

199. B. A. Shepherd, "Britain's Cosmetic Growth," *Drug and Cosmetic Industry* 65 (1949), pp. 160–1.

200. Scott, *Fresh Lipstick*, p. 222.

201. National Archives, UK (hereafter National Archives), "Toilet Preparations," draft contained in Board of Trade memorandum to D. P. Brearly, June 12, 1947, BT 64/ 1827.

202. Ina Zweiniger-Bargielowska, "The Body and Consumer Culture," in Ina Zweiniger-Bargielowska (ed.), *Women in Twentieth-century Britain* (London: Pearson Educational, 2001), p. 188.

203. National Archives, Perfumery and Toilet Preparations Industry. First Report on Post War Reconstruction, April 1944, BT 11/2327.

5

The Television Age

Over a fairly short stretch of time, from, say, 1949–1953, the way products were sold in this country was completely re-invented.

Leonard Lavin, founder of Alberto-Culver[1]

Beauty and the advertising revolution

The three decades after 1945 were times of growing affluence and relative stability in the West. Living standards surged and mass consumer societies bloomed across Western Europe and Japan under the United States' leadership of the capitalist world.[2] The global market for beauty products in the non-Communist countries grew rapidly. Over that entire period the beauty market grew much faster than overall incomes.[3]

The American market comprised well over half of the world total in 1950 and was still over two-fifths of the global industry in the mid-1970s. It was the market where most new trends began, where new product formulations in creams and color cosmetics first appeared, and where pioneering advances in therapeutic toothpaste, anti-dandruff shampoos, and much else happened.[4] It was also a profitable market. An estimate of profit margins in American consumer goods industries in 1968 suggested that the margin for health and beauty aids was 18 per cent, double that of consumer electronics and soap and detergents, and the highest of any industry except alcoholic beverages.[5]

It was not a coincidence that it was also the United States which led the postwar media revolution created by television. The first television services had emerged in the United States, Europe, and the Soviet Union during the 1930s, but almost all services had been suspended during the war. During the late 1940s, however, television service spread rapidly in the United States. At first broadcasting was local, but in 1951 coast-to-coast transmission became possible. The business model adopted by television followed that used in American radio, with three large television networks controlling a system funded by corporate sponsorship.[6]

The spread of television followed elsewhere, but with a lag. Color television was launched in America in the mid-1950s but only reached many European countries during the following decade.[7] In Europe governments often controlled broadcasting and permitted little or no advertising. Britain was one of the first European countries to allow commercial advertising, in 1955, but the publicly funded BBC remained the main provider of services for many years. The rollout of television elsewhere occurred in stages. At the other extreme, television made little impact as a mass medium in India until the 1990s.

Television's impact on the beauty industry was multi-faceted and profound. Thanks to Hollywood and fashion magazines such as *Vogue*, *Cosmopolitan*, and *Good Housekeeping*, the new medium greatly contributed to the diffusion of Western, and especially American, ideals of lifestyle, fashion, and beauty. The United States became a major source of television programming for other countries, with programs dubbed or subtitled into local languages. As a result, decades before the invention of home videos, television took older Hollywood movies, and their celebrities, into the intimacy of people's homes. The media corporations' distillation of the American way of life was transmitted to growing numbers of individual homes around the world. The picture they presented was highly selective—African-American actors, for example, were rarely seen on television before the 1960s,[8] whilst non-whites generally were strictly limited to the kind of roles that they could play in Hollywood movies[9]—but that did not lessen the impact of this diffusion.[10]

Television became especially important in turning beauty pageants into international media events. A British-based Miss World contest was launched in 1951.[11] A US-based Miss Universe followed in 1952, and within three years it was broadcast on network American television. In time both pageants were televised in many countries. Feminine grooming was turned into a widely watched media spectacle which set expectations and defined aspirations.[12] At a global level, the paler skins and wider eyes favored in both these contests reflected and reinforced the pre-eminence of Western beauty ideals. Scandinavian women were the first winners of both contests. The first nine winners of Miss World included six Europeans and three pale-skinned contestants from Venezuela, Egypt, and South Africa. The winners of Miss Universe were also overwhelmingly pale-skinned contestants from the United States, Europe, and Latin America.[13]

The pageants were not outliers in these biases. Barbie dolls, created in the late 1950s, were blue-eyed and (predominantly) blonde until 1980, even though the early prototypes, designed in Japan, had distinctly East Asian features.[14] Even when non-whites began winning beauty pageants, as did Miss Japan and Miss Thailand in the Miss Universe contests of 1959 and 1965 respectively, both contestants seemed to fit into what has been called a "Miss Universe standard of beauty" in terms of face, figure, proportions, and posture.[15] As in the case of the Miss Europe contest held in Paris in 1929, beauty ideals showed strong evidence of convergence.

Television also drove new waves of innovation in make-up. Max Factor's son, who ran the company after his father died in 1938, introduced the first make-up designed for television commercials. In 1947 the company launched the cream-based Pan-Stik make-up in a stick form, designed to be applied as easily as lipstick. It was the first make-up developed for use in all three theatrical arenas—movies, stage, and television—as well as for sale in the general retail trade. As color television was launched in the mid-1950s, Max Factor developed the make-up that became the standard for the whole American television industry, and it was soon diffused into the wider market. In 1954 the company launched Erace, a concealer applied underneath make-up to hide shadows and blemishes.[16] The company worked closely with the televised beauty pageants. It sponsored Miss Peru, the winner of the 1957 Miss Universe contest, on a tour of Latin America, and sponsored Miss Japan to tour Japan on its behalf two years later.[17]

Television's impact on advertising was transformational. The effect was felt first and most intensely in America. "We went from being a vast nation, where word-of-mouth, traveling salesmen, and regional print and radio broadcast advertising were the only resources available to manufacturers and distributors," Leonard Lavin, the founder of the hair care company Alberto-Culver, later observed, "to being a small, accessible national community, linked by the most powerful advertising and marketing tool in the history of mankind."[18] Television advertising and sponsored game shows drove advertising budgets upwards, and beauty was a big part of those budgets. By the 1960s American cosmetics companies were spending an average of 15 per cent of their sales on advertising.[19]

The companies which sold mass-marketed consumer goods understood the opportunities to take their brands into people's living rooms. Gillette moved rapidly to use televised sports to advertise its razors. It held the exclusive television rights to baseball's World Series between 1950 and 1959. In order to reach the female consumers of the Toni brand of hair care, acquired in 1949, Gillette secured exclusive television rights to the Miss America pageant. The pageant became the basis for marketing campaigns such as the "Miss America Beauty Book" in 1960, which was offered free to purchasers of Toni's home permanent-wave kit.[20]

In color cosmetics and skin care, television was rapidly perceived as a vital marketing tool. Beauty is a fickle lover. Some categories of product bred more brand loyalty than others. Like a good man, a good foundation was hard to find, and when women found one, they tended to stick to it because foundation was expensive and needed to be a close match with skin tone. Eye and lip cosmetics, on the other hand, were cheap and easy: "fun" products which consumers could take for a ride around town without committing themselves to any one in particular. Innovations rarely delivered sustained advantages for long. This point was succinctly made by Hazel Bishop, whose distinctive No-Smear lipstick, marketed as "Stays on you, not on him," briefly captured one-quarter of the American lipstick market after its launch in 1950. "Anytime you come into the cosmetics industry with a product which is a success," she later wrote, "it will be copied very quickly. You can't keep your exclusivity for long."[21] Television advertising was one of the best chances to keep brands novel and alive in a highly competitive, restlessly innovating market.

Bishop was one of the first American entrepreneurs to use television advertising; the advertisements appeared to show that her lipstick indeed did not rub off as easily as competing products. This marketing success was also her downfall. Bishop was forced out of her own company shortly afterwards by the advertising executive she had given a 20 per cent stake to, in return for advertising space on television.[22] Larger firms soon followed the Bishop model. Pond's launched its first television show in 1951, a 15-minute program first shown in New York and then in Philadelphia and Chicago. By the following year the company had a television budget of $1.2 million, which was used to buy spot advertisements in 16 key markets. In 1955 Pond's switched to network television, launching *Pond's Theatre* on NBC, one of the three major networks.[23]

5.1 Hazel Bishop applying her "Kissable Lipstick," the innovative No-Smear lipstick, 1951.

Photograph by Robert Isear © Robert Isear

Leonard Lavin demonstrated the potential of television to grow new brands fast. As a young man, Lavin had become interested in the prospects of the beauty industry after looking at the lipsticks and other cosmetics in the front windows of shops in Chicago. He joined a start-up fragrance business shortly before the outbreak of World War II and rejoined it after war service. Subsequently he moved on to sell other products, including permanent waves, and established his own sales company. While visiting a West Coast drugstore, he encountered a shampoo which appeared to be selling well even though it was not advertised. In 1955 he bought the tiny firm of Alberto-Culver, which made the hairdressing formula Alberto VO5, along with many other products, for $500,000, with borrowed money from angel investors.

Lavin was a consummate salesman rather than a man of refined feelings: on his wedding night, as he later recalled, he gave his wife one of the permanent waves he was selling, and the following morning left her in the hotel in order to pursue a sales opportunity. He also had a clear perception that, though his industry sold "nonessentials," it had great commercial potential because it "helped people feel better about themselves."[24] After taking control of Alberto-Culver, Lavin discontinued everything except the hairdressing brand and relocated the company to Chicago. He immediately bought three TV spot announcements a week in Philadelphia. In 1956 he spent over $300,000 on advertising to generate $1.5 million sales volume. By 1960, his sales had reached $15 million, while his television advertising budget was over $10 million. In the previous year his company had joined the list of the 100 largest national advertisers in the United States.[25]

Lavin showed how television advertising could overcome powerful incumbents. By 1960 VO5 had taken 45 per cent of the market in hair conditioners, reducing Helene Curtis's once-dominant Suave to a 20 per cent share.[26] There were other striking examples as well. In 1961 Noxell's successful launch of Cover Girl, a mass-market medicated make-up promoted by leading fashion models, was driven by television advertising.[27] In 1972, in yet another radical innovation with major implications for the entire industry, Lavin forced American television companies to abandon selling only 60-second spots, introducing 30-second ones, which opened up further chances for smaller firms to compete with the consumer products giants such as P & G.[28]

Of all the postwar beauty entrepreneurs, no one demonstrated the power of television advertising more dramatically than Charles Revson. By the late 1940s Revlon had become a broad-based cosmetics company. By introducing new colors of lipstick and nail polish every fall and spring fashion season, Revlon was able to turn the fickleness of fashion to its advantage. The brilliance of Revlon's strategy was to make trendiness a high customer priority, and then to generate the trends that satisfied its customers' restlessness—albeit only till next season. In 1952, Revson raised the sensual and sexual component of cosmetic advertising to a new level when he introduced Fire and Ice, a deep red lipstick color. The advertisements featured a beautiful woman in a low-cut gown, and asserted that the brand was "for you who love to flirt with fire... who dare to skate on thin ice." The advertising copy was written by a woman, Kay Daly, one of the few female executives who survived for long in Revson's company.[29]

The Fire and Ice advertising campaign had a great impact. But it was Revson's sponsorship of *The $64,000 Dollar Question* game show, which began broadcasting on the CBS television network in 1955, that truly transformed his firm's fortunes. The game offered the largest amount of cash ever awarded by a radio or television show to a contestant, who was asked increasingly difficult questions on a subject of their choice. Contestants could win up to $64,000, but even losers received a Cadillac car as a consolation prize. During the program, an actress pitched Revlon's products. The company saw its sales grow from $34 million in 1954 to $134 million in 1960.[30]

In time, it emerged that the game show was manipulated and the outcomes fixed in advance. There was a public outcry, and the scandal even became a subject of Congressional hearings. Revson was never formally shown to have been involved in the fixing, and he emerged with no impact on his business. The allegations were par for the course for Revson. Entrepreneurs in the beauty industry have often been colorful characters, and many sport obsessive personalities. Revson's character stood out as commercial in the most ruthless sense. He was sued for corporate espionage, and in 1961 even his own brother sued him.[31] Revson was rumored to tap the telephones of his own managers, let alone competitors, including Hazel Bishop.[32]

By the early 1960s the American beauty industry was spending $152 million ($1 billion in 2008 dollars) on television advertising. This was more than the amount spent in any other industry except food.[33] Television advertising could deliver success in the marketplace, but the cost could also take its toll on firms. Coty, for example, found that television had a greater impact on its costs than its revenues. In 1946 Yvonne Cotnaréanu placed her capable brother-in-law in charge of both the American and international companies. Even so, repairing the damage and regaining the old glory remained elusive. In the United States, Coty's sales grew to reach nearly $25 million in 1957, but it also went into the red, with the management blaming the high cost of advertising without corresponding revenue increases. Losses forced the firm to move towards selling cheaper fragrances in drugstores, further eroding its reputation and paving the way toward its sale to Pfizer in 1963.[34]

Television had a wider impact than simply on the performance of individual firms. It served to make explicit what the industry's critics had long perceived as the manipulative nature of advertising. This challenge to the legitimacy of the industry was not simply a matter of crooked game shows. The cost of television advertising was accompanied by a further professionalization of marketing. America led the world in advanced marketing research, which employed psychological methods to understand human desires, and to segment markets on the basis of income, social class, ethnicity, and geography.[35] Television was ideal for crafting marketing messages to segmented markets. In beauty, perhaps even more than in most consumer products, this encouraged a proliferation of products which differed in artifice, such as packaging, rather than in functionality. Meanwhile the broader claims made, primarily to keep a woman looking younger than her natural age, remained hyperbole.

As social mores in American society became more liberal, the visual nature of television tempted advertisers to move more explicitly towards employing sexual innuendo to tempt consumers to buy their brands. Noxell's relaunch of its Noxzema aerosol shaving cream was an iconic, but not atypical, advertising campaign in this respect. A commercial using a former Miss Sweden saying "Take it off. Take it all off" ran on network television in the US from 1966 to 1973.[36] The way television could access people's living rooms and psyches seemed to make it more explicit than ever that the industry rested on selling "hope."[37]

While television transformed advertising, it was an expensive tool. As the ability to sustain large advertising campaigns emerged as critical, many smaller cosmetics firms needed more money than they could generate internally to use the new advertising medium. There was a sudden rush to go public, as Revlon did in 1955, or else issue some shares on the market while retaining family ownership, which was the path taken by Leonard Lavin. There were also mergers to gain scale. Chesebrough and Pond's merged to create Chesebrough-Pond's in 1955. The new firm proceeded to acquire smaller brands, including Prince Matchabelli and, in 1960, Northam Warren, the maker of the Cutex nail care brand. There were also sales to larger firms, who began seeking attractive brands behind which to fund big advertising budgets. Clairol's sale to Bristol-Myers in 1959 was a harbinger of this new trend.[38]

Interestingly, the fastest-growing sector of the American market made less use of television advertising. Direct sellers, led by Avon, increased their share of the American market from 15 to 23 per cent between 1950 and 1970.[39] As a growing number of women worked outside the home, this retail channel offered convenience to women who had less time to shop, and to mothers with young children at home. Avon's business expanded from rural areas to middle-class suburbia, driving the growth in sales from $16 million in 1945 to $240 million by 1957.[40] The launch of the successful "Ding Dong! Avon Calling" television commercial in 1953 was important in propelling the company's overall market share from 5 per cent in that year to 11 per cent by 1965.[41]

While American cosmetics companies spent an average of 15 per cent of sales on advertising in the 1960s, Avon spent only 2.7 per cent, as it could rely on the promotional literature it produced for its sales representatives.[42] Avon's army of female sales representatives, which reached over 300,000 by the early 1970s, and which was carefully incentivized to keep growing sales by progressive expansion of the earnings of representatives per customer, enabled the company to reach segments that other firms found challenging. Strikingly, it held 40 per cent of the $400 million African-American perfume and cologne market in the early 1970s.[43]

The smaller direct-selling companies spent even less on advertising than Avon did. This was especially true of the firms which followed earlier models, developed by Stanley Home Products and Tupperware, of using parties in people's homes to sell products. These included Jafra, founded by Jan and Frank Day in Malibu, California in the mid-1950s, which focused on skin care products,[44] and Mary Kay, founded by Mary Kay Ash in Dallas, Texas in 1963. Kay, an evangelical Baptist, emphasized a set of strong ethical values based on the principles of "God first, family second, job third," and a strong commitment to "enriching women's lives."[45] Mary Kay had a salesperson present products at a party of consumers organized in one of their homes. Each guest completed a skin questionnaire to determine her own skin type, and the hostess would then demonstrate the system and teach each guest how to use the products. This direct sales method enabled Mary Kay to reach more people in less time than Avon was able to do with its one-to-one method, and, adding further reinforcement to the selling dynamic, the party plan gave guests a sense of obligation to the hostess.[46]

Overall, it would seem that the direct-selling alternative to advertising, if effectively managed, was profitable, although building a sales force took much longer. In 1981 Avon's revenues of $2.6 billion delivered a return on capital of almost 25 per cent, whilst Revlon's $2.4 billion revenues produced a return of less than 12 per cent. Mary Kay had a smaller business of $235 million revenues, but a high return on capital at 35 per cent.[47]

The impact of television was felt first on the American market. In Europe, commercial advertising on the airwaves spread unevenly between countries.[48]

Commercial advertising began in Britain in 1955. The first commercial screened in that country was for Unilever's Gibbs SR toothpaste. In 1981 the beauty industry in Britain allocated three-quarters of its total consumer market advertising spending of $128 million to television.[49] In Sweden, commercial television advertising was prohibited until 1990. In France even advertising on the radio was initially prohibited, leaving companies to try to reach their consumers though the privately owned Radio Luxembourg, located outside the country.[50] The use of television advertising remained lower than in Britain, partly because the many small firms could not afford big advertising budgets.[51] As elsewhere, toiletries were heavily advertised on television, but even during the 1970s only around one-fifth of advertising for fragrances was on television. By 1980 L'Oréal had become France's largest single corporate advertiser in any industry, but only 20 per cent of its total $34 million advertising budget was spent on television, compared to the two-fifths spent on radio and one-quarter on the press.[52]

Television's ability to reach far more people than ever before served as a major new force for expanding sales of the beauty industry. It also increased the potential for manipulative advertising. Successfully used, it could turn a medium-sized firm into a large firm in less than a decade. The costs and complexity of television advertising carried major implications for companies. The need for big advertising budgets encouraged a premium on scale rather than creativity per se. Meanwhile it raised the entry barrier to the world's largest market for foreign brands, for whom success in America now rested on levels of advertising expenditure far beyond those in their domestic business.

The fragrance revolution

Both the American market and television played important roles in widening the market for fragrances, taking their place alongside less visible causes of change that radically determined how the industry functioned.

A shift in the size, scope, and nationality of large supplier firms was one of the most significant if least visible of these changes. Grasse's firms had exercised a quasi-monopoly over the global supply of natural essences and aromatic florals, which were obtained from Grasse, from neighboring Italy, and from French colonies. The war, however, disrupted the relationship between Grasse and its clients outside France. After 1945 there were new challenges, including soil erosion in Grasse itself, and the disruption of supplies from French North Africa as these colonies achieved political independence. In the mid-1960s the Grasse complex was still substantial, with an estimated 6,000 flower producers supplying some 30 factories and three-fifths of the production exported. However the small, family-owned Grasse firms were too undercapitalized to develop new sources of supply elsewhere or to invest in new technologies.[53]

After the war, the pace of technological innovation intensified—with further advances in solvent extraction as well as the development of new synthetic fragrance compositions, often by-products of the petrochemical industry—and a new cohort of supplier firms flourished, often with close ties to petrochemicals and scientific research. Although their names were unknown to the purchasers of perfume brands, these firms emerged as major players in the industry. The largest of these firms was International Flavors and Fragrances (IFF). This American company had its origins in a small business created by Arnold Lewis van Ameringen, a Dutchman who had emigrated to the United States in 1917. After working briefly for a Dutch exporter of essential oils to the United States, he set up his own firm in New York, which in time developed a business with the Wertheimers as well as other fragrance firms.[54]

International Flavors and Fragrances assumed its modern form when Ameringen merged his company with his original Dutch employer in 1958. By 1963 IFF had sales of $47 million, of which perfumery accounted for $32.5 million, making it the single largest supplier firm to the fragrance industry. Meanwhile, Universal Oil Products, another US-based firm, used its petrochemicals expertise to build a synthetic fragrance business. In 1967, it acquired the historic Chiris business in Grasse from the family.[55]

In Europe, Switzerland, the home of a large chemicals and pharmaceuticals industry, also developed a cluster of large essential oils houses. The leaders included Firmenich and Givaudan, both of which traced their histories back to the 1890s. In 1963 the latter was acquired by the Swiss pharmaceutical giant Hoffman La Roche, and a year later Hoffman also acquired the Roure-Bertrand business in Grasse.[56] The acquisitions of these firms and others in Grasse further intensified the competitive pressures on the remaining independent Grasse houses.[57]

Unbeknownst to consumers, these supplier houses assumed an increasingly important role in the creation of scents. Many fragrance companies grew to rely on the laboratories of these firms, which included large facilities located near the head offices of the major companies in Paris and New York, for their fragrance preparation. In a typical development process, a fragrance company would invite several supplier houses and their "noses" to participate in what was basically a contest to see who could develop a scent that matched most closely the description set forth in a brief developed primarily by the marketing department and advertising agency of the fragrance company. The brief would include the desired level of cost for the "juice," based on the expected retail price and the cost of other items, especially the bottle and packaging. Numerous iterations of a scent would be constructed, refined, and market tested before a fragrance went into commercial production. An idiosyncratic feature of the industry was that no formal contract was ever signed between the two sides, but the business of the supplier houses was widely regarded as "highly profitable," not least because once they had supplied the fragrance, they bore no risk if the resulting scent failed to work as a successful brand. By the 1980s almost all the fragrance companies, apart from outliers such as Guerlain and Chanel, outsourced their creation of scents to the supplier houses.[58]

The growth of supplier houses did not challenge the continued importance of French brands. France remained a huge market for fragrance. This reflected both a high rate of per capita consumption—twice that of Britain and Germany even in the 1970s—and a strong preference for prestige fragrances, which made the mass-market segment smaller than elsewhere in Europe.[59] Paris's historical legacy as the capital of beauty, its cluster of creative talent, and its discerning consumers continued to give the French industry a unique importance. The historical districts of Paris itself, so important to brand images, were renovated and restored by urban planners from the late 1940s.[60]

Postwar French governments also understood the importance of the country's fashion and beauty industries. They facilitated a speedy recovery of the creative industries from wartime disruption by financing exhibitions to display the work of new designers such as Christian Dior, whose House, wholly financed by a wealthy textile magnate, opened in 1946. Dior's "New Look," featuring full hips, bare shoulders, and thin waists, swept the Western fashion world and the wardrobes of Hollywood celebrities.[61] Meanwhile a separate fragrance company successfully launched Miss Dior perfume shortly after the success of the "New Look" collection.[62] Dior and other Parisian designers depended on exports; success in the American market in particular was critical. The American market in fragrances was also vital. By 1970 it was worth $459 million, or 15 per cent of the total market.[63]

The French fragrance houses understood the significance of the American market, and by the late 1940s were ramping up to supply it. However, as will be explored in the following chapter, they lacked the resources, or even the inclination, to undertake the level of advertising now required in the market. They also proved unable to seize the opportunities for expanding sales of perfume by creating a market for more accessible brands, and the firms which did explore this strategy ended up tarnishing their brands rather than creating new sales.

Instead, a new mass market for perfumes was built by domestic firms such as Max Factor and Prince Matchabelli during the postwar decades. In 1955 Max Factor launched its first fragrance, Electrique, which was a commercial success. The company used television to grow the brand, which was sold in drugstores rather than department stores. A series of successful perfume launches followed and, in 1961, Max Factor reinforced its success in the category by buying Parfums Corday.[64]

The creation, at this time, of American luxury brands was as remarkable as the building of a mass fragrance market in the United States. Estée Lauder was one of the most important figures in the initial stages of this process. Born Josephine Esther Mentzer in New York, the daughter of poor Hungarian Jewish immigrants, she worked in the family's small retailing businesses and then, in 1924 aged 16, joined her uncle's small venture making skin creams and other beauty products. She experimented with making her own skin creams, which she sold to beauty parlors. By the mid-1930s she was convinced that her creams needed to be sold in attractive containers, and she came up with the idea of opal white jars with black lids. Around this time she formally changed her name to Estée Lauder, designed to hint at a European identity.[65]

In 1946 she and her husband, whom she had briefly divorced during the war years when she fell in love with another man, launched Estée Lauder Cosmetics. A relentless emphasis on perfection, fashion, and quality became the hallmark of the new firm. The first line of products was the Just Red line of skin creams, face powder, and other cosmetics, which they made themselves in a former restaurant.

Rather than establishing her own salons, Lauder sought access to premium department stores which, among other advantages, issued charge cards which allowed consumers to buy products on credit, facilitating impulse purchases. She targeted Saks Fifth Avenue, where she persuaded a skeptical buyer at the store to place a small initial order by donating 80 of her lipsticks as table gifts to a charity luncheon at which she was speaking in the exclusive Waldorf-Astoria hotel on Park Avenue. The wealthy lunch guests were struck by the unusual packaging as well as the color and texture of the product, and promptly walked two blocks west from the Waldorf to Saks to buy it.[66] Lauder initially undertook most of the selling herself, visiting stores constantly, and establishing personal rapport with their buyers, who were almost always women.[67]

Lauder had a deep awareness of what was needed to create and sustain a luxury brand. Her essential starting points were always the high quality of the product and of the packaging. Her female customers were not "sex kittens," but "elegant achievers. They were independent."[68] Exclusivity was essential. "Less is more" was one of her sayings. She also viewed service as key to the brand. "When a woman walks into a store," she told New York's Fashion Institute, "she wants to see a smiling face that greets her by name and remembers her by name and gives her her card. It's service."[69]

Lauder's entry into fragrances became her big breakthrough and the opportunity which enabled her to put this philosophy into operation. In 1953 Estée Lauder launched Youth Dew bath oil. The step was made possible by the support of Arnold Ameringen, whom she had met and become friends with a decade previously, and the scent was believed to have been created by one of his "noses." The high concentration of essential oils in the product meant that the scent lasted for up to 24 hours on the skin. As a result, the product immediately struck home with consumers, as it appeared to deliver value. It was also packaged less expensively than French perfumes, and women were encouraged to use it lavishly on a regular basis. In a clever marketing gambit, Lauder initially offered it as a free gift with the purchase of her less successful skin treatment products.[70] Youth Dew, which would become one of the world's best-selling fragrances, laid the basis for Lauder's dominant position in department stores. Within three decades of launching her company, Lauder's overall sales had reached $200 million.

After Lauder had opened the doors to the creation of a prestige American fragrance business, it was Charles Revson who really brought the vision to fruition. In 1957 Revson launched his first perfume, Intimate, which he soon began to promote through television advertising. Three years later he purchased a controlling interest in Les Parfums Pierre Balmain in France. In 1968, in a further radical move, Revlon launched a scent named after the prominent designer Norman Norell, which was advertised as the "first designer scent." The sales of the brand never went above $11 million, but the creation of an American designer scent was a total marketing innovation, which Revson used to challenge Lauder in department stores.[71] It signaled the transformation in the status of the New York fashion industry, as American and European fashion magazines increasingly covered the fashion shows in New York, and designers such as Bill Blass, Ralph Lauren, and Calvin Klein began attracting global acclaim.[72] By the early 1970s, confidence in American designers and the prestige associated with their brands was so great that Suzanne Grayson, a leading American beauty marketing analyst, proclaimed that French prestige fragrance was a "myth" and that the traditional marks of a beautiful perfume were "dogwash." By 1982 one-third of an estimated 500 American perfumes carried designer labels.[73]

In 1973 Revson launched the Charlie fragrance. The new brand, given a masculine name and containing a strong perfume composition, was targeted at the modern independent woman, and advertised with explicit sexual imagery. Acclaimed as the first modern lifestyle fragrance, its impact was transformational. The new fragrance had sales of $10 million in its first year. By 1975, the year Revson died, the brand had $55 million of sales in its domestic market. Within five years of its launch it also had $100 million of international sales. In 1980 the annual sales of Revlon's Charlie surpassed those of Chanel N°5.[74]

The rise of American fragrances to global stature in the luxury category crowned New York's position as a global beauty capital with stature equal to Paris. It was the head office location of a roll-call of leading firms, including Estée Lauder and Revlon, alongside Avon, Colgate-Palmolive, Coty, Elizabeth Arden, Helena Rubinstein, and many others. It was a unique hub of creative talent, of major suppliers such as IFF, and of affluent consumers who could shop in many of the world's most prestigious department stores. The beauty business was in constant dialogue with related industries also clustered in the city, including fashion, publishing and Madison Avenue. New York was the corporate headquarters of three major television networks, and it was intimately linked to Hollywood through finance and acting schools, and as the filming location of innumerable movies.

New York's stature did not rest on the demise of Paris, and as the two hubs continued, both complemented and interacted with one another. Rather than being rivals, they offered alternative visions of beauty. New York epitomized accessibility, while Paris provided style. Both cities had their vitality constantly refreshed by immigrant talent, and firms based in both cities sought markets in the other.

Paradoxically, by the time Grayson ridiculed the pretensions of French luxury brands, there was also renewed creativity in Paris, driven especially by the couture houses. The Paris design houses had been handicapped by limited financial resources, whilst facing growing competition from American designers as well as the strength of Italian fashion houses such as Gucci and Giorgio Armani. Licensing became the financial mainstay for many designers, and perfume sales also provided a major source of profits.[75]

Among the new generation of couture houses, Yves Saint Laurent stood out. The Algerian-born Saint Laurent had come to Paris in 1954, and a year afterwards, aged only 19, was recruited as a designer at Christian Dior. Two years later Dior's sudden death resulted in the young man being appointed to run the firm. His meteoric rise came to an abrupt halt in 1960, when his conscription into the French army resulted in a nervous breakdown, as well as the loss of his job at Christian Dior. In 1962 Saint Laurent founded his own firm along with his personal and professional partner Pierre Bergé. He grew to be the single most important creative influence on female fashion in the world, popularizing such fashion trends as the "beatnik" look, safari jackets for men and women, tight pants, and tall, thigh-high boots.[76]

It was a vivid demonstration of the closely interlocked worlds of Paris and New York that it was the American market which shaped Saint Laurent's successful entry into fragrances. In 1965 Saint Laurent's original financial backer sold his 80 per cent share of the couture house to Charles of the Ritz, which launched an entire line of skin care and make-up under the Yves Saint Laurent Beauté brand. Shortly after the pharmaceutical company Squibb acquired Charles of the Ritz in 1971, Saint Laurent and Bergé took full control of their couture house, but the beauty business remained with Squibb.

Saint Laurent worked closely with the American owners as the fragrance business was developed. In 1971, the designer himself posed nude and floppy-haired, wearing only his trademark thick black glasses, for the launch of YSL pour Homme. He was also the creative influence on the launch of Opium perfume in 1978, which was aimed specifically at the American market. The name itself was considered scandalous for glamorizing drug use, while the price of $150 an ounce was considered outrageous at the time. Opium was highly potent, being the first prestige French fragrance to raise the level of concentrate in the perfume to 30 per cent. Designed for a woman who "wanted to be feminine again," it was launched simultaneously at Saks and Blooming-dale's in New York and backed with a big advertising budget. It became an instant commercial success.[77]

The American market was the key battleground for prestige fragrances. It was also an expensive battleground. While fragrances were still sold through small, family-owned perfumeries in many European countries, in the United States department stores formed the key distribution channel. Lauder's "gift-with-purchase" marketing set the market off on an expensive route which encouraged consumers to be more interested in promotions than in the fragrance itself. The competition between Revlon and Lauder further drove up the cost of doing business in department stores, which forced companies to spend between 15 and 20 per cent of their sales for point-of-sale displays, giveaways, and other promotional devices, including the salaries of sales staff.[78]

It became hugely expensive to launch a prestige perfume into the highly competitive American market. Low levels of brand loyalty and high seasonal-ity of sales encouraged ever growing numbers of product launches.[79] The high costs of promotion meant that even successful perfumes took two or three years to break even. In most cases, profits were only made if, over time, a brand launched in a top department store could be sold in drugstores.[80]

The creation of American luxury brands, and the creation of a large American mass market for fragrances, were transformational events. Paradox-ically, these changes also promoted, in contrast to trends seen in fashion and other beauty categories, a divergence in consumer preferences. American fragrance demand had formerly been met by imports or by American-made products directly inspired by trends in Europe. Lauder and, initially, Revson emulated fragrance ideas from Europe in terms of olfactory selection. During the 1970s, however, American fragrances diverged from European ones, per-haps reflecting domestic shifts in sexual and societal mores in the United States, as well as the rise in confidence of successful American firms, who became increasingly sure of their ability to launch new American concepts. American fragrances, especially following the launch of Charlie, emerged as more sporty and independent than their French equivalents, and easier for consumers to understand.[81]

Hair care and the rise of L'Oréal

During the postwar decades there was an enormous growth in the market for products which cleaned, managed, and dyed hair. By 1960 the market in hair care products was worth $365 million in the United States, and made up the single largest category in the beauty business. By the end of the 1960s hair care sales were worth a further $969 million, still the largest category, and represented one-third of the overall market.[82] In mid-1960s Germany and Britain, hair care products also represented about a third of the total industry, with sales of $90 million and $73 million respectively.[83]

In the United States, the use of shampoo to wash hair became widespread after World War II. Many of the leading brands were increasingly sold in the consumer market as well as in salons. Helene Curtis established an early lead in postwar America, initially selling to salons and then in retail channels. Its sales soared from $11 million in 1946 to $49 million in 1958. Suave shampoo eventually sold its billionth bottle in 1972, becoming the biggest-selling shampoo ever in the United States. There were also successful dandruff shampoos, hair sprays, and other products, but the firm stumbled badly when it tried to develop businesses beyond hair care. Between 1956 and 1960 it acquired a diverse collection of businesses, including Lenthéric and a Los Angeles-based door-to-door cosmetics firm, Studio Girl, all with disappointing outcomes. In 1964, Helene Curtis's wrinkle-removing cream was seized by regulators on the grounds that the company was making false claims for its efficacy.[84]

These problems left the American shampoo market open for others. Shifts in hair fashions facilitated ease of entry. Redken Laboratories Inc., launched in California in 1961 by Paula Kent Meehan, became the most successful of many new brands sold to professional salons. Redken listed the ingredients on product labels, an unusual practice at the time, and sought to teach the chemistry of hair to stylists, to whom it sold exclusively.[85] By the 1970s only 5 per cent of the overall hair care market was represented by professional salons, although they remained important for developing and testing new products and concepts.[86] The larger retail market for shampoos and related hair products also attracted many entrants, including some of America's most consummate users of television advertising. Alberto-Culver entered with a full range of cream rinsers, hair-setting products, and shampoos. In 1961 P & G, which had had a small shampoo business since the 1930s, launched the anti-dandruff shampoo Head & Shoulders, which both looked and smelled bad, but was functionally highly effective. The firm's mastery of television advertising helped the brand to capture a quarter of the American shampoo market, and together with its smaller brands, the firm held one-half of the market by 1970.

The challenge for a mass marketer like P & G was that it had limited understanding of how the shampoo market could shift under the influence of new fashions and trends. The invention of the hair dryer led women, in particular, to wash their hair more often. With this historically unprecedented level of hair-washing, shampoos quickly became more specialized and the market more segmented. Head & Shoulders, as a broadly pitched brand to people who could admit to their dandruff problem, lost its position atop the market. The new shampoos came from a wide variety of manufacturers: the small Mennen Company launched America's first conditioning shampoo, Protein 21; Clairol launched the highly fragranced Herbal Essences; and finally Johnson & Johnson entered the market with Baby Shampoo, which was initially aimed at teenage girls and new mothers but ultimately seized overall market leadership. By the early 1980s P & G was even considering divesting themselves of shampoos altogether.[87]

The hair dye market was the category that underwent the greatest transformation during the postwar period. In 1950 Clairol introduced the Miss Clairol Hair Color Bath, which lightly tinted, conditioned, and shampooed hair in a single step, eliminating the pre-lightening process and taking only 20 minutes. The small company lacked the financial resources for a major advertising campaign, and instead advertised the brand in association with two chains of beauty salons located within major department stores. This gave the brand exposure and associated it with prestigious stores, even though many American women still doubted the legitimacy of hair coloring. Gelb and his two dozen sales staff spent the first half of the decade evangelizing: they toured the country to demonstrate the benefits of one-step hair coloring to salons and beauty shows.[88]

An intriguing advertising campaign with the arresting slogan "Does she . . . or doesn't she?," launched in 1956, took the Clairol brand out of salons and into the consumer market. The new campaign was created by Shirley Polykoff, a New York-born daughter of poor Russian Jewish immigrants, who built a career as a fashion writer before joining a prestigious advertising agency. The advertising copy featured a mother and child, rather than the professional women who had always featured in the brand's campaigns, and carried the suggestion that married women could be as interested in being sexually attractive as professional women. The second line, "Hair color so natural only her hairdresser knows for sure," focused attention on the actual product. This first advertising campaign to sell hair dye to a mass audience had a major impact, and there was enough money to start television advertising the following year. The company continued to place great emphasis on relationships with hairdressers, but the case for hair dyeing was now taken into the mass market.[89] Self-reinvention had never before been so openly and guiltlessly promoted.

Clairol, with its noteworthy advertisements, became a major force for persuading millions of American women to "be blonde beautifully." By the 1970s hair coloring was a $250 million market, split equally between home use and salon products, and nearly one-third of American women dyed their hair regularly. Clairol held a 60 per cent market share which, unlike shampoo, was not easy for other firms to surpass because of Clairol's established relationships with salons and distributors and the need for competitors to offer as many shades of coloring in their product lines as those offered by the market leader. Alberto-Culver, the nearest challenger, held a mere one-tenth of the market.[90]

Beyond the United States, shampoo consumption also rose with the rising incomes of the postwar decades, as did the practice of hair dyeing, albeit with societal and cultural differences that led to consumption varying widely even between countries with similar income levels.[91] European companies retained strong capabilities in both the technology and the fashion of hair care, employing these skills to delight consumers and offer them growing choices.

As in the United States, the European shampoo market saw multiple entrants as the market experienced rapid growth. In Britain, it was estimated that nearly 100 companies were selling 400 different brands by the mid-1970s, though the top six held half of the market. The brands of the large consumer products firms, led by Unilever's Sunsilk, were pre-eminent, supported by heavy television advertising.[92] Elsewhere in Western Europe, powerful local incumbents dominated several markets. They often placed a higher emphasis on research than many of their American counterparts, and the business models of the major firms continued to emphasize their close relationships with hairdressers, which served as a major barrier to entry from foreign firms. There was, however, a general trend over time towards launching brands into the consumer market, and, in the case of some of these firms, in seeking product portfolios wider than hair products. The relationship with salons was one factor behind lower spending on television advertising in many markets. In the German hair care market in the 1970s, for example, over half of total advertising spent was on print media, and only a third on television.[93]

It was a striking testament to the strength of path-dependency in the beauty industry that the long-established German leaders in hair care were able to rebuild their businesses after their near-destruction during the war. The market leaders Schwarzkopf and Wella resumed business, relocated their factories, rebuilt relationships with salons, and resumed their emphasis on the science of hair. There were also new entrants. In 1948 Hans Erich Dotter, a young German entrepreneur, launched a start-up called Goldwell with a lotion, sold exclusively to salons, which enabled people to shape their hairstyle at home. The company, which remained a salon brand, flourished with a high-quality aerosol hairspray that met the popularity of back-combed hairstyles, and would later, during the 1970s, stun the world of hairdressing when it launched the only permanent-wave solution in the world that turned to foam on contact with air.[94]

Schwarzkopf, whose Berlin factory had been partly destroyed during the war, managed to resume making shampoo within months of the end of the conflict, by setting up improvised production sites. There was further disruption when the firm lost its plant in West Berlin in 1949, and was forced to dissolve its agencies in East Germany in 1950 due to the insurmountable economic and political difficulties caused by the Communist takeover. The local manager was able to rescue the factory machinery and even the building materials, which were dismantled and collected by the employees only hours prior to the Communists' expropriation of the firm and its assets.[95] The company's ownership structure fragmented into three independent but co-operating private companies, a situation which lasted for two decades.[96]

The desperate circumstances of postwar Germany worked to encourage creativity rather than dampen it, as Schwarzkopf and others strove to salvage once-respected businesses. In 1947 Schwarzkopf launched the world's first cold permanent-wave product. Two years later it came out with Germany's first crème shampoo in a tube, a major step in making the product accessible to a wider range of consumers. During the following decade it helped drive the growth of the hair care market by offering an increasing range of products segmented for different types of hair and needs. In 1955 the first formulation of a new hair spray, soon extended to a line of three different formulations adapted to various weathers, was launched. Its brand name, Taft, became synonymous with hair spray in Germany. In 1962 the company's shampoos began to be sold in formulations for specific hair types.[97]

Schwarzkopf had flirted with cosmetics during the interwar years,[98] but hair products, including hair salon equipment, now became its exclusive concern. Schwarzkopf, like Clairol, modified its previous reliance on the salon business. In 1961, it founded a separate subsidiary to sell hair products for home use in the growing supermarket, grocery, and self-service mass market, becoming one of the first German beauty companies to recognize the importance of the emergent mass market in consumer products.

The key constraint on the firm's growth, as in the case of many family-owned firms, was lack of capital. The family was approached by several firms as potential outside investors, particularly from the United States, but it finally chose the chemicals giant Hoechst as a partner, both because it was already the firm's largest supplier of raw materials, and because it promised to allow the firm continued autonomy. Hoechst signed a licensing agreement with Schwarzkopf in 1968 under which it agreed to manufacture and sell the latter's products in a number of foreign markets using its own subsidiaries. In the following year the family sold 25 per cent of the equity to Hoechst.[99] In 1970 Hoechst bought another 24 per cent following the death of a member of the Schwarzkopf family.[100]

Wella's business, located in Soviet-occupied Germany, was completely lost after the war. The Ströher family fled to West Germany. By 1949 they managed to rebuild the business sufficiently to begin selling hair dryers to salons. New hair brands followed, beginning with Koleston, a major innovation based on the coloring agent being suspended in a creamy substance similar to a conditioner, which was sold exclusively through salons for their customers to use at home until 1971. As consumers shampooed their hair more often and changed their hairstyles more frequently, it responded with the Wella Privat product line, also sold through salons. The strong relationship between the firm and the profession was reinforced by the training courses offered each year to thousands of domestic and international hairdressers.[101]

It was L'Oréal which emerged as the largest European hair care company. Eugène Schueller engaged in careful succession planning. He only had one daughter, Liliane, who married the French politician André Bettencourt in 1950. He began grooming one of his managers, François Dalle, to succeed him soon after the end of the war. Dalle was the son of a prosperous brewer who had been educated at a private boarding school, where he had met and forged close friendships both with Bettencourt and François Mitterrand, who much later became President of France. In 1942, at the age of 24, he was recruited to Monsavon after an introduction by Bettencourt, and soon became its head. He worked hard to expand sales, which was no easy task in a country where rationing only ended in 1950, and where—as he complained—French consumers used only a fifth as much soap to wash themselves as did their Dutch and British neighbors.[102] When Schueller formally merged L'Oréal and Monsavon in 1954, Dalle was made deputy managing director of the combined business.

Unlike many family firms, when Schueller died in 1957 Dalle was ready to take over L'Oréal. The fact that Schueller only had one child, and that she was committed to the future of the firm, proved a crucial factor that prevented L'Oréal experiencing the same fate as many family firms when their founders died. Dalle proved a good choice. Like François Coty, he combined an extreme attention to the details of every aspect of his business and a wider vision. In what was emerging as a standard pattern in the company, he was autocratic, but he was able to listen to others and draw on their talents.

The outlines of Dalle's strategy were soon apparent. He saw that the firm could grow by offering products across all distribution channels, including salons, self-service retail, pharmacies, and perfumeries. This made sense because, although all consumers might want to invest in making themselves more attractive, they differed in their ability and willingness to pay for products and advice. The key, as he emphasized from the start of his tenure, lay in careful positioning of brands within each channel.[103] Focus and innovation were also central concerns. Dalle sold the Monsavon soap business to P & G, a company that he admired as a "veritable model," and used the cash to invest in research.[104] Capacity was expanded by building a new factory at

5.2 Eugène Schueller, founder of L'Oréal, 1956.

© L'Oréal / DR

Alnay-sous-Bois, just outside Paris. It became the largest cosmetics plant in Europe.[105]

Dalle paid considerable attention to keeping the relationship with hairdressers vibrant. By 1962 L'Oréal's salon sales had reached 2 billion francs (around $400 million). The company operated demonstration centers throughout France where thousands of hairdressers were trained. These centers kept particular focus on providing education in salon-based coloring, which was perceived as key to expanding demand. In 1964 a new professional hair care brand called L'Oréal Recherche was launched, renamed Kérastase three years later, which offered customers individualized advice and service, and was designed to capture the salon shampoo and conditioner market just as the firm had captured colorants. In 1966 Dalle added products for home use which were also sold in the salon. Dalle successfully gambled that hairdressers would not see this as competition but as an additional source of income and an extension of their own treatments after customers had left their salons.[106]

Dalle expanded his portfolio of brands both by developing new brands and by acquisitions. Among the first of the former was Elnett hair spray. A few years before it was launched in 1960, the company's laboratories had developed a polymer-based product that they called hair lacquer, which had been introduced in the salon trade but without success. Believing that the failure lay in execution rather than in concept, Dalle had the product market-tested in containers which did not reveal its failed past. After favorable results, he launched the new brand, which he had initially named Ellenett, based on the French word for "she," but then shortened the name to Elnett, because this looked better when printed on the bottle. The emphasis on speed, execution, and detail was to become characteristic.

Elnett proved to be an enduring success in both the salon trade and retail channels, where it was sold in perfumeries and upscale pharmacies and drugstores. Through the experience of Elnett, Dalle further developed his strategy of market segmentation. He began to divide the company's portfolio into two categories which were referred to internally as "products on the right" and "products on the left." The former were mass brands such as Dop which were sold in mass channels such as supermarkets. The products "on the left" carried the brand name L'Oréal and were sold in department stores, fine perfumeries, and salons. He sought to make these products the highest quality, both technically and in their presentation. Elnett's original formulation was so effective that it remained unchanged for the rest of the century.[107] The strategy delivered dominance of the domestic hair care market. By the 1970s L'Oréal's hold on the French hair care and colorants market was strong. It controlled three-quarters of the domestic colorant market, over one-half of the French hairspray market, and one-half of the shampoo market.[108]

While Dalle was able to run his business with almost complete autonomy from the family, his ability to develop and market new products, let alone expand internationally, was constrained by lack of capital. Dalle's first response was to try to access the capital markets without losing control. In 1963 a part of the group went public as L'Oréal SA, which took the ownership of parts of the French business and all patents and trademarks. As only one-fifth of the stock was issued to the public, the family remained in control. A private company owned the remaining activities in France, including a small perfumery business. Another private company owned the equity of the foreign subsidiaries. Mme Bettencourt held around one-half of the shares of these private companies, with the remainder held by family and close friends.[109]

Dalle used his new funds to acquire small, family-owned and sometimes poorly managed firms in France. The acquisitions began with Cadoricin, which made shampoos and a mass-market colorant called Mousse Color, in 1961. This acquisition and the sale of Monsavon were concluded on the same day, as Dalle needed the funds from the sale to buy the company. Between 1965 and 1973 Garnier, Parfums Guy Laroche, André Courrèges, Biotherm, and the worldwide rights for the Gemey brand were swept up, taking the company into cosmetics and perfume on a small scale. Typically, Dalle would persuade their owners to sell by agreeing only slowly to build up his shareholding, enabling founding families to retain their involvement over a period of years.

In 1965 Dalle also took a more radical step by acquiring Lancôme, which marked his first move into luxury. Armand Petitjean had proved better at creating a prestigious luxury brand than sustaining it. During the 1950s his rejection of the new technology of packaging lipstick in plastic roll-tubes, opting instead to retain gold and silver dispensers, decimated the firm's lipstick business. The construction of a new factory facility in Chevilly-Larue, which became known as the Versailles of Perfumery, left the firm in serious financial trouble by 1961. The company's bank threatened to close it down unless other members of the family took it over, which Petitjean's son reluctantly agreed to do. Although Lancôme was approached by Revlon and others, it was Dalle who managed to make the deal.[110]

The acquisition of Lancôme enabled Dalle to enter the skin care category. Many years previously, he had tried to create a competitor cream to Nivea when he ran Monsavon during the German occupation. Its development was cancelled after the end of the war due to raw materials shortages. Lancôme provided a chance to pick up the concept, but this presented both scientific and marketing challenges. While hair colorants were the products of chemistry, Dalle now needed biologists, who were not produced in great numbers by French universities at the time. Moreover, when his first attempt, Absolue, came onto the market it failed. The affluent female consumers who bought expensive skin care products sought individualized creams that fitted their own needs rather than an all-purpose cream. The product was then reimagined as a face cream for women to use in the morning. Bienfait du Matin was launched in 1969. Dalle was not prepared to aim for the 50,000 to 100,000 units typically sold in the first year of a luxury brand, and instead aimed and achieved one million units by the second year.[111]

Dalle was also able to overcome the constraint on capital caused by the firm's shareholding. By the mid-1960s he was seeking to persuade a large company to invest in L'Oréal, yet grant it autonomy. He almost secured such an arrangement with Unilever, whose French management reached a provisional deal that offered to pay $84 million for a minority shareholding in L'Oréal for ten years, and to acquire a majority after Dalle had retired. However, after an extended period of negotiation, Unilever's top management rejected the agreement, whose price was considered excessive given that only a minority shareholding—which Unilever rarely accepted—was offered. The Anglo-Dutch company's executives had convinced themselves that the fragmented hair care and cosmetics categories would in time follow the path set by toiletries and converge towards powerful mass brands, which the firm could develop organically. It was a serious misjudgment.[112]

Dalle pursued other options. In 1969 L'Oréal SA, in which Mme Bettencourt's shareholding had fallen to 25 per cent, was merged with the domestic private company, in which Mme Bettencourt still owned 70 per cent, to give her 45 per cent of the shared group, which, combined with a family trust holding of 11 per cent, gave her the majority. Five years later Dalle persuaded Nestlé, the large Swiss consumer goods multinational, to acquire a 25 per cent stake in the business.

The timing reflected a French presidential election which seemed likely to result in François Mitterrand, the Socialist candidate, winning on an agenda that included nationalizing large companies. The new structure gave majority control jointly to Nestlé and the family trust, alongside a smaller public holding.[113] The government, which by then had become sensitive to foreign ownership of beauty companies, permitted the arrangement so long as Bettencourt retained an overall 51 per cent ownership of the company for the duration of her life. It was agreed that if she died before 1994, her only daughter could not sell the company until that year. In addition, Nestlé became the majority owner of Cosmair, a private US company which had the exclusive license to distribute L'Oréal's brands in the United States.[114]

When Dalle retired as chief executive in 1984, L'Oréal was among the largest of the world's largest beauty companies. It not only had a presence in luxury, but also in cosmetics, skin, and perfume. In the late 1970s Dalle had also made equity investments in magazine publishing companies, and in 1984 even taken a 10 per cent stake in the French pay television company Canal Plus. A series of investments, beginning with the acquisition of 53 per cent of Synthélabo, which made products for arterial diseases and hospital equipment, had made L'Oréal the third largest pharmaceutical company in France, an achievement which Dalle came to consider as the real jewel of the entire business. Yet L'Oréal still remained primarily a hair care company which was heavily dependent on sales in France and Europe. Dalle always regarded skin care and cosmetics as confined to the smaller luxury component of the company.[115]

On both sides of the Atlantic, then, hair care companies were successful in persuading consumers to wash their hair with shampoos rather than soap and water, and to apply hair sprays and other products. In contrast to the consumption of fragrances, there was a strong convergence between countries in fashions in hair care, but at this stage the brands sold in the American and European markets remained distinct. Hair products provided the basis for many successful businesses. Dalle, in particular, built L'Oréal by combining its capabilities in research with well-crafted market segmentation whilst enjoying freedom from predators due to family ownership, and, later, by his success in bringing in Nestlé as a major shareholder.

The geography of beauty

Big firms like L'Oréal co-existed with numerous small companies in each country. There were many new entrants to the industry during the postwar decades. As markets also remained local in many ways, new ventures were regularly inspired by products and strategies pursued in other markets. A growth of contract manufacturing facilitated start-ups by alleviating the need for large-scale investment in manufacturing capacity.[116] In the mid-1960s France had 430 companies producing cosmetics and toiletries, Spain had 560, Germany had 140, and the Netherlands 50.[117] A decade later, a thousand cosmetics firms marketed 20,000 different brands in the United States, although ten firms accounted for more than one-half of total industry revenues.[118]

Firms clustered in many cities, but none matched New York or Paris in terms of the numbers of head offices located there, the depth of creative talent and, especially, their aspirational status. In the United States, for example,

Cincinnati was handicapped by its location in America's Midwest and its perceived dearth of style, fashion, and cosmopolitan lifestyle. Los Angeles was a lot more cosmopolitan, as well as the home of Hollywood, but the city's cultural and fashion world was notoriously overshadowed by New York.

Chicago was the home of major hair care firms, including Helene Curtis and Alberto-Culver. It was also the historic center of the African-American beauty industry, which continued to see new entrepreneurial endeavors, including John H. Johnson's launch of *Ebony* magazine in 1945. However, the segregated nature of the American beauty market constrained the potential of such a cluster to contribute towards making Chicago a beauty capital with wider national or global recognition.[119] African-Americans remained excluded from Miss America altogether until the late 1960s, and the first African-American to win even a state title was the 1970 Miss Iowa.[120]

In Europe, too, a challenger to Paris never emerged, although Germany was the home of leading brands, especially in hair and skin care. These were rebuilt as the consequences of the disastrous Nazi era faded. Beiersdorf renewed the Nivea brand and launched new product lines. The controlling families were also able to stabilize the shareholding by persuading the insurance company Allianz to take a 25 per cent equity stake, leaving the Troplowitz–Mankiewicz family prominent in the senior management.[121] The German industry, though, was spread over the country and was not clustered in a single hub. Moreover, after the Nazi era, the notion of constructing a new aspirational German beauty ideal was strictly *verboten*.

There were clusters of beauty firms in other European cities, but they lacked the aspirational appeal that could either attract creative talent from afar, or become the basis of a beauty ideal with widespread international appeal. Sweden's locally owned beauty industry, for example, had many small and medium-sized entrepreneurs. A high standard of living also made the small country a prosperous market, two-thirds of which was supplied locally in the 1960s.[122] Stockholm, however, was the modestly sized capital of a country on Europe's periphery, most widely known for cold and dark winters and for being a welfare state. Notoriously high tax rates also discouraged entrepreneurship and provided little attraction for creative talent to come from elsewhere.

These circumstances encouraged entrepreneurs to emphasize associations with Paris rather than Stockholm as they built brands. Such was the case for

Knut Wulff, sometimes called the father of Swedish cosmetics, who built a beauty company out of his father's defunct hairdressing and perfumery business. Motivated by a conviction that he wanted to "strengthen people's self-confidence" by making them feel beautiful, Wulff launched a new skin care and color cosmetics business in 1946, after he had already successfully transformed his father's salon business into a chain of women's prestige beauty salons, where the latest Paris hair fashions were offered alongside advanced skin care and other beauty treatments. The company employed the name of a French entrepreneur, Pierre Robert, whom Wulff had met while attending a course at L'Oréal's hairdressing academy in the 1930s. He began by selling skin creams and an aftersun lotion called Lait de Beauté, or simply LdB.[123] By the 1970s Wulff held nearly half of the Swedish skin care market and over one-third of the hair spray and lipstick markets.[124]

A significant factor in Wulff's success was his adroit use of a carefully cultivated Parisian image. In 1963 he opened an Institut de Beauté Scandinave in Paris adjacent to Hermès in the fashionable rue du Faubourg Saint-Honoré. It offered beauty courses, as did the one he opened in Sweden, and sought to transform the element of Swedishness and Scandinavian beauty rituals, reflected in the provision of a sauna, facials, manicure, and pedicure, into a source of appeal that transcended Swedish borders. He built close contacts with French fashion magazines in pursuit of his strategy of always "being seen." He worked closely too with several haute couture fashion houses preparing models for shows. In this way, Wulff could trade simultaneously on the appeal of Scandinavia in Paris, and on the ideal of Paris for his business and reputation in Sweden and elsewhere.[125]

Other entrepreneurs left Sweden altogether. In 1967 Oriflame was founded in Stockholm by Robert and Jonas af Jochnick and Bengt Hellsten. Unlike many founders of beauty firms, they had received formal training in management studies, from the Stockholm School of Economics, Harvard Business School, and INSEAD, the leading business school located near Paris, respectively, but lacked any prior knowledge of cosmetics. These three men had started discussing an entrepreneurial venture, and just at that time heard of problems at a direct-sales company which an American entrepreneur was starting up in Sweden, in which Jonas had invested. It turned out that the venture, which had recruited some former employees of Tupperware, was fraudulent, but Jonas concluded that the business concept was sound. The Oriflame founders, aware of Avon's success,

5.3 Knut Wulff, the founder of Swedish cosmetics company Pierre Robert and owner of the beauty salon chain Wulff's Salonger, with one of his hair models Anita Ekberg. Ekberg went on to become Miss Sweden in 1951, and later became a prominent Hollywood actress, circa 1950.

Photograph by Sixten Sandgren © Sixten Sandgren

decided to encourage the distributors who had been fooled by the old company to become investors nevertheless in the new company.

Sweden at that time only used direct sales for big-ticket items, like vacuum cleaners sold by Electrolux. The brothers decided to use the same home party strategy as Tupperware to sell quality products at a lower price than Pierre Robert. The new company was able to start rapidly by subcontracting its production to a British affiliate of a US-owned contract manufacturer. From the start, they conceived of basing the company on natural products, and they found a beautician who formulated some product concepts based on the use of natural ingredients.[126]

The business model worked, but the founders saw their future outside Stockholm rather than in it. They first grew sales elsewhere in Scandinavia and then went to Britain. Oriflame was incorporated in Luxembourg in 1970, primarily to avoid the extensive regulation on foreign investment then prevalent in Sweden. The head office was located in Brussels, to where the two brothers drove from Sweden in their car. A leading American bank, which at that time was looking for venture capital opportunities, took 10 per cent of the equity and gave them a loan facility. The new company was successful in Britain, which became their biggest market outside Sweden within a decade. In 1982 it was listed on the London Stock Exchange.[127]

In contrast to Stockholm, Milan developed strong aspirational appeal in the world of fashion after World War II. Rising incomes also led to wider use of cosmetics. By the mid-1960s the Italian beauty market was worth $240 million, and was the fourth largest in Europe. Yet a beauty business did not emerge to match that of fashion, although a large cosmetics contract manufacturing industry developed. The Italian market was dominated by foreign brands, whilst Italian brands rarely sold outside Italy. Societal values may have hindered the beauty industry. The all-powerful Catholic Church continued to reinforce women's traditional roles as wives and mothers, and expressed disapproval of excessive use of make-up and perfumes. The fragmentation of the Italian industry posed a more prosaic constraint, with several thousand firms making small quantities of soaps, toiletries, and cosmetics. Distribution channels were also highly fragmented. While toiletries were sold by grocery stores, cosmetics were sold through numerous independent perfumeries and pharmacies, as department stores were virtually non-existent. This resulted in lipsticks, perfumes, and other products being sold at much higher prices than in Western Europe.[128] Finally, Italian firms spent little on research and development.[129]

Meanwhile, London remained overshadowed by Paris. The country was an important and often lucrative market, but one in which French and American brands were widely sold. Postwar London was an austere capital of a country whose colonial empire was being dismantled and whose economy looked increasingly weak.

Unlike Italy, Britain did possess a significant locally owned industry. Gala, Outdoor Girl, Goya, and Yardley were widely sold cosmetics brands in the domestic market.[130] In 1952, Boots relaunched its No 7 brand, which had almost disappeared during the war. A new gold-and-yellow packaging was heavily influenced by Hollywood.[131] There was also an unexpected renaissance of the Rimmel brand. The residual British company, separated from its French directors during the war, had finally gone into liquidation. The rights to the brand name were bought by a British businessman, who persuaded the owner of the advertising agency whom he had initially employed to rebuild the business to take over running the company. Robert Caplin, the advertising executive, and his sister, Rose, repositioned the brand from its luxury-and-fragrance heritage by a new focus on "beauty on a budget" and color cosmetics. They also came up with the idea of a self-selection counter dispenser.[132] All these homegrown brands held significant shares of the mass market, especially in color cosmetics, but they were typically positioned more as cheaper versions of American brands than as celebrations of a British beauty ideal. They therefore provided limited opportunities for an autonomous beauty cluster to emerge along the lines of Paris.

There seemed a moment when London's status in the world of beauty might be transformed, when the city blossomed anew during the 1960s as a center of creative fashion with a distinctly youthful beauty ideal. The designer Mary Quant launched the miniskirt on the world fashion scene. The Beatles and the model Twiggy added to the atmosphere of "swinging London." The Myram Picker group, which owned Gala, launched Mary Quant cosmetics. Aimed at younger women, the company distinguished itself by using the hard colors of black and silver and by appealing to the "new, liberated, independent mood of mini-skirted women."[133] Even Yardley appeared reinvigorated, promoting a so-called London look of a pale, unmade-up face with a heavy focus on the lips. It employed a trendy British fashion model, Jean Shrimpton, to promote the brand in the United States. Meanwhile, Vidal Sassoon transformed the hairdressing business in London, and then globally, by developing a new style which complemented the natural structure of a woman's face.[134]

In the end London, alas, did not become the new Paris. Creative talent sought greener pastures elsewhere. Vidal Sassoon opened his first salon in New York in 1964 and over time shifted most of his business to the United States. The prospects of an autonomous beauty culture were further reduced

THE CAMOUFLAGE KIT Everything you need for the Camouflage look The latest from MARY QUANT

5.4 Mary Quant, 1960s British fashion icon and founder of the mod look, launched a color cosmetics brand, advertised here with a provocative androgynous image of female power, circa 1970.

by the UK's highly developed market for corporate control. In time, the owners of Rimmel, Gala, and other brands sold out to larger, often non-beauty, firms. Few brands flourished under their new owners, let alone provided a basis for developing a globally attractive beauty ideal.[135] The corporate powerhouses of the domestic beauty industry were multinational sellers of mass toiletries like Unilever and Beecham. Brands such as Lux, Sunsilk, and Brylcreem hair oil were triumphs of mass marketing, and mass marketing was not the way to build a Paris-style beauty culture.

Both in America and Europe, then, there remained important clusters of firms in cities other than New York and Paris. Yet Stockholm, Milan, Chicago, and even London did not become beauty capitals. The forces of path-dependency and agglomeration proved powerful protectors of the status of Paris and New York. The clustering of creative talent, suppliers, related industries, retail outlets, and consumers in these cities, combined with their heritages, served as a self-reinforcing mechanism. In the beauty and fashion industries, lifestyle and location are critically important. Creative talent wants to be near similar people. It wants to live in cosmopolitan cities, dine in fine restaurants, and date stylish people. The consumers of beauty brands wanted to be associated with cities which symbolized aspiration and fashion.

The beauty miracle in Japan

The three-decade-long transformation of the impoverished postwar Japanese economy into the fearsomely competitive producer of motor vehicles and consumer electronics ranks as one of the most remarkable episodes in the economic history of the twentieth century. The scale of the growth of the Japanese beauty market in this era was almost as miraculous.

During the war, cosmetics manufacturing was virtually eliminated by the government, as resources were switched to the war effort with none of the regard for civilian morale evident in democratic countries. The postwar years proved challenging to companies trying to rebuild businesses. Club Cosmetics, the former market leader, never recovered, and went bankrupt in 1954. Despite Shinobu Suzuki's conviction that his Pola brand could be best understood if it was sold directly to consumers, he was forced to abandon direct selling completely for several years, as he was unable to find suitable workers.[136]

As economic growth resumed in the early 1950s and rationing and price controls were eased, consumers began purchasing cosmetics and toiletries in increasing amounts. By the mid-1950s the industry was growing at 17 per cent per annum. A survey of Tokyo women in 1958 showed that nine-tenths were using face cream, and three-fifths wore lipstick.[137] The market reached over $300 million in 1966. It was about to become, and remain, the world's second-largest beauty market.

Since the nineteenth century Japanese companies had marketed their brands as aspirational symbols of modernity. Paris in particular, and the West in general, had been their primary inspiration, although the process of translating these ideals to Japanese consumers had been orchestrated by locally owned and managed firms. After 1945 the Western impact on Japan became even stronger. In time, iconic American brands such as McDonalds, Coca-Cola, and Disney would become as familiar to Japanese consumers as to their American counterparts. A similar Westernization or Americanization was observable in the beauty industry but, as previously, local firms remained the orchestrators of the process. Western and Japanese practices and preferences continued to co-exist in a fluid dialogue which shifted over time and varied between companies.

The Japanese industry became far more exposed to American-style marketing after World War II. Max Factor, which opened a Japanese branch in 1949, had a catalytic effect. A campaign for Roman Pink lipstick at the end of the 1950s opened the eyes of many managers to the power of a well-funded and professional advertising campaign.[138] Western fashions also entered Japan with greater intensity. Hollywood films, extensively watched in Japan, diffused Christian Dior's "New Look" to Japanese women in numbers which fashion magazines never matched.

Japanese companies responded with products designed to persuade their buyers that they would look like the actresses and models they saw on cinema and television screens. Shiseido's new make-up made eyes larger and rounder-shaped, with pink-overtoned face powder encouraging a resemblance to European skin. Shiseido also made extensive use of models of mixed Japanese and Western ethnicity to advertise products designed to Westernize Japanese faces.[139]

American-style television advertising also reached Japan after a lag. Although not one of the first companies to use television advertising, Shiseido launched itself into the medium in 1958 by becoming the sole sponsor of a television musical show targeted at women aged 18 to 29, which became a major hit.[140] During the mid-1950s Pola also abandoned its previous reliance on word of mouth and aired its first radio commercial. Television advertisements followed. The phrase "Hello, this is the Pola salesman!" became well known to viewers and listeners.[141] Lion, which had a joint venture with Bristol-Myers enabling it to distribute the latter's toiletries products, scored a huge success in 1962 with its launch of the Vitalis men's hairstyling brand in a burst of television and other media advertising.[142]

In Japan, firms drove market growth by new brand launches, innovation, promotion schemes, and distribution strategies rather than by price competition. In 1952 the industry was exempted from the laws prohibiting price-fixing which the Allies had imposed on Japan, and this remained the case for the following three decades. Firms competed fiercely to reach customers by other means. Shiseido utilized its large voluntary chain store network. Pola rebuilt its direct sales force, which reached 3,000 in 1955 and over 90,000 a mere decade later. Loyal customers were rewarded with souvenir gifts.[143]

There were also new entrants. Among the most successful was Kosé, founded in 1946 by Kosaburo Kobayashi. From the start, the company emphasized high quality standards and, rather than selling through wholesalers, created a nationwide system of "ring stores" which were given exclusive access to Kosé products. By the 1950s it was launching prestige cosmetics brands, employing, as usual, French names such as La Bonne. Kosé also began building a cadre of female beauty advisers.[144]

The large textile company Kanebo also entered the fray. Kanebo had made toilet soap, skin creams, and hair products during the 1930s, but at the end of the war these operations were spun off into a separate company.[145] In 1961 it reacquired its former company. Kanebo had the financial and management resources to grow a beauty business quickly, as well as a corporate culture said to be faster-adapting than that of the market leader Shiseido. Kanebo's management had strong competitive instincts, both internally—to catch up with Kanebo's textile division—and externally, to catch up with Shiseido. Kanebo's cotton textile business had also given it extensive experience in employing and motivating young female workers. This experience could, to some extent, be transferred to the young female beauticians which the company used to sell its products in department stores and specialized chain stores.[146]

The upshot was a fast entry into the market. By 1966 cosmetics had already reached 10 per cent of total group sales. The firm built its own chain store system. By 1964 it had 10,000 chain stores. A Paris research facility was established in 1965, and two years later Kanebo launched a store in fashionable Ginza to open up a market in Tokyo. The pace of growth was so fast that substantial losses were incurred, and at times exiting the business was discussed.[147] Still, by 1977 Kanebo had captured almost one-fifth of the domestic Japanese beauty market.[148]

The intermingling of Japanese and Western creative influences during this era is evident in the formative stages of the business of Shu Uemura. He had developed an early interest in acting, theatre, and make-up, but in his early twenties, just after the end of World War II, he was struck down with tuberculosis, and remained under medical treatment until he was 25. "I had time to think a lot about health and the human body," he later reflected.

"I had always liked beautiful things to begin with. The central idea of my philosophy became simplicity or pureness."[149] He went on to attend make-up school as the only male member of his class. Uemura became involved in cinema make-up after working on a collaborative American–Japanese war film which Frank Sinatra starred in and directed. When shooting on location in Hawaii was over, the production team moved to Hollywood to finish the film. There Uemura worked with the Westmore family and other leading American make-up artists.

In the early 1960s Uemura decided to start a business in Japan. He began by teaching make-up in a picture-card-show style to professionals working in beauty salons. He built a studio to teach make-up techniques in the garden of his father's house in Tokyo. It was modeled on similar studios in Hollywood and initially used imported materials from small cosmetic companies around Hollywood. In 1965 he established the Shu Uemura Make-Up Institute in Tokyo as the first Hollywood-style make-up atelier in Japan. In 1968 he launched his first Mode Make-up, with a distinctive vision to achieve a harmony between creativity and beauty. The manufacture of his own skin care products, characterized by astounding colors packaged in minimalist clear plastic, followed, and in 1972 he organized the first "make-up show" in a hotel in Tokyo.[150]

Shu Uemura, like Shiseido and the other Japanese firms of the era, were diffusers and interpreters of American beauty ideals and practices, but this diffusion continued to rest also on Japanese cultural traditions. As elsewhere, the full homogenization of consumer preferences was a long way off. Japanese consumers continued to be far more interested in buying skin products than their American counterparts, who were far more interested in color cosmetics and fragrances. During the 1960s three-fifths of the total Japanese beauty market was held by skin preparations. Moreover, a preference for pale skin made skin lighteners, virtually unknown in the West until recently except for the African-American market, a major product.

It was also striking that Japan's emergence as the world's second-largest economy by the 1970s was not mirrored in the growth of Tokyo as a global beauty capital of stature equal to New York and Paris. By then the leading Japanese companies featured high up in the rankings of the world's largest firms, but this was primarily because of the size of their domestic market. In 1980 less than 4 per cent of Shiseido's sales were made outside Japan, and two decades of trying to extend its brands to the United States and Europe had proved frustrating.[151] Tokyo was emerging as a fashion and beauty capital of increasing importance for the surrounding region, but Western consumers continued to regard Japanese brands as more exotic than aspirational. The problem might have rested fundamentally, as some thought, on the mismatch between Tokyo's historical image in the West of geisha women, ancient temples, and other traditional images or symbols, and the emergent reality in Tokyo of a modern, and far from attractive, bustling city with chic, trendy fashions.[152]

Summing up

During the postwar decades, Western and Japanese consumers celebrated the return of peace and prosperity with a splurge of spending on beauty products. As incomes rose, the industry enticed consumers with television advertising which employed in-depth research on consumer demographics and desires. Television drove the further democratization of the beauty market, which was particularly noticeable in the case of fragrance consumption. It also contributed to the further erosion of moral objections to the use of transformational products. In hair products especially, the combination of product innovation, marketing, and consumer education through salons served to expand the market rapidly. The segmentation of markets by income and distribution channels also made beauty products more accessible to wider ranges of consumers.

There were both remarkable changes and striking continuities during these years. The former included the strong growth of American prestige fragrances and the stunning growth of the Japanese market. There were, however, few radical changes to the long-established borders of beauty. The industry's attention was heavily focused on women between their late teens and mid-thirties, whom it promised to make more attractive, and, as they aged, to keep looking young. This female age range accounted, according to one article on the American market in 1973, for one-half of the total fragrance, eye shadow, and sun care products, 60 per cent of the mascara, and 80 per cent of the shampoo consumed.[153] A survey of the American male market concluded with "the blunt fact that the market has been nearly static for 50 years."[154] The largest Western beauty companies were all focused on white people's features, skin, and hair, which Japanese companies offered their own consumers the opportunity to emulate. Paris and New York remained the capitals of beauty.

Television now joined Hollywood as a diffuser of fashions and celebrities. Not surprisingly, there was evidence of convergence in consumer markets. The use of shampoo to wash hair increased everywhere as incomes rose. Yet there was no sudden burst of homogeneity between countries. Whilst per capita consumption of toothpaste in the US was broadly similar to that in Switzerland during the 1970s, for example, it was nearly double that of France and Italy.[155] Germans retained an idiosyncratic preference for bath preparations, with a particular liking for liquids with foaming properties, and scented with herbal extracts such as pine.[156]

Markets continued to differ even more widely on what products could, and should, be applied to body and skin. American women rarely set foot out of their doors without make-up. By the early 1960s an estimated 86 per cent of American girls aged 14 to 17 already used lipstick, 36 per cent used mascara, and 28 per cent used face powder.[157] In Japan women made far greater use of skin creams than color cosmetics. The Japanese face cream and lotion market was worth $1.3 billion at the end of the 1970s, making it the largest in the world. In contrast, the American face cream market was worth $525 million, even though it had twice the population of Japan.[158] In Europe skin products were also used much more widely than color lines, but huge variations persisted between countries in the region in usage of creams as well as cosmetics. Meanwhile there was an actual divergence in scent preferences between the United States and Europe. Although television had enabled the peoples of the world to see each other as never before, it had clearly not resulted in any sudden surge in homogenization.

Notes

1. Leonard H. Lavin, *Winners Make It Happen. Reflections of a Self-Made Man* (Chicago: Bonus Books, 2003), p. 53.

2. Victoria de Grazia, *Irresistible Empire: America's Advance through Twentieth-century Europe* (Cambridge, Mass.: Harvard University Press, 2005), ch. 7.

3. Adjusting for inflation, whilst the GDP per capita of the United States and Japan rose by 2.4 and 6.9 per cent per annum respectively between 1950 and 1976, their beauty industries grew by 5.8 and 10.7 per cent per annum. See Geoffrey Jones, "Blonde and Blue-eyed? Globalizing Beauty, c.1945–c.1980," *Economic History Review* 61 (2008), p. 133.

4. Avon Archives, Hagley Museum, Wilmington, Del., Avon Products Inc., Accession number 2155 (hereafter AVON), Record Group II: Historical Files, Series 9: Library Resources, "Overview of the Over-the-Counter Cosmetic Industry," March 13, 1974, Box 127.

5. Frost and Sullivan, *The Cosmetics and Toiletries Industry Market* (New York, August 1972), Exhibit XVII. The category of health and beauty aids included the beauty industry as defined in this book along with various over-the-counter products such as first aid and foot care preparations.

6. Thomas K. McCraw, *American Business since 1920: How it Worked* (Wheeling, Ill.: Harlan Davidson, 2009), 2nd edn, pp. 101–2; Regina Lee Blaszczyk, *American Consumer Society 1865–2005* (Wheeling, Ill.: Harlan Davidson, 2009), pp. 234–8.

7. Wilfried Feldenkirchen and Susanne Hilger, *Menschen und Marken: 125 Jahre Henkel 1876–2001* (Düsseldorf: Henkel KGaA, 2001), p. 264.

8. Linda Scott, *Fresh Lipstick. Redressing Fashion and Feminism* (New York: Palgrave Macmillan, 2005), p. 269.

9. Mary Caudle Beltran, "Bronze Seduction: The Shaping of Latina Stardom in Hollywood Film and Star Publicity," unpubl. doctoral diss., University of Texas at Austin, 2002, ch. 3.

10. Grazia, *Irresistible Empire*, p. 429.

11. Neville Hoad, "World Piece: What the Miss World Pageant Can Teach about Globalization," *Cultural Critique* 58 (Fall 2004), pp. 61–2.

12. Stephen Gundle, *Glamour. A History* (Oxford: Oxford University Press, 2008), pp. 257–8.

13. <http://www.perfectmiss.extra.hu/world/world6os.htm>, accessed March 20, 2009.

14. Christopher Varaste, *Face of the American Dream: Barbie Doll, 1959–1971* (Grantsville, Md: Hobby House Press, 1999), p. 17; M. G. Lord, *Forever Barbie* (New York: Morrow and Co., 1994), p. 162.

15. Penny van Esterik, "The Politics of Beauty in Thailand," in Colleen Ballerino Cohen, Richard Wilk, and Beverly Stoeltje (eds), *Beauty Queens on the Global Stage: Gender, Contests, and Power* (New York: Routledge, 1996), p. 215. Miss India for 1966 became the first "darker-skinned" winner of Miss World.

16. Fred E. Basten, *Max Factor. The Man Who Changed the Faces of the World* (New York: Arcade, 2008), pp. 145–8.

17. Procter & Gamble Archives (hereafter P & G), *Max Factor Reporter*, IV, 5, October–November 1957; vol. 10, August–September 1959.

18. Lavin, *Winners*, p. 53.

19. "Cosmetics: The Brand is Everything," *Printers' Ink*, November 1, 1963.

20. Gordon McKibben, *Cutting Edge* (Boston, Mass.: Harvard Business School Press, 1998), pp. 49–52; Gillette, Annual Report, 1960.

21. Margaret Allen, *Selling Dreams* (New York: Simon and Schuster, 1981), pp. 50–2.

22. Allen, *Selling*, p. 53.

23. J. Walter Thompson Archives (hereafter JWT), Account Files, Chesebrough-Pond's Inc., Account Histories 1955–1959, "Pond's Case History," May 5, 1959, Box 3.

24. Lavin, *Winners*, pp. 37, 143.

25. "Alberto-Culver Tells of 5-Year Ad Total: $19,000,000," *Advertising Age*, April 24, 1961.

26. Lavin, *Winners*, ch. 4; JWT, New Business Records, Alberto Culver Co., 1959–1965, "The Daringest Investor in TV," *Sales Management*, December 15, 1961, Box 1.

27. Norma Gerber, "Marketing Case History: Cover Girl," *Product Management*, July 1973; P & G, *The Noxell Story. The Little Blue Jar: A Business Romance.*

28. Lavin, *Winners*, pp. 163–6.

29. Richard Tedlow, *Giants of Enterprise: Seven Business Innovators and the Empires They Built* (New York: HarperCollins, 2001), pp. 270–9; Kathy Peiss, *Hope in a Jar* (New York: Henry Holt 1998), pp. 249–51; Scott, *Fresh Lipstick*, pp. 238–44.

30. "The $16 Million Challenge," *Time*, September 30, 1957; Peiss, *Hope*, pp. 249–52; Tedlow, *Giants*, pp. 269, 279–98.

31. Tedlow, *Giants*, pp. 279–98, 299–302.

32. Tedlow, *Giants*, pp. 299–302.

33. *Standard and Poor's Industry Surveys* (New York: Standard & Poor's Corp., 1962).

34. Annual Reports of Coty Inc. and Coty International Corporation, 1957; "Personality: He Has Young Ideas in Old Line," *New York Times*, September 2, 1962.

35. Robert Fitzgerald, "Marketing and Distribution," in Geoffrey Jones and Jonathan Zeitlin (eds), *The Oxford Handbook of Business History* (Oxford: Oxford University Press, 2008), pp. 409–10.

36. Tom Reichert, *The Erotic History of Advertising* (New York: Prometheus, 2003), pp. 133–66.

37. This observation was first made by Martin Revson, the brother of Charles, in a 1950 interview: Tedlow, *Giants*, p. 474.

38. Allen, *Selling*, pp. 73–6.

39. John A. Quelch and Alice M. Court, "Mary Kay Cosmetics Inc.: Marketing Communications," Harvard Business School Case no. 9-583-068 (June 25, 1985).

40. Katina Lee Manko, " 'Ding Dong! Avon Calling!': Gender, Business and Door-to-Door Selling, 1890–1955," unpubl. doctoral diss., University of Delaware, 2001, p. 236, chs 4 and 5.

41. Manko, "Ding Dong!," p. 266; AVON, Record Group I: Archive, Series 8: Marketing, Subseries B: Product Marketing, "Five-Year Overview," March 25 and 26, 1970, Box 65.

42. "Cosmetics: The Brand is Everything," *Printers' Ink*, November 1, 1963.

43. Edward S. Rutland, "Perfume and Cologne—An Analysis of the Black Market," *Cosmetics and Perfumery* 89 (June 1974). Estée Lauder, Chanel, and Coty followed with 10, 9, and 6 per cent market shares respectively.

44. Interview with Frank and Jan Day, in Morris L. Mayer, *Direct Selling in the United States* (Washington, DC: Direct Selling Education Foundation, 1995), pp. 46–7. In 1973, when it was sold to Gillette, Jafra had sales of $8 million and 10,000 consultants.

45. Beth Kreydatus, " 'Enriching Women's Lives': The Mary Kay Approach to Beauty, Business, and Feminism," *Business and Economic History On-Line*, vol. 3 (2005), pp. 1–32.

46. Quelch and Court, "Mary Kay." The company also focused on higher-priced products than those of Avon. Sales grew from $4 million in 1968 to $53 million in 1978, by which time Mary Kay had over 43,000 beauty consultants.

47. Quelch and Court, "Mary Kay," Exhibit 2.

48. Grazia, *Irresistible*, ch. 9.

49. Frost and Sullivan, *Marketing Strategies for Selling Cosmetics and Toiletries in Europe* (New York, April 1983).

50. François Dalle, *L'aventure L'Oréal* (Paris: Éditions Odile Jacob, 2001), pp. 53–4.

51. Crédit Lyonnais Archives (hereafter CL), DEEF 79425/1, "Industrie de la parfumerie en France et dans le principaux pays industrialisés," DEEF 79425/1, Secteur Parachimie, October 9, 1972.

52. Frost and Sullivan, *Marketing Strategies*.

53. S. A. Mann, *Cosmetics Industry of Europe 1968* (Park Ridge, NJ: Noyes Development Corporation, 1968), p. 35; Centre des archives économiques et financières (hereafter CAEF), B-0065514/1, Ministère des finances et des affaires économiques, société Victor Mane et fils (1961–1968), Maurice Mane to Jean Le Guen, Direction des finances extérieures, March 12, 1965.

54. Lee Israel, *Estée Lauder. Beyond the Magic* (New York: Macmillan, 1985), p. 27.

55. Grazia, *Irresistible*, pp. 368–9. In 1977 Chiris was sold to the Dutch firm of Naarden.

56. Hans Conrad Peyer, *Roche: A Company History 1896–1996* (Basle: Roche, 1996), pp. 171, 194–5, 221.

57. In 1964 Unilever acquired Bertrand Frères. See Fred Aftalion, *A History of the International Chemical Industry* (Philadelphia: Chemical Heritage Press, 2001),

pp. 354–5; Geoffrey Jones, *Renewing Unilever* (Oxford: Oxford University Press, 2005), pp. 207–11.

58. Allen, *Selling*, pp. 235–6; Geoffrey Jones and David Kiron, "Bernd Beetz: Creating the New Coty," Harvard Business School Case no. 9-808-133 (December 8, 2008).

59. AVON, Record Group I: Archive, Series 1: Administration, Subseries C: Conferences, 1973–1978, Boca Raton Conference, May 1979, Box 4; Frost and Sullivan, *Cosmetics and Toiletries*. In 1981 the French fragrance market was worth $450 million, while the German and British markets were both worth $300 million. See Frost and Sullivan, *Marketing Strategies*.

60. Rosemary Wakeman, "Nostalgic Modernism and the Invention of Paris in the Twentieth Century," *French Historical Studies* 27:1 (Winter 2004), pp. 139–44.

61. Tomoko Okawa, "Licensing Practices at Maison Christian Dior," in Regina Lee Blaszczyk (ed.), *Producing Fashion: Commerce, Culture and Consumers* (Philadelphia: University of Pennsylvania Press, 2007), pp. 84–95.

62. Edwin T. Morris, *Fragrance: The Story of Perfume from Cleopatra to Chanel* (New York: Charles Scribner's Sons, 1984), pp. 210–11.

63. "Perfumes, Cosmetics, and other Toilet Preparations," *The US Industrial Outlook for 1969* (Washington, DC: Washington, Business and Defense Services Administration, 1970), p. 185.

64. Basten, *Max Factor*, pp. 148–50.

65. Nancy Koehn, *Brand New* (Boston, Mass.: Harvard Business School Press, 2001), pp. 149–65.

66. Koehn, *Brand New*, pp. 174–6.

67. Lindy Woodhead, *War Paint* (Hoboken, NJ: John Wiley, 2003), p. 350.

68. Estée Lauder, *Estée: A Success Story* (New York: Random House, 1985), p. 149.

69. Both quotes are from Lauder's visits to Hazel Bishop's class at the Fashion Institute of New York, where Bishop had built a new career as an educator in 1978. See Schlesinger Library, Radcliffe Institute. Hazel Bishop, Papers, MC 518, "Lauder Entrance," n.d., notes taken by Bishop during Estée Lauder's visit to her class, Box #10.7. Bishop was appointed to the Revlon Chair in Cosmetics Marketing in 1980.

70. Israel, *Estée Lauder*, pp. 40–1; Koehn, *Brand New*, pp. 166–83.

71. Kathy Larkin, "Kathy Larkin Analyzes European Penetration of the American Perfume Market," *Europe*, March–April 1982, pp. 14–16.

72. Norma M. Rantisi, "The Ascendance of New York Fashion," *International Journal of Urban and Regional Research* 28 (2004), pp. 86–106.

73. "Kathy Larkin Analyzes."

74. Morris, *Fragrance*, p. 278; Steve Ginsberg, *Reeking Havoc* (London: Hutchinson, 1990), p. 10; CL, DEEF 79426/1, "Industrie française des produits de parfumerie, de beauté et de toilette," February 16, 1982.

75. François Baudet, *Fashion: The Twentieth Century* (London: Thames and Hudson, 1999), pp. 238–46.

76. Baudet, *Fashion*, pp. 192–5.

77. Morris, *Fragrance*, pp. 278–9; Richard Stamelman, *Perfume* (New York: Rizzoli, 2006), pp. 301–2; comments by Chantal Roos in "Yves Saint Laurent, the Legend," *Women's Wear Daily*, June 3, 2008.

78. Ginsberg, *Reeking*, pp. 9, 95.

79. In the 1970s 47 per cent of all fragrance sales in the United States were made in October, November, and December: Frost and Sullivan, *The Hygiene and Grooming Aids Market* (New York, January 1974), p. 30.

80. "Kathy Larkin Analyzes."

81. This paragraph draws heavily on conversations in July 2008 with Celeste Lee, a New York-based fragrance consultant.

82. "Perfumes," *US Industrial Outlook for 1969*, p. 185.

83. Mann, *Cosmetics Industry*. This source only gives retail figures for France, which suggests that hair products were over 30 per cent of the total market.

84. Allen, *Selling*, p. 150.

85. "Beverly Hills Business: Profile of Paula Kent Meehan," *Beverly Hills Courier*, December 24, 2004; Allen, *Selling*, pp. 146–7.

86. Frost and Sullivan, *Cosmetics and Toiletries*, p. 59.

87. Davis Dyer, Frederick Dalzell, and Rowena Olegario, *Rising Tide* (Boston, Mass.: Harvard Business School Press, 2004), pp. 93–4, 111, 261–3.

88. P & G, *50 Colorful Years: The Clairol Story* (1982).

89. P & G, *50 Colorful Years*.

90. Frost and Sullivan, *The Hygiene and Grooming Aids Market* (New York, January 1974).

91. Geoffrey Jones, "Blonde and Blue-eyed? Globalizing Beauty, c.1945–c.1980," *Economic History Review* 61 (2008), p. 134.

92. F. V. Wells, "Shampoos: The European Market," *Soap/Cosmetics/Chemical Specialities*, October 1976.

93. Frost and Sullivan, *Marketing Strategies*.

94. <www.goldwellusa.com>, accessed February 23, 2009.

95. Henkel Archives (hereafter HA), D440 Schwarzkopf Dokumentations Forschungsgeschichte, "Schwarzkopf: Chronologie—Schwarzkopf Heute (in Stichworten)," September 1976.

96. HA, D440, "Aktennotiz, Betrifft: Firma Hans Schwarzkopf," Steeger to Kobold, Hellwig, Mueller, Werdelmann, Siehler, Ludwig and Jacobi, November 10, 1967.

97. HA, D440, "Hans Schwarzkopf: A Schwarzkopf Chronology," 1988.

98. HA, D440, Schwarzkopf-Firmengeschichte, n.d. In 1938, Schwarzkopf launched a cosmetics and skin care line called Onalka.

99. Hoechst Annual Reports, 1969, p. 58; HA, D440, "Schwarzkopf: Chronology."

100. Hoechst Annual Reports, 1969 and 1970.

101. Wella Corporate Archive (hereafter WA), company publication entitled "Wella International," n.d. (1965?); "Wella International," n.d. (1972?); Wella AG, *Wella History. Wella AG's History from 1880 until Today* (Darmstadt: Wella AG, 2001), pp. 13–29.

102. Dalle, *L'aventure*, pp. 41–59.

103. Dalle, *L'aventure*, p. 90.

104. Dalle, *L'aventure*, p. 27. L'Oréal applied for 600 patents in France and abroad between 1948 and 1962, by which time it was employing 200 people in its laboratories: CL, DEEF 74156/1, "L'Oréal" (Paris: L'Oréal, 1963).

105. CL, DEEF 74156/1, "L'Oréal."

106. Dalle, *L'aventure*, pp. 111–14.

107. Dalle, *L'aventure*, pp. 98–102.

108. By the 1970s L'Oréal controlled three-quarters of the colorant market, over one-half of the French hairspray market, and one-half of the shampoo market.

109. As a result, the total sales of the entire group—estimated at 750 million francs ($150 million) in 1964—were much greater than for L'Oréal SA: Unilever Archives Rotterdam (hereafter UAR), Memo on Lolo, October 1, 1964, AHK 1798.

110. Jacqueline Demornex, *Lancôme, Paris* (Paris: Éditions Assouline, 2000), pp. 14–18; Jean Laudereau, "Mémoire de L'Oréal 1907–1992," unpubl. MS, pp. 269–74.

111. Dalle, *L'aventure*, pp. 135–40; Laudereau, "Mémoire," p. 278.

112. Jones, *Renewing*, p. 33; UAR, Private Note of Discussion, May 24, 1966, AHK 1748.

113. The structure was achieved by increasing the holding of Gesparal, the family trust, to 51 per cent and exchanging 49 per cent of Gesparal for 5 per cent of Nestlé.

114. Frost and Sullivan, *Cosmetics and Toiletries in Europe*, vol. 2 (New York, January 1985), pp. 346–7.

115. Interview with Lindsay Owen-Jones, January 22, 2009. On the pharmaceutical investments, see Caroline Plé, "L'Oréal, premier groupe français de cosmétique: Étude d'une société multinationale du mondial au local," *CERUR*, vol. 3 (1999); Florence Charue-Duboc, "Repositioning of European Chemical Groups and Changes in Innovation Management: The Case of the French Chemical Industry," in L. Galambos,

T. Hikino, and V. Zamagni (eds), *The Global Chemical Industry in the Age of the Petrochemical Revolution* (Cambridge: Cambridge University Press, 2007), pp. 276–7.

116. In 1960 around 20 per cent of the total output of the American beauty industry was accounted for by contract manufacturers. See *Industrial Outlook* 1960.

117. Mann, *Cosmetics Industry*.

118. *Industrial Outlook* 1978.

119. The American ethnic cosmetics market, which in this period primarily sold products specially formulated and marketed to African-Americans, was still only 2.3 per cent of the total market in 1977: Frost and Sullivan, *Ethnic Cosmetics and Toiletries Market* (New York, September 1988), p. 3. See also Susannah Walker, *Style and Status* (Lexington, Ky: University of Kentucky Press, 2007), ch. 3.

120. Quote from Dawn Perlmutter, "Miss America: Whose Ideal?," in Peg Zeglin Brand (ed.), *Beauty Matters* (Bloomington, Ind.: Indiana University Press, 2000).

121. By 1957, 30 per cent of corporate sales derived from products developed after 1949: Beiersdorf AG, *100 Jahre Beiersdorf, 1882–1982* (Hamburg: Beiersdorf, 1982), pp. 73–6.

122. Mann, *Cosmetics Industry*, pp. 88–92.

123. Arne Högberg, *Skönhetens entreprenör: Knut Wulff berättar om sitt liv* (Malmö: Corona Förlag, 2004), pp. 50–1.

124. Högberg, *Skönhetens entreprenör*, p. 88.

125. Högberg, *Skönhetens entreprenör*, pp. 65–8.

126. Telephone interview with Robert af Jochnick, April 20, 2007; "Oriflame is to Obtain a Listing on the London Stock Exchange Soon," *Financial Times*, April 28, 1982.

127. Telephone interview with Robert af Jochnick, April 20, 2007; "Oriflame is to Obtain," *Financial Times*. In 1982 sales were $6 million.

128. Emanuela Scarpellini, "Selling Fashion and Beauty: Avon International," paper presented to the joint annual meeting of the Business History Conference and European Business History Association, Milan, June 11–13, 2009.

129. CL, DEEF 79425/1, "L'industrie chimique italienne," August 24, 1970.

130. Richard Corson, *Fashions in Makeup* (London: Peter Owen, 2003 edn), pp. 530–1; Allen, *Selling*, p. 81.

131. Frost and Sullivan, *Cosmetics and Toiletries Markets in Europe* (New York, 1986); Frost and Sullivan, *Marketing*, p. 118.

132. Coty Archives (hereafter COTY), Rimmel & Coty History, Presentation, July 1, 2004—Dublin; Peter Reyder, "A History of Rimmel," commissioned by Robert Caplin (c.1982).

133. James Foreman-Peck, *Smith & Nephew in the Health Care Industry* (Aldershot: Edward Elgar, 1995), p. 136. Allen, *Selling*, pp. 79–81.

134. Allen, *Selling*, pp. 138–40.

135. See Chapter 9.

136. *Eien No Bi Wo Motomete—POLA Monogatari* (*A Quest for Everlasting Beauty: POLA Corporation's History of 50 Years*) (Tokyo: Pola, 1980; in Japanese), pp. 95–221; *Keshohin Kogyo 120 nen no ayumia* (*Course of 120 Years of the Japanese Cosmetic Industry*) (Tokyo: Japan Cosmetics Industry Association, 1995); *Club Cosmetics Hachijyunenshi* (*Club Cosmetics—80 Years of History*) (Osaka: Club Cosmetics, August 1983); *Hyakkaryoran—Club Cosmetics Hyakunenshi* (*Club Cosmetics, 100 Years of History—Profusion of Flowers*) (Osaka: Club Cosmetics, December 2003).

137. JWT, Samuel W. Meek papers, International Offices, Japan, Tokyo: Market Research, 1951–1962, "Japan's Face Cream and Face Powder Market," May 1958, Box 3.

138. *Keshohin Kogyo*, pp. 319–20.

139. *The Shiseido Story: A History of Shiseido 1872–1972* (Tokyo: Shiseido, 2003), pp. 51–92.

140. *The Shiseido Story*, p. 77.

141. *POLA Monogatari*, pp. 95–221.

142. Junichi Mizuo, *Keshohin no Burandi Shi* (*Brand History of Cosmetics-From Cultural Enlightenment to Global Marketing*) (Tokyo: Chuou Krosha, 1998), pp. 133–4.

143. *POLA Monogatari*, pp. 95–221.

144. Kosé Corporation, *Sozo to Chosen—Kosé 50 nen shi* (*Imagination and Challenge—Kosé 50 year history*) (Tokyo: Kosé Corporation, 1998), pp. 1–30.

145. *Kanebo Hyakunen shi* (*Kanebo Hundred-Year History*) (Osaka: Kanebo, 1988), pp. 287, 651–68.

146. Interview of Nakatsu by Masako Egawa, July 5, 2007; interview with Kazuhiko Toyama by Masako Egawa, June 26, 2007.

147. *Kanebo Hyakunen shi*, pp. 651–68, 820–36.

148. Mary Tradii, "The Lifestyle Company Kanebo," in Tina Grant (ed.), *International Directory of Company Histories* 53 (London: St. James Press, 2003), pp. 187–91.

149. Interview with Shu Uemura, Tokyo, March 23, 2007.

150. Interview with Shu Uemura, March 23, 2007.

151. See Chapter 7.

152. Interview with Carsten Fischer, Tokyo, March 20, 2007. Fischer became chief of Shiseido's international division in 2007.

153. AVON, Record Group II: Historical Files, Series 9: Library Resources, "Beauty and the 18–34 Market," *Redbook Beauty Study 1973*, Box 127.

154. Peter Vautin, "Men's Toiletries are Undersold," *Drug and Cosmetic Industry* (April 1962), pp. 409, 518.

155. Frost and Sullivan, *Cosmetics and Toiletries.*

156. During the 1960s, 7 per cent of the total German beauty market was represented by this category, which was far higher than in any other European country: Mann, *Cosmetics Industry.*

157. Jones, "Globalizing Beauty," p. 135.

158. P & G, Olay Worldwide Overview Presentation, September 16, 1980.

6

Global Ambitions Meet Local Markets

What is right for one country is not necessarily right for the next door neighbor.
Ogilvy, Benson & Mather presentation to Avon, 1975[1]

Brave new worlds

Despite their belief in the international appeal of their brands, the leading entrepreneurs in the beauty industry faced considerable obstacles to globalizing their business. These men and women were often cosmopolitan figures who frequently moved easily between countries and saw the profit to be made from the universal desire to be beautiful. They were equally at home in Paris, the capital of fashion, as in Hollywood, the imperial seat of illusion, but there were innumerable homes in between, each one with slightly different needs than the rest, and finding a way to sell beauty globally in a such a diverse world was never going to be easy.

As companies took their brands international, it became apparent that brand success at home did not necessarily translate into brand success abroad. Like all firms, beauty companies had seen their businesses, and their brands, disrupted by war and economic crises during the interwar years. Yet even in the best of times, companies found that while the human desire to be attractive might be universal, markets were local. As there was little multinational retailing or distribution, companies needed to access distribution systems and retail outlets country by country. The aspirations encouraged by Paris and Hollywood might be widely shared, but consumer preferences for specific scents, products, colors, names, and much else were shaped by deep-seated cultural and societal traditions. "Beauty is only skin deep," as the saying goes, but the implications are much deeper than that. Even though human beings are biologically the same inside, our skin-deep differences of skin tones and hair texture mean that many products need to be reformulated for different markets. There were also local incumbents in most markets and limitations on the availability of raw materials, whilst import and other restrictions prevented international firms from fully exploiting their advantages in terms of scope.

The new era following the end of World War II seemed set to shift once more the balance between the challenges and opportunities of globalization. The wider political and economic context continued to exert an overall constraint on the industry. The Communist world, for example, was simply closed. The Soviet Union possessed a large toiletries and cosmetics industry which was in the hands of state-owned companies that exported to the new Communist countries of Eastern Europe. In East Germany, the state-owned firm of Londa, formed out of the expropriated Wella properties, also built a substantial beauty business and exported to neighboring Communist markets.[2]

In China, also, foreign firms were expropriated after the Communists seized power in 1949. The manufacture of toiletries by state-owned companies grew considerably, but in a one-party state that saw luxury as bourgeois decadence the range of products was often limited to the basics of hygiene. The allocation of one firm to supply an entire region resulted in the creation of giant enterprises, such as Shanghai Toothpaste, whose production of toothpaste was almost as much as the entire Japanese industry and represented 40 per cent of China's market. In contrast, cosmetics production was suppressed, especially during the Cultural Revolution of the 1970s.[3]

In many other developing countries, tariffs and exchange controls made for unattractive markets, although Western toiletry companies with factories in these countries were often able to grow successful toiletries businesses. Newly independent India was heavily influenced by socialist ideology also, but although the government endorsed state planning and the diversion of resources to build capital-intensive industries, cosmetics were not banned outright as in China. Instead, Jawaharlal Nehru, India's first prime minister, requested that the Tata business group, one of India's largest postwar businesses, create an Indian-owned cosmetics business. The result was Lakmé, named after the French opera of the same name, which itself was perhaps ironically based on an Orientalist novel that treated foreign settings as exotic locales. In 1961 the French-born Simone N. Tata, who had married into the family, joined the board of the company, and became the chief executive three years later. As Lakmé blossomed into India's leading cosmetics enterprise, Simone Tata became known as the "Cosmetics Czarina of India."[4]

India, which had numerous rural poor alongside a smaller and richer urban population, offered only a modest market for cosmetics, and there were also cultural issues regarding consumption. It was considered unseemly for un-married women to use cosmetics regularly, especially outside major towns. The Indian distribution system was also extremely fragmented, consisting primarily of millions of small shops called *kiranas* that supplied toiletries, food, and medicine. Most consumers did not own cars and wanted to shop locally, and often needed to buy using the credit these firms offered.

In South Korea, also, a locally owned beauty industry emerged. Amore-Pacific was founded in 1945 by Suh Sung-whan and launched its first branded product, Melody Cream, in 1948.[5] It was already the largest company in the Korean market when, in 1963, it launched direct selling, which it came to dominate. It was a pioneer in mass-market advertising, launched Korea's first beauty magazine in 1958, and co-hosted the first Miss Korea pageant in 1976. High levels of protection, government policy excluding foreign firms from the market, a complex distribution system, and demanding and idiosyncratic health regulations virtually excluded foreign companies from the Korean market, providing the basis for a large domestic industry to grow.[6]

It was a different story in the main Western markets, where the barriers to trade and capital flows which had previously beset international commerce were progressively dismantled.[7] The growing ease of international travel and communication, the spread of television, the worldwide triumph of Dior's New Look, and the advent of international beauty pageants all suggested that further convergence in consumer preferences was under way. Many entrepreneurs recognized the new potential of international markets. Max Factor's strong global ambitions had been blocked by the war, but the firm was able to open a branch in Mexico City as early as 1944, and then resumed rapid international expansion once the war had finished.[8] Wella, which like all German firms had once more lost its international business, reopened its small manufacturing plant in the United States during the late 1940s.[9]

The industry's potential for global growth also attracted renewed attention from several of the multinational consumer product companies, especially Unilever. This company had miraculously survived the forced separation of its business into two halves during the Nazi occupation of Continental Europe during the war. The company, which was still the largest corporation in Europe, remained primarily a manufacturer of household soap and branded foodstuffs, but its toiletries business, which included the hugely successful Lux toilet soap, was quite large in its own right, although fragmented into many small affiliates in different countries. In 1944 it expanded its small toothpaste business by spending $10 million ($86 million in 2008 dollars) to buy Pepsodent, the owner of one of the leading toothpaste brands in the United States.

In 1950 a group of senior Unilever executives were asked to investigate the global prospects of the cosmetics and toiletries industry, which they were amazed to discover was already worth $1 billion. It also appeared to them to have great growth prospects, as there was "a direct relationship between the standard of living and the usage of toilet preparations." The commercial potential appeared even greater because the technology was not sophisticated, the fixed capital requirements were limited, and the industry was highly fragmented. The industry was, the executives concluded, a "Unilever business."[10]

The following decades witnessed a further surge in the globalization of the industry, yet it also became clear that the brave new world of globalization was destined to remain a challenging one even as markets soared. The beauty industry was not alone in this regard. Lopes has shown, in the case of alcoholic beverages for example, that markets remained highly fragmented, and that "global brands" with consistent positioning were very rare until the 1980s.[11]

Luxury in flux: balancing exclusivity and globalism

As the Western world returned to peace and prosperity, the international markets for luxury brands, whether Christian Dior fashion, Rolex watches, or French cognac, began to re-emerge from wartime austerity. The markets for expensive perfumes and cosmetics also revived. The export market was essential for the French houses, even more so after the destruction in Europe, and most were quick to rebuild their businesses as soon as markets returned to normal. By 1947 Guerlain alone was selling $800,000 worth of products in the United States, employing a local agent to get its products into the market.[12]

Perfume was the main category in which prices were sufficiently high, and the importance of country of origin in brands sufficiently great, for exporting to be a possibility. France exported one-fifth of its total production during the postwar decades, making it by far the largest exporter of beauty products in the world.[13] Perfume from France was virtually the only product category which the United States imported: total imports contributed less than 1 per cent of the total American market during the 1960s.[14]

The American market presented both the biggest opportunity and the biggest challenge for the sellers of luxury brands. The war had left it by far the largest and most affluent market for luxury brands in the world. "There is no future," Lancôme's Petitjean asserted bleakly, "without the United States." He launched a perfume into the market in 1946.[15] Yet the market contained many perils also. The importance of advertising in the United States, and the increasing cost of doing business in department stores, imposed huge costs on smaller firms. It acted as a constant temptation for the owners of brands to widen their distribution and lower their prices. As in the case of Coty in the interwar years, however, this potentially threatened the exclusivity and identity of their brands. The question was how to undertake the advertising and promotion necessary to sell in the American market, and elsewhere over time, whilst retaining the luster of an exclusive brand. During the late 1960 and early 1970s, for example, a strategy to widen the market for Chanel N°5, which included distributing it in drugstores in the United States, almost killed the brand, leaving it with only around 4 per cent of the American market by the mid-1970s.[16] That was not the kind of exclusivity that Chanel wanted.

Petitjean represented one extreme of the approaches taken to these challenges. In pursuit of international markets, he moved rapidly to establish distribution companies in other European countries, and later elsewhere, and to build awareness of his brand after the end of the war. Already during the war he had founded a school to train a select group of young women in both the scientific and artistic aspects of the beauty business. They were trained in anatomy and physiology, product technology and composition, skin massage and theatrical make-up, as well as sales technique and commercial strategy. The mission of these "ambassadrices," as they were called, was to take Lancôme "to the entire world."[17]

The Lancôme women staffed beauty institutes that the company created in major capitals and cities outside France. They combined the roles of celebrity spokespersons for the brand with more business-oriented skills, including securing local import agents and training local personnel. By 1955, the Lancôme brand was sold in 98 countries via 33 agents and nine fully controlled

6.1 Armand Petitjean, founder of Lancôme, appears here with his cadre of ambassadrices, the female spokespersons trained at the school he founded in 1942, 1950s.

© Archives patrimoine Lancôme, 2009

subsidiaries.[18] By the end of the 1960s exports accounted for an estimated two-thirds of the brand's total sales of 110 million francs ($22 million).[19]

The commitment to globalization, however, was matched by an extreme emphasis on retaining both the French identity and the exclusivity of the Lancôme brand. As a result, Petitjean would not allow any production outside the country, nor any mass-market-style advertising.[20] Petitjean would countenance neither advertising his brands nor producing them outside France, a view which prompted his co-founder Guillaume d'Ornano to leave and form his own company, Orlane, in 1946. In the United States, Petitjean refused to sell anything but perfume, considering the competition from Elizabeth Arden and Max Factor in cosmetics and skin care too strong.[21] The lack of local production, a refusal to sell anything but perfume, and no advertising proved far from a winning formula in America. Distributed by Saks Fifth Avenue, and sold in a dozen other highly selective points of sale, the brand made little progress during the postwar years.[22] When Lancôme's American management defied Petitjean's strict policies for the brand by widening its accessibility, including selling make-up and skin care, the subsequent conflict led to their departure from the company.[23]

At the other extreme, the risks posed to a luxury brand by excessive accessibility were demonstrated by Wertheimer-owned Bourjois. It launched a show on American television for its Evening in Paris perfume as early as 1953, but it made the brand so accessible that demand fell away. By the early 1960s it had virtually disappeared from department stores in the States.[24]

Most strategies fell somewhere in between those of Lancôme and Bourjois. Firms mostly saw the need to retain premium prices. In 1954 Guerlain, Corday, Lenthéric, and several other firms were investigated by the US Department of Justice for keeping prices 400 per cent above those in Paris.[25] They advertised their brands, but predominantly in fashion magazines rather than on television. While the emphasis on exclusivity meant that the development of wider markets was left to American competitors, the strategy continued to give French firms an edge in the luxury perfume market over their more widely distributed American counterparts, who were perceived as lacking sufficient cachet.[26] Chanel was one of the few companies which launched itself into the world of television. By the late 1950s Chanel had begun advertising in that medium and these adverts became increasingly sophisticated as leading fashion photographers were hired. The elegant French actress Catherine Deneuve was persuaded to become the face of Chanel in the American market in 1968. Even then, Chanel spent less of its advertising budget on television than its American counterparts.[27]

Although the fortunes of individual brands fluctuated, and the development of new prestige American fragrances provided powerful new competitors, the United States remained a key market for luxury French perfume brands at least until the 1980s, when Asian markets rose in importance. The American market contributed over one-quarter of Guerlain's total revenues of $130 million during the early 1980s. By then, more than two-thirds of Guerlain's overall sales came from exports.[28]

In color cosmetics and skin care, it was also more difficult for expensive French brands to compete in the American market given the grip of local incumbents on the department stores. This was apparent after L'Oréal acquired Lancôme and, during the 1970s, sought to grow its business in categories other than perfumery. L'Oréal, which operated through Cosmair, a licensee which primarily sold hair care, was unable to break the stranglehold of the local incumbents, especially Estée Lauder, over the leading American department stores. Annual sales could not get beyond $250,000. L'Oréal Paris also made slow progress against the local incumbents, Revlon, Maybelline, and Cover Girl.[29]

A similar challenge was faced by Shiseido, which entered the American mainland in 1965 with an invitation to participate in a "Far East Festival" held at Macy's in New York to promote Japanese brands, including Shiseido. Shiseido displayed its recently created Zen perfume, which targeted foreign markets as well as Western women living in Japan. Zen sold well during the Macy's event, but because the Shiseido counter was relegated to a corner of the store, sales fell after the event was over, while its skin care and make-up products found few takers. An attempt to take the brand into more stores went on to tarnish its reputation. The task of rebuilding the brand's reputation in America only began after Shiseido was able to open a counter at the high-end Neiman Marcus store in Houston, Texas in 1982.[30]

In the case of Lancôme, it was not until the early 1980s that a new manager, Lindsay Owen-Jones, was able to finally convince Macy's to give Lancôme the same amount of space as Lauder. Owen-Jones was an unlikely manager for L'Oréal: as his name suggests, he was not French but British. He had joined the company in 1969, after studying French and German at Oxford and taking an MBA at INSEAD, where, he later recalled, he first heard of L'Oréal from someone who told him that one could get paid to watch girls undress for the Ambre Solaire advertisements.[31] After starting as a product manager for Elnett in France, he worked at subsidiaries in Belgium, Italy and, finally in the early 1980s, the United States.

Owen-Jones's strategy was to demonstrate to Macy's how the American market was changing. He was able to point out that the spread of European clothes and cars like BMW into affluent suburbs suggested that their customers were "ripe for some European sophistication" as represented by Lancôme. He made the case that the brand was the only one with the full-range attraction that could challenge Estée Lauder, and that Macy's volume would be much greater if the two brands fought it out on equal terms. Macy's accepted the argument. Owen-Jones, in full recognition that losses would initially be made, tripled the advertising budget and further raised awareness of the brand by hiring the actress and model Isabella Rossellini to endorse it. Between 1983 and 1988 Lancôme's sales in the American market grew annually by 30 per cent, and by 1988 US sales made up 35 per cent of the brand's global takings.[32]

As the luxury American brands pursued international markets, they also faced the challenge of access to foreign department stores. Although brands such as Elizabeth Arden and Helena Rubinstein had long been sold, newer brands needed to fight their way in. Brands that lacked consumer awareness needed to secure floor space in a good location, which usually meant displacing brands with whom department store buyers had pre-existing relationships. In some European countries, department stores did not even sell beauty products. In Germany, for example, expensive cosmetics were sold primarily through small perfumeries. As her company sought access to European markets, Estée Lauder had to go in person to negotiate with the department store buyers, just as she had done previously with American department stores.[33]

Estée Lauder rarely took no for an answer as she sought to break into exclusive stores. When the cosmetics buyer at Galeries Lafayette in Paris refused even to meet her to discuss her products, Lauder resorted to a tactic pioneered by François Coty many years previously. She became friendly with one of the saleswomen, and whilst showing her Youth Dew, she later recalled, "a good bit of the bath oil spilled in the floor. They said later that I did it on purpose. I'll never tell."[34] As shoppers began to ask the saleswomen where they could buy the product, the buyer relented, and within a few weeks Lauder opened her first counter at Galeries Lafayette. In Sweden, Knut Wulff's son recalled how his father came home from work one day in the 1960s and complained that "a crazy American lady is here giving away lipsticks for free!" To compete with Pierre Robert, Lauder personally visited Swedish department stores to give away a free lipstick with each purchase of one of her products.[35] It was only in 1981 that Estée Lauder got her products into a major German department store. This was the first time a prestige cosmetics range, from any country, had been sold in such a store.[36]

None of the leading American firms shared Petitjean's reluctance to manufacture locally. By the 1970s Lauder had four factories outside the United States to support her sales in Europe and Mexico. Revlon opened its first foreign factory, in Mexico, in 1948. When the company entered Germany in the early 1950s, it employed a licensing agreement with Henkel. By 1971 the firm's brands were manufactured in 12 countries and sold in 84, and one-third of its sales were made outside the United States.[37]

Both the difficulty of accessing distribution channels, and the importance of country of origin, made the acquisition of brands the most realistic strategy for firms which wanted to build a luxury business. However, such acquisitions were fraught with danger. The value of such brands frequently rested on the creativity of their founders or, if the brand had persisted longer, on a small group of people who controlled it. This was a fragile and intangible asset which could be lost if the brand passed into other hands. Brand value that depended on a carefully cultivated image of exclusivity was also very vulnerable if a new owner sought to expand sales.

The extent of these dangers was shown by the experiences of several large firms which bought luxury brands only to see their value disappear in front of their eyes. Unilever acquired an unenviable track record of destroying value in such acquisitions. Most of the luxury brands it acquired before World War I, such as Vinolia, were in time destroyed by strategies to mass-market them, which, as one manager later observed, served only to erode "their elegance."[38] Atkinson's and Pierre Robert, acquired in 1975, suffered similar fates.[39]

American companies seeking to buy French prestige brands eventually encountered a further problem. In 1960 Revlon acquired Les Parfums Pierre Balmain, and in the following year Max Factor acquired Corday. In 1962 the now 92-year-old Félicie Vanpouille sold Parfums Caron to Jean-Paul Elkann, a banker, who took it public in 1964, and in 1966 it was acquired by American investors.[40] In 1969 Morton-Norwich acquired Orlane, which sold cosmetics and toiletries as well as perfumery. By then, one estimate was that only four of the 15 largest French perfume companies remained French-owned.[41] This spate of acquisitions provoked a reaction. France deemed beauty a national concern and moved to protect it from foreign, or rather American, values. In 1970 Helena Rubinstein's proposed acquisition of 80 per cent of the equity of Parfums Rochas was blocked by the government, and a few months later the French pharmaceutical company Roussel-Uclaf acquired it. Thereafter, attempted foreign acquisitions of French perfumery firms were regularly blocked.[42] The major exception was Nestlé's large investment in L'Oréal. During the negotiations involving the government, strict assurances had to be given that the businesses would remain autonomous from one another, while it was stressed that Nestlé's large global presence would facilitate the rapid international expansion of L'Oréal.[43]

Meanwhile a new distribution channel appeared. Critical to the further expansion of the luxury market, and indeed a crucial development for all luxury industries, was the emergence of "duty-free," or travel retail. The first duty-free shop opened at Shannon Airport in Ireland in 1946. These shops offered a diversion to trans-Atlantic passengers who were stranded at the airport while their planes made refueling stops. The first duty-free counter at London's Heathrow Airport appeared in 1959. The democratization of air travel drove the expansion of these new retail facilities as increasing numbers of travelers passed through airports.

The concept of duty-free shopping was further expanded when two American entrepreneurs created Duty-Free Shops (DFS) in Hong Kong in 1960. Duty-Free Shops secured the exclusive concession for duty-free sales in Hawaii in the early 1960s. Positioned to focus on the emerging Japanese traveler, who was not only beginning to become affluent but also belonged to a society where gift-giving was the norm rather than a seasonal exception, this move created a business breakthrough for DFS. The emergence of new groups of consumers from specific regions became a key driver of the travel retail market for beauty products. The number of Japanese international travelers doubled in the decade after Tokyo's Narita Airport opened in 1974, and by the 1980s the affluent consumers of Japan's "bubble economy" had become massive consumers of luxury products, including beauty. They were joined by the affluent consumers and travelers from the oil-rich Arab Gulf.

Travel retail provided an important means to grow the market for luxury fragrances and cosmetics because it exposed many new potential customers, often male international business travelers, to brands for the first time, and at prices without tax. Overcoming consumers' reluctance to buy international, rather than local, beauty products became easier as consumers themselves became more international. One estimate is that by 1982 one-fifth of total French fragrance exports were from sales in duty-free shops and on board airplanes. The global size of the duty-free market, of which the beauty industry represented around one-quarter, was nearly $7 billion in 1985, and $13.5 billion four years later.[44] The top sales locations, London Heathrow and Honolulu airports, symbolized the importance of European and Asian, especially Japanese, travelers in the market, with Americans remaining decidedly less enthusiastic about making such purchases when they traveled internationally.[45]

The huge American market, as well as the growth of travel retail, provided major opportunities for luxury brands. But their globalization was no easy matter. The American market was expensive, and unforgiving. Everywhere companies faced the challenge of accessing distribution channels. There was also the tension between expanding markets and remaining exclusive. When the goal is to seem exclusive, Estée Lauder is right: less is usually more.

The mass market

During the postwar decades some sellers of mass-market toiletries, hair care, and cosmetics made a renewed drive to take their brands into international markets. Typically, a combination of import duties, currency restrictions, and the need for some local adaptations in formulation and packaging encouraged firms to manufacture locally. It was the norm rather than the exception for firms in the mass market to manufacture locally in foreign markets once sales rose to a certain volume. The toiletry and other consumer products companies such as Colgate-Palmolive, Unilever, and Bristol-Myers, in particular, developed widespread foreign manufacturing. Frequently they could manufacture small quantities of personal care products in the context of larger businesses in household soap. As many developing countries were decolonized, they often imposed high tariffs, enabling the large Western firms which built factories inside those markets to capture strong market positions with limited competition.[46]

As in the luxury sector, access to distribution channels was key. Distribution channels continued to differ widely between countries, but they were also in transition. The broad trend was for mass-market toiletries and shampoo products to move from pharmacies and small shops into supermarkets and chain stores, but this proceeded at very different rates in different countries.[47] In the United States supermarkets steadily gained in importance at the expense of drugstores. By 1972 supermarkets accounted for one-third of total beauty sales.[48] Government regulations affected distribution channels. In most of Europe the independence of pharmacies was protected by laws designed to prevent multiple retailing. In France, for example, only pharmacies could sell treatment or medicated shampoos—around one-quarter of the shampoo market.[49]

In Europe, the distribution channels of Italy and Britain were at opposite extremes. In Italy, there was a high level of fragmentation. The majority of outlets, most of which were individually owned, were small perfumeries, hairdressing salons, pharmacies, and grocery stores. Britain had few perfumery shops, but supermarkets progressively increased in importance. While pharmacies in Italy and other European markets were mainly individual units, in Britain the large Boots chain, which had a shop in almost every town in that country, accounted for one-third of total retail sales of beauty products during the 1970s. In Germany, specialist stores known as Drogerien accounted for 35 per cent of the market, primarily selling cheaper brands, although the supermarkets' share began to increase from the 1960s on. Sweden was different again, with many cosmetics and toiletries sold through the drugstores known as Apoteket, which were nationalized in 1970.[50]

The marketing of brands was also complicated by major differences in the availability and regulation of television advertising. A firm like Alberto-Culver, which had driven its rapid domestic growth almost entirely by using this medium, was obliged to adapt as it expanded abroad from the early 1960s. "Wherever possible," one executive noted, "we schedule television. But in some countries we must order it a year in advance. In others, where commercial TV is not available—Greece, Turkey, Scandinavia, for example—we must use cinema. And in still others—West Germany and England—we schedule print advertising to reinforce TV."[51] In some developing countries, companies had no choice but to use other mediums to reach large numbers of customers. In India, Unilever and Colgate-Palmolive needed to advertise their toiletries in cinemas, which reached millions of consumers, rather than on television.

The broadest level of globalization remained in toiletry brands. Toiletries were the only category other than perfume in which foreign companies were able to hold a significant share of the American market. Toiletries were also the main category sold by Western companies in developing countries. By the 1950s Colgate-Palmolive's Palmolive and Unilever's Lux toilet soaps were sold in numerous countries. Toothpaste was also heavily globalized. Colgate toothpaste was sold in many countries. Unilever also took the American brands it acquired to Europe first and then elsewhere, including Pepsodent and later Stripe, the rights to which it acquired in 1958. Colgate-Palmolive and Unilever held between them large shares of dental markets across the world.[52] In some markets these companies also fought Beecham and its Macleans brand, which briefly captured 8 per cent of the American market during the 1960s, initially by encouraging sampling of the toothpaste by giving a tube away free with its Brylcreem hairdressing product.[53]

As these companies took their brands into foreign markets, they diffused consumption habits. As incomes rose and distribution channels matured, companies would introduce more expensive products. Toothpaste would follow toilet soap. Shampoo would follow toothpaste. At some stage a market for cheaper brands of cosmetics would develop. The relationship between income levels and the type of consumer product which could be sold was understood, providing companies with a rough and ready guide to when a market might be ready for the introduction of a particular category and brand.[54]

Individual firms sometimes exercised a formative influence on markets at their early stages. In male toiletries, for example, J. B. Williams took its shaving cream and Aqua Velva after-shave lotion around the world. Its sales beyond North America increased from less than $300,000 in 1941 to $3.5 million in 1956, or one-third of the total, and its brands were sold in 73 countries by then, typically by contracting production to local manufacturers.[55] Colgate-Palmolive virtually created the toothpaste market in many developing countries in Asia: it held well over four-fifths of both the Thai and Philippines markets at the end of the 1950s.[56] A number of companies were instrumental in diffusing the use of deodorants, which had been confined primarily to the United States before World War II.[57] Bristol-Myers' Mum was rapidly globalized after its launch in 1952. Both Gillette's Right Guard aerosol deodorant, launched in 1960, and Unilever's Rexona underarm deodorant, launched in 1965, were taken around the world.[58]

Although levels of globalization in toiletries were substantial, the limitations were also striking. As in other categories, although some brands were taken international, markets stayed highly differentiated. The practice of using deodorants, for example, was much slower to spread in Europe than in the United States. There was particular reluctance to use deodorants (and soap) in France, which was only partially overcome after L'Oréal launched its own product, Printil, in 1964. The company was careful to avoid marketing that used American-style threats of broken relationships resulting from bad body odor, opting instead to emphasize the feeling of well-being in one's own skin.[59]

For even the most internationalized company, only some brands were thought capable of being globalized. While Lux was a global giant, Unilever's strategies with other brands reflected a persistent belief in the dissimilarities rather than the similarities among markets. Like all consumer products companies, Unilever understood that markets differed, but the belief in local autonomy and decentralized decision-making became a core value within the company. As a result, although brands and knowledge were certainly transferred between affiliates, the process often moved slowly and rested more on personal connections within the firm than on centralized direction.[60]

The case of the Dove brand provides one example. In 1957 Unilever launched the Dove synthetic soap bar in the United States, and sold it at over twice the price of Lux. This product was marketed as a luxuriously feminine cleansing cream which was much kinder to the skin than other soaps were. Its distinctive white color helped make it a household name in the United States, although a failed brand extension into dishwashing liquid during the mid-1960s helped tarnish the brand for a couple of decades. Unilever resolutely declined to transfer Dove toilet soap to other markets, as it became folklore within the firm that consumers elsewhere would not pay a premium price for a toilet soap. As a result, it was sold only in the United States until the late 1980s.[61]

Meanwhile, despite the belief by some managers that beauty was a "Unilever business," the company missed successive opportunities to acquire firms that might have taken it into categories beyond toiletries. The decision not to invest in L'Oréal in 1964 was followed by further missed opportunities, including the failure of a poorly prepared hostile takeover bid four years later for the pharmaceutical company Smith & Nephew, the owner of the British rights to the Nivea brand.[62]

Unilever spent the 1970s on a half-hearted search for an American cosmetics company to buy, but dismissed all the potential targets as too expensive, too closely held and thus unavailable, or problematic because of perceived poor ethical standards. This inaction reflected, in part, major organizational failings within the company. Its major affiliate in the United States was poorly managed, with declining market share and profitability in its primary business of laundry soap. Meanwhile the European parent allowed this situation to persist throughout the 1970s due to a combination of the firm's strong belief in local autonomy and an exaggerated fear of the antitrust implications if it intervened in the management of its American business.[63]

Meanwhile, the largest American consumer products company remained cautious about international markets. During the 1950s P & G stayed heavily focused both on the North American market and on laundry soap and synthetic detergents, where it had secured a worldwide technological lead in the late 1940s. P & G's Camay toilet soap brand was a success in North America, and was sold in parts of Europe, Latin America, and the

Philippines, but not as widely as Palmolive and Lux. When P & G expanded its overall business into Continental Europe during the 1950s, this was driven by detergents and, from the 1960s, Pampers diapers. While Pampers was sold in more than 70 countries by 1980, Head and Shoulders shampoo and Crest toothpaste were only sold in half a dozen countries outside the United States.[64]

There were a number of reasons why P & G held back from international-izing its toiletry brands at a faster rate in this period. In general, the company, based in the Midwestern city of Cincinnati, was more focused on its large-volume business in its domestic market than excited about global markets. As the company tried to expand its international business after the war, it was handicapped because, as one manager later recalled, "Americans were very hard to persuade to go overseas... because of this shadow over people out of the mainline domestic business until the 1960s—they were afraid they would lose their place in line in the US organization."[65]

As a company which—in contrast to Unilever—preferred to centralize decision-making, P & G was especially reluctant to invest in any developing country where political instability or high inflation might disrupt standardized routines. The fear of high inflation rates kept the company out of Brazil, for instance, until 1988.[66] As P & G took its business to Western Europe and later elsewhere, detergents and diapers were highly capital-intensive businesses which left few resources for managers to devote to small volumes of toilet soap.

There was also a rapid internationalization of shampoo and other hair care brands, although here first-mover advantages proved weaker, and regional rather than global strategies prevailed over time. Helene Curtis and Colgate-Palmolive, whose shampoos included Halo and Lustre Crème, took the lead during the 1950s.[67] Helene Curtis products were manufactured under license and sold in 25 countries by the mid-1950s, and ten years later it had licensed manufacturing in 81 countries. Helene Curtis virtually created the market for shampoo in many developing countries. It was able to respond to rising tariffs by subcontracting production. In Thailand, where it licensed manufacturing of its brand to a local firm in 1960, it held over half of the market for the next 20 years.[68]

The global shampoo market, however, was subject to the same level of disruption caused by fashion shifts and new entrants as domestic markets. Helene Curtis's use of agency agreements to gain rapid access to markets limited its growth potential, as its brand was usually only one of many made and sold by subcontracted firms.[69] In Thailand, for example, the brand's position was eroded over time at the cheaper end by local competitors who developed markets in rural areas beyond the capital city by devices such as giving away free samples, and at the higher end by mass-market toiletry companies. In the world as a whole, the mass-market brands of L'Oréal and the large toiletry companies, such as Unilever's Sunsilk, a hugely successful shampoo launched in 1954, undermined Helene Curtis's early lead. These firms had captured substantial shares of the overall European and Latin American markets by the 1970s.[70]

In Southeast and East Asia, Japanese toiletry companies helped overturn Helene Curtis's early start. Both Kao and Lion began international expansion during the late 1950s. Given that Communist China was wholly blocked to them, both focused on the growing Southeast Asia market, using Thailand as a regional hub. In 1957 Kao began exporting Kao Feather Shampoo, a brand launched with enormous success two years previously in Japan, to Thailand, Singapore, and Hong Kong. In Thailand, Kao first exported intermediary products manufactured by a local firm, and then opened its own factory in 1964.[71] By the 1980s it had replaced Helene Curtis as the market leader, although elsewhere in the region the lack of distribution facilities posed many challenges. In Indonesia Kao discovered that most daily merchandise was sold in roadside stands, and it needed to employ special vehicles in return for cash to sell its products.[72] Lion Dentrifice pursued a similar strategy for its shampoo and toothpaste brands.[73]

In Europe, L'Oréal and the German hair companies were powerful local incumbents who soon overshadowed Helene Curtis's technological and marketing capabilities. By the early 1960s L'Oréal's hair care brands were available in 60 countries, and it was manufacturing either by itself or under contract in about half of them, although two-thirds of its revenues were still being generated in France. Typically, the company entered new markets through salons, which enabled it to establish its credentials as hair care specialists, as well as to gain knowledge of the local market. It would then introduce its retail brands through separate channels, normally using heavy discounts and heavy promotional spending directed at retailers. The company would use different sales forces for each distribution channel, and sometimes for each product category, in each country.

L'Oréal's first international success after François Dalle replaced Schueller at the helm was Elnett hair spray. As the brand was rolled out, Dalle developed an international marketing strategy based on his "theory of the foothold." A brand such as Elnett was used to make a "breach" in a foreign market, and to develop a "foothold." The next stage was to "bundle" or put together a package of brands which could be sold in that market. Dalle insisted that launches be made without delay, and that sales forces become imbued with the ethos of "conquerors" who are able to convey their enthusiasm to their salon and retail customers. Dalle was also convinced that markets were won by emphasizing quality rather than price, and indeed opted to charge premium prices when building markets. In Germany, for example, Elnett was sold at twice the price of competitor products, a tactic, he later observed, which worked to "wear the competition out while we made all the money." In the face of skepticism by the managers of local affiliates, Dalle was able to use Elnett to substantiate his argument that when a brand succeeded where first launched in an international market, so achieving "the foothold," it would go on to succeed also in every other country where it was launched, as long as the strategy of imitating the original success was faithfully followed.[74]

The theory was primarily tested in Europe, where the bulk of the company's sales continued to be made. In the United States, the company had no direct business at all, and instead acted through an agent. Cosmair had been formed in 1954 to act as an exclusive licensee to distribute L'Oréal's hair products to beauty salons. It was initially owned by Schueller and another French entrepreneur, Jacques Corrèze, who had joined L'Oréal in 1950.[75] This arrangement was predicated on the assumption that the earnings flow from the American business were likely to be less predictable than that from L'Oréal's business in the rest of the world, as the US market required big investments to launch new brands, while it was so big that it might in time become even larger than its parent. It was therefore decided to keep Cosmair separate from the rest of the business.[76]

Cosmair struggled to grow its business. The American distribution system, where local middlemen rather than national distributors delivered to salons, was a major challenge. The company had few relationships with such middlemen, while hair salons and their clientele were unfamiliar with the L'Oréal brand. In contrast to most European countries, therefore, its sales representatives had no access to the salons. By 1963, Cosmair had $6 million in US sales, but it remained a minnow in the market. In 1974 Nestlé joined the family shareholders and Corrèze. The strong support of Nestlé helped grow the firm. It expanded into the consumer hair care market, launching a major new colorant line called Préférence with what would become an iconic slogan, "Because you're worth it." However, at the time, the slogan was used only once and then rapidly forgotten, and never used at all outside the United States. In 1978 L'Oréal still held only 18 per cent of the American colorant market, compared to Clairol's 62 per cent.[77]

L'Oréal also struggled to make an impact in Japan against the strong local incumbents. In 1963 Dalle entered an alliance with Kosé to sell L'Oréal products to the professional hair care market, but the company's hair colorants made little progress in a country whose consumers were at that time primarily interested in covering grey hair rather than using multiple shades and colors. The Lancôme brand was introduced in 1978, but market share and profitability proved elusive. Kosé's branding and marketing capabilities, on the other hand, were greatly strengthened by what became a long-term relationship with the French company.[78]

The German hair care companies also took their brands to other countries, primarily in Europe and sometimes in Latin America. Schwarzkopf's strategy, like L'Oréal's, of entering new countries through the salon business was useful as it did not require expensive advertising, which was important since the firm was capital-constrained, but it was also slow, because the company needed to build knowledge of its brands with salon owners one by one by offering training in the use of their products. As the brand became known, Schwarzkopf would also launch its shampoos and hairsprays through retail channels such as drug and department stores, although its prestige brands and hair coloring products remained exclusive to salons.

Schwarzkopf's modest capital resources meant that it often needed to sell through independent distributors and licensees, and it was only after Hoechst took an equity stake in 1969 that the company was able to speed up its strategy to take over the manufacturing facilities of its local distributors. By 1976 it had nine fully owned subsidiaries, eight in Europe and one in Australia, plus a further two minority holdings in firms in Austria and South Africa. Hoechst's foreign affiliates also became licensed manufacturers for Schwarzkopf products.[79] Schwarzkopf was no more successful than other European companies at the time in breaking into the American market on a large scale.[80]

Wella pursued a more aggressive internationalization strategy, with a primary focus on Europe and the Americas. In Latin America, fully- or majority-owned production firms were started in Chile in 1952, Brazil in 1954, Argentina in 1957, and Mexico in 1961, and a holding company was set up in Panama in 1955.[81] By the late 1960s, the company had manufacturing plants in 46 countries, sold in far more, and sales in international markets was approaching three-quarters of its total, although it, like its European competitors, also made little progress in the United States.[82]

The postwar diffusion of hair care brands, therefore, was striking, but limited. The American and Japanese markets remained dominated by local incumbents. In Europe, also, local incumbents were dominant. L'Oréal dominated the French hair care market. Wella, Schwarzkopf, and Henkel together held over one-half of the German retail hair market. L'Oréal and others were usually able to develop shares only in some categories in foreign countries. In Germany, for example, L'Oréal held a bare 7 per cent of the hairspray market, and 3 per cent of shampoos, during the 1960s.[83]

Hair care provided the primary category in which Western firms were able to secure small toeholds in Communist Eastern Europe. After 1974 L'Oréal, for example, sold concentrates to state-owned manufacturers for its products to the Soviet Union, where they were made locally.[84] However, the leading example originated with the German firm of Olivin, which made Bac deodorant and other toiletries.[85] It signed numerous licensing agreements with foreign firms from the 1950s, beginning with Turkey in 1954, and in 1967 with Communist Yugoslavia. Agreements with Czechoslovakia and Hungary followed.[86] Olivin was sold to Britain's Reckitt & Colman in 1972, which sold it to Schwarzkopf three years later. The venture's presence in Hungary, where the local Communist regime became more tolerant of the market than elsewhere, grew particularly strong. Schwarzkopf was able to build a market for its hair brands, and in 1985 it became the first Western firm to acquire the majority of its joint venture with a local state-owned firm.

In both mass skin care and color cosmetics, a few internationalized brands intermingled with many more local or regional ones. In skin care, the familiar names continued to expand their geographical reach. By the mid-1950s, Pond's Cream was sold in nearly 120 countries, supplied from two plants in the US and four abroad.[87] The merger with Chesebrough further widened its global reach, as did acquisitions of other firms. Cutex nail polish, for example, was sold in 109 countries, and manufactured in nearly 40, when it was acquired in 1959.[88] Other major US skin cream brands had less international exposure.

Noxzema Skin Cream, dating from 1917, was a major brand in America, but before 1956 its international sales were confined to Canada and limited exports outside North America, directed by a single manager in Baltimore. As late as 1977 less than one-tenth of Noxell's total sales, including Cover Girl cosmetics, were made outside North America.[89]

Pond's major European competitor, Nivea, was once more devastated by the sequestration of Beiersdorf's trademarks in foreign countries. Beiersdorf took up the strategy of introducing a single one of its new, postwar beauty brands, such as the hand cream Atrix, into foreign countries as a way towards rebuilding its presence in beauty markets even without Nivea, often using its Tesa adhesive business as a platform.[90] It was not until the 1970s that Beiersdorf more or less restored its international business and regained many of its lost trademarks, as we will see in greater depth later on. By then it had 18 foreign subsidiaries as well as 22 licensing agreements to produce its brands in local markets, including a joint venture that it made with Kao to take its brands into the Japanese market.[91]

There were also newcomers to the international market in mass skin care. Among the most unusual cases, and in some respects a forerunner of more complex patterns of globalization, was the international spread of the Oil of Olay brand. This brand had originated in the wartime research of a chemist in South Africa, who developed a topical skin treatment to prevent dehydration of burn wounds on pilots. Afterwards he and his wife developed in their home a new type of skin cream designed to moisturize more effectively than the greasy skin creams on the market, and conceptualized as a product that was more feminine than most existing preparations. Joined by an advertising agency account executive, they launched the product as Oil of Olay, initially sold through door-to-door selling and by word of mouth. Their Adams National Company, a modestly sized firm, took the brand international, beginning with Australia in 1957, and reaching five other countries, including Britain, Germany, and the United States, by the end of the 1960s.

In Australia, the local management of a larger American company saw and was intrigued by the brand. Richardson-Merrell, which purchased Adams National in 1970, was itself an unusual company whose predecessors included the makers of Vicks Vapor Rub. The company had diversified into the beauty industry in the early 1940s, buying Prince Matchabelli among other brands, and sold them on again by the late 1950s. Richardson-Merrell now staged a spectacular entry into mass skin care. Oil of Olay was positioned in the medium-price mass market in the United States, cheaper than an Estée Lauder cream but dearer than a Noxell mass cream. Costs were kept low by manufacturing in the US Caribbean territory of Puerto Rico, where the firm received large tax breaks. During the 1970s US sales rose from $3 million to $60 million, while total Olay sales rose from $7 million to $117 million, as the brand was also taken to ten new countries including France, Italy, Brazil, and Mexico.[92]

In color cosmetics also, there were a number of highly international brands. By 1958 Max Factor was sold in 106 countries; by 1971 it was manufactured in eight foreign countries and sold in 143, while international sales had reached 54 per cent of its total.[93] However, two of the largest American mass-market color cosmetics brands stayed focused on their domestic business. Despite the domestic success of the Cover Girl make-up, Noxell was slow to globalize the brand, relying on exporting or licensing agreements to sell modest amounts abroad. The first foreign sales branch was only opened in Britain in 1964, and it took a further 14 years before local manufacture began in that market.[94] Maybelline, which accounted for one-third of the American eye cosmetics market, especially after the launch of the successful Great Lash mascara in 1971, also had only a small international business.[95]

In Europe there were many firms with strong local franchises but with more limited international businesses, largely confined to Europe. In France, Gemey and Bourjois were leaders in color cosmetics, but their business elsewhere was mostly elsewhere in Europe. This was true of the domestically successful mass brands in Britain such as Rimmel, which, although sold in 90 countries by the early 1980s, held a large share only in its domestic market.[96] The giant US conglomerate ITT, which acquired Rimmel in 1971, tried to take the brand to America, only to withdraw it again within two years.[97] There was little interest in any British color cosmetics brand in the American market. Yardley's attempt to exploit the "swinging London" image in the American market during the 1960s by building a color cosmetics business resulted in heavy losses.[98]

Like their toiletry counterparts, the Japanese skin care and cosmetics brands also became primarily focused on the regional market. In 1957 Shiseido revived its global ambitions when it established an affiliate in Taiwan. In the following year it started local production and began selling vanishing cream and pomade. However, as cosmetics were much more expensive than shampoo and toothpaste, the more prestigious companies were initially more interested in developed markets until, as in the case of Shiseido, the challenges became apparent. Kosé's global expansion began in Hong Kong in 1962, initially using a combination of direct sales and retail, before focusing on Southeast Asian markets, including Singapore, where it was decided to position Kosé as a prestige brand sold in department stores.[99]

The postwar decades, then, saw a significant internationalization of mass brands, but one with distinct limitations. In countries lacking powerful incumbents, foreign brands became widely sold. In Britain the leading US cosmetics firms were household names. In 1959 Max Factor alone accounted for 40 per cent of total sales of face powders, lipstick, and foundation in independent British pharmacies. Revlon and Coty held a further 11 per cent and 8 per cent respectively.[100] Foreign brands, however, were not able to gain a significant share of the large American, French, and Japanese color cosmetics and skin care markets given the strength of the local incumbents. Avon, the largest foreign firm, held 5 per cent of the French cosmetics and toiletries sector at the end of the 1960s.[101] In Japan, Avon and Revlon, the two largest foreign companies, held less than 2 per cent of the cosmetics market.

Managing global brands

As firms sought to expand their business, they began to face the challenge of how to manage business and brands which were sold in many countries. Most firms were, by later standards, quite fragmented. The name L'Oréal was not even used in most of its foreign subsidiaries, for example. The company was named SAIPO in Italy, Golden in Britain, and Haarkosmetik und Parfümerie in Germany.[102] It was common for the same product to be given different brand names in different countries. Companies also marketed multiple brands using different brand names in different countries. It was the norm rather than the exception for brand positioning to vary between countries. Local managers frequently exaggerated the need for local adaptations, sometimes simply to defend their own turfs, but often also because their understanding of the market gave them a greater understanding of what would be successful in their own area.

Many of Unilever's international brands lacked consistent positioning or formulation during the postwar decades, although it had more success maintaining consistency across countries in several toiletry brands than in its much larger detergents and foods businesses. Unilever was able to maintain brand discipline over the Sunsilk shampoo brand, which was manufactured in nearly 30 countries by the early 1970s, and sold in many more, although not in the United States. Lux toilet soap, which was sold on five continents by 1960 and was the largest-selling toilet bar soap, was also marketed worldwide with a consistent brand positioning as the "soap of the stars."[103] In an unusual reversal, it was the highly centralized P & G that experienced more problems with the less widely sold Camay. The former head of their export division later observed how P & G during the postwar decades "kept going from right to left on Camay...I did not recognize the Camay in Australia or in Germany because they were different."[104]

Beiersdorf was one company whose fragmentation of its brands was forced upon it by exogenous events. The "ring firm" strategy had disastrous consequences in the aftermath of World War II, when some formerly trusted associates decided to run the businesses for their own profit employing Beiersdorf trademarks. The worst case was in the United States, where Carl Herzog's Duke Laboratories bought the trademarks and ran the Nivea business in that country until 1973. He opted to keep his sales steady at around $5 million, not using any advertising or mass-marketing approaches. Herzog transformed the Nivea brand into a specialty pharmaceutical product distributed primarily to dermatologists. Taking advantage of the gap left in the skin care market with the exit of the original Nivea cream from most mass retail locations, Johnson & Johnson's Neutrogena redesigned its packaging to resemble the classic blue Nivea jar.[105] Only when he had reached the age of 88, in 1973, did Herzog sell his trademarks back to Beiersdorf, for $4 million.[106]

Beiersdorf slowly bought back other local companies that had obtained the Nivea trademark. In 1952 it reacquired the trademark in the Netherlands, and in 1958 in Argentina and Brazil, but it took far longer in other markets, including France (1974) and Thailand (1977). The consequent fragmentation of the brand identity of Nivea took decades to repair. In Denmark, Beiersdorf's trademarks were expropriated and acquired by the former licensee. The new firm reached a new licensing agreement with Beiersdorf, as a means of accessing know-how, but pursued its own brand identity strategy for Nivea. It used models in explicitly sexual positions and employed highly stylized, orientalized settings featuring Egyptian furniture meant to convey "an Eastern routine of perfected beauty care." Neither brand image conformed to the athletic, tanned, and fresh Nivea woman at the center of the brand identity built by Beiersdorf. It was only in 1966, following the death of the local owner, that Beiersdorf was able to reacquire the Danish Nivea and other trademarks.[107]

When it was not possible to reacquire a former subsidiary or buy the company that had bought its trademarks, Beiersdorf sought to establish a good working relationship with such firms. In Britain, Smith & Nephew acquired the former "ring firm" which held the British and British Commonwealth rights to Nivea, in 1951. After failing in its attempts to buy back the brand, Beiersdorf reached an understanding with Smith & Nephew in 1958 to share information on the manufacture and distribution of Nivea worldwide.[108] However, the positioning of the brands later diverged considerably. While Beiersdorf continued to use the well-known blue Nivea tin in outdoor locations to advertise the product and link it to its use during outdoor activities in all seasons, during the 1970s Smith & Nephew placed the Nivea brand within its recently acquired Gala cosmetics business, which targeted as consumers young, modern women on a budget.[109]

By the 1970s Nivea had a claim to be amongst the world's largest brands of all-purpose skin creams. It had extended internationally the range of products available under the brand to include sunscreen and baby creams, soaps and moisturizers, making it amongst the largest brands in the beauty industry.[110] Yet the legacy of fragmentation persisted until the end of the century. Beiersdorf only recovered ownership of the Nivea brand in Britain and India in 1992, and in Poland five years later. Smith & Nephew continued to distribute the brand in Britain until 2000.[111]

Pond's was one of the mass-market firms which emphasized, perhaps more strongly than during the interwar years, the need to maintain consistency in branding and marketing between countries. The firm and its agency, J. Walter Thompson, strove to maintain their core marketing strategy—such as endorsements by high-society women—despite local pressures for alternative approaches from local managers in postwar Europe and elsewhere.[112] This approach was maintained when it launched new products such as Angel Face, a face powder created in 1946. It began selling the face powder in Latin America only three years later, and it was sold in 30 countries by 1961, using an almost identical advertising and brand image in each country. "We like

Chesebrough-Pond's to have a uniform image," an executive observed in 1961, "to look the same everywhere." It has been estimated that about 50 per cent of Angel Face's advertisements internationally used artwork and copy themes created by the J. Walter Thompson agency in the United States.[113]

In luxury brands, the challenge remained the tension between keeping brand identities consistent internationally and yet relevant to consumers in each market. The people who could afford to buy such brands frequently travelled internationally. They expected to see their favorite brands looking the same, being sold at similar price points, and with the same spokespeople in advertisements, in different countries. The growth of the travel retail channel made the need for such consistency even greater. Yet some degree of local adaptation was almost always required, if only to meet local regulatory requirements. As always, there was a strong temptation for local managers to try to boost their sales by seeking to adapt brand identities to what they perceived would work in their markets.

In mass cosmetics and toiletries, even in cases when brand positioning was consistent, such as Lux toilet soap, product formulation was typically adapted to local conditions. This was often required by government regulations and the cost and availability of raw materials, let alone local consumer preferences for scents, colors, and other features. Large Western companies, however, rarely reformulated for non-Caucasian skin and hair types, thus leaving the field open for others. African-American firms, for example, seized the chance to export to Africa and the African diaspora in the Caribbean and Latin America. In 1960 a "Hollywood Beauty Culture Center" was opened in Accra, Ghana. In 1962 the Miami-based Sunlight School of Beauty opened a center in Kingston, Jamaica. These firms found a niche by being able to claim relevance both from their African descent and from the aspirational benefits of being from the United States.[114]

As the era of colonialism wound down and non-Western nations grew in confidence, Western companies did begin to show an interest in ethnic differences in hair and skin. In West Africa, Unilever, Max Factor, and Pond's began experimenting with specially formulated make-up during the 1960s.[115] The same trend was evident in India. Unilever's affiliate Hindustan Lever, which was partly locally owned, and Colgate-Palmolive had manufactured global brands of toiletries and other consumer products locally for decades, and were the prime beneficiaries of the high levels of protection which kept other foreign firms out. Hindustan Lever had established its own research facilities in India from the 1950s, which developed alternative sources for raw materials to replace expensive imports, including new chemical processes to use local lemongrass to make perfume. During the 1970s Hindustan Lever began launching its own distinctly Indian shampoo and toothpaste brands as well as brands from Unilever's global portfolio, including Close-up toothpaste.[116]

In 1978 Hindustan Lever also launched one of its most successful beauty products, albeit one which would later arouse controversy. Fair & Lovely was a skin-lightening cream designed to appeal to a traditional regard for fairer skin in India. The origins of such preferences lay deep in Indian history, some tracing them back to the very origins of the caste system two and a half thousand years ago, when fair-skinned foreigners established a class system with the indigenous darker-skinned local population at the bottom. Hindu mythology depicted fair-skinned gods fighting darker-skinned devils. Much later, the era of British rule introduced a new set of rulers with lighter skins. The emphasis on fairness became extremely important in the highly developed Indian market for arranged marriages, where references to "fairness" regularly preceded references to a woman's educational level, while dowry valuations were calculated on the fairness or darkness of a woman's skin.

Hindustan Lever applied its scientific and branding capabilities to translate such cultural preferences into a highly successful brand, which became the best-selling skin care brand in India. Fair & Lovely was based on a patented formulation containing an active ingredient which controlled the dispersion of melanin in the skin. The brand's advertising promised greater fairness within six weeks of using the product, and from the beginning the brand emphasized the improved marriage prospects of fair-skinned women. Considerable use was made of endorsement by celebrities from the huge Indian cinema industry known as Bollywood, whose leading actors and actresses were overwhelmingly fair-skinned.[117]

Fair & Lovely thus typified many of the complexities of the international beauty business. On the one hand, it was made specifically for the Indian domestic market by a locally adapted unit of Unilever that also locally produced the firm's global brands. Like American products, it was pitched by movie stars, but at least they were homegrown. On the other hand, it reinforced colonial-era prejudice in favor of lighter skin. Yet this, too, drew on

6.2 Advertisement for Hindustan Lever's skin-lightening cream Fair & Lovely, 1989.

older, caste-based Indian traditions. Although Unilever may have been too decentralized for its own good at times in terms of overall brand management, it followed the right basic approach in India: cultivate deep local knowledge and tailor products and marketing to local needs, while also keeping global brands recognizable.

Direct selling

The growth of direct selling across borders was a new strategy after 1945, and one which proved a highly effective means of expanding sales of beauty products in developing countries. Avon, the world's largest direct-selling beauty company, took the lead in taking the strategy to other countries. The company, which before World War II operated outside the United States only in Canada, considered several options before going global, including expanding domestically through new channels such as supermarkets. In 1954 it opened in a Spanish-speaking market, the US territory of Puerto Rico. It then decided to expand internationally, and moved quickly. In 1958 a separate International Division, named Avon International, was established in Rye, New York, to manage the firm's global growth.

Avon opened for business in a succession of Latin American markets including Venezuela, Cuba, Mexico, and Brazil. Avon's decision to focus initially on Latin America reflected the competitive advantage held by direct sellers in such markets. On the one hand, distribution channels were weak. On the other hand, whilst average income levels restricted cosmetics sales to urban elites, they were willing consumers of aspirational brands. By 1960 Avon had secured strong market positions in many countries, including Venezuela, where it held 50 per cent of the cosmetics market, and it began local manufacturing in that year.[118] The major setback at this time came in Cuba, where a business opened in 1955 had grown so fast that a factory was opened a mere three years later. Avon's entire business was then nationalized after Fidel Castro took power in 1959.[119]

Avon's entry into new markets followed an established pattern. It began with acquainting representatives and customers with the Avon line. This was typically attractive to potential representatives, as it was new and exciting. Avon sought to provide representatives with the "best possible line of products at an attractive price" and thus an attractive earning opportunity. Products were transferred from the United States, but with local variation to suit markets, and fewer products were made available than in the American market. As markets began to become saturated—which Avon defined as coverage of one representative per 1,000 people—new products and packaging became important for giving representatives the means to open the way for reorders. The company would then implement selective product mixes and launch loss-leader strategies to create maximum pricing impact.[120]

This standard pattern was modified to take account of local circumstances. For example, when Avon sought to open in Mexico in 1958, local legislation required the company to equip a factory and recruit and train its staff before a single representative could be appointed. It also found that local knowledge of how to use or even buy cosmetics was weaker than in Puerto Rico and Venezuela, requiring a major educational effort. The sheer size and poor domestic transportation of Brazil, where Avon also opened in 1958, presented severe logistical challenges to making deliveries and receiving payments. The company responded by setting up its own carrier system. Brazil also obliged Avon to create a new accounting system in response to inflation rates, which by the early 1960s had reached 5 per cent a month.[121]

After gaining experience in Latin America, Avon entered Europe. It opened in Britain and Germany in 1959. These countries provided the macro-economic stability which a country like Brazil lacked, but they were also mature markets with numerous incumbents and well-developed distribution systems. It was initially unclear how either market would respond to direct selling. In both countries, there were cultural issues to be dealt with. In Britain, Avon blamed a slow start on a cultural feeling that "direct selling was akin to 'hawking' or being a 'fishmonger'." Avon also reported problems caused by "the very conservative, traditional reserve and attitude of the Englishman about having his wife go out and ring strange doorbells." In response to such challenges, Avon devoted considerable resources to promotional materials, training, and other tools to hire and motivate representatives. In Germany, where the company entered in 1959, this also had to include extensive translation of materials into German.[122] In 1966 Avon also entered Italy. It recruited 24,000 Avon ladies within three years, first in the northern cities, and soon covering the whole country.[123]

A key challenge for Avon in Europe, as elsewhere, was to recruit and retain representatives. This involved responding to many inter-country differences in the region. A survey of the motivation of Avon consultants, for example, established that earning money was the most important reason in all countries, although far more so in France than in Germany. However, while the representatives in Britain also ranked highly making friends, this was quite insignificant in Germany, France, and Italy. In Germany, working with beauty products was rated almost as highly as making money, while this was far less important than in France.[124]

Like other beauty companies, Avon struggled with the tension between local relevance and international branding. During the 1960s Avon's foreign subsidiaries began to assume increasing responsibility for advertising and merchandising, and sales materials increasingly began to reflect local perspectives on consumer needs and preferences. Merchandising proposals submitted by the subsidiaries to the head office at Avon International began to call for alterations to packaging as well as the development of entirely new products, which the local managers deemed necessary or appropriate in order to maximize penetration and overall growth in these markets.

Products intended for different markets were developed and merchandised within Avon using three different profiles. A "blue profile" indicated that a product had undergone "major modification in appearance from the US line," as when a cricket helmet was used instead of an American football as a decanter shape for a male fragrance in countries where cricket is a major sport. A "yellow profile" meant that a product had an exact or similar US counterpart, although minor modifications were common. And a "pink profile" was for products that were never planned for the United States, and were unique to the country and market for which they were intended.[125]

However, whilst seeking local relevance, Avon's management also sought uniformity in management customer service and packaging. It started by trying to standardize products sold in Europe, and creating a London-based marketing organization to oversee the whole region in 1972. Avon moved its entire export business from New York to Britain when it opened in that country. In the same year it began to centralize Latin American marketing in New York. "The domestic US marketing experience," a senior executive affirmed in 1973, "is considered the foundation for our policies, our techniques, and our success in all markets throughout the world."[126]

Avon's senior management retained its belief that consumers everywhere were basically the same in their need for social recognition, but during the 1970s this was balanced or qualified by explicit discussions of cultural differences among the European countries, and between Europe and the United States. The European product line showed a high degree of product specificity with multiple individual-country lines.[127]

By the 1970s international sales contributed nearly a third of Avon's total sales and a quarter of its profits. The company sold in 14 countries through over 400,000 representatives. It had secured one-third of the British fragrance market and one-fifth of the German and Italian, though less than one-tenth of the French.[128] In France the company encountered a strong dislike of direct selling, which was not helped by legislation which prohibited the presentation of the direct selling method on television.[129] It had built brand awareness in some countries even where it had no direct selling business, as in Malaysia, where it sponsored Miss Malaysia beauty pageants.[130]

The wide variation in Avon's profitability between countries was one indication of the challenges faced in trying to build an international direct selling business. In 1971 US gross margins were 63 per cent. By contrast, in Western Europe as a whole they were 21 per cent, rather higher in Germany (26) and lower in France (16). In Latin America they were 20 per cent, but ranged from 31 per cent in Mexico to 8.7 per cent in Brazil and negative in Argentina.[131]

Avon was by far the most globalized direct seller by this time, but several other companies expanded into neighboring countries. Jafra Cosmetics expanded from California to Mexico, where it built a strong presence, although the firm's purchase by Gillette in 1973, and the subsequent move of the head office to Boston, resulted in a loss of momentum.[132] Mary Kay's first international subsidiary, in Australia, came only in 1971, followed by Canada seven years later.[133]

Among the non-American direct sellers, Oriflame and Pola stood at the opposite extreme. The Swedish company went international from the start, though not listing its shares in Britain, where two-fifths of total sales were located, until 1982. In contrast, Pola proceeded with extreme caution. It looked first to Hong Kong, drawing on its experience in Taiwan before World War II. In 1958, it reached an agreement with a local company to sell Pola products through direct sales, and the following year a shop was opened. In 1961 Pola also went into business in Hawaii, which had both a large ethnic Japanese population and a long exposure to direct sales. A Los Angeles branch was soon opened, and in 1966 Pola also opened in Bangkok.[134] Even though the scale of its domestic business made the company the world's second-largest direct seller, its foreign businesses remained small due, as a later chief executive observed, to the way in which "top management thought," with a heavy emphasis on its domestic business.[135]

Direct selling emerged as an important diffuser of beauty products during these years. It had the ability to reach consumers far beyond those who frequented retail distribution channels, and it became a source of supplemental income to tens of thousands of women. Avon in particular had a major societal impact on Latin America and, later, other developing countries. It provided employment for numerous women, serving as an incubator of entrepreneurship, and it served as a model for the creation of local firms such as Brazil's Natura and Thailand's Mistine. Direct selling was so transformational in such contexts because it provided a bridge between the modern commercial beauty industry and the traditional worlds of local neighborhoods and societal structures. This proved both a powerful means to build markets and an important means of social change. Likewise the ideals which Avon sold, and the business methods involved in direct selling, diffused a powerful set of images of modernity for women in societies which were very different from those of the United States.[136]

Summing up

During the decades after the end of World War II, there was a renewed drive to globalize the beauty industry. The results were mixed. By the 1970s a number of brands, including Sunsilk, Pond's, Avon, and Max Factor, had become widely available. Toiletry companies and direct sellers built a market for mass-market toiletries, hair care, and cosmetics in many Latin American and other developing countries. As a result, the practice of using shampoo to wash hair was widely diffused by companies that made shampoo. The advent of travel retail also provided an entire new distribution channel for luxury brands, contributing to both growing and extending their markets.

Still, the tensions between global ambitions and local markets continued. Consumer preferences remained far from homogenous. Markets for most brands were more regional than global. With the exception of some luxury brands and toiletries, local firms dominated the markets of the United States, France, and Japan. It was often difficult to gain access to foreign distribution channels, whether department stores or professional salons. Many brands that were sold in multiple countries looked like, and were, quite different products in different countries. As a result, though by the 1970s almost all of the top 30 beauty firms had some international business, a surprising number remained heavily focused on their domestic markets. These included both consumer products giants, such as P & G, as well as the rapidly growing Japanese firms such as Shiseido and Kao. Even L'Oréal, which had grown to be Europe's largest beauty firm in the industry, had limited business outside Europe, and did not even own its small American operation. During the last decades of the twentieth century, much of that was set to change.

Notes

1. History of Advertising Trust (hereafter HAT), Ogilvy, Benson & Mather, Strategic Planning Options, Presentation to Avon on August 5, 1975.

2. Wella AG, *Wella History: Wella AG's History from 1880 Until Today* (Darmstadt: Wella AG, 2001), p. 14.

3. Fang Wenhui, *Keshouhinkogyou No Hikakukeieishi* (Tokyo: Nihon Keizai Hyouron-sha: Tokyo, 1999; in Japanese), pp. 185–6.

4. <www.tata.com/htm/Group_milestone.htm?sectid=0Xw9Kk6LW6s=>, accessed March 10, 2009.

5. The company took the formal name AmorePacific in 1993.

6. Pankaj Ghemawat, David Kiron, and Carin-Isabel Knoop, "AmorePacific: From Local to Global Beauty," Harvard Business School Case no. 9-706-411 (November 21, 2006).

7. Geoffrey Jones, *Multinationals and Global Capitalism* (Oxford: Oxford University Press, 2005), pp. 92–101.

8. Procter & Gamble Corporate Archive (hereafter P & G), Max Factor—Historical Events.

9. Wella Corporate Archive (hereafter WA), A 334 "Gründungsdaten der ausländischen Wella-Firmen," March 3, 1960; *Wella History*, p. 20; Erich Körner, unpubl. company history, p. 82.

10. Geoffrey Jones, *Renewing Unilever* (Oxford: Oxford University Press, 2005), pp. 32–3; Geoffrey Jones, "Blonde and Blue-eyed? Globalizing Beauty, c.1945–c.1980," *Economic History Review* 61 (2008), pp. 130–1; Andrew Knox, *Coming Clean: A Postscript after Retirement from Unilever* (London: Heinemann, 1976), pp. 155–61.

11. Teresa da Silva Lopes, *Global Brands: The Evolution of Multinationals in Alcoholic Beverages* (Cambridge: Cambridge University Press, 2007).

12. Chambre de Commerce et d'Industrie de Paris (hereafter CCIP), CPA case no. 2492, "Parfumerie Guerlain," June 11, 1948.

13. S. A. Mann, *Cosmetics Industry of Europe 1968* (Park Ridge, NJ: Noyes Development Corporation, 1968).

14. *The U.S. Industrial Outlook for 1964* (Washington, DC: Washington, Business and Defense Services Administration, 1965). *The U.S. Industrial Outlook for 1965* (Washington, DC: Washington Business and Defense Services Administration, 1966).

15. Jean Laudereau, "Mémoire de L'Oréal 1907–1992," unpubl. MS, p. 271.

16. Dave Mote and M. L. Cohen, "Chanel S.A.," in J. Pederson (ed.), *International Directory of Company Histories*, 49 (Farmington Hills, Mich.: St. James Press, 2003), pp. 83–6; Dana Thomas, *Deluxe: How Luxury Lost its Luster* (New York: Penguin, 2007), p. 150.

17. L'Oréal Archives (hereafter L'Oréal), "60 ans de Lancôme: Le roman de la rose," *En Direct* 145, March 1995, p. 4.

18. Jacqueline Demornex, *Lancôme, Paris* (Paris: Éditions Assouline, 2000), pp. 10–15; L'Oréal, "60 ans."

19. Unilever Archives Rotterdam (hereafter UAR), L'Oréal. A Company Study, April 1971, OS 71002.

20. Laudereau, "Mémoire," pp. 269–70.

21. L'Oréal, "Lancôme aux États-Unis: Petite histoire d'une grande réussite," *En Direct* 111, March 1988, p. 13; Laudereau, "Mémoire," pp. 272–3.

22. L'Oréal, "60 ans," p. 6.

23. Laudereau, "Memoire," p. 271.

24. Helen Marie Caldwell, "The Development and Democratization of the American Perfume Market 1920–1975," unpubl. doctoral diss., University of Connecticut, 1995, p. 221.

25. "Time Clock," *Time*, June 7, 1954.

26. "Packaging and Selling," *Drug and Cosmetic Industry* 76:3 (March 1955), p. 343.

27. Bruno Abescat and Yves Stavridès, "Derrière l'empire Chanel...La fabuleuse histoire des Wertheimer," *L'Express*, April 7–August 8, 2005, available at <www.lexpress.fr/actualite/economie/la-fabuleuse-histoire-des-wertheimer_485301.html>, accessed February 2, 2007; Caldwell, "Development," pp. 308–13.

28. My estimates, based on DAFSA, *L'industrie mondiale de la parfumerie*, fourth quarter 1986.

29. L'Oréal, "60 ans," p. 6.

30. Yoshiharu Fukuhara, *The Journey of My Life* (Tokyo: Shiseido, 1999), p. 87; Geoffrey Jones, Akiko Kanno, and Masako Egawa, "Making China Beautiful: Shiseido and the China Market," Harvard Business School Case no. 9-805-003 (April 12, 2007).

31. Telephone interview with Lindsay Owen-Jones, January 22, 2009.

32. L'Oréal, "Lancôme aux États-Unis," p. 13; Richard Tomlinson, "L'Oréal's Global Makeover," *Fortune*, September 30, 2002; telephone interview with Lindsay Owen-Jones, January 22, 2009.

33. Nancy F. Koehn, *Brand New* (Boston, Mass.: Harvard Business School Press, 2001), pp. 174–6, 197–8.

34. Estée Lauder, *Estée: A Success Story* (New York: Random House, 1985), p. 118–19.

35. Gefle Dagblad, "Det doftar succé för Pierre Wulff," January 27, 2008, accessed at <www/gd/se/Article.jsp?article=124492>

36. Frost and Sullivan, *Marketing Strategies for Selling Cosmetics and Toiletries in Europe* (New York, September 1983), pp. 308–33.

37. Frost and Sullivan, *The Cosmetics and Toiletries Industry Market* (New York, August 1972); Susanne Hilger, *Amerikanisierung deutscher Unternehmen* (Stuttgart: Franz Steiner Verlag, 2004), pp. 158–9.

38. Knox, *Coming Clean*, p. 157.

39. Jones, *Renewing*, p. 63. The brand Pierre Robert ultimately disappeared. A few of the other brands, including LdB and Jane Hellen, survived, to be purchased and revived in 1998 by Wulff's friend and neighbor Kent Widding, the owner of the Swedish firm Hardford. See Arne Högberg, *Skönhetens entreprenör* (Malmö: Corona Förlag, 2004), pp. 93, 102.

40. Caldwell, "Development," p. 298.

41. Charles Torem and William Lawrence Craig, "Developments in the Control of Foreign Investment in France," *Michigan Law Review* 70 (1971), n. 187, pp. 331–2.

42. Hubert Bonin, "Equipment Goods and Mass Brands: American Business Spreading Modernity into France?," paper delivered to the Helsinki Congress of the International Economic History Association, August 21–5, 2006.

43. Centre des archives économiques et financières (hereafter CAEF), B-0065523/1, Ministère des finances et des affaires économiques, Direction des finances extérieures, Investissements étrangers en France, société SA Gesparal (1974–1982), Projet d'accord entre Mme Bettencourt, L'Oréal et Nestlé Alimentana, Paris, January 5, 1974.

44. Crédit Lyonnais archives (hereafter CL), DEEF 79426/1, "Industrie française des produits de parfumerie, de beauté et de toilette," February 16, 1982; Europe Strategic Analyse Financière (Eurostaf), *L'Industrie Mondiale de la Parfumerie et Cosmétologie*, 1991.

45. L'Oréal, *En Direct* 153 (April 1997), pp. 14–17.

46. Jones, "Blonde and Blue-eyed?," p. 136.

47. UAR 3110, World Toilet Preparations Survey 1959–1960.

48. Frost and Sullivan, *Cosmetics*.

49. Frost and Sullivan, *Cosmetics*; F. V. Wells, "Shampoos: The European Market," *Soap/Cosmetics/Chemical Specialities*, October 1976.

50. The pricing of the pharmaceutical products sold in these independent drugstores had been state-regulated for centuries.

51. "Making Big Advertising Pay," *Sales Management*, March 1, 1963.

52. Jones, "Blonde and Blue-eyed?," p. 137.

53. Jones, *Renewing*, p. 33; Peter Miskell, "Cavity Protection or Cosmetic Perfection?," *Business History Review* 78 (Spring 2004).

54. Jones, *Renewing*, pp. 162–3.

55. University of Connecticut Archives (hereafter UConn), J. B. Williams Collection, Box 1, Folder 6, Annual Report 1956; "Williams Business Brazil," *J. B. Williams Newsletter*, December 11, 1958, Box 3, Folder 32.

56. Jones, "Blonde and Blue-eyed?," p. 137.

57. HAT, JWT, Chesebrough-Pond's, J. Walter Thompson, Review of Personal Deodorant Markets, February 1962, Box 70.

58. Rexona had been launched in nearly 30 countries by the end of the 1970s: Jones, *Renewing*, pp. 33, 126–7, 166; Jones, "Blonde and Blue-Eyed?," p. 138.

59. François Dalle, *L'aventure L'Oréal* (Paris: Éditions Odile Jacob, 2001), pp. 104–7; Jones, "Blonde and Blue-eyed?," p. 135.

60. Jones, *Renewing*, pp. 38–50.

61. Jones, *Renewing*, pp. 25, 134–5, 145–6.

62. Jones, *Renewing*, pp. 34, 301–3; James Foreman-Peck, *Smith & Nephew in the Health Care Industry* (Aldershot: Edward Elgar, 1995), pp. 217–19.

63. Jones, *Renewing*, pp. 69–77.

64. Davis Dyer, Frederick Dalzell, and Rowena Olegario, *Rising Tide* (Boston, Mass.: Harvard Business School Press, 2004), pp. 101–6; P & G, *Hedley Moonbeams*, Christmas 1952.

65. P & G, Walter Lingle, Oral History, September 29, 1987.

66. P & G, Lingle, Oral History.

67. UAR, World Toilet Preparations Survey 1959–1960.

68. "Cosmetics—Local Products Now Accepted," *Bangkok Bank Monthly Review*, 19:4 (April 1978), pp. 159–63.

69. "Helene Curtis Enters a New Era of Innovation," *Drug and Cosmetic Industry* (August 1996).

70. Jones, "Blonde and Blue-eyed?," p. 139.

71. Tsunehiko Yui, Akira Kudo, and Haruhito Takeda, in association with Eisuke Daito and Satoshi Sasaki, *Kaoshi Hyakunen (1890–1990)* (*Hundred-year History of Kao (1890–1990)*) (Tokyo: Kao Corporation, 1993; in Japanese), pp. 430–3.

72. Yui *et al.*, *Kaoshi*, pp. 806–8.

73. Lion Company, *Lion Hyakunen Shie* (*Lion 100-Year History*) (Tokyo: Lion, 1992), pp. 109–11; *Lion Hyakunen Shie*, pp. 356–61.

74. Dalle, *L'aventure*, pp. 102–4.

75. "Jacques Corrèze, L'Oréal Official and Nazi Collaborator, Dies at 79," *New York Times*, June 28, 1991.

76. Telephone interview with Lindsay Owen-Jones, January 22, 2009.

77. Dalle, *L'aventure*, pp. 230–4; interview with Béatrice Dautresme in "Mass, Class and the 'Politique' of L'Oréal," *Adweek*, February 1985; interview with Patrick Rabain, Paris, June 17, 2008. Cosmair's sales reached $665 million in 1985. See "Cosmair Makes a Name for Itself," *New York Times*, May 12, 1985.

78. CL, DEEF 79425/1, "Industrie de la parfumerie en France et dans les principaux pays industrialisés," Secteur Parachimie, October 9, 1972; Interview with Patrick Rabain, Paris, June 17, 2008.

79. HA, D440 Schwarzkopf Dokumentations Forschungsgeschichte, "Schwarzkopf: Chronologie—Schwarzkopf Heute (in Stichworten)," September 1976; interview with Hans Peter Schwarzkopf by Christian Stadler, March 27, 2007.

80. HistoCom Archives, Schwarzkopf Lizenzverträge 9, James P. Lewis to Gerd and Hans Peter Schwarzkopf, re: Schwarzkopf Inc., Culver City, USA, "Schwarzkopf Inc. Business Plan," June 17, 1992.

81. *Wella History*, p. 20; WA, Accession A 334, "Gründungsdaten der ausländischen Wella-Firmen," March 3, 1960.

82. WA, "Wella International," n.d. but likely printed in 1965; Körner, unpubl. company history, p. 82; "Wella International," n.d., but dated to c.1972 by the Wella archivist.

83. Frost and Sullivan, *Cosmetics*; Wells, "Shampoos."

84. L'Oréal, "Éclairages," interview with Gérard Chouraqui, *En Direct* 118, July–August 1989.

85. Olivin was owned by the pharmaceutical company C. H. Boehringer & Sohn.

86. HA, Schwarzkopf, K-Akte Ungarn, Lizenzvertrag Kosmetikai/Caola, "Vertrag," "Zwischen Olivin Wiesbaden, Zwiegniederlassung der Firma C.H. Boehringer Sohn ... und Firma Kozmetikai es Haztartasvegypari Vallalat, Budapest XI/Ungarn, vertreten durch Chemolimpex, Budapest/Ungarn," May 24, 1971/June 11, 1971.

87. JWT, Howard Henderson papers—Clients—Chesebrough-Pond's, "History: The Pond's Extract Company," February 15, 1960, Box 4.

88. JWT, New Business Records, Milton Moskowitz papers—Cutex, Northam Warren Corporation; "New Business Call Report," June 3, 1959, Box 1.

89. Noxzema Annual Report, 1962; P & G, *The Noxell Story. The Little Blue Jar. A Business Romance*, p. 12.

90. Beiersdorf AG, *100 Jahre Beiersdorf, 1882–1982* (Hamburg: Beiersdorf, 1982), pp. 87–8. A development of the clear tape launched in the mid-1930s, Tesa had only been introduced in Germany in 1941 and had few sales outside Germany in 1945, so the trademark was not expropriated. The first postwar manufacturing subsidiaries founded in the mid-1950s were Tesa subsidiaries.

91. Beiersdorf AG, *100 Jahre*; Yui *et al.*, *Kaoshi*, pp. 512–16.

92. Richardson Merrill Annual Report 1971; Olay Worldwide Overview Presentation, September 16, 1980, P & G; "Oil of Olay's Secret: Price and Positioning," *New York Times*, September 1, 1980.

93. Max Factor Annual Reports, 1958 and 1971.

94. Noxell Corporation, Annual Reports, 1962 and 1979.

95. "Mascara and Maybelline," *Drug and Cosmetic Industry* (1978), pp. 26–9.

96. Coty Archives (hereafter COTY), Rimmel and Coty History, Presentation, July 1, 2004, Dublin.

97. "ITT Ending US Sales of Rimmel Cosmetics," *Wall Street Journal*, May 18, 1978.

98. Interview with Eric Morgan, London, May 11, 2006; Budget Submission, Cosmetics Operating Group, July 7, 1984, BAT Industries files, Tobacco Control Archives, University of California, San Francisco.

99. Kosé Corporation, *Sozo to Chosen—Kosé 50 nen shi* (*Imagination and Challenge—Kosé 50 year history*) (Tokyo: Kosé Corporation, 1998), pp. 93–5.

100. HAT, JWT, Chesebrough-Pond's, J. Walter Thompson, Cutex and L'Onglex, Survey of the Cosmetic Market, June 13, 1962, Box 470.

101. Frost and Sullivan, *Cosmetics*.

102. Jones, *Renewing*, pp. 38–42.

103. Jones, *Renewing*, pp. 142–6, 165–6.

104. P & G, Samih Sherif, Oral History, September 8, 1996. Sherif was head of Export and Special Operations, based in Geneva. See "Samih Sherif: Entrepreneur Extraordinaire," *Moonbeams* (internal newsletter), March 1988, pp. 3–6.

105. Hellmut Kruse, *Wagen und Winnen: Ein hanseatisches Kaufmannsleben im 20. Jahrhundert* (Hamburg: Die Hanse, 2006), p. 140.

106. Kruse, *Wagen*, pp. 138–41, 174.

107. Kruse, *Wagen*, pp. 155–6.

108. Foreman-Peck, *Smith*, pp. 129–32; Beiersdorf Archive, The Company, *Ninety Seven and Counting. The Story of Beiersdorf in the UK* (Hamburg: Beiersdorf, 2003).

109. Foreman-Peck, *Smith*, pp. 136–7.

110. Harm Schröter, "Erfolgsfaktor Marketing: Der Strukturwandel von der Reklame zur Unternehmenssteuerung," in Wilfried Feldenkirchen, Frauke Schönert-Röhlk, and Günther Schulz (eds), *Wirtschaft, Gesellschaft, Unternehmen: Festschrift für Hans Pohl zum 60. Geburtstag*, vol. 2 (Franz Steiner Verlag: Stuttgart, 1995), pp. 1101, 1111, 1125; Beiersdorf AG, *Nivea: Evolution of a World Famous Brand* (Hamburg: Beiersdorf AG, 2001), pp. 60–1, 70–1; Kruse, *Wagen*, p. 186.

111. <www.beiersdorf.com/Area-About-us/Our-History/NIVEA-Reacquisition-od-Trademarks.aspx?l=2>, accessed March 12, 2009.

112. JWT, Howard Henderson papers—Clients—Chesebrough-Pond's, Clippings 1933–1961, Memorandum by Howard Henderson to all offices, December 17, 1952, Box 10.

113. "Defying a Popular Success Theory," *Printers' Ink*, December 8, 1961.

114. Jennifer Malia McAndrew, " 'But You Don't Look Like a Negro': African American Entrepreneurs in Female Beauty Culture in the Mid-Twentieth Century," paper presented at the Business History Conference, Cleveland, June 2007.

115. David K. Fieldhouse, *Merchant Capital and Economic Decolonization* (Oxford: Clarendon Press, 1994), pp. 537–9.

116. Jones, *Renewing*, pp. 169–74.

117. Kavita Karan, "Obsessions with Fair Skin: Color Discourses in Indian Advertising," and Natasha Sheyde, "All's Fair in Love and Cream: A Cultural Case Study of Fair & Lovely in India," *Advertising & Society Review* 9:2 (2008), available at <http://muse.jhu.edu/journals/advertising_and_society_review/v009/9.2>, accessed April 11, 2009.

118. Avon Archives, Hagley Museum, Wilmington, Del., Avon Products Inc., Accession number 2155 (hereafter AVON), Record Group II: Historical Files, Series 7: Conferences, Hays Clark, International Division, "Avon Around the World," June 17–21, 1963, Box 124.

119. AVON, "Avon Around the World."

120. AVON, Record Group I: Archive, Series 11: Avon International, Subseries B: Conferences, "Plans for Market Penetration—Puerto Rico," International Division Merchandising Conference, March 1968, Box 69.

121. AVON, "Avon Around the World."

122. AVON, Record Group I: Archive, Series 11: Avon International, Subseries D: Sales Promotion, Campaign Mailings for Avon, Germany 1959–1964, Box 85.

123. Andrea Colli and Emanuela Scarpellini, "Investing in a Developing Economy: US and European Direct Investments in Italy during the 'Economic Miracle' (1950–1970)," paper presented at the Helsinki Congress of the International Economic History Association, August 21–25, 2006.

124. HAT, Ogilvy & Mather Research Materials, Avon Unprocessed, Attitude Survey, Europe, May 19, 1975.

125. AVON, Record Group I: Archive, Series 11: Avon International, Subseries B: Conferences, "Presentation on Product, Packaging, and Development," 1968 Avon International Merchandising Conference, New York City, March 25–29, 1968, Box 69.

126. AVON, Record Group I: Archive, Series 11: Avon International, Subseries B: Conferences, Comments by L. V. Consiglio on Marketing Objectives Setting, Avon World Management Planning Conference, June 4–8, 1973, Box 4.

127. AVON, Record Group I: Archive, Series 1: Administration, Subseries C: Conferences, "Europe in the 1980s—Marketing," Avon Boca Raton Conference, May 1979, Box 4.

128. HAT, T. D. Mustard, Fragrance Terminology Study in Europe—1973, March 30, 1973, HAT, Ogilvy & Mather Research Materials, Avon Unprocessed.

129. HAT, Ogilvy & Mather Research Materials, Discussion Document. A 1974/75 European Research Programme for Avon, July 1974.

130. AVON, "Meet Miss Malaysia," *Avon and You* (September–October 1965).

131. AVON, Record Group I: Archive, 1: Administration, Subseries C: Conferences, 1973 Planning Meeting, Box 4.

132. Gordon McKibben, *Cutting Edge: Gillette's Journey to Global Leadership* (Boston, Mass.: Harvard Business School Press, 1998), pp. 45, 70.

133. Wendy Stein, "Mary Kay," in Tina Grant (ed.), *International Directory of Company Histories*, vol. 84 (Farmington Hills, Mich.: St. James Press, 2007), pp. 251–6.

134. *Eien No Bi Wo Motomete—POLA Monogatari* (*A Quest for Everlasting Beauty: POLA Corporation's History of 50 Years*) (Tokyo: Pola, 1980; in Japanese), pp. 206–7.

135. "Garelli Shapes Skin Care Tactics," *Drug and Cosmetic Industry* (January 1, 1990), p. 15; interview with Satoshi Suzuki, March 3, 2007. In 2000 foreign sales represented only around 4 per cent of total sales.

136. Kathy Peiss, "Educating the Eye of the Beholder: American Cosmetics Abroad," *Daedalus* 131 (Fall 2002), pp. 101–9; Ara Wilson, *The Intimate Economies of Bangkok: Tomboys, Tycoons, and Avon Ladies in the Global City* (Berkeley: University of California Press, 2004), ch. 5.

7

The Uncertain Identity of Beauty

The whole idea of being linked with up-market beauty products and fragrances
rather embarrassed the tough business executives who operated in Unilever House.
Eleanor Macdonald, a Unilever executive[1]

Beauty at the crossroads

Even as the beauty market boomed, the identity of the industry remained
unclear. The industry's lack of a clear identity was rooted in its historical
origins in quite distinct product categories. During the nineteenth century
firms such as Colgate and Rimmel had initially covered the whole spectrum
of products from perfume to toilet soap. Later, as the industry grew in scale
and developed mature distribution channels, and as the science behind
the products became more complex, few firms were able to span all the different
categories, and none were successful in more than a few of them. The
marketing of toothpaste in drugstores had come to require a quite different
set of skills than the launch of a prestige fragrance in a department store.

In some countries companies sought to build collective organizations to
enhance the legitimacy of their business and to frame their activity as an
industry. In the United States, a perfumers' association was established in 1894,
and extended its membership to cosmetics and toiletry firms in 1922.[2] In 1945 a
Toilet Preparation and Perfumery Manufacturers Association was formed in
Britain.[3] In France, three separate trade organizations were formed. These
were the perfumers, which were highly exclusive; the makers of decorative
beauty products; and the manufacturers of toiletries. It was not until 1974 that
they joined in a federated organization, and soon thereafter the professional
hair care sector, cosmetic firms in the pharmacy sector, and direct sellers'
syndicates joined the federation as well.[4] It was not surprising that in France

the different categories were rarely considered as a collective entity, given the historically high rank of the perfumers.

Beauty, then, was slow to grow as a category defined by a shared understanding of the identities of the firms, their products, the rules for inclusion, and the similarity and comparability of products in a particular domain.[5] This had dual implications for the future of the industry. It added to the challenges faced by firms that wanted to diversify from one category to another. Meanwhile, the lack of a distinct identity encouraged firms from other industries to invest in it.

Yet although the boundaries of the industry may have been indistinct, the broad terrain of the market appeared increasingly attractive structurally. Compared to many other consumer industries, the products were not technologically complex, labor costs were low, capital expenditures were minimal, and consumers seemed to want a range of products—and were willing to pay large premiums to buy them. The high degree of fragmentation in the industry presented apparent opportunities to roll up successful brands into larger units.[6]

By coincidence, it was increasingly easy to buy into an industry in which extensive family ownership had formerly made acquisitions difficult. This situation began to change as many early pioneers became infirm or died. Helena Rubinstein died in 1965, and Elizabeth Arden in the following year. In a handful of cases, families found ways to stay in the industry, obtain funds for expansion, and arrange smooth successions. The family owners of L'Oréal and Schwarzkopf persuaded larger companies from beyond the beauty industry to invest in them.

Estée Lauder, in contrast, remained utterly committed to keeping her business totally private and family-owned, even as sales soared to $40 million by the end of the 1960s.[7] In 1973, however, she did hand over the presidency of her company to her son Leonard, whilst remaining the company's public face. The firm's continued private ownership facilitated the strategy of growing new brands, as the losses which such growth typically involved could be absorbed without attracting criticism from outside investors.[8] Clinique, launched in 1968 as an allergy-tested, fragrance-free line of cosmetics sold by sales consultants wearing white lab coats, was reported to have lost $3 million by 1975, when sales began to increase rapidly.[9]

Many families sought an exit from the industry once the founder died. Even if spouses or siblings shared the passion and creativity of the original founders, success demanded high levels of advertising and media spending, and many family-owned firms found themselves cash-constrained, with the future growth of even treasured brands dependent on deeper pockets. Some families also faced crushing inheritance tax bills, such as the $35 million owed by the estate of Elizabeth Arden, which left her inheritors with nothing unless they were able to sell her company.[10] In other cases, families, especially those with multiple claimants on the succession, simply wanted to monetarize their inheritance.

The desire of families to exit the industry occurred at precisely the time when the market for corporate control took off, especially in the United States and Britain. Moreover, management consultants and others were propounding the (then) conventional wisdom that it was important for large firms to diversify and build multi-product businesses.[11] The result, starting from the 1960s, was a radical upheaval in the ownership and organization of the industry. It was only much later that management researchers would establish that, across the broad sweep of industries, many acquisitions, perhaps up to one-half, would fail in some sense.[12] The beauty industry provides an important case study of the management challenges which caused so many acquisitions to fail.

The end of the affair: beauty and drugs go their separate ways

For hundreds, indeed thousands, of years, beauty and health had been closely integrated. Fragrances had been drunk as well as applied; skin creams and cosmetics had been curative as well as decorative. Medical and beauty knowledge had been closely entwined and were based on common knowledge of flowers, herbs, and oils. However, industrialization resulted in beauty and health becoming separate domains. Medical knowledge turned to the application of modern science, seeking to move beyond craft knowledge and towards drugs which could intervene powerfully to counter disease and preserve life. Efficacy, not myth, became the mantra of medicine. The beauty industry went in the opposite direction. Although functionally effective products were developed, such as toothpaste and, later, sunscreen, the beauty industry for the most part became more focused on aspirations and image. The salespeople selling Clinique in department stores wore white coats but were not doctors; the faint green packaging looked almost medical, but the contents did not require FDA approval.[13] Hope, not efficacy, was the mantra of beauty.

Yet a number of companies continued to straddle the areas of beauty and health. Bristol-Myers, Lehn & Fink, and Squibb in the United States, and Beecham in Britain, had product portfolios during the postwar decades spanning toiletries, cosmetics, non-prescription drugs, vitamins, disinfectants and, in some cases, antibiotics. Hoffman-La Roche, a large Swiss pharmaceutical company which had become a major pioneer in the manufacture of vitamins during World War II, launched Pantene shampoo as a by-product of the synthesis of the vitamin panthenol in 1945. This grew as a successful brand of hair lotion sold at a premium price in Europe.[14]

Beiersdorf and Johnson & Johnson were major examples of another type of firm which spanned health and beauty. The pharmacy origins of Beiersdorf continued to be reflected in its postwar product portfolio, which covered wound care, deodorizing soaps and skin creams, as well as adhesives. The twin themes of health and beauty lay at the heart of the identity of the Nivea brand.[15] Johnson & Johnson, whose origins also lay in wound care, had become the leading firm in skin care products for babies after the launch of Johnson's Baby Cream in 1921. From the late 1950s the firm also moved rapidly into over-the-counter (OTC) drugs and pharmaceuticals, by buying drug manufacturers—including those who made a non-aspirin pain reliever called Tylenol—as well as a large feminine hygiene business.

From the late 1950s, pharmaceutical companies began a major move into the beauty industry. Bristol-Myers' acquisition of Clairol in 1959 signaled the start of a wave of acquisitions. In 1963 Pfizer, a pioneer of penicillin production, bought Coty as part of a diversification process which transformed it into a manufacturer of consumer products, including OTC consumer remedies.[16] American Cyanamid, another large pharmaceutical firm, acquired John Breck in the same year, followed by Shulton in 1970. Plough acquired Maybelline in 1967. Following a merger with Schering in 1971, this combined company also bought the cosmetics businesses of Germany's Chicogo and Britain's Rimmel, in 1974 and 1980 respectively. Bidding wars broke out for valuable brand franchises. When Elizabeth Arden's management approached American Cyanamid to acquire it, there was a larger counter-offer from Eli Lilly, yet another leading pharmaceutical manufacturer, which eventually won.[17]

Many within the industry perceived a compelling business logic for these acquisitions. It was assumed that the large research capabilities of pharmaceutical companies would facilitate product development.[18] There were also predictions that government regulation over cosmetics in the United States would grow further, and that as a result the regulatory expertise of pharmaceutical companies would be valuable.[19] As pharmaceutical and chemicals firms were also suppliers of raw materials to the beauty industry, it was believed that vertical integration down the value chain into more lucrative consumer products made financial sense.[20]

As so often happens, a corporate trend that began in the United States soon found its followers in Europe. The health care company Smith & Nephew, which owned the British rights to Nivea, first unsuccessfully tried to create its own skin and color cosmetics brands, and then, in 1971, bought the majority of the Myram Picker Group, whose Gala and Mary Quant cosmetics brands were widely sold in the British market.[21]

On a larger scale, Beecham began building a cosmetics business. In 1965 it acquired three-quarters of the equity of Margaret Astor, a medium-sized German cosmetics company founded in 1951, which held almost one-third of the German lipstick market. Two years later it acquired Lancaster, a luxury cosmetics brand established in Monaco in 1946. There followed other acquisitions, especially of small companies in bath preparations, in France, Germany, and the United States. A more radical departure came when Beecham acquired the controversial Jovan brand in 1979. Founded less than a decade earlier, this Chicago-based fragrance start-up had taken one-third of the male and one-tenth of the female fragrance market in the United States by mass marketing its perfumes like packaged goods, employing sexually explicit advertising, and incorporating large quantities of musk into its perfumes with the claim that the ingredient chemically enhanced sexual attraction.[22]

Hoechst, Germany's largest chemicals and pharmaceutical company, also became a convert to the beauty industry. It had long been a supplier of raw materials to toiletries and cosmetics manufacturers. During the 1960s Hoechst's management became convinced that the future lay in building a business which spanned the whole spectrum of activities from raw materials to consumer goods, including cosmetics.[23] The licensing agreement and equity investment in Schwarzkopf was followed during the 1970s by acquisitions of German cosmetics brands including Marbert, Jade, and Mouson, as well as the Madame Rochas fragrance house, acquired in 1974 as part of Hoechst's assumption of a majority equity stake in Roussel-Uclaf, then the leading French pharmaceutical concern.[24]

7.1 An advertisement for Jovan Musk for Men, launched by the Chicago start-up Jovan Inc., became famous for its use of erotic imagery to boost fragrance sales to male consumers, 1988.

The outcomes of this flow of pharmaceutical money into the beauty industry were decidedly mixed. In some cases, valuable brand equities were destroyed by their new owners. Squibb's Lenthéric experienced heavy losses in the early 1950s, especially after introducing a cheap make-up.[25] As a result of the US Justice Department's action against price-fixing in 1954, Squibb signed a consent decree to sell its British and French affiliates.[26] The rest of the business was sold to Helene Curtis in 1956. Breck shampoo was even more damaged by its new owners. American Cyanamid first reformulated and repositioned it as a budget brand, and then spent little on marketing it. The brand was left behind by competitors selling herbal-based shampoos during the 1970s, whilst provoking feminist disdain for the traditional "Breck girls" used in its advertisements.[27] Smith & Nephew's attempt to take Gala cosmetics into the American market during the 1970s, about which it knew little, resulted in major losses and the sale of the brand in 1980.[28]

In some cases, beauty brands benefited from the stability and resources provided by their new owners. Clairol flourished under the ownership of Bristol-Myers. Richard Gelb, the son of Clairol's founder, joined Bristol-Myers after the acquisition, and was given the autonomy to develop its business further. After mishaps elsewhere in Bristol-Myers, Gelb was appointed chief executive of the entire company in 1972. By the next decade, cosmetics and toiletries contributed a fifth of the firm's overall revenues.[29]

The fragrance business, subject to the high costs and uncertainty of fragrance launches, seemed to benefit from ownership by cash-rich larger companies. Coty, for example, experienced a renaissance under Pfizer's ownership. This relationship had got off to a bad start when, following the acquisition, Coty had been merged into the main pharmaceutical business, an arrangement which had to be undone "when it discovered that merchandising cosmetics was a different operation entirely from selling drugs."[30] Thereafter, the new owners provided the resources for a successful business to be developed that was based largely on the cheaper end of the American fragrance market. In 1965 Coty launched Imprévu, its first new perfume in 25 years. In 1981 Coty, which by then had established itself as second only to Revlon in female fragrances in the American market, had further success with the launch of Stetson, a successful men's cologne scent featuring images of cowboys wearing the famous hat. Later during that decade, Yves Saint Laurent launched his controversial and highly successful Opium perfume under Squibb's ownership.

Despite such successes, fundamental differences in corporate culture and organization proved challenging. The beauty divisions were usually only a small unit within the pharmaceutical corporation, whose senior executives struggled to understand a consumer products business in which successful brands needed to demonstrate much more than functional effectiveness. Roche, for example, expanded its successful Pantene brand into conditioners, hair sprays, skin creams, after-shaves, and sun creams, but the beauty business remained its smallest division. Roche's senior management was reluctant to grow Pantene very much because of potential conflict with its sales of essential oils to other beauty firms. A still greater constraint was the pharmaceutical-based corporate culture which gave managers limited experience of—or even interest in—consumer products. By 1981 Pantene products were sold in department stores and professional hair salons in many countries, but their total sales of just over $60 million represented only 3 per cent of Roche's total turnover.[31]

Whilst allowing autonomy to beauty affiliates made sense within chiefly science-based companies, many companies struggled to make that relationship work in practice. Hoechst, for example, found the management of its beauty business perplexing. An initial approach of seeking to impose a centralized management structure ran into difficulties because of the highly diverse portfolio of companies which had been acquired, as well as their partial ownership by others in some cases. In 1974 a more decentralized model was adopted, with the creation of a cosmetics division that was given responsibility for global strategy and branding. The managements of individual components, such as Schwarzkopf and Marbert, served as profit centers, and were allowed to manage their brands without close supervision.[32]

Managerial problems persisted, however. Hoechst's relationship with Schwarzkopf fluctuated but was rarely untroubled, and tensions increased rather than decreased over time. Hoechst initially helped the brand's internationalization by buying its distributors in foreign countries, and sometimes it used its own subsidiaries to roll out brands. In return, Hoechst sought greater control over Schwarzkopf's strategy, including capital investment, acquisitions, marketing, and human resources.[33] The Schwarzkopf family came to feel that the larger company did not care sufficiently for their brands and kept going back on its promise to leave their firm autonomous.[34] As Schwarzkopf's profitability tumbled in its own core domestic salon business, the relationship deteriorated further.[35]

The underlying problem was that it proved hard to generate synergies between pharmaceutical and beauty. Johnson & Johnson, which had strong managerial capabilities in both consumer marketing and pharmaceutical research, was able to combine successfully its non-prescription drugs, first aid, toiletry, and baby care products under the broad category of health care, which the company defined as "encompassing products related to health and well-being."[36] During the 1970s its baby care brand was successfully translated into a mass-market shampoo. Johnson & Johnson was a rare case. Overall, the laboratories of pharmaceutical companies did not become major sources of innovation for cosmetics companies. "The R & D companies never brought anything to the party," one analyst of the cosmetics industry later concluded. "It is marketing that sells products, not a breakthrough in lipstick technology."[37]

The lack of synergy was sharply exposed as the costs rose in both industries during the course of the 1970s. The oil price rises during that decade created unstable macro-economic conditions, including bouts of inflation and unemployment, which made the high advertising expenditures required to support brands in the beauty industry very evident. Meanwhile, the rising cost of pharmaceutical research gave firms a new interest in raising cash in order to fund it.[38] Opportunities in health care and pharmaceuticals began to appear more lucrative.

By the early 1980s pharmaceutical companies began selling off their beauty brands in increasing numbers. The trend was encouraged by the high prices they could get for beauty brands because, as will be shown later, a new generation of buyers were willing to pay large sums for even the most tarnished of franchises. In 1982 Roche sold the Pantene brand to Richardson Vicks. In 1986 Squibb sold Charles of the Ritz to Yves Saint Laurent, reuniting the beauty and fashion business of the designer under one owner.[39] In 1987 Eli Lilly sold Elizabeth Arden to Fabergé. Although Arden's brand was evidently suffering from high corporate overheads and years of spending a mere 10 per cent of sales on advertising, a rumored 30 firms showed interest in buying the company.[40] Unilever acquired Fabergé/Elizabeth Arden only a year later.[41]

As the prices for cosmetics brands soared, the rush to offload them intensified. In 1988 Schering-Plough also sold Rimmel and Chicogo to Unilever. Maybelline was sold in the following year to Wasserstein Pirella, a recently founded financial advisory boutique which became interested in buying up unwanted cosmetics brands. In 1990 American Cyanamid sold Shulton and Breck.[42] Beecham sold its cosmetics division in 1990.

By the end of the decade, the once huge pharmaceutical ownership of beauty companies had largely, but not entirely, ended. In Germany, Schwarzkopf's financial position was so bad by 1988 that a merger with Henkel was considered, but instead Hoechst bought out shares of some of the members of the Schwarz-kopf family who had decided to cash out, giving it majority control in 1990, and with it the chance to introduce management changes it had long sought.[43] Bristol-Myers, even after merging with Squibb in 1989, also retained its large business in toiletries, cosmetics, and hair care. In 1994 it even acquired Matrix, a leading hair care brand in the American salon market.[44] Johnson & Johnson also continued to build both its health care and beauty businesses. In 1993 it purchased RoC, the maker of hypoallergenic skin products, from LVMH, and the following year it acquired the larger Los Angeles-based Neutrogena Corporation, which made dermatologist-recommended skin and hair care products.[45]

The relationship between the beauty and pharmaceutical industries took its most intimate form in France. Dalle's investment in Synthélabo formed part of a wider relationship between the two industries. Another pharmaceutical company, Pierre Fabre, which had strong dermatological interests, launched successful skin care brands, beginning with Galénic in 1977. In 1980 it also took the initiative in forming a joint venture with Shiseido to sell the latter's products in France.[46]

The most wide-ranging relationship between pharmaceuticals and beauty was orchestrated by the French government as part of an industrial policy designed both to enhance domestic capabilities and to restrict foreign owner-ship in industries that were deemed strategic. In 1973 the government created Sanofi as a subsidiary of the state-owned oil company Elf-Aquitaine, with a mandate to strengthen the French pharmaceuticals and health care industry. Sanofi also became a vehicle to block foreign investment in the beauty industry by taking equity stakes in firms which otherwise might have had to resort to the capital markets to raise funds and thus become exposed to foreign predators. The 13 companies in which it invested in its first three years included cosmetics ventures as well as pharmaceuticals.[47]

Sanofi's first investment was in Yves Rocher, a pioneering natural beauty company.[48] Anxious to avoid a public listing of his company, Rocher sold 62 per cent of his company to Sanofi in 1973 but retained the majority of the company's voting rights and, therefore, management control. As other companies looked vulnerable, Sanofi moved to invest in them. In 1976 Sanofi acquired Roger et Gallet. By 1980 companies controlled by Sanofi held the second-largest share of the French domestic beauty market, although this was much smaller than L'Oréal's one-third share.[49]

Sanofi grew as a well-managed corporation which was able to keep political interference in its affairs at arm's length. It became increasingly cash-rich as its pharmaceutical sales rose rapidly, facilitated by joint ventures in the United States and Japan which enabled it both to buy further companies and extend its reach beyond France. As American companies sold brands, Sanofi bought them. In 1987 it acquired from American Cyanamid the luxury Swiss skin care brand La Prairie and Jacqueline Cochrane, whose fragrance brands included the US distribution rights of Nina Ricci, the Parisian perfume and haute couture fashion house. In 1988 it bought a 38 per cent stake in Nina Ricci itself, leaving Robert Ricci, founder Nina Ricci's son, with majority control.[50] Two small Italian perfume firms, which sold in exclusive department stores in Europe and in the USA, followed.[51] Sanofi also purchased Parfums Stern from Avon in 1990. Then, most spectacularly, three years later it acquired the entire Yves Saint Laurent fashion house and beauty business, which had been afflicted by falling profits.[52]

This French experience did not prove an exception to the overall difficulty of achieving synergies between pharmaceutical and beauty companies. Sanofi's added value lay in providing a corporate vehicle to enable the fragmented French industry to survive a transition to a larger size without selling out to larger, foreign firms. L'Oréal's investment in the pharmaceutical industry never translated into a source of innovation in beauty products, even if it laid the basis for a successful French-owned pharmaceutical company.[53]

For a time, then, there had seemed an unstoppable convergence between health and beauty. The beauty industry seemed set, for a time, to become a subdivision of the pharmaceutical industry. However, it turned out that there was little synergy to be obtained from the common ownership of beauty and drugs firms. The same lack of synergy became apparent whether it was a pharmaceutical company or a beauty company which orchestrated the relationship. The enormous investment by pharmaceutical companies in the beauty industry on both sides of the Atlantic turned out, for the most part, to be the corporate equivalent of an evolutionary dead end.

Beauty in the age of the conglomerate: diversification for its own sake

The beauty industry also found itself intimately involved in the enthusiasm for wholly unrelated diversification which swept American and European business between the 1960s and the 1980s.[54] Cosmetics companies became for a time a target of highly diversified firms, sometimes known as conglomerates, which assumed that their management skills and financial discipline could be applied to almost any industry with equal effect. Meanwhile, some beauty companies themselves also diversified into wholly unrelated industries.

The creation of both the Christian Dior and Kanebo beauty businesses after World War II demonstrated that conglomerate-style investment in the beauty industry was not entirely new. Yet as the fashion for diversification swept the corporate world during the 1960s, conglomerates began to look with increasing interest at the potential of beauty brands as they sought to buy what they regarded as undervalued assets which could then be used to borrow funds against and to make more acquisitions.

In many cases the owners of cosmetics brands were more than willing to sell, if the price was right. The family owners of Gala cosmetics, for example, sold out to Reckitt & Colman, a diversified British business spanning food and drink, household products, OTC drugs, and toiletries, in 1969. In what would later become a familiar pattern, the acquisition proved disappointing, and the brand was sold again, eight years later, in a much weakened form.[55] Rimmel's sale to ITT also proved transient, and the company was resold to Schering-Plough in 1980.[56] In Germany, Quandt, the conglomerate which owned the auto company BMW amongst much else, acquired Mouson from its founding family in 1972, only to sell it to Hoechst six years later.[57] J. B. Williams also became a brand that was passed from one owner to another. Acquired by a New York pharmaceuticals company in 1957, it was sold to Nabisco, the large food manufacturer, in 1971 and then, after a deteriorating performance, sold to Beecham a decade later.[58]

Large tobacco companies, anxious to diversify out of an industry which was attracting growing criticism on health grounds, also bought into the beauty industry. There was a considerable irony here, given the damaging impact of smoking-generated free radicals on the aging of skin. Philip Morris acquired Burma-Shave in 1963. This once-iconic American company, founded in 1925 and famous for a brushless shaving cream, was already a fading force. By the time the brand was sold in 1977, Burma-Shave was completely tarnished, and it languished thereafter.[59] Andrew Jergens seems to have survived better after it was acquired by American Brands, but by 1988 the business was sold, this time to Japan's Kao.[60]

British American Tobacco (BAT), the largest British-based tobacco company, moved beyond merely buying and selling brands to make an attempt at building a new organization in the beauty industry. In the early 1960s BAT began to diversify, first into paper and printing, where it had long been involved through its core cigarette business, and then into quite different industries.[61] In 1964 it took a one-third stake in the Lenthéric fragrance house in Britain, acquiring the remainder three years later. Over the following two decades BAT spent $120 million acquiring small and medium-sized cosmetics and fragrances firms, usually buying out the families that owned them. The acquisitions included, in Britain, Morney and Yardley. Germaine Monteil, an American brand founded by a French fashion designer working in New York, followed in 1969.[62] In almost every case, the brands had long and proud heritages, but had faded in more recent years.

In 1970 these acquisitions were merged into one wholly owned subsidiary, British American Cosmetics (BAC). Eric Morgan, who had begun his career with P & G in Europe in the 1950s, became managing director. A cohesive business began to be built which was managed, like BAT itself, on a decentralized, geographical basis.[63] Few managers were transferred from the tobacco parent, but quite a number were recruited from the British affiliates of other consumer products companies, including Unilever, P & G, and Beecham. Surprisingly, synergies were also achieved with other parts of the BAT group; in particular, information was shared about consumer marketing and retailing trends at group-wide training sessions. By demonstrating how a beauty business could be built by acquiring tired brands and managing them more professionally by recruiting managers trained in highly regarded consumer marketing firms, the episode proved a precursor to the larger and ultimately more sustained diversification of Benckiser into the beauty industry after 1990.

BAC's largest component, and most serious initial challenge, was Yardley. The company continued to do well in its home market, introducing fragrance mini-sprays among other innovations, and it had profitable markets in Colombia, Venezuela, South Africa, and the Middle East. However, the entry of Revlon's Charlie into Britain left it with a customer base amongst older women. It was also burdened by the legacy of the former owners' misjudged expansion into color cosmetics in the United States, where continuing losses absorbed profits made in other markets. In contrast, Morgan was able to reinvent the Lenthéric brand as a mass market fragrance business sold through drugstores, and it became a market leader in Britain by 1977.[64]

The drawbacks of ownership by BAT became apparent as the focus of diversification shifted elsewhere. Attention shifted to retailing, resulting in a string of acquisitions including, in 1973, Saks Fifth Avenue. Morgan was soon struggling to find funds to make further acquisitions.[65] During the early 1980s a major restructuring of Yardley, the merger of its management with the more successful Lenthéric business, and the creation of a worldwide marketing operation contributed to creating an increasingly profitable company. BAC sold in over 140 countries and manufactured in 37 of them, with a product range spanning fragrances, men's products, luxury toiletries, make-up, and skin care products.[66] Yet it was a minnow within its parent corporation, which by the early 1980s had grown to be Britain's third-largest company.[67] BAT's shift into financial services, including the acquisition of one of the largest British insurance companies in 1984, led to the sudden sale of BAC to Beecham later that year.[68]

The combined business of BAC and Beecham included a wide range of toiletry, cosmetics, and fragrance brands with a considerable international business. There were significant managerial improvements after Beecham put its own cosmetics business under the more effective management team of Yardley Lenthéric. By 1989 Beecham's overall cosmetics and toiletries business had reached $1.5 billion in sales out of the corporate total of $4 billion. However, by then the company's strategy had switched to building a pharmaceutical powerhouse. In 1989 the acquisition of the American pharmaceutical company SmithKlein resulted in the decision to sell the entire cosmetics division to help fund the transaction, although the toothpaste business was retained. Wasserstein Pirella, a recently established American financial boutique, took most of the former BAC business organized as Yardley Lenthéric, whilst Astor Lancaster's brands went to Benckiser.

The other major conglomerate investors in this era included the American firm of Norton Simon. In 1973 it swooped on the still family-owned Max Factor, which had suffered a collapse of profitability following an inventory crisis at its large Japanese affiliate, and over the following decade further beauty and fashion businesses were acquired. The results were dismal. A succession of senior executives were hired, and then fired. Unsuccessful product launches drove Max Factor into losses by the end of the decade.[69]

During the 1980s the takeover frenzy in the United States reached a high point as newly devised financial instruments, especially so-called junk bonds, allowed a new generation of entrepreneurs to make hostile acquisitions for companies, break them up, and make huge profits in the process.[70] In 1983 Esmark, whose own interests extended from phosphate mines to women's intimate apparel, acquired Norton Simon.[71] Max Factor was relocated to Stamford, Connecticut and placed under the Playtex bra division. Esmark was itself soon acquired by yet another diversified company, Beatrice Foods, which was then taken over by the private equity firm Kohlberg Kravis Roberts, which proceeded to dismember the organization and sell off individual assets. Max Factor was sold to Revlon in 1988, and the head office moved back to Los Angeles.

The fashion for unrelated diversification also gripped many beauty companies. In 1969 Chesebrough-Pond's started down this path when it bought a spaghetti sauce company. It made further acquisitions in children's apparel, shoes, and—in 1982—a company which made 40 per cent of the tennis racquets sold in the United States. In 1985 $1.25 billion was paid for a large manufacturer of weedkillers and pesticides.[72] Charles Revson was a serial diversifier. In 1957, even as cosmetics sales boomed, he acquired a shoe polish company. He proved less successful in shoe polish than in nail varnish, and the venture was sold 12 years later, but this did not deter Revson, who went on to buy firms making electric shavers, women's sportswear, and other products; none of these acquisitions worked out. Pharmaceuticals attracted Revson in particular. In 1966 he paid $67 million in stock, worth nearly half a billion dollars today, for a pharmaceutical company which produced a drug for diabetes. Five years later he sold this to Ciba-Geigy in exchange for a portfolio of other drugs which the Swiss pharmaceutical company had been required to divest for antitrust reasons.

Revson's conviction that the future of Revlon lay in diversification was demonstrated by the man he chose to succeed him. As he began to suffer from the pancreatic cancer from which he eventually died in 1975, he looked beyond Revlon, his sons, and the beauty industry and recruited Charles Bergerac, previously chief executive of ITT's European operations, to run the company. Under Bergerac's stewardship, Revlon made numerous acquisitions in health care, optical lenses, and medical equipment, reducing the share of cosmetics and toiletries in Revlon's revenues to only one-half by 1980.[73] Avon diversified out of both cosmetics and direct selling. In 1979 it acquired Tiffany's, the New York prestige jewelry store. It was sold five years later after a disappointing performance, but this did nothing to prevent more acquisitions of mail order, clothing and, especially, health care companies. A large health care company acquired in 1982 had to be sold three years later after causing Avon after-losses of $60 million, but once more this did not prevent a new wave of acquisitions in nursing homes.[74] Avon's acquisitions spree took the company to the brink of disaster. In 1988 it had a pre-tax loss of $800 million as a result of its poorly performing health businesses, which all had to be sold, as was the entire retirement home business in 1989.[75] The company was so weakened that both Mary Kay and Amway started acquiring its stock. Amway made a formal takeover bid, which was rejected, but an investor group which included Mary Kay was not conclusively defeated until 1991.[76]

Avon was far from alone in generating losses from its acquisitions. Chesebrough-Pond's was fatally weakened by the poor performance of its acquisitions, contributing to the firm's sale to Unilever in 1987.[77] The cosmetics business of the once-mighty Revlon was also crippled. By early 1980s its market share in cosmetics was in decline as insufficient funding caused it to fall behind both Estée Lauder in department stores and Cover Girl in the mass sector, as the firm's health business began to take precedence over beauty. In 1985 the weakened Revlon was acquired in a hostile takeover bid by one of the most aggressive corporate raiders, Ronald Perelman, using a recently acquired Florida food chain, which was then sold off to help pay for the $2.7 billion spent on buying Revlon. Perelman took the company private, and then rapidly sold off its health and drug investments to pay off more of his debt in junk bonds.[78]

Perelman proceeded to fall in love with the glamour of the beauty business. He launched a relentless campaign of hostile acquisitions to expand Revlon's brand portfolio. An aggressive attempt to buy Gillette during 1986 and 1987 was ultimately beaten off by the beleaguered Boston firm.[79] However, as other firms divested themselves of now-unwanted businesses, he was able to acquire notable brands, including Max Factor, Yves St Laurent fragrances, and Charles of the Ritz. It proved much easier to buy firms than to rebuild Revlon, which had been burdened with huge debt as a result of his takeover. In 1991 Perelman had to sell Max Factor to P & G. In the following year an attempt to raise funds through an IPO failed.[80]

The one partial exception to the story of poor outcomes of diversification occurred in the special instance of the French luxury industry. The origins of what would become LVMH began in 1971, when Moët et Chandon, a champagne company which had recently acquired Parfums Dior, merged with a large cognac producer to create Moët-Hennessy. Although continuing to acquire alcoholic beverages firms, the new company also bought RoC, a cosmetics firm specializing in hypoallergenic make-up, in 1978. In 1987 LVMH was created when Moët-Hennessy merged with Louis Vuitton, the French luxury fashion and leather goods company which had acquired the Maison Dior business from the French government three years previously.

Soon afterwards Bernard Arnault took control of the company. After graduating as an engineer from the elite École Polytechnique, Arnault had joined his father's construction company, which he proceeded to transform into a real estate venture, moving it to the United States after the socialist François Mitterrand became President of France in 1981. In the US he became intimately acquainted with the aggressive takeover strategies of corporate raiders and others.[81] Arnault, who had a particular interest in artistic creation and high standards of quality,[82] returned to France three years later to become chief executive of a small luxury goods company.

This proved only the start of Arnault's ambitions. Soon afterwards he acquired control of the almost bankrupt Boussac textile company for a small sum. He rapidly sold most of the assets, keeping only the Christian Dior fashion business and the Le Bon Marché department store. He later claimed to have become convinced of the global potential of the Dior brand when he arrived in New York for the first time in his life and his cab driver did not know the name of the French president but said he knew Christian Dior.[83] Shortly after the creation of LVMH, he was able to exploit tension between the former chief executives of Moët Hennessy and Louis Vuitton and, following the October 1987 stock market crash, was able to take over two-fifths of LVMH's capital.[84]

Arnault became a master of using acquisitions to grow his business, which spanned alcoholic beverages, fashion, and beauty, but always in the luxury sector. He controlled the entire undertaking through a pyramid of financial holding companies in which ownership was shared with minority share-holders, such as the bank Crédit Lyonnais, which provided capital to fund acquisitions. Within this complex structure, Arnaud's personal holding com-pany owned just over two-fifths of a financial holding company, Financière Agache, which owned just over half of other subsidiaries, including LVMH and Christian Dior, whose ownership and management still contained many members of the original founding families. Arnault himself was at the center of the co-ordination and direction of the entire venture.[85] This organizational and financial model enabled Arnault to keep acquiring companies to add to his portfolio, such as Guerlain in 1994.

As the market for corporate control grew, it therefore became increasingly easy to buy beauty companies and their brands, and for beauty companies to buy into other industries. In the wider management literature, the conglomer-ates and unrelated diversifiers of this era came to be heavily criticized, as the belief grew that firms should focus on their "core businesses," which they understood and knew how to manage. More recently it has been argued that such highly diversified firms and conglomerates performed, in aggregate, much better than their critics alleged.[86] Certainly LVMH, and perhaps even BAC, would count as support for this view. It was equally clear, however, that some brands were badly tarnished by poor management within conglomerates, and by being passed from one owner to another. It proved equally problematic for managers of firms such as Revlon and Avon to divert resources and managerial attention from their beauty brands to other industries. As advertising costs soared and competition intensified, beauty became even more of an unrelent-ing industry than in the past. In an industry in which constant attention to fashion shifts, innovation, heavy spending on advertising, and the recruitment and retention of creative talent were essential for success, brands needed to be the focus of corporate attention.

The difference in toiletries

Surprisingly, the "soapers" and other consumer products companies which sold toiletries played only a marginal role in the acquisition frenzies of the 1960s and 1970s. After all, they had marketed their soaps, toothpaste, and other

17. Max Factor's "Pan-Cake Make-Up" advertisement featuring the movie star Merle Oberon (1944).

18. Advertisement for Revlon's Fatal Apple face powder, invoking "the look of Eve" and featuring an apple as a symbol of erotic seduction (1946).

19. Illustration from a sales catalogue of Avon, showing a representative calling on her customer in the United States (1956).

WHEN YOUR AVON REPRESENTATIVE CALLS

Mrs. Marie Russell Lehner, fashion coordinator of Buffalo, New York, takes time out to select the Avon fragrance that is right for her . . . with the help of Mrs. Madeline Pritchard, her Avon Representative. Mrs. Lehner, a busy executive, appreciates the convenience of selecting Avon cosmetics for the whole family, in the privacy of her home.

20. L'Oréal's hairspray Elnett was the firm's first great success in the hair care mass market, displayed here in an advertisement from the brand's launch year (1960).
© L'Oréal

L'ORÉAL PRÉSENTE **Elnett** *Souple*

nuage fixant

véritable révolution pour le maintien et la beauté de votre coiffure

L'ORÉAL, grâce à ses chimistes, vient de créer ce produit extraordinaire et, grâce à ses ingénieurs, vous l'offre à un prix très, très abordable !

L'Oréal avec ses laboratoires qui sont les plus grands du monde, a trouvé le produit qui permet à toute femme de faire tenir sa coiffure sans le « gommage ».
L'Oréal avec ses procédés de fabrication, les plus puissants du monde, a pu baisser son prix de revient et, par conséquent, son prix de vente.

ELNETT vous permet une fixation merveilleusement souple et légère de votre coiffure... et laisse aux cheveux un toucher très, très agréable !

En vaporisant un nuage d'ELNETT sur vos cheveux avant votre coup de peigne du matin, vous faciliterez votre coiffage.
Si vous vaporisez un peu d'ELNETT sur votre coiffure terminée, elle tiendra toute la journée.
En touchant vos cheveux avec vos mains, vous constaterez qu'ils sont doux et qu'ils rendent souples.

Elnett *coiffure belle et nette*

PRIX MAXIMUM : 7,50 N.F.

21. Poster advertisement for Pierre Robert's LdB, the popular skin and body lotion created by Knut Wulff in 1945, whose name is an abbreviation of "Lait de Beauté." Invoking erotic imagery as well as an association to health and nature, LdB is advertised here with a picture of a woman with glowing skin (*c.* 1965).

Photograph by Georg Oddner © Georg Oddner

The one lotion that's cool, exciting
—brisk as an ocean breeze!

The one-and-only Old Spice exhilarates...gives you that great-to-be-alive feeling...refreshes after every shave...adds to your assurance... and wins feminine approval every time. Old Spice After Shave Lotion, 1.25 and 2.00 plus tax.

Old Spice —the shave lotion men recommend to other men!

SHULTON

22. Advertisement for Old Spice® for men, a prominent spice cologne shaving lotion launched in 1938 by maker Shulton and acquired by P & G in 1990 (1962).

23. Facial cosmetics advertisement for Shiseido, illustrating the preference at that time for models with Western features including round eyes and short hair styles inspired by the London mod look (1966).

24. Avon advertisement displaying an expanded range of color cosmetics developed to appeal to the preferences of African-American women (1978).

25. Revlon's global bestseller Charlie, launched in 1973 using explicit sexual imagery and targeting the modern independent woman (1988).

26. Original 1977 bottle for YSL Opium, the lifestyle perfume launched by Yves Saint Laurent Beauté.

© YSL Beauté.

27. Shu Uemura, the make-up artist who founded the color cosmetics firm in 1967 under the name Japan Makeup. The firm was renamed Shu Uemura Cosmetics in 1983, and was later sold to L'Oréal (2000).

© L'Oréal and Akira Okimura.

28. Wella acquired the Rochas fragrance brand in 1987, and targeted male consumers with Aquaman by Rochas, launched in 2001.

29. Advertisement for Rimmel make-up featuring the celebrity model Kate Moss (2007).

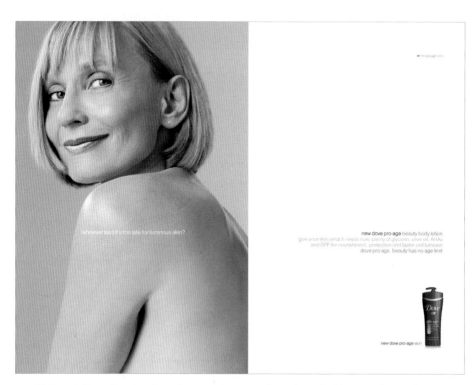

30. Unilever's Dove Pro-Age line of personal care products, launched in 2007, featured a campaign using senior women (2007).

Photograph by Richard Phibbs © Unilever and Richard Phibbs.

キラリ、華やぐ唇でパーティーへ！マキアージュの新しいリップコンパクト。
クリスタライジングリップコンパクト 4種 新発売

ドレスコードは、唇。

31. Advertisement for Shiseido's Maquillage brand, showing the increasing preference for Japanese rather than Western models (2007).

32. L'Oréal Paris' skin brightening cream White Perfect advertisement for China, with company celebrity spokesperson Michele Reis (2007).

toiletries as beauty aids for decades. In contrast to the pharmaceutical companies, they had great experience in consumer marketing. Their absence is even more surprising given that the market potential of shampoos, skin creams, and cosmetics was well understood. Henkel, Germany's largest soap and detergents company, launched shampoos soon after the end of the war, and in 1949 it acquired Therachemie, a recently founded company which made home hair coloring. Expansion into other hair care products followed, and what became named the Thera Poly brand was extended into new skin care and cosmetics products. In 1954, Henkel also launched Fa soap, a new type of toilet soap made from high-quality vegetable oils and animal fats. In the following year it agreed to become a distributor of Revlon cosmetics in Germany.[87]

In the United States, Gillette, whose business had previously been confined to razors and blades, also saw opportunities in a wider range of beauty products. In 1949 it acquired Toni, a recently founded company which had developed a home permanent-wave kit which was enormously successful in the American market. Within a few years, Gillette had extended the Toni brand into shampoos and skin cleansers. Deodorants and hair sprays followed.[88]

Yet this early postwar activity did not translate into a sustained push into the rest of the beauty industry. Companies struggled to make a success of the brands they had acquired. The top management of Unilever walked away from an opportunity to buy L'Oréal. Henkel's efforts in cosmetics and skin care made little progress. In 1960 Revlon cancelled the distribution agreement with Henkel, and began manufacturing in Germany itself.[89] During the following decade Henkel, like Unilever, regularly scanned the corporate world for potential cosmetics acquisitions, even entering negotiations with some German firms, but without ever consummating a deal.[90]

As for Gillette, it began selling shaving creams in 1953 and deodorants in 1960, when the successful Right Guard aerosol deodorant was launched. However, it repeatedly stumbled in the market for cosmetic products for women. The Toni division waned as the fashion for home perming declined. An attempt to enter the luxury business with the purchase of the small Eve of Roma prestige cosmetics business in 1967, including an Italian factory and a number of Italian salons, proved very unsuccessful.[91] Six years later Gillette purchased the Californian direct seller Jafra, only to disrupt its business badly by moving the head office to Gillette's Boston headquarters.[92]

The other large consumer product companies focused on building mass-market shampoo, toothpaste, and deodorant businesses, but stayed firmly away from skin care, cosmetics, and fragrances. This was true of both P & G and Colgate-Palmolive. The former showed a particular determination to stay within product areas in which technological and marketing capabilities could be developed organically. An antitrust case, arising from P & G's acquisition of a household bleach company in 1957, led P & G to abstain from making acquisitions until the start of the 1980s.[93] In Japan, the leading companies broadly followed the P & G model. Kao's Feather Shampoo, launched in 1955, and Halo toothpaste, launched in 1967, proved marketing triumphs, but did not tempt Kao further into cosmetics. Lion created joint ventures with Bristol-Myers during the 1960s, which enabled it to distribute the latter's toiletries products such as the deodorant Ban, but it did not follow the American company's expanding interest in other categories beyond small experiments in skin and hair care.[94]

The lack of a clear identity for the beauty industry as a whole provides the key to understanding why the makers of toiletries were unwilling to, or incapable of, extending their business into other categories. Even if their businesses in soaps, toothpastes, and shaving creams were marketed as beauty aids, their much larger businesses in detergents, razors, diapers, or margarine were pre-eminently functional. These products were sold in large volumes into mass-distribution channels markets in which customers placed most value on their functionality.

As a result, these companies primarily identified themselves as belonging with other fast-moving consumer-packaged goods industries rather than the more fashion-oriented and creative segments of the beauty industry. P & G, for example, invested massively in building a new diaper business. Unilever invested in a wide range of industries, from animal feeds to road haulage, but it was especially interested in building scale in processed and frozen food.[95] Lion also diversified from the late 1960s into branded foodstuffs, especially spices, salad dressings, and other Western-style seasonings.[96] It was not easy for managers interested in growing the small beauty businesses in these big firms to gain access to resources in competition with larger and more successful parts of their businesses, nor did the best managers tend to gravitate towards small product categories. Meanwhile, attracting the creative talent necessary for building fashionable beauty brands to work in cities such as Cincinnati or Düsseldorf remained a challenge.

The corporate culture of these companies also exhibited a "maleness" which may have been a factor in the lack of understanding of, and sometimes disdain for, fashion-driven categories. The disdain was discernible in the packaged goods companies. Eleanor Macdonald, a Unilever executive, observed that Unilever was a "very much a male orientated company."[97] Even two decades later this company had high rates of resignations among female managers, ascribed internally to "male chauvinistic attitudes that are deeply rooted."[98]

Gillette's original business of selling razors and blades to men also contributed to a very male culture. It was a pioneer of using endorsements of male sports figures as a marketing device; it was the leading sponsor of boxing programs on American television between 1944 and 1964; it sponsored World Series baseball in America, bullfighting in Mexico, soccer in Brazil, and horse racing in Colombia.[99] Gillette "is as masculine as you can get," an article on female employment in the company observed in the house magazine in 1957.[100] In 1972 J. Walter Thompson noted the "strong current perception that Gillette is a male oriented company."[101]

A renewed interest by toiletry companies in the wider beauty industry emerged during the second half of the 1960s. Management consultants emphasized the growth and profitability of the cosmetics industry.[102] Henkel bought small German brands, such as Manuela in 1964, and formed another subsidiary to manage its licensee business with American firms. Five years later Henkel acquired the Khasana brand, which Bristol-Myers had acquired a decade earlier and run with little success. Henkel's acquisition of Khasana proved challenging. Adopting a strategy inspired by the marketing methods of P & G and Colgate, Henkel launched brands below market prices in order to achieve large market shares quickly. But with a few exceptions, such as a short-lived success of the all-purpose skin cream Crème 21 against Nivea and the continued success of Fa, the beauty business remained loss-making.[103] While some of Khasana's brands survived in the new cosmetics division, Henkel-Khasana itself was liquidated in 1980.[104]

Henkel's misfortunes were matched by others. In 1971 Kao formed a separate fragrances and cosmetics division, which initially began to develop more cosmetic images for functional brands. Kao launched a research program to develop skin care products, and in 1980 Sofina skin cosmetics was launched. Like other toiletry companies, Kao found the market difficult. Kao did not have a distribution channel for such products. The initial decision to establish a separate division had to be reversed and the operation merged into the rest of the firm in order to benefit from the latter's reputation for quality.[105]

However, the most catastrophic experience was that of Colgate-Palmolive. In 1971 a new chief executive launched a strategy of diversification into textiles, surgical dressings, sports equipment, foods, and health care. Three years later Helena Rubinstein was acquired from the founder's eldest son and her nephew for over $140 million. An unsuccessful attempt was launched to remold the brand on the lines of a mass-market toiletry brand. A number of innovative, but unsuccessful, initiatives were also introduced. One was a new skin line called Madame Rubinstein marketed, rather too explicitly, for women over 50. Another was the introduction of an electronic beauty-scanner which purported to provide an individual analysis of the right skin care and make-up needs for customers. Both initiatives incurred heavy losses. A move of the head office from Manhattan to Nassau County on Long Island proved highly disruptive, and had to be reversed three years later. In 1979 the Helena Rubinstein business lost $20 million on sales of $200 million, and Colgate-Palmolive put it up for sale.[106]

In 1980, after trying but failing to dispose of the business to both L'Oréal and Kao, the brand was sold to a private buyer for $20 million. In a remarkable proof of the destruction in value, only $1.5 million was paid on signing, $3.5 million in two equal installments, with the balance paid annually until 1996. Finally, in 1984 L'Oréal bought the Helena Rubinstein operations in Latin America and Japan, followed four years later by the worldwide operations. The brand was renewed over time, but its reputation in the United States was badly tarnished. Colgate-Palmolive spent the 1980s trying to recover its vitality by selling non-core assets, and rebuilding and renewing its laundry and toiletry businesses.[107]

It seemed for a while that the other companies would follow Colgate-Palmolive and divest from the beauty industry, even from many toiletries. P & G's internal discussion during the early 1980s concerning withdrawing from shampoo had its counterpart at Unilever. By 1980 Unilever's beauty revenues, overwhelmingly derived from toiletry sales, were only 4 per cent of total corporate revenues.[108] In 1984 the issue of whether to divest from the category altogether was on the table at Unilever: it was considered the most likely option if no major American acquisition could be made.[109]

The rush of large-scale acquisitions by the toiletry companies during the mid-1980s was therefore surprising. The changing overall business climate was one important factor. The Reagan administration's relaxation of antitrust policy in the United States relieved P & G and other companies of concerns that acquisitions would get them sued. Corporate managements, even of the largest blue chip companies, came under new pressure from financial analysts to "deliver value" to shareholders. In 1980 P & G made its first significant acquisition in 17 years when it bought a soft drinks business.[110] Two years earlier, Unilever's acquisition of a large American chemicals company had served to raise the confidence of its senior management in their ability to make successful acquisitions in the United States.[111]

Both Unilever and P & G however, were more interested in OTC health care than in beauty. P & G bought a pharmaceuticals company with a large OTC business in 1982.[112] The same interest lay behind a hostile takeover bid by Unilever for Richardson Vicks in 1985. Unilever's over-aggressive approach, however, led the Richardson family to seek an alternative, "white knight" suitor. That other suitor turned out to be P & G, which acquired Richardson Vicks in 1986 in its largest-ever acquisition. P & G thus acquired a portfolio of modestly-sized beauty brands, including Oil of Olay skin cream and Pantene shampoo, as well as the licensing rights to the Vidal Sassoon brand, which the hairdresser had sold to Richardson Vicks in 1982.[113]

The Richardson Vicks acquisition happened at a fortuitous time, just as P & G's shampoo business, from which the company had considered withdrawing earlier in the decade, was showing signs of turning around. The company's researchers were close to perfecting a major technological breakthrough involving a 2-in-1 shampoo, where the conditioner and shampoo were combined in one product which both cleaned the hair and left it feeling silky. The technology was first put into an existing unsuccessful brand called Pert, which was rebranded as Pert Plus. The renamed Pert Plus brand was launched nationally in the United States in 1987 as a functionally proficient "2-in-1" shampoo and conditioner, achieving a respectable growth before a host of similar products from other companies appeared.[114] The Richardson Vicks acquisition now gave P & G other shampoo brands to work with—Vidal Sassoon and Pantene. In order to exploit this technology quickly, and in Asia in particular, P & G put the technology into whatever brand name worked best.

P & G's new technology scored a resounding triumph when it was put together with Pantene in Taiwan and matched with a winning advertising campaign. When acquired, Pantene was still the minor prestige brand with a health-oriented image which Roche had developed. P & G's Asian regional management suggested to its small subsidiary in Taiwan, a country which it had only entered for the first time in 1985, that they should try to use Pantene as a third brand to build their tiny hair care business alongside Head & Shoulders and Pert Plus, both of which emphasized functional effectiveness. The brand management team took elements from Pantene campaigns in other markets to develop a brand based on a beauty platform which stressed its ability to deliver healthy, shiny hair. Pantene Pro-V was launched in Taiwan in 1990. It proved successful and spread to other markets around the world.[115]

By then P & G was acquiring other brands. Between 1989 and 1991 it bought Noxell, the Shulton division of American Cyanamid, Max Factor, and Betrix. In reaction, Unilever, which had looked at Chesebrough-Pond's as a target for some years but had been deterred because of its diversified portfolio, cast aside its reputation for slow-moving caution and became in turn a "white knight" after another firm made a failed hostile bid for that company. The successful acquisition of Chesebrough-Pond's gave Unilever the mass skin-care brands Pond's and Vaseline, as well as smaller brand properties such as Cutex and Prince Matchabelli cosmetics. Within a year Unilever had recouped around one-third of the acquisition price by selling practically all of the non-beauty businesses.[116] During the late 1980s Unilever returned to the luxury sector with the acquisitions of Calvin Klein Cosmetics, a business started by the designer earlier in the decade, and Fabergé/Elizabeth Arden.[117] Meanwhile Kao acquired Andrew Jergens in 1988, and built a professional hair care business in Germany, first acquiring professional hair care firms in a joint venture with Beiersdorf, and then buying Goldwell in 1989.[118]

The last substantive acquirer of beauty brands during these years was Benckiser, a long-established German family-owned chemicals business which was reinvented as a successful detergents and consumer products company through multiple acquisitions over the course of the 1980s. In 1990 it was decided to diversify the company once again into the beauty industry. Astor Lancaster was acquired from Beecham, and other acquisitions followed, including Coty in 1992. In 1996, having been outbid by L'Oréal for Maybelline, Unilever's color cosmetics business, including the Rimmel brand, was bought. In that year Benckiser was floated on the stock market, with the family retaining a 15 per cent shareholding, while Coty was spun off as a separate US-based holding company, wholly owned by the family, as a vehicle to hold the fledgling $1.5 billion beauty business which had been assembled.[119]

Thus, during the first four postwar decades, the senior managements of the largest consumer products companies making toiletries had seen more future in diapers, detergents, and ice cream than in lipstick, mascara, or perfume. The corporate culture of many of these firms, as well as perceived conflicts of interest and some very bad experiences in shampoo and cosmetics, all contributed to this situation. This changed in the mid-1980s, and within a few years P & G, Unilever, Benckiser, and Kao had become major owners of brand properties in cosmetics, skin and hair care, and fragrances. It still remained unclear, however, if these new owners would have any more success than their predecessors in managing their new brands.

Summing up

The ownership of the world beauty industry experienced enormous change between the 1960s and the 1980s. Numerous small and medium-sized cosmetics, fragrances, and toiletries brands were bought and sold, sometimes multiple times. It was clear that a large company from a different industry, whether pharmaceuticals, tobacco, or soap, could buy a good collection of cosmetics and fragrances brands. It was also clear that the real challenge was to manage them properly. This frenetic activity was more than a game of corporate musical chairs. More fundamentally, it was a story of a search for identity by an industry whose borders were still unclear. It was also a search for the right business model needed to take the industry, whatever its identity was, to the next stage.

For a time, it seemed that this model would involve the reuniting of beauty and health. The world's largest pharmaceutical companies purchased some of the most iconic brands of cosmetics and fragrances. Charles Revson and François Dalle invested in pharmaceutical companies. Avon bought health care companies and nursing homes. It turned out, however, that beauty and health had diverged too much from their common origin in the past to be reassembled, at least at this time. The sudden appearance in the mid-1980s of the leading toiletry companies as major acquirers of cosmetics, fragrance, and skin and hair care brands marked the beginning of a new business model. However, it remained to be seen if these companies possessed the cultural and organizational capabilities which would make them any more successful than their pharmaceutical and conglomerate predecessors.

Notes

1. Eleanor Macdonald, *Nothing By Chance! An Autobiography of a Pioneer Business Woman* (Alton, Hants: Nimrod Press, 1987), p. 122. Macdonald was recruited to Unilever's Atkinson's fragrance company in the late 1940s. During a 20-year career with Unilever, she also worked for the United Africa Company, its large Western African trading company, as its Women's Adviser with a mandate to understand the needs of the female consumers in the region.

2. In 1935 this took the name of the Toilet Goods Association (TGA). The TGA was renamed the Cosmetic, Toiletry, and Fragrance Association (CFTA) in 1971, and in 2007 the Personal Care Products Council.

3. This was renamed the Cosmetic Toiletry and Perfumery Association in 1978. See Hilda Butler, "Cosmetics through the Ages," in Hilda Butler (ed.), *Poucher's Perfumes Cosmetics and Soaps,* 10th edn (Dordrecht: Kluwer, 2000), p. 59.

4. Bénédicte Corbier, "La Fédération des Industries de la Parfumerie," in François Berthoud (ed.), *Parfums et cosmétiques: Une industrie du rêve et de la beauté* (Paris: Les éditions d'Assalit, 2005), p. 173.

5. The substantial management literature on "new market categories," and the economic significance of well-understood categories, can be approached through P. DiMaggio, "Cultural Entrepreneurship in Nineteenth-Century Boston," *Media, Culture and Society* 4 (1982), pp. 33–50, and E. Zuckerman, "The Categorical Imperative: Securities Analysts and the Illegitimacy Discount," *American Journal of Sociology* 104 (1999), pp. 1398–438.

6. Frost and Sullivan, *The Cosmetics and Toiletries Industry Market* (New York: August 1972).

7. Lee Israel, *Estée Lauder: Beyond the Magic* (New York: Macmillan, 1985), pp. 76–7.

8. Subrata N. Chakravert and Mike Tuthill, "Not by Style Alone," *Forbes*, November 18, 1985.

9. Israel, *Estée*, pp. 74–5.

10. Lindy Woodhead, *War Paint* (Hoboken, NJ: John Wiley, 2003), pp. 413–14.

11. The causes and consequences of the growth of large, diversified firms has generated a vast literature. Richard Whittington and Michael Mayer, *The European*

Corporation: Strategy, Structure, and Social Science (Oxford: Oxford University Press, 2000), ch. 3, provides a critical assessment of the evidence.

12. Michael C. Jensen and Richard S. Rubback, "The Market for Corporate Control: The Scientific Evidence," *Journal of Financial Economics* 11 (1983), pp. 5–50, was a pioneering paper which showed that, on average, acquisitions benefited the shareholders of acquired firms rather than acquiring firms.

13. Israel, *Estée*, pp. 72–4.

14. Hans Conrad Peyer, *Roche: A Company History 1896–1996* (Basle: Roche, 1996), pp. 171, 194–5, 221.

15. Between the 1950s and 1970s, between two-fifths and one-half of Beiersdorf's total sales were in personal care. See Geoffrey Jones, "Blonde and Blue-eyed? Globalizing Beauty, c.1945–c.1980," *Economic History Review* 61 (2008), p. 153; Beiersdorf AG, *100 Jahre Beiersdorf, 1882–1982* (Hamburg: Beiersdorf, 1982), p. 93; Beiersdorf Annual Reports, 1970–1980.

16. Alfred D. Chandler, *Shaping the Industrial Century* (Cambridge, Mass.: Harvard University Press, 2005), p. 190.

17. "Cyanamid Fighting Lilly's Plan to Buy Cosmetics Maker," *New York Times*, October 21, 1970.

18. "Squibb Beech-Nut Plans to Acquire Lanvin-Charles," *Wall Street Journal*, October 27, 1970.

19. Frost and Sullivan, *Cosmetics*, pp. 139–40.

20. "Nation's Chemical Industry Sheds Its Anonymity," *New York Times*, April 5, 1964.

21. James Foreman-Peck, *Smith & Nephew in the Health Care Industry* (Aldershot: Edward Elgar, 1995), pp. 136–8; Margaret Allen, *Selling Dreams* (New York: Simon and Schuster, 1981), pp. 81–2.

22. "Jovan Maneuver Catapults Beecham onto the World Scene," *Advertising Age*, September 3, 1979; Tom Reichert, *The Erotic History of Advertising* (New York: Prometheus Books, 2003), pp. 260–7; "Jovan Moves Out New Fragrances, Steps into After-Bath Products," *Advertising Age*, September 13, 1976.

23. HistoCom Industriepark Höchst, formerly the Hoechst corporate archive, Frankfurt (hereafter HistoCom), IW 1802: Hans Schwarzkopf GmbH, Hamburg (January 1, 1972—December 31, 1991); W. von Pölnitz, "Gedanken zur Organization des Consumer-Geschäftes von Hoechst unter Einschluss der Kosmetik-Aktivitäten," December 17, 1979.

24. Hoechst Annual Reports; HistoCom, IW 1201.1, Summary Sheet for Marbert, in Marbert GmbH, Düsseldorf, January 1, 1972 and June 30, 1972.

25. "Perfume and Powder Purveyors Introduce Novelties," *Wall Street Journal*, August 24, 1951; "Squibb's Foreign Earnings Growing More Important," *Barron's National Business and Financial Weekly*, August 13, 1951. In 1952 Squibb was acquired by the Olin Mathieson Chemical Corporation.

26. "Trade-Mark Infringement: The Power of an American Trade-mark Owner to Prevent the Importation of the Authentic Product Manufactured by a Foreign Company," *Yale Law Journal* 64:4 (February 1955), pp. 557–68.

27. "Reviving Breck: New Bottles, No 'Girls'," *Wall Street Journal*, June 1, 1993.

28. Foreman-Peck, *Smith & Nephew*, pp. 136–8; Allen, *Selling*, pp. 81–2.

29. Sandy Schusteff, "Bristol-Myers Squibb Company," in Tina Grant (ed.), *International Directory of Company Histories*, vol. 37 (Farmington Hills, Mich.: St. James Press, 2001), pp. 41–5; Chandler, *Shaping*, pp. 216–17.

30. Frost and Sullivan, *Cosmetics*, p. 139.

31. Frost and Sullivan, *Marketing Strategies for Selling Cosmetics and Toiletries in Europe* (New York, April 1983), pp. 105–6.

32. HistoCom, IW 1802, W. von Pölnitz, "Gedanken."

33. HistoCom, IW 1802, K. Lanz, "Schwarzkopf/Auslandsgesellschaften—Umsatz und Ergebnisplanung bis 1976, Notiz KDA vom June 14 1972," July 3, 1972; W. von Pölnitz, "Notiz über eine Gesellschafterbesprechung mit den Mitgliedern der Familie Schwarzkopf...," May 16, 1978; K. Warning to the Hoechst Management Board, "Schwarzkopf," March 7, 1990.

34. Interview with Hans Peter Schwarzkopf by Christian Stadler, March 27, 2007.

35. HistoCom, IW 1802, "Hans Schwarzkopf GmbH, Hamburg. Stärken und Schwächen," December 16, 1982; Schwarzkopf Lizenzverträge 9, Martin Frühauf and Uwe Jens Thomsen to the Schwarzkopf family and heirs of Peter Schwarzkopf, November 18, 1988; Uwe Jens Thomsen, "Hans Schwarzkopf GmbH, Hamburg," July 17, 1984; Uwe Jens Thomsen to Kurt and Hans Peter Schwarzkopf, September 7, 1984.

36. Johnson & Johnson, Form 10-K, year ending December 31, 1978.

37. "Drug Companies Leave Cosmetics," *New York Times*, December 28, 1989. The quotation is by Jack L. Salzman, cosmetics industry analyst of Goldman Sachs.

38. Chandler, *Shaping*, p. 196.

39. "Charles of the Ritz Sold to Yves St. Laurent," *New York Times*, November 19, 1986.

40. "Fabergé Pays Premium to Buy Elizabeth Arden," *New York Times*, August 6, 1987.

41. Geoffrey Jones, *Renewing Unilever* (Oxford: Oxford University Press, 2005), p. 298.

42. "Clorox Buying Brands of Cyanamid Division," *New York Times*, June 21, 1990; "Cyanamid Completes Shulton Sale," *New York Times*, September 11, 1990.

43. HistoCom, IW 1802, Martin Frühauf, "Schwarzkopf," December 18, 1989; "Henkel übernimmt die Mehrheit bei Schwarzkopf," *Frankfurter Allgemeine Zeitung*, August 12, 1995.

44. Matrix had been founded by Arnold ("Arnie") Miller, a hairdresser and entrepreneur in Cleveland, Ohio, in 1980: Geoffrey Jones, David Kiron, Vincent Dessain, and Anders Sjöman, "L'Oréal and the Globalization of American Beauty," Harvard Business School Case no. 9-805-086 (February 2, 2006).

45. "Johnson to Buy Skin-care Line," *New York Times*, November 19, 1993; Brian O'Reilly; "J & J is on a Roll," *Fortune*, December 26, 1994, pp. 178–92.

46. Geoffrey Jones, Akiko Kanno, and Masako Egawa, "Making China Beautiful: Shiseido and the China Market," Harvard Business School Case no. 9-805-003 (July 3, 2008). Shiseido took full ownership of the joint venture in 1996.

47. Chandler, *Shaping*, p. 257; "French Firms View Bid as a Big Deal," *Washington Post*, January 2, 1988.

48. See Chapter 9.

49. CL, DEFF 796261-1, Industrie française des produits de parfumerie de beauté et de toilette, February 16, 1982.

50. "Sanofi Buys Nina Ricci Holding," *Financial Times*, April 12, 1988.

51. These were Fendi Profuma and Florbath Profumi Di Parma: "Sanofi Purchases Italian Perfume Companies," *Chemical Marketing Reporter*, February 18, 1988.

52. "French Giant is Acquiring St. Laurent," *New York Times*, January 20, 1993.

53. Telephone interview with Lindsay Owen-Jones, Chairman of L'Oréal, January 22, 2009.

54. Whittington and Mayer, *European*, ch. 3.

55. Derek F. Channon, *The Strategy and Structure of British Enterprise* (London: Macmillan, 1973), pp. 63, 190–1; Allen, *Selling*, p. 77.

56. "ITT Ending US Sales of Rimmel Cosmetics," *Wall Street Journal*, May 18, 1978.

57. HistoCom, IW 208.3 Mouson Cosmetic GmbH, Frankfurt am Main, Mouson Cosmetic GmbH summary sheet; and Rolf Sammet to the Hoechst Board of Supervisors, March 8, 1978. On Quandt, see Whittington and Mayer, *European*, p. 199.

58. Frost and Sullivan, *Cosmetics and Toiletries Markets in Europe* (New York, 1985), pp. 324–5.

59. "Burma-Shave Rhymes are Reborn for TV," *New York Times*, July 8, 1997.

60. "American Brands Bids Time," *New York Times*, August 17, 1983.

61. Whittington and Mayer, *European*, pp. 140–1.

62. Germaine Monteil had launched a range of make-up and skin care products in 1935 and promoted the idea that "beauty is not a gift, it is a habit:" Kate Mulvey and Melissa Richards, *Decades of Beauty* (New York: Octopus, 1998), p. 93.

63. BAT Industries files, Tobacco Control Archives, University of California, San Francisco, Budget Submission, Cosmetics Operating Group, July 7, 1984.

64. Allen, *Selling*, p. 241.

65. Morgan was able to buy Swiss-based Juvena, only to discover that its reported sales and profits were based on creative accounting. Interview by author with Eric Morgan, former Chief Executive BAC, London, May 11 2006.

66. BAT Archives, London, "All About BAT," September 1984.

67. Beauty products never exceeded 2 per cent of BAT's overall corporate revenues, and 1 per cent of the profits.

68. British American Tobacco, *1902–2002: Celebrating Our First 100 Years* (London: BAT, 2002), pp. 94–5.

69. Allen, *Selling*, pp. 104–8; Steve Ginsberg, *Reeking Havoc* (London: Hutchinson, 1990), pp. 90–3.

70. Thomas K. McCraw, *American Business since 1920: How it Worked*, 2nd edn (Wheeling, Ill.: Harlan Davidson, 2009), pp. 194–6.

71. "Acquisition Strains at Esmark," *New York Times*, October 7, 1983.

72. Carol I. Keeley, "Chesebrough-Pond's USA, Inc.," in Paula Kepos (ed.), *International Directory of Company Histories*, vol. 8 (Farmington Hills, Mich.: St. James Press, 1994), p. 106.

73. Gillian Wolf, "Revlon, Inc.," in Tina Grant (ed.), *International Directory of Company Histories*, vol. 17 (Farmington Hills, Mich.: St. James Press, 1997), pp. 402–3.

74. Laura Klepacki, *Avon: Building the World's Premier Company for Women* (Hoboken, NJ: John Wiley, 2005), p. 30. In 1986 beauty products still provided more than 70 per cent of Avon's sales and 80 per cent of its profits, but in the same year Avon also began buying nursing homes.

75. Klepacki, *Avon*, pp. 28–31; Allen, *Selling*, pp. 115–16.

76. Klepacki, *Avon*, pp. 39–41.

77. Jones, *Renewing*, pp. 306–8.

78. "Suit Filed on Revlon Contract; Cosmetics Pact is Disputed," *New York Times*, November 22, 1985, p. D4; "Revlon Plan For Bond Deal," *New York Times*, June 29, 1991, p. 36; Riva D. Atlas, "Perelman Said to Buy Back Bonds in Big Bet on Revlon," *New York Times*, December 14, 2000; and "Perelman's Endless (and Costly) Love," *New York Times*, December 17, 2000.

79. Gordon McKibben, *Cutting Edge* (Boston, Mass.: Harvard Business School Press, 1998), chs 7 and 8.

80. Wolf, "Revlon Inc.," p. 403.

81. Dana Thomas, *DeLuxe. How Luxury Lost Its Luster* (New York: Penguin Press, 2007), pp. 42–3; Whittington and Mayer, *European*, p. 109.

82. Bernard Arnault, *La passion créative* (Paris: Plon, 2000), p. 25.

83. Arnault, *La passion*, p. 27.

84. Thomas, *DeLuxe*, pp. 46–9; Teresa da Silva Lopes, *Global Brands: The Evolution of Multinationals in Alcoholic Beverages* (Cambridge: Cambridge University Press, 2007), pp. 82–4.

85. Whittington and Mayer, *European*, pp. 160–2.

86. Whittington and Mayer, *European*, ch. 5.

87. Susanne Hilger, *Amerikanisierung deutscher Unternehmen* (Stuttgart: Franz Steiner Verlag, 2004), pp. 151–3, 159; Wilfried Feldenkirchen and Susanne Hilger, *Menschen und Marken* (Düsseldorf: Henkel KGaA, 2001), p. 126.

88. McKibben, *Cutting*, pp. 45–6; Gillette Archives (hereafter GA), *The Gillette Company 1901–1976* (Boston, Mass.: Gillette, 1977), p. 22; *Toni 25* (Boston, Mass.: Gillette, 1969).

89. Hilger, *Amerikanisierung*, p. 159.

90. Henkel Archives (hereafter HA), 455/21 Gründung Kosmetik, 1962–1967, Sihler to Kobold and the Persil management board, "Betr.: Projekt Kosmetik: Kauf einer Körperpflegemittelfirma," June 4, 1968, Hilger, *Amerikanisierung*, p. 163.

91. Gillette Annual Report, 1967; McKibben, *Cutting*, p. 70; "Gillette Makes Tricky Switch to Selling Women's Products," *Wall Street Journal*, November 5, 1981.

92. McKibben, *Cutting*, pp. 45, 70.

93. Davis Dyer, Frederick Dalzell, and Rowena Olegario, *Rising Tide* (Boston, Mass.: Harward Business School Press, 2004).

94. Lion Company, *Lion Hyakunen Shie* (*Lion 100-Year History*) (Tokyo: Lion, 1992), *passim*.

95. Jones, *Renewing*, pp. 24–32.

96. Lion used a licensing agreement with McCormick & Co., a leading American producer. See *Lion Hyakunen*.

97. Macdonald, *Nothing*.

98. Jones, *Renewing*, p. 263.

99. GA, *The Gillette Company*, pp. 18–19; Gillette Annual Report, 1962.

100. GA, "Women...in a Man's World," *The Blade* 4:5 (May 1957).

101. J. Walter Thompson Archives, John W. Hartman Center, Duke University (hereafter JWT), Corporate Vertical Files, JWT Chicago office: Gillette PCD Corporate Image, c.1972, Gillette Studies, Box 9.

102. For the case of Henkel, see Susanne Hilger, "Reluctant Americanization? The Reaction of Henkel to the Influences and Competition from the United States," in Akira Kudo, Matthias Kipping, and Harm G. Schröter (eds), *German and Japanese Business in the Boom Years* (London: Routledge, 2004), pp. 206–7; HA 314/130, SRI Report.

103. Hilger, *Amerikanisierung*, pp. 164–6; Harm Schröter, "Erfolgsfaktor Marketing: Der Strukturwandel von der Reklame zur Unternehmenssteuerung," in Wilfried Feldenkirchen, Frauke Schönert-Röhlk, and Günther Schulz (eds), *Wirtschaft, Gesellschaft, Unternehmen: Festschrift für Hans Pohl* (Stuttgart: Franz Steiner Verlag, 1995), pp. 1106–11; HA D516—Henkel-Khasana Dokumentationsmappe, Szymczak to Sihler, "Bruttofremdumsatz und Bruttoergebnis II S-KOS," August 2, 1977.

104. HA D516—Henkel-Khasana Dokumentationsmappe, Landesgericht firm registration form HR B 11801.

105. Tsunehiko Yui, Akira Kudo, and Haruhito Takeda, in association with Eisuke Daito and Satoshi Sasaki, *Kaoshi Hyakunen (1890–1990)* (*Hundred-year History of Kao (1890–1990)*) (Tokyo: Kao Corporation, 1993; in Japanese).

106. Allen, *Selling*, pp. 86–97.

107. David E. Salamie and Frank Uhle, "Colgate-Palmolive Company," in Tina Grant (ed.), *International Directory of Company Histories*, vol. 35 (Farmington Hills, Mich.: St. James Press, 2001), pp. 110–15.

108. Jones, *Renewing*, p. 63.

109. Jones, *Renewing*, p. 98.

110. Dyer, *Rising Tide*, p. 192.

111. Jones, *Renewing*, ch. 4.

112. Dyer, *Rising Tide*, pp. 193–4.

113. Jones, *Renewing*, pp. 305–6; Dyer, *Rising Tide*, pp. 194–5.

114. Dyer, *Rising Tide*, pp. 261–70.

115. Dyer, *Rising Tide*, pp. 274–8. See Chapter 10.

116. Jones, *Renewing*, pp. 98, 306–7, 313–14.

117. Dyer, *Rising Tide*, pp. 283–4; Jones, *Renewing*, pp. 99–101.

118. Yui *et al.*, *Kaoshi*.

119. Geoffrey Jones and David Kiron, "Bernd Beetz: Creating the New Coty," Harvard Business School Case no. 9-808-133 (December 8, 2008).

Part 3

Beauty Reimagined

8

Challenges from New Quarters

I hate the beauty industry. It is a monster industry selling unattainable dreams.
It lies. It cheats. It exploits women. Its major product lines are packaging and
garbage.

Anita Roddick, founder of The Body Shop[1]

The rise of skepticism

While the beauty industry was busy searching for a suitable business model, as
we saw in the last chapter, a new set of challenges arose: the industry's
fundamental assumptions were under new forms of attack. As we have seen
throughout the book, beauty has regularly presented a problem for forces of
conservative morality and tradition. What changed in the 1960s and 1970s is
that it became a political problem from the left as well.

Against the historical backdrop of tradition, aristocracy, and royal courts,
the mass production of beauty has been a force for the democratization of
personal aesthetics. It enabled a growing number of people, for the first time in
human history, to make choices about how they looked and smelled and to
participate in social definitions of taste, fashion, and style. What was once the
sole power of the sovereign became the right of every individual—to make
choices about personal appearance and standards of beauty. And it granted to
every man and woman new powers of self-reinvention: to change the color of
one's hair, the redness of one's lips, and the scent of one's body. Ordinary
people living everywhere were encouraged to imagine that they were the kings
and queens of the modern world.

Yet there was another side to the story, one that regarded the industry as
complicit with the crimes of Western imperialism, American racial segregation, and fascism. New forms of political consciousness arose in the decades

after World War II. Consumer activists, feminists, environmentalists, people of color, and colonized peoples articulated new messages and found international platforms for their messages. Beauty had always been attacked by the forces of tradition; now it was being attacked by the forces of social revolution as well. These new critiques of the beauty industry from the left accused it of offering consumers choices that were constrained by bigoted assumptions about age, gender, ethnicity, and class. Promises of efficacy and safety were held to be resting on little more than advertising copy. Critics were holding the mirror up to the beauty industry, and the reflection was not pretty.

The industry's enormous advertising budget was an obvious starting point for critical scrutiny. It was focused on promising women between their teens and late thirties that its products would make them more attractive and, as they aged, keep them looking younger than their age: "whether you are 25 or 65 (or 75!) your skin can have a youthful beauty never possible before," as a typical Revlon ad of the 1960s put it.[2] It was hardly surprising that consumer groups identified cosmetics advertising as amongst the most misleading.[3] Growing skepticism may have been encouraged by the departure from the industry, through death or retirement, of many of the figures who had lent their names to brands, and their replacement by anonymous corporate behemoths.

The scale, cost, and increasing sophistication of the advertising industry, of which the beauty industry was such an important component, stimulated growing hostility as consumer activist and feminist movements gathered steam. In 1958 the American economist John Kenneth Galbraith launched a major critique of advertising promoting "unreal" needs.[4] Galbraith's arguments were taken up in Europe where, from the 1960s on, consumer movements criticized the cost and manipulative nature of advertising.[5] The result was a growth of regulations designed to prohibit false and misleading advertisements, although with many national variations in enforcement. While German laws, for example, enforced a literal interpretation of truth, French laws allowed more expressive freedom.[6] In Britain a system of voluntary regulation was put in place. In the United States, there was also a surge of tight regulations, although by the 1980s a reversion to high tolerance of advertising claims was evident.

The beauty industry, then, found itself especially exposed to criticism that it made "unreal promises" to meet "unreal" needs. As a result, these decades saw the beginnings of a skepticism and a changing focus which would, in time, greatly change some aspects of the industry.

Science and nature

During the nineteenth century the emergent beauty industry had employed modern science to offer consumers both wider and safer choices than in the pre-industrial era. Yet as companies searched for efficacy, there was always the risk of unintended side effects and reactions. Indeed, the stronger the intervention in appearance, the greater the possibility that such reactions might happen. The consumer safety legislation which appeared during the 1930s, especially in the United States, had identified this issue, but without providing robust protection to consumers. This situation continued to prevail as the industry boomed after World War II, although there were occasional expressions of concern about the potential health risks of products. In 1948 the American Medical Association, for example, established a committee on cosmetics to look specifically at health issues.[7]

During the 1960s the emergence of the consumer movement on both sides of the Atlantic brought with it rising concerns about safety in many industries, as a perception emerged that many manufactured products were harmful. P & G, Unilever, and other manufacturers of synthetic detergents came under attack for the environmental damage caused by the chemicals used in their products.[8] A series of catastrophic incidents highlighted the risks to personal health of certain products and reinforced the growing skepticism concerning the safety of the science which lay behind industrial products. In Europe, the drug Thalidomide, marketed between 1957 and 1961 as a remedy for morning sickness during pregnancy, turned out to produce horrific birth defects. In France, a talcum powder marketed in 1972 as talc Morhange killed 36 children and injured a further 240.[9] This talcum powder contained hexachlorophene, which the Food and Drug Administration (FDA) in the United States had issued a major warning against two years previously.[10]

This chemical compound was also widely used in other cosmetic products. It was the major ingredient in Cover Girl cosmetics, which needed to be reformulated when the use of the chemical was banned. It also featured in the new category of vaginal deodorants, whose sales had boomed after Alberto-Culver launched them in the American market in the late 1960s.

The FDA warning caused a temporary collapse in Alberto-Culver's sales, though the product was later reformulated.[11] The very concept of a vaginal deodorant was widely criticized as both unnecessary and unsafe.[12]

By the 1970s consumer skepticism about the safety of consumer products had reached such a level that governments responded with new regulations requiring rigorous testing and the provision of greater consumer information. Until the early 1970s, American manufacturers of beauty products did not voluntarily label ingredients, despite the passage of the 1966 Fair Packaging and Labeling Act (FPLA), by which the labeling of cosmetic product ingredients was, in theory, mandated.[13] In 1971, in reaction to widespread calls for regulation and disclosure, the American trade association, recently renamed the Cosmetic, Toiletry and Fragrance Association (CFTA), agreed on a system of voluntary regulation under which both members and non-members voluntarily supplied information on various issues, including data on the composition of finished products and details of customer complaints.[14] Mandatory labeling of cosmetic products was instituted in 1973 under the FDA's enforcement of the FPLA, although important exceptions to the law remained, including products for professional salon use only and product samples. Firms could also apply for exceptions, citing protection of trade secrets. Fragrance ingredients were exempted altogether from this labeling legislation.

In Europe, there was often a greater reliance on government legislation. In both Germany and France there was an explosion of consumer-related laws during the 1970s. In Germany, the Law on Food and Cosmetics in 1975 imposed standards on safety and labeling, and regulated additives and advertising, though the beauty industry was left to self-regulate its conformity to these standards. In France, there was a greater reliance on direct government enforcement as it focused on consumer products considered especially dangerous. The talc Morhange incident resulted in the Law on Cosmetic and Hygiene Products in 1975, which required new products to be approved by the Ministry of Health and information about new products to be distributed to anti-poison centers throughout the country.[15]

As legislation to reassure consumers grew, the discovery of further health risks continued to undermine consumer confidence that modern science, and the brands sold by big companies, were safe. By the mid-1970s there was mounting scientific evidence concerning the potentially carcinogenic ingredients used in hair dyes.[16] American research on mice found that the paraphenylenediamines

(PPD), or aniline dyes, used in permanent hair dyes were carcinogens when ingested in large quantities. The main chemical under scrutiny was the most frequently used of the four paraphenylenediamines, which ensured the proper color results desired by consumers who sought darker, black and brown, hair tones.[17] There was parallel, widely reported research about the dangers of hair dyes in other countries.

This research caused a temporary crisis for the major hair dye brands, which had to reformulate their products. Clairol, the market leader in the United States, declared on its packaging that the product had been changed. The color of Clairol's modified dyes was lighter, and the slogan "New clear formula, same great color" was printed on the bottle label.[18] In 1980 the FDA publicly expressed its view that the frequent use of an almost identical chemical as a replacement did not resolve the health issues.[19] PPDs remained in use. Two decades later hair dyes based on them accounted for four-fifths of the products sold in the United States and Europe.[20] They were regulated in the latter jurisdiction but not in the former.[21]

In Europe, L'Oréal, which had always put a heavy emphasis on employing science to develop functional but safe chemicals for cosmetic uses, was highly skeptical of the research on colorants. Charles Zviak, the company's top research scientist, explained both to employees and to the public that the animals used in tests had been fed massive doses of hair colorants, constituting the equivalent of a person "eating or drinking 30 to 40 bottles or tubes of hair dye every day for their entire lives!"[22] François Dalle was also initially dismissive of the scientific evidence. In a 1977 internal memorandum to his employees, he responded fiercely to a recent attack by a French journalist on L'Oréal's shampoos, in which a common ingredient was declared to be unsafe. He dismissed the scientific arguments behind this "unjust attack," which he concluded was "a scandal of radio and television."[23]

Whilst the controversy surrounding hair dyes raged, other health alarms further damaged public confidence in the safety of products. These included the discovery that chlorofluorocarbons (CFCs), the main aerosol used in a host of products from refrigerators to cosmetics, was destroying the ozone layer. Aerosols had been enormously important in the beauty industry since Bristol-Myers' Ban and Mum and Gillette's Right Guard aerosol deodorants were launched in the 1950s.[24] In 1978 the United States banned CFC aerosols, and this step was soon followed by European nations, beginning with Sweden in 1979. In 1980 the personal care industry was further devastated when a deadly new illness called toxic shock syndrome was directly linked to the use of P & G's Rely tampon, launched the previous year as the first "super-absorbent" tampon. The brand was withdrawn from the market.[25]

The twin side of growing consumer skepticism about the safety of the chemical ingredients used in cosmetic products was the emergence of a renewed interest in the use of natural ingredients. The first stirrings of a reaction against the use of chemical ingredients, and a return to using more "natural" ingredients, appeared primarily in postwar Europe where, interestingly, it was not consumers or their advocates who took the lead, but a new generation of entrepreneurs. A preference for nature over artifice had longer roots in Europe. It can be seen in Nazi discourses which raged, for example, against the artificiality of Hollywood make-up, but this had been combined with an often perverted use of science. The new interest in the potential of organic or botanical ingredients in cosmetics was as much a reaction against the horrors of interwar Europe as against the use of chemicals.

The concept of green cosmetics began on a very small scale. Many of the first founders had formal education in science, and the scope of this concept evolved over time. One of the pioneering firms was Biotherm, started in 1950 by a French biologist who made a skin care product using a mineral water from the thermal springs at Molitg-les-Bains in the Pyrenees. A dermatologist, Jus Julin, had identified the springs' unique "Thermal Plankton" as a skin rejuvenator, and they became a key ingredient in the Biotherm skin care range.[26] In the United States in 1948 Emil Bronner, a scion of a soapmaking family going back five generations, founded what became Dr. Bronner's Magic Soaps in Los Angeles, selling liquid peppermint soap and health food seasonings.[27]

As the 1950s progressed, other small ventures were launched, mostly in France and neighboring countries. The use of plants, fruits, and flowers featured prominently. Jacques Courtin-Clarins founded Clarins in 1954. As a young medical student, he had noted that when patients were treated for circulatory problems with massage, their skin looked better. He started a business with botanical body oils. Opening the first Clarins Institut de Beauté in Paris, he developed treatments and products for his salon using plant-based formulas first for the body and the face.[28] Also in 1954, Edmund Georg Locher founded Juvena out of a pharmaceutical laboratory in Zurich. The new company began by using natural ingredients to create light skin creams instead of heavy fatty creams.[29]

During the mid-1950s Yves Rocher also started a company in the rural village of La Gacilly in the French region of Brittany. After leaving school and starting work as a clothing salesman, he used a traditional recipe to create, in the attic of his family's house, a hemorrhoid cream using ingredients from plants. He advertised the product in a Parisian magazine and sold it through mail order. The business was so successful that by the early 1960s Rocher had extended his range to skin care and cosmetics. Driven by the idea of creating jobs to revitalize the region, Rocher steadily expanded production in the village. A reliance on natural ingredients became a hallmark of the firm's products, which remained mail-order-only until the late 1960s, when he opened his own shops.[30]

These and other early green ventures were tiny businesses on the margins of the industry. The great majority of consumers initially showed little interest in natural ingredients in an era when glamorous, highly made-up female models prevailed in cosmetics advertising. During the 1960s, however, there was a growing concern in fashion for the environment, and for things regarded as "natural," such as all-natural fibers and denim blue jeans. A "hippie" youth culture embraced pacifism, flower power, and all things perceived as friendly to the environment. The exclusive use of natural ingredients, however, remained a marginal passion which was mostly pursued by ventures located at a distance from major centers of fashion and capitals of beauty in Europe. In Sweden, a country where the environmental movement was particularly strong, a number of natural brands appeared during the 1960s. Knut Wulff launched Naturelle, a pioneering "natural" hair care brand based on the use of herbs.[31] The founders of Oriflame also saw their business from the beginning as being based on the use of Swedish natural herbs in the formulation of products, with minimal use of perfume and no animal testing.[32]

The mainstream industry also began to reflect some of these new attitudes in their marketing, if not their ingredients. After the hexachlorophene in Cover Girl was banned, the brand launched a Clean Makeup campaign which emphasized outdoor scenes and "natural look."[33] In Britain, Mary Quant launched Starkers make-up in 1968, which emphasized its natural appearance with an advertisement featuring a completely naked young woman.[34]

By the 1970s "natural," although not exclusively meaning the use of all-natural products or avoidance of animal testing, had become a recognized psychographic segment in both the luxury and mass markets. In 1973 Elizabeth Arden opened a new hair salon on the tenth floor of its building on Fifth Avenue which was designed as a botanical environment with hanging plants, flowering crab-apple trees, and seasonal plants at the entrance.[35] The d'Ornano family, having sold Orlane to the Americans, returned to the beauty industry in 1976 when Michel d'Ornano founded a new luxury venture named Sisley, which employed botanical ingredients to make extremely expensive skin creams and other beauty products.[36] By then many mass market firms had joined the "natural" bandwagon. During the late 1970s Clairol captured a large share of the American shampoo market with Herbal Essences, a green shampoo with a high fragrance content based on the essences of sixteen herbs and wildflowers.[37]

Companies had never ceased using natural ingredients in their products, because it was understood that plant extracts contained active ingredients that affected skin and hair and performed other cosmetic functions.[38] As companies responded to growing consumer interest in "natural" products, they typically just added plant extracts to the same chemical formulas used in their existing products, not least because the use of pure natural products greatly raised the cost and complexity of cosmetics, due to problems of spoiled ingredients. Without the employment of synthetic preservatives, plant-derived formulations, especially if not tested on animals, carried health risks unless treated carefully. This encouraged a feeling in the mainstream industry that the "natural" movement was little more than a naive fad based on weak intellectual and scientific foundations. There was, and remained, a major problem of definitions about what natural beauty care really means, with no regulation specifying the percentage of natural ingredients in a formula necessary for it to be natural.[39]

Skepticism was the initial sentiment at L'Oréal. Dalle fulminated in internal newsletters about the "scandal" of "so-called natural products." He disputed the distinction between natural and synthetic ingredients, arguing that natural substances were often synthesized and that manufactured production allowed better quality control than did natural products.[40] However, as consumer interest in natural ingredients persisted, the company responded by experiments with natural brands. In 1978 the hair care brand Kérastase launched two new plant-extract-based products.[41] Within a few years the new emphasis on natural ingredients could be seen in new skin care product launches in both the luxury and mass segments. Even so, throughout the following two decades L'Oréal's approach towards green cosmetics remained cautious.

There was also a new cohort of companies which, although still marginal, would in time exercise a major influence on the industry as a whole. In 1976 Olivier Baussan, a young literature student, founded l'Occitane in the southern French region of Provence. The firm made shampoos, colognes, and bath essences and was founded on the principle of pure products and principled business ethics. In 1980 the first l'Occitane shop was opened in the small village of Volx.[42] In 1975 Tom and Kate Chappell, who had created Tom's of Maine five years earlier by making a phosphate-free laundry detergent, launched their first natural toothpaste on the market. Natural deodorants, mouthwash, and shaving cream followed. The company also exemplified the further widening of the green concept, as it emphasized the recycling of packaging and dedicated one-tenth of its pre-tax profits to charitable causes. Like a number of American firms, there was a religious dimension to the endeavor. Tom Chappell had a master's degree from Harvard Divinity School, and the philosophy behind the business was decidedly evangelical. Chappell's book, *The Soul of a Business*, promoted "common good capitalism," and proclaimed that at "Tom of Maine's, doing good is at the center of the business enterprise."[43]

Two other companies, The Body Shop and Aveda, emerged as iconic "natural" firms of the era. In 1976 Anita Roddick, the daughter of Italian immigrants to Britain, established a store selling skin and hair care products in Brighton, on the south coast of England. She had previously been involved in women's rights issues in developing countries while working for an international agency in Geneva, and had later traveled throughout Africa and the South Pacific. The decision to open a beauty shop was made after she and her husband Gordon sold their small hotel business to finance his wish to spend two years riding on horseback from Buenos Aires to New York City.[44]

Roddick's vision was straightforward. She wanted to sell cosmetics in different sizes, rather than big bottles, and she wanted to use cheap containers, believing that many women felt "conned," as she did, because much of the cost of cosmetics was due to "fancy packaging." She was also

8.1 Anita Roddick, founder of The Body Shop and pioneer of the ethical consumer movement, the banning of animal testing, and fair trade business practices, 2007.

© The Body Shop

determined to use natural ingredients, an idea inspired by seeing the traditional beauty practices of women in Tahiti and elsewhere during her travels. "It was a revelation to realize," she later wrote, "that there were women all over the world caring for their bodies perfectly well without ever buying a single cosmetic." After approaching cosmetics manufacturers, including Boots, to make products for her, and being told that the ingredients she proposed were "ridiculous," she employed ingredients made from a radical young local herbalist and frustrated make-up artist, Mark Constantine, who became a major supplier to the firm before founding his own company, Lush, in 1994.[45] Roddick prepared product batches in her own kitchen, and packaged them in the cheapest containers she could find—urine-sample bottles.[46]

The first store—named The Body Shop—worked well, and when her husband returned in 1977 after his horse died crossing the Andes, the couple pursued a new strategy of franchising their business. Roddick's conviction that business practices needed to be guided by "feminine principles" of love and intuition—not to mention cheap packaging and natural environmentally friendly ingredients—proved a powerful marketing success, as did her explicit denunciation of the industry for exploiting women by making false claims. After the first international franchise, a kiosk in Brussels, was opened in 1978, shops were opened in Stockholm and Athens the following year, and by 1982 two new stores were opening every month. All the early franchisees were women. By 1984, the year before it went public, The Body Shop had a turnover of almost $7 million with 45 outlets in Britain and 83 abroad.[47] The Body Shop's retail model was later used by other companies selling green brands, such as the clothing retailer Limited Brands, which founded a natural-toiletries store chain called Bath & Body Works in 1988.

A different approach was taken by Horst Rechelbacher, whose father had been a shoemaker and his mother a herbalist in Austria in the Nazi period. Poverty ended his schooling early and led to an apprenticeship as a hairdresser. Aged 17 in 1958, he moved to Rome and London to work in salons, and five years later to New York. In 1965 an accident set in motion a chain of events that led to corporate success for the itinerant hairdresser. Whilst attending a hair show in Minneapolis, he was hit by a car. Hospitalized for six months and with huge medical bills to pay, he stayed in the Midwestern city and opened his own salon business there.

While living in Minneapolis Rechelbacher became interested in Eastern meditation. After hearing the Swami Rama, a prominent Indian guru, speak at the University of Minnesota, Rechelbacher followed him to India in 1970 and stayed for six months. There he studied the use of herbs and plants to promote health and longevity. When he returned to the United States he began developing products for his salons using the essential oils derived from plants, introducing American consumers to Ayurvedic philosophy and aromatherapy. In 1977 he established an Ayurveda-inspired cosmetology school.

Aveda Corporation—a name inspired by Rechelbacher's India experience—was founded in 1978. The first product, a clove shampoo, was formulated in his kitchen sink. Over the following years Aveda played an important role in popularizing the concept of aromatherapy, which linked the sense of smell to health and well-being. Aveda's products, which expanded from hair care to other beauty products, were first sold through Rechelbacher's chain of hair salons in Minnesota. Later, they were sold at Aveda's chain of "esthetiques" stores, which were renamed "lifestyle" stores in 1995.[48] Both Aveda and The Body Shop made financial pledges to environmental programs and supported environmental campaigns.

Direct sellers also became important in the green movement. Natura was established in 1969 by Antonio Luiz da Cunha Seabra as a small laboratory and cosmetics store in the city of São Paulo in Brazil. After a period of experimentation, the company opted to follow the direct-selling model. As Natura mounted an increasingly successful challenge to the incumbent Avon in Brazil, it placed increasing emphasis on sustainable methods and obtaining ingredients from the Amazon, as well as developing a broader social vision for a country marked by huge disparities in wealth.[49] Among other direct sellers was Nu Skin, founded in 1984 in Provo, Utah. The desire to make skin care products that contained "All of the Good, None of the Bad" was the motivation of Nedra Roney, who founded the company with her brother Blake and Sandie Tillotson.

By the 1980s green cosmetics remained far from a mainstream market segment. The impact on the American market, in particular, was limited. The use of botanicals remained primarily a European phenomenon, mainly reaching fashionable New York stores as imports from Europe.[50] This may have reflected in part the lack of a US equivalent of a pharmacy channel, which was important in European countries, as well as US consumer interest in the transformational effect of make-up rather than skin care.[51]

Nevertheless, a great deal had changed. The scientific legitimacy of beauty products had been partially discredited for many consumers, who at best had come to rely on regulations rather than brand reputation for assurances of safety. There had also been a rediscovery that the herbs, plants, and flowers used in the past could be as effective and safe as, if not more than, products employing modern science. The hippies were not the only ones relying on flower power. Entrepreneurs whose business model gave them intimate access to consumers, such as retailers, hairdressers, and direct sellers, were especially prominent in identifying the interest of some consumers in natural products. They also widened the concept of greenness to include recycling, environmentally friendly packaging, the avoidance of animal testing, and the support of green causes. Two modern but alternative visions of beauty were now in competition.

Decolonizing beauty

Until the 1960s the Western beauty industry's preoccupation with light skin and light hair had been a constant since its emergence. This did not mean that markets had not been sought outside the West, or that local models or celebrities were not occasionally employed, but the industry had never formulated products for different ethnicities and had not wavered from the assumption that the benchmarks of beauty were white Europeans and their descendants.

By the 1970s both the legitimacy and commercial viability of such assumptions about the ethnicity of beauty were rapidly eroding. Societal and political changes accelerated in the United States following the Supreme Court's 1954 decision against segregation in schools and the Civil Rights Acts of the 1960s. The result for the beauty industry was a blurring of the strict ethnic divide which had prevailed for so long. African-American-owned cosmetics companies began to use both white and black models in advertisements, and some beauty salons offered services to both ethnicities. In 1968 the *Ladies' Home Journal* became one of the first white-owned women's fashion magazines to put an African-American on its cover.[52] A slow racial integration of beauty pageants began, although the first African-American winner of Miss America, Vanessa Williams, was only crowned in 1983.[53]

The ending of legal forms of racial segregation was accompanied by a new confidence in celebrating African-American identity, typified by James Brown's 1968 single "Say It Loud—I'm Black and I'm Proud." The "Afro," an unstraightened hairstyle, emerged as a political statement of black pride, its popularity paralleling the growing interest in looking "natural."[54] A new generation of black entrepreneurs entered the beauty market. These included John H. Johnson, the founder of the first black-owned mass circulation periodical, *Ebony*, who launched Fashion Fair Cosmetics after he noticed that the models in his publishing company's traveling fashion show had to mix foundations to create the right blend to match their complexions. The new line, which was marketed to upscale department stores, had sales of $8 million by the mid-1970s.[55]

There was also a renewed interest in the African-American market from white-owned companies. A handful of such companies, including Plough, Maybelline, and Clairol, had carved out market positions during the postwar decades.[56] During the 1970s Max Factor and Revlon also entered the market with specific products and brands for African-Americans, and L'Oréal launched the Radiance brand of hair strengtheners, which it claimed was "specially formulated for the black woman's delicate hair."[57]

Avon was the firm that invested most heavily in the African-American market. Avon had begun to use African-American models in *Ebony* advertising in 1961.[58] In the early 1970s the firm created a new senior management position of Director of Inner City Markets, specifically designed to target the millions of African-Americans who had migrated to Midwestern, Northeastern, and Western cities from the South.[59] In 1974 a black-owned advertising agency was retained to manage Avon's ad campaigns for the black market.[60]

Avon was able to benefit from the added credibility it gained from the many black women in its army of neighborhood sales representatives. Although Avon's sales materials in the 1950s used white women to illustrate its woman-to-woman educational and service-oriented selling approach, by the following decade the sales brochures used by black representatives depicted black women selling to other black women.[61] These brochures, in the hands of a salesperson who evoked high levels of trust due to her own connection to the community, became powerful marketing tools. Avon performed especially well in the large African-American market for fragrances. By 1971 the company held a 40 per cent share of the black fragrance market, vastly ahead of Chanel N°5, which held second place with 10 per cent. Avon differed from many companies by not making specific products and brands for African-Americans, but instead selling brands which appealed to consumers of all ethnicities. By contrast, most other companies only pitched their products to white women. Avon's popular fragrance Sonnet, for example, was positioned with the same theme in both the black and white media—a romantically involved couple in a country landscape—but with black models for the black media, and white models for other media.[62]

During the 1970s, then, the American beauty industry began to evolve towards a more complex pattern which acknowledged a diversity of ethnicities. This reflected a wider shift in American self-image, from being less of a "melting pot" to more of a "mosaic."[63] The change in the beauty industry did not occur overnight. It took several more decades before the distinctive requirements of Asian and Hispanic consumers began to attract major attention. Moreover, American beauty salons continued to be largely segregated along ethnic lines, as did distribution channels. During the 1970s and 1980s Korean immigrants began buying beauty supply stores in black communities and, in time, most of the distributors which supplied them.[64]

The American industry's evolving attitudes towards ethnicity were echoed globally. As the peoples of Africa and Asia secured their independence from European colonial empires, Western companies began to show more interest in specific products for different ethnicities. Unilever, for example, launched research projects into the needs of particular ethnic groups, such as powder shampoos for South and Southeast Asia, skin lighteners, and special products for African hair and skin.[65]

The advertising of beauty companies in international markets also showed a shift towards a more diverse presentation of ethnicity. For example, as Avon went international, it initially used American sales materials, including design, content, and white models. Only the language was translated.[66] Then in the 1970s local models began to appear in their sales brochures, especially in foreign markets considered challenging. In Japan, for example, Avon did not use local models in its materials when it opened in the country in 1969, although one product display featured two Japanese wooden dolls. By 1974, the first images of Japanese women at the selling scene appeared, and one campaign sales brochure featured only Japanese models.[67] By 1977 sales brochures that featured only Japanese models alternated with brochures that used a mix of Japanese and white models.[68] A similar trend was discernible in Avon's materials in Latin America. Avon was not alone among American companies in introducing more ethnic diversity in its international marketing. In Britain, Prince Matchabelli advertised its Cachet brand in the 1970s as "a perfume no two women can share" using a collage of four women—three white and one black.[69]

A major shift in the treatment of ethnicity by the beauty industry began during these years. It was particularly noticeable in the United States, where the formal segregation of beauty had been so stark, but everywhere the industry began displaying a greater awareness of diversity and a greater interest in selling to diverse ethnicities. As in the case of green cosmetics, this was the time when such ideas began to gather momentum rather than becoming mainstream, but it was a momentum which in time reshaped the industry.

8.2 A 1970 fragrance advertisement by the American beauty direct seller Avon for its operations in Brazil. The eight women featured represent a wide range of ethnicities found in Brazil.

Women's liberation, or women's enslavement?

The movements for civil rights in the United States, consumer empowerment, environmentalism, and decolonization all posed challenges to the beauty industry, but the women's liberation movement struck right at the heart of the industry's traditional market base. The question being asked by women of every class, ethnicity, and background was whether the beauty industry did more to liberate or enslave them. Anita Roddick personified some of these tensions. She denounced, as had many before her, the exaggerated claims made by advertising and its impact on the self-confidence of women. "We have an entire industry," she wrote, "that in order to justify its own spurious existence, must believe that the world is filled with women desperate to cling to their fading youth, eager to believe nonsense dreamed up by cynical advertising copywriters and willing to pay ever bigger prices for ever smaller portions of lotions not much more effective than any old grease you care to think about."[70]

Roddick herself provided a gendered explanation behind what she regarded as the manipulative advertising of the industry:

> The industry is now controlled by men, even though, ironically, it was founded by a handful of powerful women.... Helena Rubinstein, Elizabeth Arden, Coco Chanel and Estée Lauder. Most of the cosmetics houses they set up are now no more than baubles in a string of multinational companies. The businessmen who run them betray little grasp of the fact that the notions they are trading in—age, beauty, self-esteem—are more often than not an emotional powder keg for their customers.[71]

Yet the same industry provided the avenue for her, as for many women before her, to build a successful business and, in her case, use that business as a platform to promote environmentally friendly causes. In 1985, the year The Body Shop went public, it started sponsoring posters of the environmental activist group Greenpeace.[72]

By the time Roddick launched The Body Shop, the so-called second wave of feminism, sometimes called the women's liberation movement, was in full swing. The National Organization for Women, formed in the United States in 1966, with similar organizations elsewhere, campaigned to reduce sex discrimination in employment and to legalize abortion, among other measures. Feminists devoted to legal reforms were generally not hostile to the beauty and fashion industry, but a more radical critique emerged which maintained

8.3 Feminist protest at the Miss America contest in Atlantic City, New Jersey, 1970. Photograph by Jo Freeman, <www.jofreeman.com> © Jo Freeman

that any form of decoration was oppressive. These radical feminists demanded liberation from subjection by elimination of patriarchy. They explicitly criticized the industry in that it offered women no choice but to aspire to be young and beautiful or to feel like a failure.

Feminists staged ritual protests at events regarded as demeaning to women. A demonstration against the Miss America beauty pageant in 1968 culminated in the crowning of a live sheep.[73] More broadly, many educated young women in Western countries expressed their resistance by no longer wearing make-up or plucking and shaving body hair, and instead proudly displaying hairy legs and armpits. Even so, most women continued to see the beauty industry as offering them possibilities of self-expression, even if the choices were circumscribed by society's perceptions of what was expected and allowed.[74]

In practice, the norms expected of female beauty showed few signs of being changed in creative directions. The well-established emphasis on thinness grew stronger, with a noticeable trend towards favoring thinner, tubular shapes. The beauty industry's use of models and promotion of beauty pageants encouraged this trend.[75] The thin, short-haired, and androgynous British model Twiggy symbolized a new emphasis on a young and adolescent body as a symbol of beauty. The female celebrity figures of the era, whether Jackie Kennedy or the actresses featured in the James Bond movies, emphasized the association between beauty, youthful thinness, narrow hips, and wide eyes.[76]

However, beauty advertising and marketing did manifest a new interest in showing independent professional women and the entry of women into traditionally male occupations. Chanel N°19, launched in 1970, was positioned as appealing to assertive and independent women in control of their own lives.[77] Estée Lauder and Max Factor advertisements of the 1970s included images of fashionable women getting out of their own expensive sports cars, and well-made-up women as bosses rather than secretaries in offices.[78] There were still plenty of traditional feminine images, but the range of lifestyle choices being offered in the ads had expanded.

The shifts in fragrance advertising for women, where romantic and sexual promises had always featured prominently, whether implicitly or explicitly, were especially noteworthy, with the emphasis in some cases moving from attracting men to being in control of oneself and one's life.[79] The most successful fragrance of the era, Revlon's Charlie, appealed to the independent and assertive woman rather than merely offering promises of romance. The theme of the assertive woman was taken further during the 1980s with the Charlie advertisement of a woman patting a man on his backside, featuring the caption "Cheeky Charlie." Although the New York Times declined to run the advisements, arguing that they were sexist, they formed part of a wider swathe of advertisements emphazising women's sexual assertiveness.[80]

There was some crossover of products from the female to male markets. During the late 1960s Clairol was able to expand the male market for hair color with the brand Great Day, which stressed the advantages in the workplace of covering up grey.[81] The privately owned firm Combe developed a male hair dye business by acquiring the license to the pioneering home-use men's coloring brand Grecian Formula in 1961, followed in 1987 by Just for Men.[82] Male use of skin care products was also encouraged as companies launched gender-specific brands which made men more comfortable buying them. Estée Lauder's pioneering Clinique Skin Supplies for Men brand, launched in 1976, was followed by many other brands. The male market saw a continuation of the steady rise of male consumption which had been apparent since the interwar years.[83]

The radical feminist critique of the industry, then, made no headway in convincing the great majority of female consumers that the use of beauty products was so exploitative that they should stop buying them. If anything, this critique co-existed uneasily with an increasing emphasis in the fashion and beauty industries on the body shapes, ideally thin and tubular, of women. Instead, the most interesting change was the industry's new emphasis on images of assertive, professional women, who were able to be as sexually assertive as their male counterparts. It was a step towards an equality of sorts.

Summing up

The decade of the 1970s represented an important moment in the history of the beauty industry. Despite the best efforts of radical critics, there was no shift away from heavy advertising and expensive packaging of brands. Women remained the largest consumers of beauty products, and gender differences in consumption patterns remained strong. However, fundamental assumptions of the industry were challenged. There was a widening of the choices offered by the industry. Consumers who feared or disliked chemical ingredients were able to buy brands using natural ingredients. There was a new interest in products which were more appropriate for ethnicities other than white. Men and women of color began to appear in advertisements for brands which had previously been pitched only to whites. There was a widening in the range of possible representations of women in brand advertising, from being feminine and submissive to being assertive and in control.

This reimagining of some of the borders of the beauty industry reflected, as always, the broader canvas of societal and political changes. In this period, these changes were wrought by a range of movements that swept the world. In its responses to these various challenges—whether compelled by government regulation or driven by new ideas among consumers—the industry as a whole continued to thrive economically and to spread its reach further to the four corners of the globe. What was different was that more of the globe was talking back, and the smarter firms were listening and adapting.

Notes

1. Anita Roddick, *Body and Soul. Profits with Principles: The Amazing Success Story of Anita Roddick and The Body Shop* (New York: Crown Publishers, 1991), p. 9.

2. Penny Dade, *All Made Up* (London: Middlesex University Press, 2007), p. 68.

3. Gunnar Trumbull, *Consumer Capitalism: Politics, Product Markets, and Firm Strategy in France and Germany* (Ithaca: Cornell University Press, 2006), p. 117.

4. John Kenneth Galbraith, *The Affluent Society* (Boston, Mass.: Houghton Mifflin, 1958).

5. Geoffrey Jones, *Renewing Unilever* (Oxford: Oxford University Press, 2005), p. 120.

6. Trumbull, *Consumer Capitalism*, pp. 114–21.

7. Florence E. Wall, "Historical Development of the Cosmetics Industry," in M. S. Balsam and Edward Sagarin (eds), *Cosmetics: Science and Technology* (New York: John Wiley, 1974), p. 133.

8. Jones, *Renewing*, pp. 342–3; Davis Dyer, Frederick Dalzell, and Rowena Olegario, *Rising Tide* (Boston, Mass.: Harvard Business School Press, 2004), pp. 108–9.

9. Trumbull, *Consumer Capitalism*, pp. 72–90.

10. Frost and Sullivan, *The Hygiene and Grooming Aids Market* (New York, January 1974), p. 68.

11. Leonard Lavin, *Winners Make It Happen* (Chicago: Bonus Books, 2003), pp. 141–51.

12. Margaret Allen, *Selling Dreams* (New York: Simon and Schuster, 1981), pp. 191–213; Frost and Sullivan, *Hygiene*, p. 69.

13. Norman F. Estrin (ed.), *The Cosmetic Industry: Scientific and Regulatory Foundations* (New York: Marcel Dekker, 1984), pp. 164–9.

14. Frost and Sullivan, *The Cosmetics and Toiletries Industry Market* (New York, August 1972), p. 47; Peter Barton Hutt, "A History of Government Regulation of Adulteration and Misbranding of Cosmetics," in Norman F. Estrin and James M. Akerson (eds), *Cosmetic Regulation in a Competitive Environment* (New York: Informa Health Care, 2000), p. 22; <www.personalcarecouncil.org/Content/NavigationMenu/About_Us/History/History.htm>, accessed March 25, 2009.

15. In Germany, 313 new consumer laws were passed between 1970 and 1978, compared to 25 in the previous 25 years. In France, the number of consumer laws rose from 37 in 1970 to 94 in 1978. See Trumbull, *Consumer Capitalism*, pp. 8–9, 89–96.

16. Estrin, *Cosmetic*, pp. 168–71.

17. "Cleansing the Cosmetic Laws," *New York Times*, December 5, 1977, p. 36; "As Hair Dyes Change, Confusion and Complaints Abound," *New York Times*, April 23, 1979, p. A19.

18. "As Hair Dyes Change;" P & G, *50 Colorful Years: The Clairol Story* (1982), p. 45.

19. "Science Watch: Hair Dyes and Cancer," *New York Times*, April 8, 1980, p. C3.

20. Harald Schlatter, Timothy Long, and John Gray, "An Overview of Hair Dye Safety," *Journal of Cosmetic Dermatology* 6, suppl. 1 (December 2007), pp. 32–6.

21. Heidi Søsted, "Allergic Contact Dermatitis to Hair Dye Ingredients," working paper publ. by the National Allergy Research Centre, Faculty of Health Sciences, University of Copenhagen, <http://polopoly3.it.ki.se:8080/content/1/c6/02/18/92/ Allergic%20contact%20dermatitis%20to%20hair%20dye%20ingredients.pdf>, accessed April 1, 2009.

22. L'Oréal Archives Paris (hereafter L'Oréal), *En Direct* 25 (January 1978), p. 13.

23. L'Oréal, *En Direct* 24 (December 1977), pp. 2–5.

24. History of Advertising Trust, J. Walter Thompson Archives (hereafter HAT/ JWT), Chesebrough-Pond's, Review of Personal Deodorant Markets, February 1962, Box 70.

25. Dyer, *Rising*, pp. 113–16.

26. L'Oréal, 1970 Annual Report; Frost and Sullivan, *Cosmetics and Toiletries Markets in Europe* (New York, January 1985), p. 357.

27. <www.drbronner.com/history_overview.html>, accessed April 8, 2009.

28. Jacques Courtin, *Une réussite en beauté* (Paris: J. C. Lattès, 2006); Adam Bernstein, "Jacques Courtin-Clarins Founded Skin Care Firm," *Boston Globe*, April 2, 2007.

29. "Color Surge in Italy Drives Nail Care Sales," *Drug and Cosmetic Industry* (May 1998).

30. M. L. Cohen, "Laboratoires de Biologie Végétale Yves Rocher," in Tina Grant (ed.), *International Directory of Company Histories*, vol. 35 (Farmington Hills, Mich.: St. James Press, 2001), pp. 262–5.

31. Arne Högberg, *Skönhetens Entreprenör: Knut Wulff berättar om sitt liv* (Malmö: Corona Förlag, 2004), p. 109.

32. Telephone interview with Robert af Jochnick, co-founder of Oriflame, April 20, 2007.

33. Linda Scott, *Fresh Lipstick* (New York: Palgrave Macmillan, 2005), pp. 274–5.

34. Dade, *All Made Up*, pp. 70–1.

35. "A New Angle on Naturalness," *Cosmetic World*, October 29, 1973.

36. Daphne Merkin, "The Cream Merchants. The d'Ornano Clan is France's Gift to Women," *New York Times Style Magazine*, Fashion and Beauty, spring 2008, available at <www.nytimes.com/indexes/2008/04/13/style/sisley>, accessed June 1, 2009. This article incorrectly identifies Michel and Hubert d'Ornano, the sons of Lancôme's co-founder Guillaume, as having founded Orlane in 1954. In fact, Guillaume founded the firm in 1946.

37. P & G, *50 Colorful Years*; Dyer, *Rising Tide*, p. 111.

38. Tala Aburjal and Feda M. Natsheh, "Plants Used in Cosmetics," *Phytotherapy Research* 17 (2003), pp. 987–1000.

39. Frost and Sullivan, *Hygiene*, p. 45.

40. L'Oréal, *En Direct* 24 (December 1977), pp. 2–5.

41. L'Oréal Annual Report 1978, p. 11.

42. Pierre Magnan, *The Essence of Provence. The Story of L'Occitane* (New York: Arcade Publishing, 2003), pp. 60–87.

43. Tom Chappell, *The Soul of a Business* (New York: Read, 1994), p. xv.

44. Roddick, *Body*, p. 67.

45. "Me and My Partner: Mark Constantine and Andrew Gerrie," *Independent*, October 13, 1999; "Lush Couple with a Shed Load of Ideas," *Guardian*, April 13, 2007.

46. Roddick, *Body*, p. 69–73.

47. Christopher A. Bartlett, Kenton W. Elderkin, and Krista McQuade, "The Body Shop International," Harvard Business School Case no. 9-392-032 (July 13, 1995).

48. Kathleen Peippo, "Aveda Corporation," in J. Pederson (ed.), *International Directory of Company Histories*, vol. 24 (Farmington Hills, Mich.: St. James Press, 1999), pp. 55–7; <www.rakemag.com/reporting/features/horst-rakish-interview>, accessed June 21, 2008.

49. Geoffrey Jones and Ricardo Reisen de Pinho, "Natura: Global Beauty Made in Brazil," Harvard Business School Case no. 9-807-029 (August 29, 2007). Natura's local competitor O Boticário, which was founded in 1977 and used franchising rather than direct sales, was equally committed to environmentally friendly causes.

50. Jane Ogle, "Beauty: Beneficient Botanicals," *New York Times*, February 22, 1981.

51. Virginia Roach, "Green Is Beautiful," *Drugs and Cosmetic Industry*, February 1991, pp. 22–3. Anita Roddick, *Business as Unusual* (Chichester: Anita Roddick Books, 2005), p. 149, called America "the ultimate consumer" with little concern for environmentally friendly business.

52. Scott, *Fresh Lipstick*, pp. 269–70. *Glamour Magazine*, which debuted in 1939, claims that when it put Katiti Kironde on its cover in 1968 it was the first major woman's magazine to put a black woman on the cover. See *Glamour Magazine* (April 2009), Editor's Note.

53. Susannah Walker, *Style and Status: Selling Beauty to African American Women, 1920–1975* (Lexington, Ky: University Press of Kentucky, 2007), ch. 5. For some American critics who regarded "whiteness" as a social construct, this process was more a case of expanding the definition of "whiteness" or inviting "women of color into the carefully guarded boundaries of white femininity" than a recognition of true ethnic diversity. See Sarah Banet-Wesier, *The Most Beautiful Girl in the World* (Berkeley: University of California Press, 1999), p. 207.

54. Walker, *Style*, ch. 6.

55. "The Many Faces of Black Beauty," *Product Management* (March 1976); <www.fashionfair.com/assembled/about_history.html>, accessed June 20, 2007.

56. "Schering-Plough, Clairol Top Ethnic Marketers," *Advertising Age*, November 20, 1972.

57. Advertising Archive, London. Advertisement for L'Oréal's Radiance brand, 1970s.

58. Walker, *Style*, pp. 175–6.

59. Avon Archives, Hagley Museum, Wilmington, Del., Avon Products Inc., Accession number 2155 (hereafter AVON), Record Group II: Historical Files, Series 9: Library Resources, Randy Cameron, Avon Director of Inner City Markets, "How to Reach the Black Consumer," *NAM Reports*, November 12, 1973, Box 127.

60. AVON, Record Group II: Historical Files, Series 1: Administration, Official Data/Annual Meetings 1962–1983, "Corporate Social Responsibility: The Avon Commitment," 1974, Box 110.

61. AVON, Record Group I: Archive, Series 7: Advertising, Subseries A: Advertising Scrapbooks, Box OS-71.

62. Edward S. Rutland, "Perfume and Cologne—An Analysis of the Black Market," *Cosmetics and Perfumery* 89 (June 1974), p. 41–3.

63. Matthew Frye Jacobsohn, *Roots Too: White Ethnic Revival in Post-Civil Rights America* (Cambridge, Mass.: Harvard University Press, 2006).

64. Robert Mark Silverman, *Doing Business in Minority Markets: Black and Korean Entrepreneurs in Chicago's Ethnic Beauty Aids Industry* (New York: Routledge, 2000); Adrienne P. Samuels, "Sells Your Weave? Koreans Capitalize on Black Beauty's Big Business," *Ebony*, May 2008, pp. 141–6, 176, suggests that there are 9,000 Korean-owned beauty supply stores in the United States.

65. Jones, *Renewing*, pp. 166–7.

66. AVON, Record Group I: Archive, Series 7: Advertising, Subseries A: Advertising Scrapbooks, Box OS-71.

67. AVON, Record Group I: Archive, Series 11: Avon International, Subseries D: Sales Promotion, Japan, 1969–1971, 1974, Box 94.

68. AVON, Sales Promotion, Japan, 1975, 1977, Box 95.

69. Advertising Archive, London. Advertisement for Cachet by Prince Matchabelli, 1970s. See also Dade, *All Made Up*, p. 85.

70. Roddick, *Body*, p. 11.

71. Roddick, *Body*, p. 14.

72. Roddick, *Body*, ch. 5. This was the beginning of the company's support for many environmental causes.

73. Kathy Peiss, *Hope in a Jar* (New York: Henry Holt, 1998), pp. 260–3.

74. Karen Stevenson, "Hairy Business: Organizing the Gendered Self," in Ruth Holliday and John Hassard (eds), *Contested Bodies* (London and New York: Routledge, 2001), pp. 137–52.

75. D. M. Garner, P. E. Garfinkel, D. Schwartz, and M. Thompson, "Cultural Expectations of Thinness in Women," *Psychological Reports* 47 (1980), pp. 483–91.

76. Stephen Gundle, *Glamour. A History* (Oxford: Oxford University Press, 2008), pp. 288–92. See also Avner Offer, *The Challenge of Affluence: Self-control and Well-being in the United States and Britain since 1950* (Oxford: Oxford University Press, 2006), ch. 6.

77. Richard Stamelman, *Perfume* (New York: Rizzoli, 2006), p. 330.

78. Dade, *All Made Up*, pp. 82–4, 94; Advertising Archive, London. Advertising for Eliage fragrance 1970s, Image 30525304.

79. Tom Reichert, *The Erotic History of Advertising* (New York: Prometheus, 2003), p. 256.

80. Reichert, *Erotic*, pp. 267–8.

81. Caroline Cox, *Good Hair Days* (London: Quartet Books, 1999), p. 221.

82. Ed Dinger, "Combe Inc.," in Tina Grant (ed.), *International Directory of Company Histories*, vol. 72 (Farmington Hills, Mich.: St. James Press, 2005), pp. 79–82.

83. Frost and Sullivan, *Hygiene*, p. 83, gives retail sales of men's toiletries in the United States in 1970 at $697 million, or just under 15 per cent of the total market. Frost and Sullivan, *Cosmetics* (1985), puts sales of men's toiletries in France at $250 million and Germany at $313 million in 1983, or 11 per cent and 11.6 per cent respectively of the French and German markets. It is impossible to estimate how many men applied some of the products bought by their female partners in the privacy of their own bathrooms.

9

Globalization and Tribalization

The ethical responsibility of a company like L'Oréal is to present to people all the options they have in changing or enhancing their original look. Beauty is so diverse, because populations are so diverse.

Béatrice Dautresme, Executive Vice-President,
Corporate Communications and External Affairs, L'Oréal[1]

Flat and spiky worlds

Today the word on everyone's lips is "globalization," but that is only half the story at the start of the twenty-first century. The other word, particularly in culturally sensitive industries like beauty, is "tribalization," and therein lies the contradiction that makes the present so beguiling. How can the world be moving—simultaneously, as some have observed—towards higher levels of both? As early as the 1960s globalization's cockeyed optimists began to recognize one side of the coin, but not the other. The accelerating spread of worldwide communications led to discussions of the "global village,"[2] yet the oxymoron at the heart of the term seems to have gone largely unnoticed. A globe and a village are, after all, opposite extremes of human organization, yet that is how many one-sidedly speak of our world. Perhaps the contradictory term is more apt than we realize.

That most of the world is now united in global systems of trade and communication is beyond dispute. Working at supersonic and light speeds, respectively, air travel and the World Wide Web move people, information, and goods around the world. The opening of Communist China to capitalism, the fall of the Berlin Wall, the dismantling of the Soviet Union, and the relaxing of tight government regulations in India and other developing countries have collectively drawn billions of people into global capitalist markets. In the case of beauty, a $25 billion global industry in 1982 became a $330 billion industry by 2008.

The new wave of globalization resembles the pre-World War I global era in some ways and not others. That war and the subsequent breakup of several empires led to the proliferation of nation-states. In the post-1989 world, the future of the nation-state was much less certain. Was it finally withering away at the end of the twentieth century? Were cultures and societies becoming homogenized? And if they were, were these trends to be welcomed or feared? The business strategist Kenichi Ohmae maintained, in 1990, that the world had become borderless. Later, the *New York Times* columnist Thomas Friedman asserted that new technology and the new political order had made the world "flat."[3]

Yet while the evidence of flattening seemed visible in everything from the worldwide spread of English to the presence of McDonald's hamburger stores in 120 countries, other commentators observed other processes at work. The globalization of the ubiquitous hamburger stimulated, around the world, a local, cultural, ethnic, religious reaction which has been termed "tribalization" by the political theorist Benjamin Barber.[4] As global markets spread, existing consumer and social groupings began to fragment as local cultures asserted themselves with greater confidence, as had political movements across the colonized world during the decolonization period. Although the global firm entered the public imagination, Pankaj Ghemawat, a leading management scholar, found most firms were pursuing primarily regional rather than global strategies as the value and necessity of local market knowledge became indisputably clear. The costs of managing distance, he asserted, had not died. The world had become "semi-globalized."[5] The economist Richard Florida, observing the clustering of economic power, innovation, and creative talent in a few of the world's cities and regions, concluded that the global economy was more "spiky" than flat.[6]

For the beauty industry, the metaphorical discourse of a flat, spiky, border-less, or tribal global economy was not an abstract debate. A flatter world promised to facilitate the rolling out of brands and products across continents. Fashions could be expected to spread with unprecedented ease. The stubborn resistance of consumer preferences against one-look-fits-all homogeneity in beauty, and the resulting complexities for corporate marketing strategies, might finally be resolved. A spiky or tribalized world, in contrast, meant that local adaptation would remain an issue, even more so than previously.

The two decades after 1990 saw frenetic change in the beauty industry, as firms sought to capture the opportunities offered by a flatter world, whilst negotiating the spikes. Familiar names fell by the wayside as beauty became even more of a big business. According to one estimate, while in 2001 the ten largest firms accounted for 43 per cent of the total retail sales in the world, by 2008 they accounted for 52 per cent. Two firms, P & G and L'Oréal, pulled away from their peers, increasing their combined grip of the world market from 16 per cent to 23 per cent over the same seven years.[7]

Megabrands and local identities

The tensions between global ambitions and local markets had been one of the most persistent features in the history of the beauty industry. It offered a perennial challenge for entrepreneurs who believed that they sold a universal product meeting a universal need, but who instead found that the marketing of their brands in different countries was complicated by cultural differences in aspirations and preferences. The globalization of communication and information flows, and the opening of the markets of formerly closed economies, now provided companies with a new set of opportunities to renew their global ambitions.

The challenge remained how best to get their brands onto the faces and lips of these new consumers. Many of the largest companies entered the new era with multiple brands, many still sold only in particular countries or regions, and often concentrated in a single product category. This meant that the huge sums needed to be spent on advertising were spread between many brands. It also meant that companies were not as well positioned as they might be to negotiate with major retailers.

The solution, a number of firms concluded, was to focus support on fewer, but larger, brands. The resulting "megabrands," as they became known, could then be expanded across the world and taken into different product categories. In pursuit of scale, companies sought to grow either organically or through acquisition into categories or segments beyond their existing brand portfolios. There was a desire to build skin care businesses in particular, in the recognition both that aging populations in the West would drive the demand for skin care, and that skin care was a prime concern for the Asian consumers who were becoming ever more important in the new global economy.

P & G, which had for decades developed high-volume brands in its other consumer products, became one of the most important examples of this strategy. Long ambivalent or uninterested in the beauty industry, the company moved forcefully to expand its presence. In 1992 Ed Artzt, chief executive between 1990 and 1995, made a major public address to a trade association entitled "Redefining Beautiful," which focused on explaining "why a 155-year-old soap and detergent company would want to venture into the world of fashion and glamour." He described beauty care as the most "dynamic sector" the company operated in, and the one with "the greatest potential for growth."Artzt predicted that it would "become an increasingly technology-driven industry," even if fashion and prestige would remain important, which was why he regarded it as "our kind of business . . . and getting more so every day."[8]

In 2000 a corporate crisis led to the appointment of A. G. Lafley as chief executive. Lafley, who had headed the beauty management group as well as the North American region, was even more focused on the industry in his nine years as chief executive. He saw the need for P & G to build its core brands as global leaders, and to focus corporate resources on sectors perceived to offer the fastest growth and the highest margins. Beauty fit these criteria well because of its combination of low capital intensity and high margins, its compatibility with P & G's strengths in branding and innovation, and the company's deep knowledge of the discount, drug, and grocery store channels in which brands were sold.[9]

P & G's acquisitions of Cover Girl and Max Factor had given the company a portfolio of beauty brands beyond toiletries and hair care, especially in color cosmetics, and it now expanded across other product categories, including both mass and luxury segments, and geographically. It began building a mass skin care business, using as its primary vehicle the Oil of Olay brand, which had initially languished after its acquisition in 1985. It also expanded its hair care business. In 2001 P & G won a battle with Kao to acquire Clairol. Two years later the Ströher family were persuaded to sell Wella, which held over one-fifth of the (then) $10 billion global market for professional salon hair care brands, and had large Latin American and Japanese businesses.[10] In 2005, in its biggest ever acquisition, it paid $54 billion for Gillette. This made P & G the world's largest men's grooming company, a position strengthened by further smaller acquisitions, including the luxury men's grooming companies the Art of Shaving and Zihr in 2009. By then, it was also the world's largest hair care company, the second-largest in oral hygiene, and the third-largest in color cosmetics and bath and hygiene. It was even the fourth-largest fragrance company, being particularly strong in mass fragrances, but it also owned luxury brands such as Hugo Boss. Beauty, personal care, and health represented one-half of P & G's total sales, compared to one-third a decade previously.[11]

The company's chosen megabrands were rolled out across a growing number of countries. The two largest, Pantene Pro-V and Olay respectively, were relative newcomers to P & G, albeit with a heritage which stretched further back. The reinvention of the recently acquired Pantene brand by P & G's Taiwan affiliate proved successful and began to be transferred elsewhere. P & G took the new brand to dozens of countries within a few years after 1990. Within a decade it became the largest hair care brand in the world.

In mass skin care, P & G's Oil of Olay was reinvented with new technology and rebranding. Instead of focusing on a single issue such as wrinkles, the company launched Olay Total Effects, which promised a holistic solution to the health and beauty of skin, and was sold in the mass market at retailers such as Wal-Mart, but at three times the previous price. By 2009 Olay, which was P & G's major skin care brand, was also sold in numerous countries.[12] By then Pantene Pro-V and Olay were the world's third- and fourth-largest beauty brands.

Despite their quite different histories and product portfolios, L'Oréal's strategies had many similarities to those pursued by P & G. In the early 1990s L'Oréal was still primarily a hair care company heavily dependent on the European market. The firm's most striking departure from its past was that it was the only large French company, in any industry, with a British national as chief executive. Dalle chose Lindsay Owen-Jones several years before his mandatory retirement age of 65 in 1984. Although Dalle spoke no English, Owen-Jones was fluent in French. The huge age difference between the two men did pose a transition problem, as Owen-Jones was only 38 in 1984. Dalle's solution was to appoint Charles Zviak, the company's chief scientist, as nominal chief executive, whilst Owen-Jones was given responsibility for worldwide sales. Dalle himself continued to serve as president of the company's strategic committee and retained close links with the family. It was not

9.1 Pantene "Shine" advertisement for Taiwan. Invented by Hoffman-La Roche in 1947, the vitamin A-based Pantene brand was acquired by P & G in 1986, and re-invented as a beauty brand in Taiwan, 1994.

until 1988, when both he and Zviak retired, that Owen-Jones could begin to exert full authority over the company.[13] Owen-Jones was ambitious and far more aware of global opportunities than his predecessor. He wanted, on becoming chief executive, "to write L'Oréal in the sky of every country in the world."[14] Like Dalle, he was a hands-on chief executive, constantly traveling and visiting stores wherever he went. He combined astute business skills with a passion for his company. At a meeting of senior executives in 1997 he spoke about how "L'Oréal for me is a lot more than a brand. It is a love story, part of my family, a great part of the direction of my life, where I spend most of my waking hours, a dream and an ambition."[15]

Like his counterparts at P & G, Owen-Jones sought to focus resources on taking a smaller number of brands global. Brands that did not fit his criteria for globalization, including pronounceability in the principal languages of the world and being market leaders in their home markets, were culled. By 1998 this process had become so dramatic that only ten brands represented 90 per cent of company sales.[16] Meanwhile, the company's investments in magazine publishing, film distribution, and art galleries were sold. A strategy to reduce the company's large pharmaceutical investments was implemented more stealthily, given political sensitivities in France as well as much support for these investments within the company itself.[17]

Owen-Jones was concerned to widen L'Oréal's business in other product categories. When he ran Cosmair at the beginning of the 1980s, he had found that there was a small make-up business being sold under the L'Oréal brand. Instead of killing it, he decided to expand the business and it proved successful in the American market. When he came back to Paris, he argued that the company could also do the same in Europe, but he had to wait until he had full control in order to develop the strategy because it faced obstacles. One was the widespread belief that hair care was the core of the company, and the other was a lack of managerial and scientific capabilities within the firm. Over several years, however, a successful L'Oréal Paris make-up business was built, partly by transferring managers from the luxury brands and partly by establishing internal make-up schools. While Dalle had seen skin care as primarily a luxury category, Owen-Jones believed L'Oréal Paris should sell skin care as well as color cosmetics in the mass market and become the equivalent of Lancôme in luxury.[18]

The next step was to expand the global reach of the firm's brands. During the early 1990s L'Oréal expanded into Eastern Europe and Russia, but the main focus initially was on the American market, where the firm's brands were still sold through the licensee Cosmair. This arrangement had become a major obstacle to globalizing L'Oréal because it greatly constrained its ability to expand its business in the United States, especially by acquisition. This was very evident in hair care, where the firm's French brands had made little progress in American salons in the face of the local distribution system and consumer unfamiliarity, but the solution of buying American brands was awkward because of the position of Cosmair.[19]

After several years, Owen-Jones was able to persuade the owners of Cosmair to sell it to L'Oréal in 1994. This was a turning point in the firm's global strategy. There followed a series of acquisitions of American brands. In professional hair care, Redken and Matrix were acquired. In 1996 Maybelline, which then held nearly one-fifth of the American mass cosmetics market and was the third-largest brand, was bought. Between 1998 and 2000 L'Oréal also purchased the top two US ethnic hair care manufacturers, Soft Sheen and Carson, obtaining one-fifth of the ethnic African-American hair care market.

These American brands were refreshed with L'Oréal technology and managers and, apart from the African-American brands, relocated to New York and rebranded. Redken became Redken 5th Avenue NYC. The formerly Tennessee-based Maybelline became Maybelline New York. The brand's most famous tag lines, "Maybe she's born with it. Maybe it's Maybelline," which had been dropped, was restored, and a radical new make-up collection was launched to transform the brand's staid and aging image. Maybelline's renewal led to it quickly becoming the leading color cosmetics brand in the United States.[20]

A second, urgent, drive to globalize the company began in 1997. During that year L'Oréal entered China and began a major push to globalize the company's mass brands, which had until then remained European-focused and fragmented. Owen-Jones used a worldwide meeting in Paris for two hundred senior managers of the L'Oréal Paris brand to announce a plan to make it one of the world's top ten brands. "It's time," he declared, "to make a quantum leap forward in our ambitions." All subsidiaries were renamed L'Oréal. The name L'Oréal Paris, which had taken second place to Elnett in hair styling and Plénitude in skin care, was now unified and globalized as an umbrella brand.

The company's brands were taken into foreign markets with a mixture of tight discipline and entrepreneurship. International brand managers, based in the country of origin of the brands, whether France or the United States, were charged with keeping the brand authentic, projecting future growth platforms, and making sure that brand integrity was maintained worldwide. Within that mission, brand managers were expected to act entrepreneurially. L'Oréal's organization, which made the brand in each country a business unit, provided a basis for this unusual combination, especially by providing young managers with early responsibility.[21]

The speed of the globalization of brands was remarkable. When Maybelline was acquired, it was being sold in only a few countries outside the United States. It was then launched in 80 new countries within five years. Worldwide sales rose from $350 million to $1.1 billion in 2000. The accessibility of an American brand, which emphasized an urban and hip New York lifestyle, was used worldwide as an entry point for consumers who were buying their first make-up. By 2008 Maybelline New York was the world's sixth-largest beauty brand in terms of sales.

The globalization process, as in the case of Pantene Pro-V, involved a complex interaction between marketers and researchers based in different countries. This complexity began with the fact that it was a French-owned company which was introducing consumers worldwide to an iconic American brand. The fast rollout of the brand was achieved partly by buying prominent local brands and then integrating them into Maybelline. Product development was also international. The brand's Japanese management, eager to respond to the local fashion for "wet lipstick," worked with product developers in the United States to create a lipstick which was both a moisturizer and had a translucent shine. The resulting Water Shine lipstick was a great success when launched in Japan in 2000, and also served as the basis for a lipstick which made lips sparkle like diamonds. Renamed Water Shine Diamonds, it was launched by Maybelline worldwide.[22]

The megabrand strategy was followed, in various forms and with varying degrees of success, by other large firms. Dove, which Unilever had only sold in the United States before 1989, was extended from toilet soap to other bath and shower products, and then into hair and body care. It was available in 80 countries by 2008.[23] Beiersdorf extended its mass-market skin care Nivea brand into men's toiletries and hair care.[24] Even Japanese companies, which had traditionally supported a large number of brands, joined this trend. In a sharp break with the past, for example, Shiseido launched megabrands such as

Maquillage, a prestige full-range make-up, and Tsubaki, a hair care brand, in 2005 and 2006 respectively.[25]

The global spread of megabrands provided powerful evidence of a new stage in the globalization of fashions and aspirations which was both deeper and faster than previously seen. The same trend was evident with the international spread of celebrity beauty brands, a category which was revitalized in fragrances by Coty. After its launch as an independent company in 1996, Coty initially struggled to create a coherent business out of the portfolio of brands inherited from Benckiser.[26] In 2001 Bernd Beetz, then chief executive of Parfums Christian Dior, and a former long-serving P & G executive, was recruited as chief executive. Beetz had the vision of creating a new, fast-moving and less bureaucratic company than the large firms he had worked for previously. Celebrity brands, a category which had languished during the previous decade compared to their designer counterparts, turned out to provide the way to achieve this vision.

Concerned to expand Coty's modest $50 million of sales in the American market, Beetz took a high-stakes gamble to create a successful women's fragrance aimed at the prestige market. The new fragrance, licensed by the singer-actress Jennifer Lopez, was developed on a nine-month rather than the normal two-year launch cycle. Launched in 2002, the JLo Glow fragrance succeeded beyond expectations, becoming the second-highest seller in the American market, and was almost immediately taken international. Beetz used this success to help foster a culture of success which became self-sustaining and attracted more executives from other companies. Many other celebrity fragrances were launched alongside designer fragrances acquired from other companies. Brands which had languished under past owners were rejuvenated, including Calvin Klein, which Unilever sold to Coty in 2005. The Calvin Klein acquisition made Coty the world's largest fragrance company and helped it to reach sales of $4 billion in 2008.[27]

The globalization of LVMH, which was ranked as the thirteenth-largest beauty company by 2008 even though cosmetics and fragrances were less than one-fifth of its total sales, was also striking. Like the smaller Chanel, LVMH remained entirely centered on luxury. Its brands were not, as a result, mass-volume megabrands, but were nonetheless taken to many new countries at speed. Bernard Arnault continued to assemble a portfolio of French luxury brands, including Guerlain, Givenchy, and Kenzo, as well as American brands such as Benefit and Fresh, and Italian and Spanish brands. These were run by a new generation of professional managers and young designers, with a heavy emphasis on profitability.[28]

LVMH was also active in globalizing the distribution of luxury brands. In 1996 it acquired the leading travel retailer DFS. Travel retail had, by then, grown to be a $20 billion business, of which beauty products accounted for one-quarter. In 1997 LVMH also acquired from Boots the Sephora chain of perfumeries in France, which was then taken international. Within a decade, Sephora was operating over 500 stores in 14 countries worldwide. Sephora opened its first US store in New York in 1998, and ten years later it had nearly 130 stores across North America. For some, Arnault's strategies were a vulgar antithesis of the traditional meaning of luxury. He regarded himself as inventing a new global luxury industry, which had previously only existed in the form of medium-sized artisanal enterprises.[29] Luxury was now more of a market tier than a claim about elite artisanal production and exclusivity.

The globalization of mega, celebrity, and luxury brands provided compelling evidence of the "flattening" of the world, even in such a traditionally culture-specific industry as beauty. Twenty years earlier it would have been unimaginable that a store such as Sephora could appear, and flourish, in cities as diverse as Paris, New York, Moscow, Riyadh, Shanghai, and Tokyo. It would have been equally unimaginable that the largest skin care and color cosmetics brands in both China and the United States could be the same— Olay and Maybelline New York respectively.[30] These brands served as carriers of the latest trends, which companies now seemed able to spread around the world regardless of cultural traditions, ethnicity, or income levels.

The French and American provenance and/or ownership of these and other leading brands emphasized the continuing appeal of the beauty ideals of these countries. As further evidence of flattening, they were now enthusiastically embraced by the millions of new consumers who had previously been starved of access to them by closed economies and/or low incomes. The emotional associations evoked by New York and Paris, America and France, seemed as powerful to a new generation of Chinese and Russian consumers as it had been to others in the past. "If you say to anyone in the world 'Paris'," Owen-Jones observed, "they still come up with a strangely similar description of Paris being the most romantic city in the world, where people live with a sense of style and beauty."[31] The continuing vitality of Paris brands was demonstrated when

Jean-Paul Agon, who succeeded Owen-Jones as chief executive of L'Oréal in 2006, paid $1.7 billion to buy Yves Saint Laurent Beauté (YSL) two years later.[32]

Shiseido enlisted Paris to bolster its long-frustrated efforts to succeed in Western markets. First, in 1980, Serge Lutens, the image creator for Christian Dior, was appointed to head Shiseido's international advertising, resulting in a striking fusion of Western and Eastern imagery. Then, in 1990, a new French affiliate, Beauté Prestige International SA, was established for the purpose of developing original perfume brands. Chantal Roos, the international marketing director of YSL who had worked on the launches of Opium and other perfumes, was recruited to run BPI. During the 1990s she launched the successful Issey Miyake and Jean-Paul Gaultier fragrances.[33]

Despite the continued importance of Paris, L'Oréal's strategy for the new global era was to offer consumers the choice of both French and American beauty. The American brands it acquired, rebranded as coming from New York, were intended not only to serve as vehicles to take substantial shares of the domestic American market, but also to be taken around the world. "We had to recognize," Owen-Jones explained, "that if we wanted to be a truly global company we would have to promote around the world American brands because that was the other great alternative in the beauty industry."[34]

The sustained appeal of Paris and New York beauty brands rested on a dynamic relationship between past and present, which companies sought to translate into evolving brand identities. Paris retained the historic buildings and romantic restaurants which featured so highly in images of the city, whilst New York retained the buzz and skyscrapers with which it had always been associated. Yet both cities were also in constant flux, with diverse populations composed of many immigrants. Both France and the US had multi-ethnic populations which symbolized the heterogeneity of the new century. For Owen-Jones, this was at the heart of the continued appeal of both the American and French beauty cultures: "As the global economy has become stronger, all sorts of countries have developed their own beauty culture. However, the more important question is whether that beauty culture is relevant to the rest of the world.... the theme of the American and French cultures is that they have found a way to be relevant while still being themselves."[35]

The determination to stay relevant was evident in the evolving identity of L'Oréal Paris as it was taken around the world. The brand remained true to its position as representative of "chic beauty," but the view that such chicness was no longer exclusively French became widespread. The majority of the global spokesmodels of the brand ceased to be primarily French, and came to include American, Spanish, Dutch, and Indian models.[36] And thus we see the paradox emerging: the more global the brand became, the more local its models had to be. People around the world wanted the name "L'Oréal Paris," but for many "Paris" was no longer necessarily in France. Did all the world's cultures each possess their own peculiar Paris inside them, their own distinctive take on what chicness looked like? Had multinational corporations' global conquests somehow sown the seeds of a worldwide democratization of personal aesthetics under the sign of the global brand?

Indeed, the spread of megabrands, and the continued diffusion of French and American beauty ideals, coincided with a new sensitivity to difference and diversity. The once homogenous mainstream American, beauty market, for example, increasingly reflected the country's rapidly growing ethnic diversity. The nearly 80 million Hispanics, African-Americans, and Asians recorded by the US Census in 2000 had already reached nearly 30 per cent of the overall American population. There was a rapid expansion of brands which sold to people with specific skin tones and ethnicities. Ethnic-specific beauty sales reached $1.5 billion in the United States in 2006, and each major brand sold to these markets.[37] Any lingering Barbie-style homogeneity in models gave way to greater diversity, especially in the range of skin tones that were recognized as being beautiful, and profitable. Worldwide, though, paler skins, rounder eyes, slim figures, and white teeth remained the benchmark of female beauty, regardless of ethnicity.

Moreover, rather than diffusing homogeneity in a crude fashion, companies became increasingly concerned that while the core claims, and usually the core technologies, of brands had to be the same worldwide, the form in which such claims and technologies were delivered, whether in jars or creams, and the scents which were employed, should be relevant and adapted to local consumers in each market. Jean-Paul Agon noted that although his company's global brands had global aspirations, "country by country, they need to take local expressions to respect local needs and aspirations."[38]

There was no uniform pattern to how brands responded to these twin pressures, even within the same company, and the response also varied between countries. In addition to its global spokespersons, for example, L'Oréal

Paris used local spokesmodels in markets which were considered to have special degrees of cultural sensitivity, including Germany, Italy, and China. Maybelline New York also made extensive use of local spokesmodels, including a Bollywood actress in India and a Japanese actress in Japan. Garnier, a third mass brand owned by L'Oréal, had a highly local identity everywhere.[39]

Luxury brands remained wary of too much localization. They remained much more cautious about using local models, but a search for local relevance was also noticeable. In China, Japan, South Korea, and Taiwan, prestige advertisements in beauty magazines began to take regularly the form of a Western global spokesmodel at the front of a magazine, but with three to six pages of local models near the end.[40]

The incorporation of local ideals concerning skin lightness into global brands provides one example of challenges arising from incorporating local identities into brands. In India, Hindustan Lever's Fair & Lovely skin-lightening cream was so successful that it continued to hold well over half of India's $200 million skin-lightening market. The brand was also now taken international by Unilever. It was launched in Sri Lanka in 1992, and then rolled out to nearly 40 countries in Asia, Africa, the Caribbean, and the Middle East by 2008. As it was rolled out to other countries, the brand's association of fairness with female beauty, and claims that it would enable women to find a better husband or job, led to criticism, as in India, that it was both racist and demeaning to women.[41]

Skin-lightening products, however, also formed a significant proportion of the sales of prestige skin care brands in East Asia, where a preference for lighter skin led to its incorporation into global brands. As in India, these preferences were rooted historically, but they have grown stronger over the recent past. In Japan, the market started to grow rapidly after Shiseido launched a successful Whitess essence cream in 1989. Many Western companies, including Chanel, Christian Dior, and Yves Saint Laurent, soon launched whitening cosmetics for the Japanese market.[42] As the Chinese skin care market boomed, Western and Japanese companies also incorporated skin-whitening effects into facial moisturizer brands. In addition, the incorporation of sun protection into skin creams was widely promoted as an agent to achieve better skin-whitening effects.[43]

A striking feature of the whitening fashion was that, to many, it was not an unwelcome relic from the past but widely associated with modernity and upward mobility, with a big market among urban professional women. From the perspective of many in the United States and Europe, the beauty companies could be seen as employing modern marketing methods to translate traditional prejudices concerning skin color, as well as gender roles, into warped aspirational values.[44] From a local perspective, different interpretations were possible. In India, the use of fairness creams was seen as providing one means for women to escape from socially imposed limitations.[45]

In Japan, skin lighteners represented a reassertion of traditional beauty aesthetics and a rejection of Western fashions for suntanning, a fashion which had now almost ceased among women.[46] Indeed, even as Japanese consumers continued to embrace Western fashion and luxury, the assertion of pride in local beauty was evident. Asian companies and consumers demonstrated increasing confidence in local beauty ideals. Pola discontinued the use of foreign models in 2000.[47] Kao undertook a successful launch of Asience shampoo with television advertisements of Zhang Ziyi, who became the first Chinese Miss World in 2007, showing off her long black hair to the jealous gasps of Western women. In 2007 Shiseido launched the blockbuster shampoo brand Tsubaki with a $40 million advertising campaign which featured famous Japanese women and the slogan "Japanese women are beautiful."[48]

The perceived growth of consumer interest in local identities and beauty cultures provided one basis for smaller, local firms to compete with global competitors. While they were often weaker in research capacity and sometimes handicapped by consumer perceptions that their brands were of lower quality than foreign ones, they could boast that they were local and that they understood the needs of local consumers.

As pride in local beauty identities grew, however, globalization also began to facilitate the diffusion of alternative beauty ideals. During the last century Paris's pinnacle as the capital of beauty and America's identification with wealth and Hollywood had limited the international appeal of brands representing other ideals. Despite the postwar success of the Japanese economy, and the existence of powerful local firms, Japanese brands never established more than a niche position in Western markets. A wider market continued to elude them even in the new era of globalization. Indeed, Japanese companies missed many of the new international opportunities, constrained both by a weak domestic economy after the collapse of the so-called "bubble economy," and also by a lack of international outlook among managers.

Shiseido, still the country's largest cosmetics company, did develop a large and profitable business in China from the early 1990s, but despite success with a new French fragrance affiliate, success in most Western markets proved elusive. While L'Oréal and P & G doubled their turnover between 1995 and 2005, Shiseido's sales remained almost flat. Kao gained in market share, and after its acquisition of Kanebo in 2007, its beauty business almost reached the size of Shiseido's.[49] Kao also remained heavily dependent on skin care, sold primarily in other Asian countries, and had limited international presence in other products.[50] AmorePacific and its competitors found it equally challenging to build a market for Korean brands outside Asia.[51]

Despite failures in the West, Asian firms did find international success in other Asian markets. In China and elsewhere in Asia, AmorePacific could benefit from "the Korean wave," the huge popularity of South Korean movies, television, and music. Both AmorePacific and its competitor Missha stressed that their products were Korean through advertisements, ingredients used, and product packaging in China and other Asian markets. But in the United States, AmorePacific felt a need to put more emphasis on its generic Asian background by incorporating green tea (rather than Korean red ginseng) as one of its main ingredients in its "AmorePacific" line, and by amalgamating Japanese and Chinese elements into its flagship spa in SoHo, New York.[52]

Despite such difficulties of selling Asian brands in the West, some Western companies pursued an alternative strategy of globalizing Asian brands. In 2000 L'Oréal acquired 35 per cent of Shu Uemura. Shu Uemura had strong international ambitions for his brand, and had opened stores in Hong Kong, Paris, and Los Angeles in 1986, but he found that the international business was rarely profitable.[53] His decision to sell to L'Oréal was, in part, designed to facilitate the globalization of his brand.[54] L'Oréal was now able to use its global platform to expand the brand globally. By 2008 nearly three-quarters of its sales were being made outside Japan.[55]

The rapid economic growth of China and India led to a search for brands from those countries which might have the potential to be globalized. In both cases, this was a difficult exercise because neither country had a strong domestic industry with aspirational brands. In China, one candidate was Yue-Sai, a department store brand founded by the prominent Chinese-American television celebrity Yue-Sai Kan in the early 1990s. Coty had invested in it in

1996 only to sell it to L'Oréal in 2004. Yue-Sai was perceived as having potential as a prestige Chinese brand which might, at some point, be taken global.[56] Meanwhile, Estée Lauder turned its attention to India. Having acquired Aveda in 1997, in 2008 it acquired a minority stake in Forest Essentials, an Ayurvedic cosmetics company founded eight years earlier, which made its products by hand in a village in the Himalaya and sold them in free-standing stores.[57] More broadly, the skin-lightening products developed for these markets began to find their way to markets in Western countries, reinvented as anti-aging products able to inhibit skin pigmentation.

If there was growing interest in the international potential of brands and concepts originating in Asia, there was also a revival in the popularity of European brands from beyond France. The Spanish perfume industry, which had stagnated under a long fascist dictatorship, and thus a poor image, between 1939 and 1975, began to recover after the restoration of democracy and the rapid economic growth of the Spanish economy. The family-owned Puig group, in particular, led the renewal, acquiring many of its domestic competitors in the process.[58] There was a growing international market for a Swedish or, more broadly, Scandinavian beauty ideal, suggestive of fair skins and healthy lifestyles. Oriflame found that its Swedish identity resonated strongly as it expanded in Eastern Europe from the 1990s. In 2007 the company moved its headquarters back from Brussels to Stockholm, in part to enhance this Swedish image.[59] In the United States, the drugstore CVS identified Finland's upscale green brand Lumene, founded in 1970, which incorporated local Finnish ingredients such as Arctic white peat, as a way to build a distinctive beauty business. After signing a deal as the brand's exclusive US retailer, CVS rolled it out in its American stores in 2003.[60]

A swathe of brands which had their origins in Britain were also successfully taken into international markets, and sometimes acquired by larger firms. In 2006 L'Oréal acquired The Body Shop, although another leading British green brand, Lush, remained independent. Kao bought the premium hair care and cosmetics brands John Frieda and Molton Brown. Estée Lauder bought Bumble and bumble, the creation of British-born Michael Gordon.[61] Coty relaunched Rimmel as a hip London brand, advertised by the native model Kate Moss, with distinctive store displays of red British telephone booths. Positioned as a mass cosmetic brand priced slightly below Maybelline, it was rolled out using multiple strategies, ranging from exclusive contracts with

Wal-Mart in the United States, to franchising agreements with Kosé in Japan and China.[62]

The evidence from the beauty industry, therefore, lent support to those who emphasized that globalization was making the world flatter; but that was not all that was happening. Large corporations both responded to this flatter world and orchestrated the flatness process themselves by, for instance, taking a brand based in Tennessee, relocating it to New York and launching it world-wide. However, the same firms can also be seen responding to, and in part shaping, tribalization. Global brands took diversity around the world, incorporated assertions of local identity, and legitimized them in the process. The globalization process worked to facilitate the diffusion of different beauty ideals around the globe. It was the firms that could respond to both the contemporary world's flatness and its tribalization that succeeded.

The dramatic opening of new markets, and the globalization of aspirations which accompanied it, provided an extraordinary opportunity. The firms which made their move to seize them and succeeded became the global leaders. Whilst in the mid-1990s, L'Oréal still made 63 per cent of its sales in Western Europe and 20 per cent in North America, by 2008 these proportions had changed to 45 and 23 per cent respectively as its business grew elsewhere. P & G still had nearly one-third of its sales in North America and a further 25 per cent in Western Europe, but expansion in China, which the firm entered in the late 1980s, and subsequently in Eastern Europe and Russia, had made it far more global by 2008.

Nevertheless, not even the largest firms in the industry were global in the sense that their business was evenly spread between regions, suggesting once more the necessity of more regional than global strategies.[63] L'Oréal and P & G both still clearly showed their European and American origins. Among other global leaders, Estée Lauder in 2008 still had over three-fifths of its total sales, Revlon one-half, and Johnson & Johnson two-fifths, in North America. Coty had half of its business in Europe, and a further third in North America. LVMH, Henkel, and Beiersdorf had one-half of their beauty sales in Europe. Both Kao and Shiseido had four-fifths of their sales in Asia-Pacific, and the Japanese market alone still accounted for two-thirds of Shiseido's revenues.

Avon was an outlier in having one-third of its sales in Latin America and only one-fifth in its North American home region in 2008. The toiletries companies Colgate-Palmolive and Unilever also stood out for the multiple regions in which they had substantial shares. The latter company demonstrated that global presence alone did not deliver success in the beauty industry. In 1990 it would have seemed more likely than P & G to succeed in the industry. However, Unilever's re-entry into luxury through Elizabeth Arden, Fabergé, and Calvin Klein was so poorly managed that it had to sell the brands.[64] More fundamentally, Unilever's leadership did not identify the beauty industry as an opportunity, perhaps because half of the company's revenues were in foods. When, in 2000, Unilever did make a major acquisition, it paid $20 billion for an American foods company.[65] Unilever remained the world's leader in deodorants and bath and shower products, but its growth was constrained by the limited number of categories in which it was now represented.[66]

New frontiers

The growth in the relative importance of the beauty markets beyond Europe, North America, and Japan was one of the most striking changes in the new global era. The rising importance of the four largest non-Western economies—Brazil, Russia, India, and China—which the investment bank Goldman Sachs predicted in 2003 would overtake the Western world in terms of overall wealth within half a century, was at the fulcrum of this change. These BRICs, as Goldman Sachs collectively described them, were already closing in on the Western world in terms of their share of the world beauty market. By 2008 Brazil, China, Russia, and India were the world's third-, fourth-, eighth-, and fourteenth-largest beauty markets, respectively. Collectively this amounted to almost one-fifth of the world market.

It would have been hard, at the start of the 1980s, to have predicted this. Russia had been a major presence in the first global economy, and the Chinese market had grown rapidly during the interwar years, but this earlier history had been buried by decades of Communism. During the early 1980s China's consumption of beauty products other than toiletries was close to zero. The Soviet Union was virtually closed to foreign firms. The Indian economy had been strangled by the "license Raj," the extensive web of government regulations put in place after independence. In the early 1980s it remained an inward-looking planned economy with discretionary spending on cosmetics limited to rich urban elites. Brazil was historically a bigger spender on beauty products, but the 1980s were a decade of "lost growth" with disastrously high inflation rates.

During the following decade, as these countries began to experience rapid economic growth, their urban middle classes began spending their rising incomes on beauty products. In China and Russia, in particular, the industry's products provided symbols of individualism and aspiration which had been denied to consumers by past regimes. These markets provided extraordinary opportunities for companies willing to seize them, which meant negotiating major logistical challenges, including sometimes non-existent distribution systems. It was a unique moment when, in contrast to the mature markets of the West, first-mover advantages could be seized and brand awareness built from scratch.

Brazil was the country which was most known to the major beauty companies. It had a historically high propensity towards high per capita income spending on beauty products. Its culture and language were derived from Western Europe, even though the legacy of slavery had helped to give the country a diverse ethnic make-up. There were also long-established Western firms in the market. Unilever had been manufacturing in the country since the interwar years, and had a large toiletries business. Avon had built a large direct-selling business since the late 1950s. However, protective tariffs, fragmented distribution channels, and political instability discouraged many other foreign companies. During the prolonged economic crisis of the 1980s most of the country's department stores collapsed, which left foreign luxury brands unable to penetrate the market beyond a few high-end malls and drugstores.

Paradoxically, Brazil's economic misfortunes provided space for locally owned firms to grow. Natura's direct-selling business, for instance, was able to recruit thousands of sales representatives from Brazil's army of unemployed workers. The company's commitment to environmental sustainability and corporate responsibility provided the basis for a business characterized by an authenticity which commanded loyalty from its direct sellers. With Western luxury brands unable to gain access to Brazilian consumers because of the distribution system, Natura's products acquired an aspirational status. In 1989 the company's sales stood at $170 million. Two decades later they were approaching $2.7 billion. Natura became one of Brazil's most valuable consumer brands, replacing Unilever as the market leader in Brazil, and was ranked among the 20 largest firms in the world industry.[67] Overall four of the ten largest firms were locally owned, although Unilever, Avon, P & G, and

9.2 Brazilian direct seller Natura launched the green brand Ekos in 2000. Sourced and produced in accordance with sustainable use practices which respect and work to preserve biodiversity, the Ekos range is made from Amazonian rain forest plants, 2007.

Colgate-Palmolive held second, third, fourth, and fifth places respectively in terms of market share as of 2008.[68]

It remained an open question, however, how fast Brazilian firms would be able to grow their own international businesses, despite strong ambitions.[69] Natura's international business remained primarily confined to Latin American countries. The company still had no operations in the United States, but did open a flagship store in Paris in 2005. The direct sales model, combined with strong and distinctive values, made growth through acquisition difficult. In 2005 it was approached with, but declined, an offer to acquire The Body Shop.[70] It was unclear also how far the Brazilian beauty culture was, in Owen-Jones's words, relevant to the rest of the world. Although Natura, and other leading companies, emphasized environmental responsibility, the continued image of the country as being "comprised of soccer, samba and naked women" posed a challenge for brands proclaiming their Brazilian identity.[71]

Given their historical background, the rapid growth of the Eastern European and Russian beauty markets was more remarkable than in Brazil. As the Berlin Wall fell in 1989, and liberalization and market capitalism spread, some of the largest Western companies moved to explore the opportunities. In 1988 L'Oréal opened a minority-owned joint venture with the still-Communist USSR to manufacture products for the mass market.[72] Soon after the opening of the Berlin Wall, Owen-Jones himself hired an East-German-made car, the Trabant, and set off exploring the new territories.[73]

In the race to enter the new markets, companies abandoned past orthodoxies. P & G, for example, broke from precedent by entering Eastern Europe regionally rather than on a country-by-country basis, with countries sorted according to which of the company's consumer products would prove most successful. The focus was on laundry, diapers, and toiletries, especially shampoo and toothpaste.[74] In Russia, L'Oréal Paris chose to enter color cosmetics rather than hair care, a major break from its past, because the lack of a local factory in Russia meant it needed higher-margin products which it could import. The company's cosmetics business accounted for half the company's sales and a much larger share of profits by the end of the decade.[75]

A particular interest in selling luxury brands to the newly rich elites emerged as businesses were privatized and economies deregulated. Here, as in most developing and transition economies, luxury brands transmitted signals of status which the newly rich craved. Estée Lauder opened a cosmetic beauty boutique in Budapest, its first free-standing store in the world, in 1989 (its first in the United States was in 1995 in Las Vegas). In the former Soviet Union beauty products had been sold in open-air markets, subway station kiosks, and grocery stores. In the absence of appropriate distribution channels, then, local distributors opened free-standing stores in Russia to sell luxury brands, which were in great demand.[76]

However, it was direct sellers who, as in Brazil, were able to take the greatest advantage of the still-underdeveloped infrastructure. Oriflame was a first mover. One of the founding brothers, Jonas af Jochnick, had decided to retire at the early age of 53, but he soon became bored, and as the Berlin Wall fell, the brothers decided they could capture first-mover advantages in the former Communist countries. "We had the advantage," Jonas's brother later observed, "of being very entrepreneurial, and very quick, and able to decide."[77] They decided to use a private company as their corporate vehicle, although with the same shareholders as the public company Oriflame, to which it paid dividends. This gambit enabled them to develop the business with less public scrutiny.

As it was not initially believed that direct sales would work, Oriflame began selling in shops when it entered Russia in 1992. However, as L'Oréal, Unilever, and other large companies moved in, it reverted to direct sales. The image of natural Swedish cosmetics helped them to attract consumers, as did the trust inspired by the direct-seller model. "In eastern Europe, you can't trust anyone, so people respond very well to someone you can trust," Robert later recalled. "In Russia, it is very important that people feel you are there for the long-term."[78] Avon arrived in Russia in 1995 and rapidly gained a foothold in the market.[79]

The extent of the globalization of the Russian market was indicated by the ranking of the ten largest firms, which held just over half of the market. P & G, following the merger with Gillette's large Russian business, was the largest, accounting for almost 12 per cent. Avon and L'Oréal followed. Henkel and Oriflame were next, with almost 6 per cent of the market, and Unilever, Colgate-Palmolive, and Beiersdorf were also in the top ten.

In contrast to Brazil, only one Russian firm, Kalina, was among the top ten.[80] This former state-owned firm had hardly survived the 1990s as its customers deserted it in droves for foreign brands, but it subsequently began building a significant color cosmetics and skin care business, competing with international brands and emphazing the scientific basis of its products. In 2005 it acquired Dr. Scheller Cosmetics in Germany, which gave it upmarket brands that it sought to sell in Russia by combining their reputation with its distribution network.[81] The acquisition also gave Kalina a significant position in German color cosmetics, which it reinforced when P & G allocated it a contract in 2008 to distribute Max Factor products in Germany.[82] There was, however, no evidence that a Russian-based beauty ideal was about to become attractive internationally.

The growth of the commercial beauty industry in China was arguably the most remarkable story of all the BRICs. As China embarked on reform and liberalization from the late 1970s, visiting Shiseido executives could perceive little difference between men and women in their dress and fashion.[83] The first foreign beauty companies arrived during the early 1980s, selling to the high-income segments in state-owned department stores in large cities, which were virtually the only distribution channel.[84]

High tariffs for cosmetics, which included import duties of 55 per cent, meant that local manufacturing was essential for all but the most expensive brands. The government initially obliged foreign companies to form joint ventures with local firms. Unilever entered a joint venture in 1987 with its former affiliate in China, which had been expropriated in 1949, to manufacture Lux toilet soap locally. However, in contrast to its success in India, the company was destined to underperform in China, becoming enmeshed with multiple underperforming joint ventures.[85] P & G entered a little later, but more successfully. As a result of the low prices of Chinese laundry products, P & G took the uncharacteristic decision to enter in beauty products, first in hair care and then skin care. As there were no national distribution facilities, it had to build its business by entering through Guangzhou, the fast-growing region near Hong Kong, where expatriate managers were initially based. It made a joint venture with a local Chinese firm to manufacture Head & Shoulders. Its sales, often in single-use sachets to enable people with low incomes to buy it, rose rapidly after its launch in 1988, as there was no equivalent on the Chinese market, and by 1990 it was already the brand's fifth-largest national market. Foreign investment in the Chinese cosmetics industry reached $68 million in 1993.[86]

As China's economy began to grow, a fully fledged consumer beauty culture emerged in the largest Chinese cities. By 1994 the Chinese market had reached $2.5 billion. Six years later it was $4.6 billion.[87] Lifestyle magazines and cosmetic surgery, including double-eyelid surgery and nose straightening and raising designed to emulate Western beauty norms, boomed.[88] Beauty contests, formerly totally forbidden, emerged and flourished. In 1988 one of the first was held in Guangdong. In 2003 China hosted the Miss World pageant for the first time, on the island of Hainan.[89]

During the 1990s, as the potential of the market became apparent, foreign firms invested heavily. Avon entered China in 1990. Shiseido formed a manufacturing joint venture with a local company in 1991. By 1993 P & G had launched two other hair care brands, the skin care brand Oil of Olay, bar soaps, and feminine care brands. It also opened a new factory which could supply the large Beijing and Shanghai markets and began building a Western-style distribution network. Unconventional marketing strategies were again deployed. Olay was sold through counters in department stores staffed by beauty counselors.

L'Oréal's entry into China in 1997 happened later than its competitors', in part because it lacked the toiletry products which its competitors could sell as the market began to develop. Its decision to commit itself to China called for an unusual entry strategy. While the company typically entered countries through professional hair care, this was not an option in China, where hairdressing had a low status and few consumers bought products from salons. Moreover, the consumer hair care market was already dominated by P & G. The decision was therefore taken to focus on skin care, which accounted for almost half of the total Chinese beauty market.[90]

Unconventional strategies were again employed. L'Oréal Paris was launched in China as a prestige brand sold in department stores. The price was half that of true luxury brands, but China became the most expensive country in the world to buy the brand.[91] Seventy per cent of L'Oréal Paris's sales in China were in skin care, which was completely out of line with its sales elsewhere, and contributed to making China L'Oréal's single largest skin care market.[92] Maybelline New York was its entry into the mass color cosmetics market. By 2003 it was the single largest color cosmetics brand in the country, although the make-up market was much smaller and less sophisticated than the skin care market.[93] Lancôme was launched in 1999, rapidly establishing itself as the leading prestige brand in the country, primarily because of its skin-lightening products, which had been launched in Japan the previous year. Overall, L'Oréal increased its sales in China from a mere $20 million in 1997 to $180 million six years later.[94]

As the Chinese economy grew as a central actor in the new global economy, it demonstrated both how the world was becoming flatter, and how it was not. The huge market for the latest Western and Japanese goods, and the rapid growth of department stores and shopping malls in cosmopolitan cities like Shanghai, were signs of flatness, as was China's membership in the World Trade Organization and other international institutions. The decisive role of the government, however, showed how far the world was from being borderless. In 2008 the 298 million Internet users in China surpassed the number of users in the United States, but the government had the world's most sophisticated system for filtering content on the Web. In 1998 direct selling was suddenly banned due to concerns about fraud, consumer losses, and social disorder. Avon, Mary Kay, Amway, and other direct sellers found their businesses in jeopardy. Avon had to restructure itself for a time as a conventional cosmetics company, establishing thousands of independently owned and operated small stores which exclusively sold Avon products. In 2005 the government allowed the direct sellers to return.[95] As the Chinese market boomed, the issue of local adaptation became more pressing. Like elsewhere, local brands had initially been perceived as poor in quality and lacking aspirational attributes. As a result, Japanese and Western brands rapidly gained market share, even if product formulations were changed and firms responded to local preferences for skin-whitening products. By the 1990s there was a growing belief that China might follow Japan in its preference for local brands. In 1994 Shiseido launched the locally made Aupres brand in China. It was positioned as being made especially for Chinese women and was advertised by Chinese models rather than the Western models used for Shiseido's imported brands. Aupres proved successful and was even adopted as the official brand for the Chinese team at the Athens Olympics in 2004.[96] Coty's acquisition of Yue-Sai in 1996 was driven by a similar assumption that as Chinese consumers became richer, they would also want to buy Chinese brands.[97]

The actual outcome was more complex. Foreign brands retained enormous aspirational value. Bernd Beetz, explaining Coty's decision to sell Yue-Sai, concluded that Chinese consumers really wanted "a Western-sounding brand, ideally coming from Western Europe or North America, which has an application and a cultural affinity to the region." Coty, as a result, opted for a strategy of Asian-specific executions of global platforms, launching, for example, a special Chinese version of its Calvin Klein fragrance as Euphoria Blossom.[98]

Many in the industry agreed with Coty's assessment, but the extent of "cultural affinity" was uncertain. As Chinese pride in the growth of their country increased, there appeared to be demand for increasing local content in brands. Many Chinese consumers wanted to see some Chinese faces as models, but there remained uncertainty about how far localization should be taken. "A big issue for us is whether we should use blonde Swedish models," Oriflame's Robert af Jochnick observed. "In China we have decided that we need a Chinese feel, so we are using both Swedish and Chinese models. It's one of the most difficult decisions in the industry."[99] L'Oréal Paris had four leading Chinese celebrities, including Gong Li and Zhang Ziyi, as spokesmodels by 2008, chosen in part to reflect the diversity of China's population.[100]

The localization of spokesmodels in China was only one aspect of the search for local identities. Western companies employed local talent for photographic shoots as a means to getting greater local aesthetic sensitivity.[101] Local ingredients were also featured in brands, not as in the past for reasons of availability and cost, but to enhance their appeal. Chinese consumers embraced the aspirational values of leading American and French brands, but they also wanted their Western shampoos to include black sesame and ginseng, or to have local herbs in their toothpaste.[102]

While the incorporation of local sensitivities into brands was a growing issue, local firms were not major beneficiaries. During the 1980s there were many small start-ups in China, for example, but health and quality problems fostered consumer suspicion of domestically made cosmetic products, especially before the government started giving production licenses only to firms which met specified hygiene standards.[103] The number of cosmetics companies in China grew from about 500 in 1980 to 2,700 in 1996, but only 40 companies had sales of over 100 million yuan ($12 million) and few had businesses which extended beyond regional markets.[104] Local firms which did build viable brands were regularly acquired for generous prices by Western firms interested in their large domestic markets and in the global potential of brands.

In 2008, ten firms held just over half of the Chinese market, as in Russia. C-Bons, a hair company, was the only local firm, and had recently been acquired by Beiersdorf. P & G held almost one-fifth of the Chinese beauty market, and almost one-half of the hair market. L'Oréal followed with 7.5 per cent, then Unilever in third place with 6.7 per cent. In China, Amway was the largest direct seller, but Avon and Mary Kay were also in the top ten, as were Colgate-Palmolive and Johnson & Johnson, which had recently acquired another local firm, Dabao. The largest remaining locally owned firm was Jiangsu Longliqi, which began by selling lotions made from snake oil and which focused on serving consumers who remained attracted to traditional products rather than the new brands offered by multinationals.[105]

For the global beauty industry, India was the last frontier. It had one of the world's lowest per capita spending rates on beauty products. A complex and fragmented distribution system, with 12 million independent shopkeepers accounting for 97 per cent of total retail sales, made reaching markets challenging. High tariffs continued to require local manufacturing, yet such manufacturing faced deep-seated problems of poor infrastructure, regulation, and corruption. There were major regional differences in ethnicity, language, and cultural preferences, with the darker-skinned women in the south of the country often more conservative, especially in the use of color cosmetics, than women in the north. The conservative nature of Indian society as a whole was reflected by the fact that it was one of the few countries where many women, although not men, still regularly wore national rather than Western dress.[106] Yet as the pace of urbanization and growing affluence accelerated, the beauty market expanded. It doubled in size between 2002 and 2007 alone.[107]

The market was dominated by Unilever's affiliate, Hindustan Lever. The top ten firms held 70 per cent of the total market, but half of that was held by Hindustan Lever. The firm's dominant position in toiletries and skin-lightening creams was reinforced in 1995 when Tata went into a joint venture with its cosmetics affiliate Lakmé, and three years later sold its remaining equity to Hindustan Lever. It had the largest distribution network in India and had access to rural areas in ways few other firms could match. Unlike the rest of Unilever, its reach extended far beyond toiletries. In 2008, it held one-third of the color cosmetics market and two-thirds of the skin care market.

The remaining nine companies in the top ten included three Western multinationals and six local firms. Colgate-Palmolive was the second-biggest firm with 6.3 per cent of the market, and locally owned Godrej was in third place with 4.5 per cent. Both P & G and L'Oréal were in the top ten, but with small shares, reflecting the fact that they were only recent entrants to the country. Nevertheless, those shares were growing, and India's potential as a market seemed clear. Distribution channels were changing as department stores and shopping malls appeared in larger cities. A direct-selling channel appeared. Oriflame entered the country in 1995 and had 100,000 sellers by 2008. Avon opened in India in 1996. The large Indian diaspora, and the international success of Bollywood cinema, suggested that brands with Indian origins had international potential. However, the divide between rural and urban India, as well as strengthening preferences for products such as skin lighteners, suggested that the Indian market would remain distinctive. Indeed, as the market developed, pride in distinctive Indian beauty ideals became ever stronger.[108]

By 2008 the four BRICs together represented virtually the same size as the American market, but it was their faster growth rates—the markets of the four countries combined grew 18 per cent in 2007 alone—which made them so important to the future of the beauty industry. As the global financial crisis beginning in 2008 took its toll on the US and other Western consumer markets, it seemed likely that the increase in the relative importance of BRIC markets could only grow. For companies which had perceived this opportunity earlier rather than later, and had been prepared to take risks and pursue unconventional strategies, the rewards were high. A firm whose brands were not significant players in these markets stood little chance of remaining a leading global firm.

Looking for real stories

There were growing concerns by consumers, some believed, for more meaningfulness in the brands they bought. There was both a wish for authenticity and legitimacy, and a feeling that claims made for products should be truthful. These sentiments may have reflected the continued disillusionment with the advertising industry which had begun decades earlier. This industry was, in any case, undermined as Internet, wireless, and cable enabled consumers both to avoid scheduled television advertisements and to compare products by price and efficacy through access to customer testimonials. This disillusion was related also to generational change, as a new generation, born in the digital age and coming of age with social networking technologies, emerged as consumers. It was also one dimension of the response to globalization, for as people embraced the global, they also sought the security of the local.

The trend was observable in the beauty industry. "Ten years ago," Lena Philippou Korres observed in 2008 as one factor behind the rapid growth of her own brand of Greek herbal-based cosmetics and toiletries, "it was all about the big brand, the big name, the big company. Now people are starting to look for products they can identify with... people are looking for real stories, for real quality in everything."[109] As brands became more distinct, consumers felt the lure of personal identification with the brands in their lives, and the surest way for companies to encourage that identification was through narrative: by telling stories about the brand. If consumers felt a strong commitment to environmental concerns, then a firm that told stories about the respect it paid to the earth and to local producers in the formerly colonized world stood a good chance of luring and securing those consumers. If consumers saw themselves as older or typical in appearance, then a firm that told stories about how it valued the beauty of older and ordinary people could likewise succeed. In recent times, the power of narrative has reshaped the way some beauty firms have presented themselves and their products to the world.

The search for real stories helped drive psychographic segmentation and market fragmentation. Lifestyle preferences grew as the basis of brands. Wellness, green, organic, minerals, skin tone, and other such segments flourished, especially at the higher-priced segments of the market. In 2007 so-called niche brands took one-quarter of the $8 billion US prestige beauty market, compared to 2 per cent in 1997.[110]

While there were numerous entrepreneurial start-ups to develop new niche brands, large firms were as much the orchestrators of this trend as its victims. The co-existence of megabrands with niche brands was well illustrated by the quirky New York pharmacy brand Kiehl's. This small family-owned brand had long flourished as a single store in New York's East Village. The products were sold in simple packaging. Its brands were never advertised, and their scarcity was a major marketing advantage. Attachment to the local community also formed a key element of the value proposition of the brand. In the original New York store, much of the wall space was devoted to local activities, including an entire wall devoted to the pictures of customers' children. The Kiehl's brand represented, in some respects, the antithesis of globalization, right there in the heart of the metropolis.[111]

The acquisition of such a brand by L'Oréal in 2000 was in itself remarkable. Its plain packaging and lack of advertising were quite different from any other brand the French company had owned, while L'Oréal had never before owned a retail business. Even more remarkable was the subsequent expansion of Kiehl's stores to other US cities, and then internationally, beginning with London in 2002. By 2009 Kiehl's was sold in 33 countries in Europe, Latin America, the Middle East, and Asia. In each store, the company replicated features of the original store, including a skeleton and a Harley-Davidson motorcycle, whilst forging links with the local community and seeking relevance to local consumers. In each city, a location was sought in a neighborhood which fit the psychographic position of the brand, where liberal-minded professionals lived or shopped.[112]

Although the brand found some markets, such as France, more challenging than others, it was successfully taken to quite different countries extending from Buenos Aires to Singapore. "Kiehl's is a cult niche brand," Jean-Paul

Agon observed, "but you can be a niche brand everywhere in the world. So you can globalize cult and niche—they love Kiehl's in Korea as much as in America."[113]

The globalization of a grassroots New York brand by a French corporate giant raised questions of authenticity. There was an uproar on both these grounds when The Body Shop was acquired by L'Oréal in 2006. Anita Roddick found herself accused, as she wrote shortly before her death at the early age of 64, of having "betrayed women." Her own answer was that she could infiltrate the larger company with her views, and that it was in L'Oréal's own self-interest not to seek to change them. "I do not believe that L'Oréal will compromise the ethics of The Body Shop," she wrote in 2006. "That is after all what they are paying for and they are too intelligent to mess with our DNA."[114]

Roddick was right to believe that it was unlikely that L'Oréal would hardly undermine a brand it had paid over a billion dollars to acquire. Moreover, by then, the concern to be shown to be engaged in real stories had led many companies to support wider social goals in ways that would have been unimaginable two decades earlier. The trend got under way in earnest in the United States with the MAC AIDS funds, launched in 1994, which had raised more than $100 million for research and outreach by 2009.[115] By then many large companies and leading brands supported medical and other charitable projects. It had become important, the brand manager for L'Oréal Paris observed, to do "meaningful things, and to have meaningful spokespeople for brands, people who have something to say and have done meaningful things in their lives."[116]

The broad search for meaningful things was evident as the two late-twentieth-century visions of beauty—scientific and green—flourished and, like everything else, were progressively globalized. The use of natural ingredients, which began as a niche fad, blossomed into an industry norm for firms large and small alike. In 1990 Estée Lauder launched Origins Natural Resources—which used recycled paper and make-up shades which emphasized natural skin tones, while avoiding animal products and petroleum-based active ingredients—with the opening of its first stores in Harvard Square and SoHo in Manhattan. By 2006, when L'Oréal purchased The Body Shop as well as the much smaller Sanoflore, green was confirmed as mainstream. The search was on for exotic flora and new ingredients. Skin care brands incorporated honey, pistachio, almonds, green tea, ginseng, cucumber, and hundreds of other natural ingredients.[117] The success of San Francisco-based Bare Escentuals, created in 1976, stimulated wide interest in the use of minerals, a fashion which spread throughout the world.[118]

Long-lost craft knowledge, almost driven underground by industrialization, was now sought and turned into modern brands. This was the origin of Korres Natural Products. Pharmacies traditionally held a special place in Greece. An estimated 10,000 pharmacies, all single units, in a country of ten million meant that there was virtually one pharmacy on every road, which sold over-the-counter drugs, cosmetics, and other products such as convenience food. In 1989 George Korres began working in one such homeopathic pharmacy in Athens, which he took over when the owner retired three years later. The reputation for the herbal products he began making for his customers spread by word of mouth. In 1996 he and his wife Lena Philippou, a chemical engineer, launched their own company.

Korres' cosmetics were based on herbs and flora, and drew on traditional knowledge of their efficacy. By 2008 they were using 350 different herbs, many unique to Greece. A yoghurt after-sun cream, for example, employed popular wisdom in Greece that yoghurt relieved sunburn. Honey, rose, sage, hibiscus, fig, watermelon, and mint tea were among many other ingredients employed. In a country with few home-grown consumer brands, within a decade Korres had edged past incumbents L'Oréal, Pierre Fabre, and Johnson & Johnson to take a leading share in the Greek pharmacy market.

An international business was also developed, overcoming concerns about a Greek company being able to make a quality consumer product. In 2000 exports began when a friend told them he thought it would prove attractive. They started selling in high-end department stores in New York, and in the following year were approached by a leading department store in London. In 2003 the firm opened its first store in Britain. Four years later the firm owned 18 stores, of which 16 were outside Greece and two were in Beijing, and had sales of $50 million.[119] Korres identified itself as a herb company. "I didn't start the company as a beauty company," George Korres observed, "but as a company with herbs that offers beauty solutions in the right way."[120]

By the new century there was a veritable gold rush as the search to uncover the extensive herbal and craft knowledge of ancient India and China began. The desire for local relevance in these promising markets drove much of this interest, as did faddish interest in these countries by Western consumers. However, there was also a feeling that industrialization and Westernization had swept away knowledge which had real commercial value, as well as an authenticity bestowed by centuries of use. Western medicine, after all, was well advanced in incorporating historic practices from both cultures, especially yoga and acupuncture, into its product offering, while a strong interest in traditional herbal knowledge flourished under the name "alternative medicine."

The beauty industry now followed in the track of medicine. Aveda had already introduced American consumers to Ayurvedic philosophy and aromatherapy. In 1992 Vinita Jain, who had a biochemistry degree from Switzerland as well as a Stanford MBA, created Biotique as an Indian herbal cosmetics company. By 2000 it had sales of $13 million, 80 per cent of which was outside India.[121] Forest Essentials, acquired by Estée Lauder in 2008, was one of a cluster of similar firms.

Both Japanese and Western beauty companies also went in search of the ancient knowledge of China. Research centers were established. In 2002 Shiseido established a research center in Beijing to study Eastern herbal medicine. In 2004 L'Oréal established a similar facility in Pudong with the specific intent of exploring the active ingredients behind traditional Chinese beauty products. The traditional knowledge contained in such products was recognized to be highly local, but international companies were well positioned to put together such fragmented knowledge from different regions of China and from around the world. They were also, importantly, able to employ modern science to discover how such ingredients worked, and to test formally both their efficacy and safety.[122] The potential learning was not restricted to products. These products were typically located within wider beauty practices in which, for example, services such as massage or acupuncture formed important components of an overall holistic vision. As a result, Western companies could potentially learn entirely new philosophies of beauty.[123]

The search for ancient craft knowledge and the rising use of natural ingredients was accompanied by a new interest in products which could be consumed as well as applied. This could also be seen as another reversion to the pre-industrial age, when perfumes had been drunk as an aid to health. In the new century beauty foods assumed a new significance as a market for "nutraceuticals" grew. One estimate suggested that the global beauty supplement market had reached $2 billion in 2006, being especially strong in Japan and parts of Europe.[124]

The belief that science was the key to efficacy in beauty remained strong even as the green movement became mainstream. A market for highly technical products known as "cosmeceuticals" grew rapidly and reflected consumer desires for effectiveness rather than hyperbole. These were also not conceptually new, but rather a new phase of products based on scientific research in which the industry had long been interested. These were now made more fashionable by a wave of entrepreneurial start-ups, including start-ups by dermatologists and other medical researchers. Overall, the world "cosmeceutical" market, about half of which was skin care, had grown to about $60 billion.[125] It was noteworthy that the two firms which grew to be the industry's biggest companies, P & G and L'Oréal, combined a deep-seated commitment to research alongside their formidable capabilities in branding and marketing.

The search for real stories also led firms to reconsider how, for the last century, they had treated older consumers and aging. As with the changing attitudes towards ethnicity, there were market forces at work. As baby boomers aged, growing attention was paid to consumers over 45. Both the scale and the nature of the launch of anti-aging products intensified. In 1999 Estée Lauder broke with its past history by launching Resilience Lift Face and Throat Crème and Lotion SPF 15, a new skin care product explicitly for women in their forties, fifties, and beyond. One L'Oréal executive in 2008 could imagine the company's target market extending from ages 15 to 90.[126]

Major differences were apparent, however, in handling the issue of aging itself. A minority in the industry proposed a radical reinterpretation of beauty norms, asserting that people could and should still be seen as beautiful even if they had wrinkles or were obese or simply did not look like young models. The pioneer of this approach was Natura. In 1992 Natura launched the concept of the "Truly Beautiful Woman" with the explicit declaration that beauty was not a matter of age but of self-esteem. It is instructive that this initiative emerged from a country in which high standards of physical attractiveness and youthfulness were emphasized. Brazil had the largest number of plastic surgeries per capita in the world, and was the second largest market for the anti-wrinkle drug Botox and the anti-impotence drug Viagra. Yet while there were evidently plenty of consumers in Brazil who were more than happy to use surgery and drugs to enhance their attractiveness, the market was responsive also to brands which promised truthfulness and authenticity.[127] The approach pioneered by Natura was taken up by Unilever for its Dove brand. During 2002 a company research project on women's responses to the beauty industry had indicated discontent with what was believed to be the widespread portrayal of women as "young, white, blonde and thin." They recruited two prominent psychologists who generated hypotheses which were tested on large surveys. A survey of 3,000 women found that a mere 2 per cent of respondents described themselves as beautiful. In response to this evidence, a series of advertisements began in the United States in 2005 which evolved into the Campaign for Real Beauty. These advertisements for Dove featured pictures of seniors, larger women, and other unconventional beauty models.[128]

It remained unclear as to what extent such marketing campaigns represented the beginnings of a fundamental shift in how the industry represents beauty. The Dove campaign had its critics. A leading New York photographer claimed that the photographs of "ordinary women" were heavily retouched. It was observed that Unilever was also the company which advertised Axe male body spray, showing a female pop music group driven into a sexual frenzy by its aroma on a man.[129] For others, the Dove campaign seemed naive in an industry which had always emphasized the importance of aspiration and feeling good about oneself.

There did seem to be a consensus that it no longer made sense to define aspiration as looking like a woman or a man in their twenties. The growing use of older spokespersons was noticeable. Estée Lauder's Resilience brand was launched in 1999 using Karen Graham, who had been the single model used by Estée Lauder for 15 years during the 1970s and early 1980s, but was 54 at century's end. This was the first time the company had targeted an advertising campaign to more mature customers. The L'Oréal Paris brand moved powerfully in that direction also. In 2006 the 60-year-old Diane Keaton and the 68-year-old Jane Fonda became spokespersons for the brand's anti-aging products, while the spokesperson in Malaysia was the 44-year-old actress Michelle Yeoh, a former Miss Malaysia. In 2008 L'Oréal Paris signed up the 54-year-old actor-producer Pierce Brosnan as a spokesperson for its Men Expert skin care range. These spokespersons were hardly "ordinary," as those representing

Dove were asserted to be, but their maturity set them apart from the models that the industry had traditionally employed.

While many found that such changing attitudes towards age represented an improvement for the industry, it was accompanied by a new interest in selling to very young women which might be considered less legitimate. A teenage consumer culture, primarily female, had already developed in the United States during the interwar years. Although cosmetics were not manufactured and marketed specifically for teenage girls until the 1940s, many used cosmetics, hair dyes, and nail varnish.[130] Subsequently, a formal teenage market for cosmetics grew. By 2000 it was estimated to account for 20 per cent of the total American beauty market. The pre-teen market of 9- to 12-year-old girls was seen as particularly promising by many companies.[131]

There were also efforts to overcome the gendered consumption of beauty products which had emerged in the nineteenth century. There were moments, as in the past, when the differences between genders seemed to be fading. The successful Calvin Klein ck one fragrance, launched in 1994, became a noteworthy example of a unisex or androgynous brand. This success did not turn into a mainstream trend, however. In 2008 the designer Karl Lagerfield asserted, announcing a new trio of unisex scents called Kapsule created with Coty, that "there is no gender in perfumes anymore."[132] Nevertheless, many in the industry thought that the overall trend at the start of the new century was more towards stronger than weaker emphasis on masculinity and femininity. Even the motivations behind buying fragrances seemed to differ sharply between genders.[133]

The industry continued to explore ways to sell products to men as broader social changes and generational shifts encouraged a continued upward trajectory of the size of the male market. By the new century US sales of male grooming products were estimated at $4 billion, and men's skin care alone reached $500 million.[134] Asian rather than Western markets were more promising for sales to men. There were strong male skin care markets in Japan and South Korea, where there was also a fashion for men buying cosmetics that made them appear delicate and pretty. Young Japanese and South Korean men bought foundation, eyelash tinting, and powdered facial paper, among other non-traditional options.[135] Companies also looked to Asian beauty rituals as a source of information concerning selling to men. In

India, for example, men—even the poorest—were traditionally major users of creams and fragrances.[136]

Shopping in a global village

A world that was flatter seemed set to offer new opportunities for beauty companies to tell their real stories to customers in many countries. In the past, differences in distribution systems and the challenges of foreign access had posed a formidable obstacle to globalization. The information revolution promised to lessen the obstacles to distribution, although it remained to be seen who would benefit the most.

The growth of concentration in retailing in most Western countries was one of the major themes of these years, providing both challenges and opportunities for the beauty industry. For companies which sold luxury brands, the mergers of department stores represented a continued shift in the balance of power in the industry. In the United States, for example, the merger of May Department Stores (owner of Filene's, Hecht's, Lord & Taylor, Strawbridge's, and other stores) with Federated Department Stores (owner of Macy's and Bloomingdales) in 2005 created a single entity with annual sales of about $30 billion and about 950 stores with a presence in 64 of the largest 65 US markets.

These big retailers demanded that beauty companies wanting to launch and sell their brands paid heavily for in-store advertising, sales personnel, and end-of-the-year buybacks. The cost of a new perfume launch in Macy's Herald Square branch in New York, the "number one surface in the world in terms of perfume sales," ran into hundreds of thousands of dollars.[137] One estimate was that a fragrance company needed a critical mass of $100 million in sales in US department stores to reach profitability.[138]

Obtaining scale was, therefore, vital if a beauty firm wanted to succeed in this arena. Coty's successful launch of the JLo Glow fragrance, and its subsequent acquisition of the Kenneth Cole and Marc Jacobs designer fragrance licenses from LVMH in 2003, were critical to the firm's ability to build a viable fragrance business.[139] On the other hand, the concentration of ownership of department stores was advantageous to the very largest beauty firms, which could both secure the best terms for the brands, and work with the retailers over a wide geographical span. "With big retail partners," the head of L'Oréal's luxury division noted, "we can invent the luxury of the future."[140] The department stores themselves, however, were not immune to the seismic shifts in distribution which were under way, as other retail formats grew. Sephora, for example, became a powerful means for new niche brands to reach consumers.

The concentration of ownership in mass channels created the same mixture of challenge and opportunity for beauty firms. The growth of mass retailers such as Wal-Mart and Carrefour provided a means to roll out new brands at speed, but on conditions determined by the retailers. Coty's Rimmel brand, for example, could be launched in the American market through an exclusive arrangement with Wal-Mart, but the retailer dictated a price which was lower than the firm's global strategy allowed.[141] As Wal-Mart, Carrefour, and other large supermarkets and hypermarkets expanded globally in Latin America, Eastern Europe, and Asia, their potential to help globalize beauty brands grew, but so did their bargaining power.

In the United States, drugstore discounters also played a rising role as a distribution channel. Longs, a drugstore which originated in 1938 and built a large chain of stores in western states such as California, moved aggressively into selling beauty in the early 1990s, putting beauty advisers into its stores. It was allowed to sell several expensive brands otherwise sold only in department stores, and it also became a launching pad in the United States for foreign niche brands. A similar role was performed by Walgreens and CVS, which acquired Longs in 2008.[142]

There was a new interest among beauty companies themselves in owning their own retail businesses. During the nineteenth century, Rimmel, Guerlain, and many other perfumers had regarded their shops as important components of their businesses, but the link between manufacturing and retailing had thereafter been broken, with the conspicuous exception of the voluntary chain store systems seen primarily in Japan.

During the 1970s The Body Shop's successful use of the franchising model again raised the profile of the retail format in the beauty industry. It became widely adopted by firms selling natural beauty brands, who saw it as a means to communicate directly about their products. L'Occitane expanded rapidly after its acquisition by a former Austrian ski champion, Reinold Geiger. Between 1996 and 2009 it expanded the number of its stores from two (both in France) to 900, spread around the world, including 28 airport duty-free stores.[143] Newcomers Lush and Korres also took their products directly to consumers in stores. While the former used franchising, the latter owned its own shops. This was an expensive strategy but seen by the owners as essential to raising brand awareness amongst consumers and the all-important beauty editors.[144]

By the new century retailing had gone mainstream. Estée Lauder became active in creating a global network of retail stores for many of the brands it had acquired, including Bobbi Brown and MAC.[145] L'Oréal entered retailing through the purchase of Kiehl's, while The Body Shop purchase took it into the channel on a large scale. The prospects of the Chinese beauty market led Shiseido, in 2004, to launch a voluntary chain store network of the kind it had built in Japan. By 2009 it had over 4,000 such stores, which sold brands aimed for the middle market rather than the more expensive brands sold in department stores.

However, the growth of the beauty industry in many emerging markets, and in rural areas especially, favored direct sellers. By 2007 direct sales of beauty products amounted to $32 billion worldwide, with half of this amount coming from Eastern Europe and Latin America.[146] Nearly 30 per cent of all beauty sales in Latin America, and over 20 per cent in Eastern Europe, went through direct sales, compared to 5 per cent in Western Europe and less than 10 per cent in North America.[147] The number of people employed in direct selling was huge. Overall, over three million direct sellers were employed in Russia by 2008.[148] Natura alone employed half a million people in Brazil.

Avon's ability to exploit this channel was important in its recovery from the near-terminal era of diversification, as was its ability to create once more a clear corporate identity as a "company for women." In 1999 Toronto-born Andrea Jung, who had first worked for the company as a consultant after an earlier career in upscale retailing, was appointed as its first female chief executive.[149] In contrast to the company's more mature markets in North America and Western Europe, where direct selling seemed to be waning and Avon's mass-market products seemed vulnerable to competition, in Brazil, Russia, and elsewhere the lack of alternative distribution facilities helped make Avon's revitalized business highly successful. However, despite Jung's best efforts at trying to raise the status of Avon's products, it remained primarily confined to the mass market.[150]

It was noteworthy that, by 2008, direct sellers Natura, Mary Kay, Amway, and Oriflame were also amongst the 30 largest beauty companies. It was also a channel in which other major Western companies were increasingly interested. In India, even P & G turned to direct selling in rural areas for Pantene Pro-V.

Many local firms also grew as direct sellers. In Russia, the second-largest local firm after Kalina was Faberlic, a direct seller positioned as a unique manufacturer of oxygen-based skin care products. In Thailand, Amornthep Deerojanawong, the former manager of Avon's large business in that country, established the Better Way (Thailand) Company in 1988, which three years later launched the Mistine brand of cosmetics.[151] He was supported financially by his friend who owned the Saha Group, the country's largest consumer products company and a major retailer, and which manufactured the new cosmetics. Aware that Thai consumers believed that foreign products were always superior to local ones, Amornthep broke from normal practice in direct selling by using mass-media television advertising, and made great play of using Thai actresses and actors to build the brand.[152] By 2000 Mistine, despite experiencing a one-fifth fall in sales during the Asian financial crisis in 1997, had captured over half of the direct-selling market, with some 400,000 sales representatives.[153]

In developed markets, it was non-store retailing which had the most radical impact on distribution channels. Television acquired a new importance as a means by which niche brands could gain access to consumers. In the United States, home shopping channels such as HSN and QVC appeared during the 1980s and later spread elsewhere. Initially, the consensus in the beauty industry was that television retailers would bring brand images down, but over time it emerged that exposure on the shopping channels tended to increase sales in stores significantly. A growing number of prestige brands began to appear in the medium, which sometimes launched new products before they were even sold in stores. In contrast, the Internet, although the iconic symbol of a flat world, continued to be used more as a marketing tool than as a retail channel. It is difficult to purchase make-up online because of the challenge of accurately choosing proper colors, and impossible to choose fragrances. However, many large firms used online retailing for facilitating repeat purchases, and niche brands distinctly used online means to reach consumers.[154]

Summing up

The growth of the beauty industry has been relentless over the last twenty years. The industry worked assiduously to reach an ever-wider range of consumers, whether seniors and pre-teens in the affluent West, or rural villagers in China and India. Megabrands could now be found across the globe, as could many niche brands. It was a striking testament to the flatness of the new global era.

The spread of megabrands over the last two decades lent support to a view that globalization was continuing the homogenization of beauty ideals which had been under way since the nineteenth century. French and American brands remained the benchmark of aspiration. Yet globalization now also seemed to work in the opposite direction, serving to diffuse alternative and local beauty ideals. Companies now saw opportunities to take, say, Chinese and Indian beauty concepts to Western markets, and they had the marketing and logistical capabilities to execute such strategies. Changing demographics and societal values also led firms to pursue new markets, including ethnic minorities, pre-teens, and seniors. The basis of segmentation was increasingly psychographic, reflecting different lifestyle choices. Big business became the orchestrators of diversity rather than its nemesis.

Consumers everywhere welcomed many benefits of globalization, but not at the cost of losing their identities. As a result, a growing reassertion of local identity accompanied the intensification of globalization. This reassertion of local ideals was especially evident in non-Western countries, whose beauty ideals and cultures had long been dismissed as second-rate. The variations between countries' consumer preferences in beauty products seen in today's industry was, therefore, less the result of the legacy of cultural and social obstacles to globalizing beauty than of the reassertion of local identities. It almost seemed that much of the previous two hundred years of the industry's history was being swept away. The gender and, especially, age borders of the beauty industry were fading. The search was on for the secrets of the herbs and flowers which had formed the basis for the pre-industrial beauty culture. However, this search co-existed with a demand for ever more powerful intervention to reverse the ravages of age on the appearances of baby boomers. Celebrity culture and advertising glitz co-existed with a search for authenticity. The result, for the beauty industry, was not the removal of the long-prevalent challenges of globalization, but their translation to a new level of complexity and contradiction.

The model for corporate success during these years rested on understanding the apparent contradictions of these decades. Seizing the new opportunities of globalization was essential, but so was understanding the marketing implications of tribalization. Above all, the beauty industry was a relentless industry which demanded focus to succeed. It was indicative that between 1989 and 2008 the number of firms for whom beauty formed only a smaller part of their business fell very sharply. While it is true that P & G was both amongst the largest firms in beauty and had diversified into many consumer products, it had also rapidly increased the share of beauty in its global business.

Notes

1. Interview with Béatrice Dautresme, Paris, June 17, 2008.

2. Marshall McLuhan, *Understanding Media: The Extensions of Man* (New York: McGraw Hill, 1964), p. 5.

3. Kenichi K. Ohmae, *The Borderless World* (New York: Harper Business, 1990); Thomas L. Friedman, *The World is Flat* (New York: Farrar, Straus and Giroux, 2005).

4. Benjamin Barber, *Jihad vs. McWorld: How Globalization and Tribalism are Reshaping the World* (New York: Times Books, 1995).

5. Pankaj Ghemawat, *Redefining Global Strategy* (Boston, Mass.: Harvard Business School Press, 2007).

6. Richard Florida, "The World is Spiky," *Atlantic Monthly* (October 2005), pp. 48–51.

7. Global Market Information Database (hereafter GMID), Company Shares (by Global Brand Owner), Retail Value RSP (% breakdown).

8. Talk by Ed Artzt on "Redefining Beautiful," January 8, 1992, Newsmaker Forum sponsored by Cosmetics Executive Women.

9. A. G. Lafley, "What Only the CEO Can Do," *Harvard Business Review* (May 2009), p. 58.

10. P & G had tried to buy Beiersdorf but had been blocked by the Herz family owners of Tchibo. See Neil Buckley, "Beauty in the Eye of the Buyer: Purchase Extends US Giant's Reach in European Market," *Financial Times*, March 19, 2003, p. 26.

11. Davis Dyer, Frederick Dalzell, and Rowena Olegario, *Rising Tide* (Boston, Mass.: Harvard Business School Press, 2004), pp. 303–8; A. G. Lafley and Ram Charan, *The Game Changer. How You Can Drive Revenue and Profit Growth with Innovation* (New York: Crown Business, 2008), pp. 77–8.

12. Dyer *et al.*, *Rising Tide*, pp. 356–60; Lafley and Charan, *Game Changer*, pp. 84–6.

13. Telephone interview with Lindsay Owen-Jones, Chairman of L'Oréal, January 22, 2009.

14. Interview with Lindsay Owen-Jones in "Father of the Feel-good Factory," *Financial Times*, March 3, 2008.

15. Speech by Lindsay Owen-Jones, L'Oréal Paris Conference, July 10–11, 1997. A recording of this speech was kindly provided to me by Patrick Rabain.

16. Interview with Owen-Jones, January 22, 2009.

17. Owen-Jones's strategy was to grow his way out of the pharmaceuticals business, and to dilute L'Oréal's shareholding through mergers. In 1999 there was a merger with Sanofi. In 2004 Sanofi-Synthélabo acquired Aventis, itself the result of a recent merger between Hoechst and the French company Rhône-Poulenc. By 2008 L'Oréal held just under 9 per cent of Sanofi-Aventis shares: interview with Owen-Jones, January 22, 2009.

18. Interview with Patrick Rabain, Executive Vice-President of L'Oréal Consumer Products Division between 1996 and 2008, Paris, June 17, 2008.

19. If Cosmair bought American brands that would present complicated issues of how to transfer the rights to the brand to L'Oréal. Moreover, if and when it merged with L'Oréal, the owners of Cosmair would become much bigger owners within L'Oréal.

20. Geoffrey Jones and David Kiron, "L'Oréal and the Globalization of American Beauty," Harvard Business School Case no. 9-805-086 (February 2, 2006).

21. Interview with Geoff Skingsley, Executive Vice-President, L'Oréal Human Resources, Paris, June 16, 2008.

22. Jones and Kiron, "L'Oréal," pp. 12–13.

23. Euromonitor International, Unilever Group in Cosmetics and Toiletries (January 2009).

24. Euromonitor International, Beiersdorf AG—Cosmetics and Toiletries (October 13, 2008).

25. Betsy Lowther, "Quiet Giant," *Women's Wear Daily*, May 18, 2007.

26. Geoffrey Jones and David Kiron, "Bernd Beetz: Creating the New Coty," Harvard Business School Case no. 9-808-133 (December 8, 2008), p. 4.

27. Jones and Kiron, "Bernd Beetz."

28. Dana Thomas, *Deluxe: How Luxury Lost its Luster* (New York: Penguin, 2007), pp. 49–56.

29. Bernard Arnault, *La passion créative* (Paris: Plon, 2000), p. 9.

30. Euromonitor International. Olay held 15 per cent of the Chinese market and 8 per cent of the American; Maybelline New York held 20 per cent of the Chinese and 8 per cent of the American market.

31. Interview with Owen-Jones, January 22, 2009.

32. PPR's Gucci Group had acquired the fragrance business from Sanofi in 1999 and renamed it YSL Beauté the following year. The sale included the fragrance licenses for YSL, Boucheron, Zegna, Stella McCartney, and Oscar de la Renta as well as Roger & Gallet.

33. Geoffrey Jones, Akiko Kanno, and Masako Egawa, "Making China Beautiful: Shiseido and the China Market," Harvard Business School Case no. 9-805-003 (July 3, 2008).

34. Richard Tomlinson, "L'Oréal's Global Makeover: How Did a Brit from Liverpool Turn an Emblem of French Chic into an Entrepreneurial Star? One Brand at a Time," *Fortune*, September 30, 2002.

35. Interview with Owen-Jones, January 22, 2009.

36. Interview with Youçef Nabi, International General Manager, L'Oréal Paris, Paris, June 16, 2008. Maybelline remained more American and New York in its identity, but it also employed Thai actresses throughout Asia, and the Chinese actress Ziyi Zhang globally. See Molly Prior, "Meet the Locals," *Women's Wear Daily Beauty Biz* 195: 78, April 11, 2008.

37. "Ethnic Shopper Sets Tone for Beauty Contest," *Financial Times*, April 12, 2005.

38. Telephone interview with Jean-Paul Agon, Chief Executive, L'Oréal, November 4, 2008.

39. Interview with Youçef Nabi, June 16, 2008.

40. Prior, "Meet the Locals."

41. "India Debates 'Racist' Skin Cream Ads," BBC World News, <http://news.bbc.co.uk/2/hi/south_asia/3089495.stm>, accessed April 11, 2009.

42. Mikiko Ashikari, "Cultivating Japanese Whiteness: The 'Whitening' Cosmetics Boom and the Japanese Identity," *Journal of Material Culture* 10 (2005), pp. 73–91.

43. Euromonitor International, Skin Care China (June 17, 2008).

44. Evelyn Nakano Glenn, "Yearning for Lightness: Transnational Circuits in the Marketing and Consumption of Skin Lighteners," *Gender and Society* 22 (2008), pp. 281–302.

45. Natasha Sheyde, "All's Fair in Love and Cream: A Cultural Case Study of Fair & Lovely in India," *Advertising and Society Review* 9:2 (2008), available at <http://muse.jhu.edu/journals/advertising_and_society_review/v009/9.2>, accessed April 11, 2009.

46. Ashikari, "Cultivating," pp. 85–6.

47. Interview with Satoshi Suzuki, Tokyo, March 20, 2007.

48. Yuri Kageyama, "Shiseido Breaks Ranks in Japan, Featuring Japanese Women in Ads," *International Herald Tribune*, August 28, 2007.

49. Kanebo had been owned by a government agency since the bankruptcy of the parent conglomerate.

50. Euromonitor International, Kao Corporation—Cosmetics and Toiletries—World (July 31, 2008).

51. Pankaj Ghemawat, David Kiron, and Carin-Isabel Knoop, "AmorePacific: From Local to Global Beauty," Harvard Business School Case no. 9-706-411 (November 21,

2006); Elie Ofek and Kerry Herman, "AmorePacific," Harvard Business School Note no. 9-507-070 (June 3, 2008), p. 4.

52. I owe this information to Grace Lee (MBA 2008), who submitted a paper on "AmorePacific versus Missha: A Tale of Two Strategies" as one of her requirements for her Harvard MBA.

53. At the time of the acquisition, Shu Uemura had sales in 20 countries, but three-quarters of them were in Southeast Asia, and most profits were made in Japan.

54. Interview with Shu Uemura, Tokyo, March 23, 2007.

55. Andrea Nagel, "L'Oréal Creates Prestige Unit for Art of Hair," *Women's Wear Daily* 193: 61, March 23, 2007, p. 7; L'Oréal, "Letter to Shareholders," no. 42 (March 2008), p. 3.

56. Telephone interview with Emma Walmsley, Vice-President, Consumer Products Division, L'Oréal China, July 1, 2008.

57. "Estée Lauder Buys Stake in India Firm," *Women's Wear Daily* (July 18, 2008).

58. Núria Puig, "The Search for Identity: Spanish Perfume in the International Market," *Business History* 45:1 (July 2003), p. 110.

59. Telephone interview with Robert af Jochnick, co-founder of Oriflame, April 20, 2007.

60. Antoinette Alexander, "CVS Expands Exclusive Beauty Brand Partnerships," *Drug Store News*, June 6, 2005; and <www.lumene.com>, accessed April 27, 2009.

61. Nancy F. Koehn and Erica Helms, "Bumble and bumble: Building a Successful Business in Beauty and Fashion," Harvard Business School Case no. 9-806-084 (February 24, 2006).

62. Jones and Kiron, "Bernd Beetz," p. 13.

63. This point is argued vigorously by Chang Hoon Oh and Alan M. Rugman, "Regional Sales of Multinationals in the World Cosmetics Industry," *European Management Journal* 24 (2006), pp. 163–73. The authors use *Women's Wear Daily* rather than Euromonitor data.

64. Arden and Fabergé were acquired for $1.6 billion in 1989 and sold in 2000 for $225 million: Geoffrey Jones, *Renewing Unilever* (Oxford: Oxford University Press, 2005) p. 314.

65. The food company was Bestfoods. See Jones, *Renewing*, pp. 361–7.

66. Cosmetics and toiletries now represent just under a third of Unilever's overall business. Hair care is its single largest beauty business, but it only sells shampoos and conditioners. While facial care accounts for three-quarters of the world skin care market, Unilever has minimal presence in it and instead only has a modest share of the smaller body care market: Euromonitor International, Unilever Group—Cosmetics and Toiletries—World (August 2007).

67. Geoffrey Jones and Ricardo Reisen De Pinho, "Natura: Global Beauty Made in Brazil," Harvard Business School Case no. 9-807-029 (August 29, 2007).

68. Local firms Natura, Botica, Belocap, and Niasi held 24.1 per cent of the market between them: Euromonitor International, Cosmetics and Toiletries—Brazil (May 2008).

69. Michael Kepp, "Best Face Forward: Brazil's Homegrown Cosmetics Companies are Building Global Brands, Step by Step," *Latin Trade*, June 2005.

70. Jones and Reisen De Pinho, "Natura;" interview with Guilherme Leal, co-founder of Natura, São Paulo, March 14, 2006.

71. Jones and Reisen De Pinho, "Natura," p. 9.

72. L'Oréal Archives (hereafter L'Oréal), "Éclairages," *En Direct* 118 (July–August 1989), p. 7.

73. L'Oréal, *En Direct*, special issue: *At the Helm, 20 Years 1986–2006*, p. 4.

74. Dyer *et al.*, *Rising Tide*, pp. 328–30.

75. Interview with Patrick Rabain, June 17, 2008.

76. L'Oréal, "La beauté se lève à l'est," *En Direct* 129 (November 1991).

77. Interview with Robert af Jochnick, April 20, 2007.

78. Interview with Robert af Jochnick, April 20, 2007.

79. Avon Russia, May 2005, <www.avoncompany.com/investor/russia_presentation_may2005.pdf>, accessed April 14, 2009.

80. Euromonitor International, Cosmetics and Toiletries—Russia (August 14, 2008).

81. Euromonitor International, Kalina Concern: Cosmetics and Toiletries—World (February 20, 2007).

82. "Kalina Posts High Growth Figures and Signs P & G Deal," Cosmetics-Design-Europe.com, March 27, 2008, <www.cosmeticsdesign.com/Financial/Kalina-posts-high-growth-figures-and-signs-P-G-deal>, accessed March 27, 2008.

83. Jones *et al.*, "Making."

84. Juan Antonio Fernandez, *China's State-owned Enterprise Reforms* (London: Routledge, 2007), p. 94.

85. Fang Wenhui, *Keshouhinkogyou No Hikakukeieishi* (Tokyo: Nihon Keizai Hyouron-sha, 1999; in Japanese), pp. 212–13.

86. Wenhui, *Keshouhinkogyou*, p. 232.

87. Jones *et al.*, "Making," p. 23.

88. "Saving Face," *The Economist* 372, October 7, 2004, p. 55.

89. Alexandra Hamey, "The China Doll Revolution," *Financial Times*, November 5, 2005.

90. Fernandez, *China's State-owned Enterprise*, p. 42.

91. Interview with Patrick Rabain, June 17, 2008.

92. Interview with Emma Walmsley, July 1, 2008.

93. Morgan Stanley Equity Research Europe, "L'Oréal China: Set for Further Strong Growth," May 28, 2004; interview with Emma Walmsley, July 1, 2008.

94. Zhigang Tao, "China Cosmetics Industry 2005," University of Hong Kong Asia Case Research Centre no. HKU413 (2004); Morgan Stanley, "L'Oréal China."

95. Tao, "China Cosmetics Industry," pp. 10–11. Avon regained a direct selling license in 2006 and rapidly built up 350,000 representatives over the following two years, but the government capped sales commissions. See Euromonitor, Avon.

96. Jones et al., "Making."

97. Interview with Peter Harf, Chairman, Coty, Boston, April 12, 2008.

98. Interview with Bernd Beetz, Chief Executive, Coty, New York, August 21, 2007.

99. Interview with Robert af Jochnick, April 20, 2007.

100. Interview with Youçef Nabi, June 16, 2008.

101. Interview with Emma Walmsley, July 1, 2008.

102. Majid Tehranian and B. Jeannie Lum (eds), *Globalization and Identity: Cultural Diversity, Religion, and Citizenship* (Piscataway, NJ: Transaction Publishers, 2006).

103. Wenhui, *Keshouhinkogyou*, pp. 191, 291–2.

104. Wenhui, *Keshouhinkogyou*, p. 287.

105. In 2008 the firm held 2 per cent of the China market: "Shanghai Jahwa: The Maxam Brand," Richard Ivey School of Business case no. 9-A98-A026 (December 16, 1998); Niraj Dawar and Tony Frost, "Competing with Giants: Survival Strategies for Local Companies in Emerging Markets," *Harvard Business Review* (March–April 1999), pp. 122–3.

106. "India," *Women's Wear Daily Beauty Biz* 196: 103, November 14, 2008, pp. 16–21.

107. Euromonitor International, Cosmetics and Toiletries—India (June 30, 2008).

108. Euromonitor, India, p. 13.

109. Interview with Lena Philippou and George Korres, Athens, March 27, 2008.

110. "L'Oréal Finds Buzz in Niche Beauty," *Wall Street Journal*, April 25, 2007.

111. Jones and Kiron, "L'Oréal," p. 2.

112. Jones and Kiron, "L'Oréal," pp. 16–18.

113. Interview with Jean Paul Agon, November 4, 2008.

114. Anita Roddick, "Every Body Goes Strong," <www.anitaroddick.com/readmore. php?sid=547>, posted March 21, 2006, accessed April 20, 2009.

115. In 1994 Estée Lauder acquired a majority equity interest in MAC (Make-up Art Cosmetics), which had been launched in Canada in 1985. In 1997 and 1998 it bought the balance.

116. Interview with Youçef Nabi, June 16, 2008.

117. "Ancient Ingredients with a Modern Twist," *Global Cosmetic Industry*, December 1999.

118. Carol Blitzer, "John Hansen: Bare Escentuals Targets Market, Opens New Store," *San Francisco Business Times*, March 6, 1992. For the popularity of minerals in the China market, see Euromonitor International, Cosmetics and Toiletries—China (June 2008), p. 4.

119. "Korres Pursues IPO to Fund Store Expansion," *Women's Wear Daily*, March 30, 2007. In 2009 Johnson & Johnson was appointed exclusive distributor in North America.

120. Interview with George and Lena Philippou Korres, March 27, 2008; Korres Corporate Presentation, January 2008.

121. "Going Herbal to Go Global," *HT City*, March 9, 2000.

122. Interview with Jean-François Grollier, L'Oréal Executive Vice-President, Research and Development, and Patricia Pineau, L'Oréal Research Communication Director, Paris, June 18, 2008.

123. Interview with Nicolas Rosselli, L'Oréal Director of Innovation, and Patricia Frydman-Maarek, L'Oréal Corporate Research Director, Paris, June 18, 2008.

124. Euromonitor International, "Nutraceuticals: Dish of the Day for the Beauty Market" (October 2007).

125. Japan was the largest market, perhaps $8 billion, while the US was $6 billion. See Jess Halliday, "Health Claims Could Drive Beauty Foods Market," foodnavigator. com Europe, <www.nutraingredients.com/Regulation/Health-claims-could-drive-beauty-foods-market>, posted October 5, 2007, accessed June 16, 2009.

126. Interview with Béatrice Dautresme, June 17, 2008.

127. Jones and Reisen de Pinho, "Natura."

128. John Deighton, "Dove: Evolution of a Brand," Harvard Business School Case no. 9-508-047 (October 10, 2007).

129. "Unilever Accused of Retouching Dove Real Beauty Pictures," <www.cosmeticsdesign.com>, accessed June 12, 2008.

130. Kelly Schrum, *Some Wore Bobby Sox. The Emergence of Teenage Girls' Culture, 1920–1945* (New York: Palgrave Macmillan, 2004), pp. 1–2 and ch. 3.

131. Lorraine Heller, "Teenage and Ethnic Cosmetics Could Boost Ailing Market," November 23, 2005, <www.cosmeticsdesign.com/news/ng.asp?id=64087-teenage-ethnic>, accessed June 21, 2008.

132. Jennifer Weil, "Lagerfield's Geometry Theorem for Fragrance," *Women's Wear Daily*, July 18, 2008.

133. According to Odile Roujol, men appeared motivated by belonging to a club, which wearing a particular brand suggested, and saw fragrances as a way to attract women. Women were more inclined to buy fragrances for themselves: interview with Odile Roujol, CEO, Lâncome, Paris, June 16, 2008.

134. Stephanie Thompson, "Nowhere But Up for Male Grooming," *Advertising Age*, June 13, 2005.

135. Guy Montague-Jones, "Dandy is Reborn in Developed Asian Markets," Cosmetics Design-Europe.com, <www.cosmeticsdesign.com/Products-Markets/Dandy-is-reborn-in-developed-Asian-markets>, posted October 8, 2007, accessed June 25, 2008.

136. Interview with Nicolas Rosselli and Patricia Frydman-Maarek, June 18, 2008.

137. Chandler Burr, *The Perfect Scent. A Year Inside the Perfume Industry in Paris and New York* (New York: Henry Holt, 2008), pp. 153–7.

138. Jones and Kiron, "Bernd Beetz," p. 4.

139. Jones and Kiron, "Bernd Beetz," p. 4.

140. Telephone interview with Marc Menesguen, President, Luxury Products Division, September 3, 2008.

141. Jones and Kiron, "Bernd Beetz," p. 13.

142. "CVS Buy Taps Bigger Beauty Opportunity," *Women's Wear Daily*, August 15, 2008.

143. Pierre Magnan, *The Essence of Provence: The Story of L'Occitane* (New York: Arcade Publishing, 2003), pp. 115, 131; interview with Reinold Geiger, *INSEAD Alumni Newsletter*, March 2007, <www.insead.edu/alumin/newsletter/March2007/Reinold Geigerinterview.htm>, accessed July 17, 2008; "L'Occitane Aims East with Hong Kong Flotation," Cosmetics design-europe.com, <www.cosmeticsdesign-europe.com/Product-Categories/Hair-Care/L-Occitane-aims-east-with-Hong-Kong-flotation>, accessed July 17, 2008.

144. Interview with George and Lena Philippou Korres, March 27, 2008.

145. Euromonitor International, Cosmetics and Toiletries—World (June 2007), p. 45.

146. Euromonitor International, Global Cosmetics and Toiletries: Facing Tougher Times Ahead (November 2008).

147. Euromonitor International, Cosmetics and Toiletries—World (June 2007), p. 158.

148. Euromonitor International, Cosmetics and Toiletries—Russia (August 14, 2008); Euromonitor International, Nu Skin Enterprises Inc.—Cosmetics and Toiletries—World (November 19, 2008); Wendy Stein, "Mary Kay," in Tina Grant (ed.), *International Directory of Company Histories*, vol. 84 (Farmington Hills, Mich.: St. James Press, 2007), pp. 251–6.

149. Laura Klepacki, *Avon: Building the World's Premier Company for Women* (Hoboken, NJ: John Wiley, 2005), pp. 47–51.

150. Euromonitor International, Avon Products Inc.—Cosmetics and Toiletries—World (May 19, 2008).

151. Amornthep Deerojanawong, *Rao Pen Tee Nueng* (*We Are Number One*) (Bangkok: South Asia Press Co., 1989; in Thai), p. 35.

152. Mistine also improved the logistics of its "sales cycle"—the process of issuing a new catalogue to a sales representative, presenting it to customers, and getting the order submitted—so it had 26 cycles in a year rather than Avon's 18. See Deerojanawong, *Rao*, pp. 114, 141–7.

153. O. C. Ferrell and Linda Ferrell, "Mistine," case no. 15, University of New Mexico, 2006.

154. Euromonitor International, Cosmetics and Toiletries—World (June 2007), pp. 47–8.

Conclusion

The Dream Machine

Entrepreneurs of beauty

Beauty, or more precisely today's multi-billion-dollar industry, is the creation of man, not nature. Beneath all the beauty rituals and the potions, creams, dyes, and perfumes that human societies have developed across the millennia lie the basic biological imperatives to attract and reproduce. Like cooking and healing, the making and applying of such products was largely undertaken in the household, although many societies turned to the special powers of the local apothecary, chemist, healer, priest, or witch. But biology and tradition do not take us very far in explaining the shape that the industry assumed in the nineteenth century. The achievement of the entrepreneurs who founded the modern industry was not to invent the rituals or concept of beauty products per se, but rather to take over from the pre-industrial world the numerous crafts, recipes, and traditions, and to transform them into a capitalist industry.

What the nineteenth century witnessed was the kind of entrepreneurship described by Joseph Schumpeter as both creative and destructive. Traditional products, processes, and markets were disrupted and transformed beyond recognition. At the start of that century, perfume was still consumed orally, used to scent gloves, and rarely applied to the skin. By the end of the century, men like Eugène Rimmel, Pierre-François-Pascal Guerlain, and their successors had turned a craft into an industry. Brands were built to convey the attributes of prestige and quality, and to be sold in wider markets than the town or village. The more expensive scents became integral components of the world of fashion and were sold in elegant bottles whose cost far exceeded the juice inside them. The range of scents available was expanded enormously by three factors: the worldwide search for exotic flowers and plants led by Chiris, a firm based in the town of Grasse in France; the development of new technologies to extract scents; and the application of science to create new synthetic scents. François Coty took a product which was still the preserve of the few and made it an affordable luxury for many more. While the craft of perfumery was ancient, the fragrance industry in the early twentieth century bore little resemblance to its predecessor a century earlier.

Perfume was not the only traditional item transformed by a century of entrepreneurialism, science, and mass production. As electrified cities and factories drew people into closer, sweatier quarters, entrepreneurs shaped brands which promised to make people look and smell better. Harley Procter and William Lever helped drive the transformation of the age-old soap industry from a craft that turned out an undifferentiated commodity into a mass producer and mass marketer of heavily advertised, branded consumer products. The soap artisans of Marseilles and elsewhere were marginalized in the process. Thomas Barratt reconceptualized soap as an aid to beauty for women. As the teeth of urban dwellers became increasingly rotten, Colgate and others provided new products and practices to clean them and make breath fresher. Meanwhile, Hans Schwarzkopf set out to clean people's hair.

Functionality gave way to artifice. Skin creams were recast as aids to femininity by Oscar Troplowitz and others. Helena Rubinstein and Elizabeth Arden transformed beauty salons from places considered the moral equivalent of brothels to palaces of opulence and style. Physical appearance could now be changed for a price. François Marcel and Karl Nessler gave women the chance of having wavy hair. Madam C. J. Walker gave African-Americans the chance to have straight hair. Eugène Schueller finally made dyeing grey hair, that most visible sign of aging, far safer and more respectable than in the past.

It remains a challenge for researchers on entrepreneurship to explain why some individuals perceive entrepreneurial opportunities where most do not. While the backgrounds, characters, and motivations of founder-entrepreneurs and their successors were diverse, the beauty industry provides some insights on cognition. Many began their careers in salons, perfumeries, pharmacies, and artists' make-up studios. This provided a basis for a close understanding of individual people's emotional and functional needs. And many of them also lived on the fringes of the worlds of artists and celebrities and in cosmopolitan cities. This is where they saw the early artistic signals of a more aestheticized future defined by fashionable styles and colors, which enabled them to perceive trends before they became trends.

Exposure to different cultures and ways of doing things was important, too. Beauty began as a very local industry, yet the founding entrepreneurs and their successors recognized that the desire to be attractive was not constrained by borders. Indeed, it was striking how many entrepreneurs were committed from the start to globalizing their brands. This commitment rested, ultimately, on the perception of the universality of beauty in human societies and the international ambitions of the entrepreneurs themselves.

Born into an age when international travel was suddenly much easier than ever before, many entrepreneurs also started businesses in countries other than their birthplaces. Eugène Rimmel, Karl Nessler, Andrew Jergens, Ernest Daltroff, Helena Rubinstein, Elizabeth Arden, Max Factor, and many others fit this description. The trend persisted long after moving between countries became a bureaucratic nightmare in the wake of World War I. Simone Tata, Vidal Sassoon, Horst Rechelbacher, and Yves Saint Laurent all built businesses away from their birthplaces. For many, entrepreneurial insights were shaped by exposure to foreign places. Paris was central to the strategy of Sweden's Knut Wulff. Shu Uemura spent his formative years in the make-up culture of Hollywood. More recently, the industry's top executives have included multi-lingual cosmopolitan figures such as Lindsay Owen-Jones and Bernd Beetz who lived and made their careers outside their country of origin.

The Jewish background of many industrial leaders, in both the United States and France, might be explained by this mobility across borders, as so many were driven abroad by anti-Semitism during the late nineteenth century and the first half of the twentieth. There were also close overlapping relationships with the worlds of fashion and movie-making, areas where there was also a strong Jewish presence, compounding sources of entrepreneurial information and resources. More generally, beauty was an industry for "outsiders." Coty and the Wertheimers arrived in Paris from distant provinces of France. Roddick started The Body Shop on the south coast of England, not in London. Originally this was because the industry grew from products whose use was widely regarded as barely respectable by many in society. The industry later gained greater legitimacy, but it retained an aura of frivolity. It was not only Unilever executives in the 1950s who were embarrassed to be involved with it.

This ambivalence was one reason why the industry featured so many female entrepreneurs. A veritable roll-call of female entrepreneurs—Harriet Hubbard Ayer, Rubinstein and Arden, Estée Lauder, Mary Kay—exercised formative influences on the American industry, as did their counterparts elsewhere— Félicie Vanpouille, Jung Suk Jung, Simone Tata, Anita Roddick, and Lena Philippou Korres. Numerous hairdressers and direct sellers also served as smaller-scale entrepreneurs in the industry. The number of female entrepreneurs reflected the easier entry to this industry than to others which societal prejudices had deemed "male." It was easier, too, because products could emerge out of kitchens, salons, and hair salons, where women spent considerable time among other women. It is much less evident that gender affected entrepreneurial cognition of opportunities in systematic ways. There were plenty of male creative and marketing geniuses also. Many male and female entrepreneurs worked closely with their personal partners. Whether or not men and women perceived beauty differently, there is some evidence that involving both genders in business decisions worked best.

People become entrepreneurs in order to make money, and there is no reason to assume that those who entered the beauty industry deviated from this general rule. A fortunate few made a great deal of money and sometimes founded family fortunes. Madam C. J. Walker and Annie Turnbo Malone were probably America's first female millionaires. François Coty left a personal fortune worth $3.9 billion today. On her death, Anita Roddick left nothing to her family but gave away $100 million to charity. The Forbes' 2008 list of billionaires included Bernard Arnault in thirteenth place and Liliane Bettencourt in seventeenth.

The great majority of beauty entrepreneurs did not become billionaires, but many did manifest a passion for the beauty industry. The passion was evident in the stories of the early efforts to develop products, from Schueller experimenting in his own kitchen when developing his hair dyes to Lavin trying out products on his new wife. Such a passion was surely an essential component of the tool kit needed to succeed in the industry. The beauty industry was subject to the same rules of branding and marketing seen in other fast-moving consumer goods, but taking the right decisions on product launches, brand names, packaging, and other essentials seemed to require intuitive under-standing and emotional engagement with consumers.

This did not mean that entrepreneurs were warm and fuzzy idealists, let alone saints. The need for fast decisions, based on intuitive understanding of markets, favored autocratic decision-making rather than consultation. Relentlessness, obsession, and ambition are the terms that come to mind to describe most of the key figures in the industry. There were plenty of dys-functional characters and flawed personalities. Divorces and broken relation-ships appear the norm rather than the exception among the leading entrepreneurs of each generation.

Yet few figures fit the stereotype of the industry's critics as cynical manipu-lators of people's desires and insecurities. Charles Revson should be seen as occupying one extreme of a spectrum which extended all the way to religious idealists such as Mary Kay, or environmental activists such as Anita Roddick and Luis Seabra. Along this spectrum there were people who rejoiced in creativity, like Max Factor and Shu Uemura, and others who were thrilled by a successful launch of new brands, like François Dalle or Leonard Lavin. Most executives expressed, at one time or another, loftier ideals. For the most part, these were people who earnestly believed in beauty and its salutary effects on all who cultivated it.

Beauty emerges as an industry which was easy to enter, but hard to succeed at. The modest capital and technological requirements meant that, generation after generation, businesses were started in people's homes, salons, or shops, and initial sales were built by word of mouth. Shifts in fashion also regularly disrupted market leadership and provided opportunities for newcomers. As P & G found with its shampoo business in the 1970s, and Unilever with its prestige fragrances and cosmetics in the 1990s, size offered limited protection if trends were missed and creativity subdued.

Growing a beauty brand was always a different matter, and a difficult one. This was an industry in which large businesses began with entrepreneurs smashing bottles on floors, claiming to have exotic and long-lost secrets, and running crooked game shows. Many entrepreneurs changed their own names to create more desirable auras around their brands. The product and the packaging had to be just right. More importantly, the story behind the brand had to resonate with potential consumers. Success rested on creating a narrative which enabled people to identify personally with brands. As markets fragmented and tribalized in recent years, building such identification became ever more important.

Beauty was an unforgiving industry in which the leading brands and firms of one generation disappeared from view in the next. The businesses built by Turnbo Malone and C. J. Walker were minor affairs by the 1930s. Eugène Rimmel's prestigious house sold cheap and cheerful lipsticks and face powder in post-1945 Britain. François Coty's multinational business empire of the 1920s turned into a modest-sized fragrance affiliate of Pfizer, until the name was used by Benckiser as a vehicle to create a "new Coty," which by coincidence included a revitalized Rimmel. Arden and Rubinstein, once leaders in luxury cosmetics, were small brands owned by others by the 1970s. Charles Revson built Revlon into one of the world's largest beauty companies, but today the company exists on the fringes of the top 30.

Context and timing always mattered. Wholly exogenous factors, or merely bad luck, could, and did, have a significant impact on corporate fortunes. The global ambitions of the German beauty industry, for instance, were seriously damaged by the expropriations of the two world wars. The path of the fast-growing Russian industry was wrecked by the Russian Revolution. The Great Depression disrupted the growing cosmopolitanism and globalization of the 1920s, and eviscerated the industry leader, Coty. Timing was always crucial. Schueller launched his sunscreen just as the French were allowed to take summer holidays. The economic misfortunes of Brazil in the 1980s provided a willing army of sales representatives for Natura, and decimated distribution channels other than direct sales. More recently, L'Oréal and P & G seized the new opportunities of globalization arising from the sudden opening of China and Eastern Europe in particular.

Globalization made big business even bigger and introduced whole new challenges. The costs of advertising and research, the complexities of globalization, and the economies of scale and scope all encouraged such growth, as in all consumer industries, but the management of scale in a creative industry poses special challenges. The spark of creativity and energy which characterized founders such as Coty or Revson was not easy to transmit to successors. In some cases, like the Guerlains and the Lauders, it seemed to pass from one generation to another, but in many other cases, beginning with Eugène Rimmel, heredity had no discernible relationship to creative genius.

The challenges of scale were amply demonstrated during the second half of the twentieth century. As founder-entrepreneurs retired or died, or simply lacked the capital required for large advertising budgets and international expansion, they sold to larger firms which saw the apparently profitable margins of the beauty industry without fully understanding the challenges of succeeding in it. The saga of the entry and exit of big pharmaceutical companies and conglomerates between the 1960s and the 1980s revealed the cultural, organizational, and creative challenges faced by very large firms in the beauty industry. It was striking also how difficult it was for firms such as P & G, Colgate-Palmolive, Henkel, and Unilever to extend their mass toiletry, oral care, and hair businesses into other beauty categories and segments. Colgate-Palmolive was brought to the brink of disaster by its encounter with Helena Rubinstein, while Unilever later proved capable only of destroying the value of the prestige fragrances and color cosmetics brands it acquired.

In contrast, during the same decades François Dalle laid the basis for L'Oréal's leadership in the industry by pulling off a remarkable feat. The investment by Nestlé, carefully negotiated in a context where the French government had become resistant to foreign encroachment in the French beauty industry, provided the outside capital and protection from bigger predators which was needed to grow the business. Meanwhile, the company was left autonomous and able to build on its established culture of innovation. The business was then grown by both acquiring and organically developing brands in different distribution channels, enabling the firm to reach consumers across the spectrum of different abilities to pay.

There was no single pathway for corporate success in the industry over the long term, as the quite different histories of today's leading firms demonstrate. Yet the evidence supports a number of generalizations. Competitive success over the long term rested on building organizations which combined product innovation and quality with capability and execution in logistics, manufacturing, distribution, and marketing. A steady flow of knowledge and learning between marketing and research was especially vital in building and sustaining brands, and an excessive emphasis on either function was a handicap. Whilst such organizational capabilities are the staples for success in many industries, the challenge in beauty was to combine them with an ability to understand and respond rapidly and creatively to frequently changing fashions and preferences. Success rested on the challenging task of combining creative people and energy with the marketing and financial discipline required of a large business organization.

Creativity, fluidity, and speed are far from easy to retain as the scale of business increases, and as firms crossed borders, retaining these was further complicated by the need to balance the local and the global in multiple changing environments. The penalties were severe for companies whose attention wandered, either through weak management or too much focus elsewhere. The strengthening of the competitive position of L'Oréal and P & G in the recent past rested especially on the fact that Lindsay Owen-Jones, Ed Artzt, and A. G. Lafley understood the importance of such focus at a time of unprecedented opportunities for the beauty industry. As hundreds of millions of new consumers entered the world beauty market, the companies that moved directly and deliberately into those markets, and into the product categories wanted in those markets, were the companies that triumphed.

Constructing the market for beauty

Raw, biological motivations for beauty notwithstanding, the historical and cultural variations in beauty ideals around the world clearly support the argument that beauty cultures are primarily constructed artifacts. How past societies derived these ideals is complex, unanswerable perhaps, and beyond the scope of this book. However, from the nineteenth century a more definable actor emerges—entrepreneurs and firms which created brands and marketed them. What was the industry's role in constructing beauty?

A starting point is to see the industry as an agent for democratization. Although the use of beauty products was quite widespread in some pre-industrial societies, only the rich and the royal would have had access to most of the beauty aids produced by handicraft technology. Most people, even the rich, lived in an environment of dirt, disease, disfigurement, and death. The Industrial Revolution set in motion fundamental shifts on both the demand and supply sides. Higher incomes and eventually growing leisure allowed more people to spend more and more on products and services which promised to attract sexual partners and to signal social aspiration. The transport revolution of the nineteenth century enabled entrepreneurs for the first time to expand their markets from their immediate localities to build regionally, nationally, and occasionally internationally.

The emergent beauty industry exploited these developments to provide growing numbers of people with a far greater variety of products which had long been used, whether perfumes, skin creams, or hair dyes. The new products were safer, more consistent, and far more accessible than their pre-industrial predecessors. The industry also invented new products, like tooth-paste, packed in new and convenient ways, and it provided extensive education to persuade people to use them. Market growth was driven during the twentieth century by more new products, whether nail varnish and mascara, or deodor-ants and anti-dandruff shampoos. In each case, firms and fashion magazines educated consumers to use them properly, and persuaded consumers to buy them. This combined educative and marketing function saw products developed in the affluent West cascading to other regions as their incomes rose and values became more Western. The process continues today as direct sellers and other firms penetrate to remote villages in China or Latin America.

It was the creation of aspirations, rather than new product developments, which proved such a powerful driver of market growth. Sales expanded as brands built associations with celebrities (whether actresses, artists, or aristo-crats), fashionable cities, and wealthy countries. These associations offered people the chance to feel that they shared a part of those worlds, that those worlds were accessible to them, and that those worlds approved of the use of these products. These aspirational associations were successful in sweeping away the moral objections to face painting by women, although not by men, in Western societies. It was striking that during World War II cosmetics products, whose use had been widely regarded as morally dubious in the late nineteenth century, were recognized by the governments of Western democracies as essentials which they had to supply to their citizens for the sake of morale.

The attractive, young faces and bodies used in advertisements also symbol-ized the industry's promises of delaying or reversing the signs of aging, with the concomitant social and sexual rewards. The creation of such aspirations also involved implicit discussion of the perceived consequences of not using such products. For every skin care and cosmetics advertisement which showed the benefits of using a given product, the subliminal message was also the dire consequences of not using it. By the interwar years, beauty companies were fully exploiting the belief held in Western societies that individuals could take control of, shape, and improve their looks, bodies, lives, and incomes. If you were not beautiful, it was your own fault.

Another key aspect of building the market for beauty was the creation of distribution channels. This began on a small scale with individual perfumeries, pharmacies, and hairdressing salons. These remained important channels to consumers: excellent relationships with hairdressers was a major foundation of the growth of L'Oréal, Wella, and other companies which supplied the salon trade. The creation of exclusive chains of beauty salons and the selling of premium products in department stores provided new means to reach consumers by World War I. Meanwhile, the development of direct selling provided a means of reaching consumers in rural areas and small towns. The spread of direct selling outside the United States opened up huge markets for the industry in Latin America and elsewhere and, after the fall of the Berlin Wall, in Central and Eastern Europe. Equally striking was the use of media to build markets. Advertisements in women's magazines, and on radio and on television, represented a steady stream of efforts to reach growing numbers of people to persuade them to buy brands.

The role of corporate marketers and communicators in shaping beauty ideals is central to many controversies surrounding the industry. The evidence presented here cautions against crude arguments that the beauty companies— or Madison Avenue and Hollywood—could invent and dictate beauty norms. Instead, companies are better seen as interpreters and reflectors of societal beliefs. Yet, as they turned such beliefs and norms into heavily advertised brands, they reinforced them, gave them a self-perpetuating quality, and diffused them internationally.

This mechanism can be seen in both the gender and ethnic assumptions about beauty which became explicit during the nineteenth century. This was a period when Western societies as a whole underwent growing gender differentiation in clothing, work, and much else. The entrepreneurs of the period identified and exploited this wider trend. However, the upshot was a considerable shift from the pre-industrial era, when products were often unisex and men were regular users of cosmetics and hair dyes. As firms advertised in the growing fashion and aesthetically oriented media targeted at women, such as women's magazines, the feminization and gender identities of products became firmly entrenched.

It would also be hard to claim that the association of beauty with Western countries, and white people, was the direct result of explicit corporate strategies. Paris had had its reputation for luxury and fashion for several centuries before the nineteenth, and the subsequent growth of haute couture and fashionable shopping arcades in that city preceded the rise of the modern Parisian beauty industry. However, as that industry grew, it both exploited those reputations and enhanced them. The reputation became self-sustaining, as did the flow of creative talent to the city and the growth of complementary hubs of suppliers. The same mechanism can be seen in the growth of New York as America's beauty capital, and its subsequent emergence as a global beauty hub. Beauty was an industry in which there turned out to be large economies of agglomeration, both in terms of reputation and talent.

The beauty companies interpreted prevailing societal assumptions in the West about ethnicity and appearance, translated them into marketing campaigns, and reinforced them. The timing of the emergence of the beauty industry and its first wave of globalization, coinciding with the high point of Western imperialism and economic dominance following the Industrial Revolution, made it all but inevitable that being white was seen as possessing superior beauty, alongside superior everything else. The firms which exported their branded soaps, and later other products to Asia and Africa, would need to have been quite extraordinary if they had not assumed Western superiority. Cleverly crafted marketing campaigns linking their brands to civilization then became reinforcers of societal and cultural prejudice, in the same way that the beauty industry in the United States interpreted its segregated society.

The result was a major homogenization of beauty ideals which the beauty companies helped diffuse and sustain around the world. It was a homogenization born more from aspiration than coercion, although there was plenty of coercion in the imperialist world in which it took hold. Still, it was striking that it was not merely in colonized countries that Western-style beauty triumphed. It also happened in Japan, which resisted colonization, yet whose government sought to change the cultural face of the Japanese people by banning tooth blackening and male use of cosmetics. When Japanese-owned beauty companies emerged, they looked to France and the United States for products and brands.

The momentum of homogenization continued after 1914, by which time the creativity of US-based companies, the attractions of American wealth, and the beauty ideals represented in Hollywood movies created a powerful new momentum. There was little threat to the global pre-eminence of Western beauty for many decades. Although the great European empires wound down during the 1950s and the 1960s, the West remained richer than the rest. Japan was an exception, but one in which French brand names and Western-style round eyes were aspirational. International beauty pageants, fashion magazines, and the growth of duty-free outlets proved to be further powerful diffusers of beauty ideals. The standing of Paris and New York remained self-reinforcing. Their clusters of creative talent, designers, fashion magazines, and complementary suppliers endured. The cities themselves evolved, becoming increasingly cosmopolitan, and so remained relevant to a changing world.

Although the momentum for homogenization was strong, it was striking that markets stayed highly differentiated by inherited social and cultural preferences. As firms pursued international businesses, they put great efforts into transferring brands and products between countries. By the interwar years wealthy and well-travelled urban elites in many countries understood the aspirational status of expensive French and American beauty brands. This became the basis for the growth of the duty-free market. But beauty as a whole resisted full homogenization. As firms invested in international markets, they could shape markets by transferring brands and products, but they also had to respond to markets. This was evident in the persistence of distinctive local consumer preferences even in countries which were host to many foreign firms and brands. There were substantial differences in the consumption even of categories such as deodorants and shampoos, let alone fragrances, where there were major and persistent variations in usage and scent preferences. The French preference for fragrance, the American love affair with make-up, the Japanese concern for skin care, all seemed impervious to radical change over the last 50 years.

The challenges of balancing the local and the global were formidable and help to explain why companies found building international businesses such a challenge. Although a number of brands were sold widely, such as Sunsilk and Pond's, they co-existed with numerous local brands, and even ostensibly international brands often looked, and were, different products in different countries. The problems of accessing local distribution channels, wide variations in advertising media, local regulations, and—especially in the case of France—government restrictions on foreign ownership all made building foreign markets a challenge. It was striking that the major markets of the United States, Japan, and France had limited foreign presence before the 1980s.

The most recent wave of globalization has seen great change. The large-scale penetration of the American market by foreign firms, the spread of megabrands around the globe, and the reopening of China and Eastern Europe to the global beauty industry were all transformational. More fundamental still was the role of globalization in facilitating more heterogeneous beauty ideals rather than simply working as a force for homogeneity. The industry was, again, interpreting political and societal shifts. Responding to the new realities of the post-colonial world, firms began employing more local models in their advertising in non-Western countries. As the racially segregated society of the United States gave way to a diverse mosaic of different ethnic groups, meeting the needs of the "ethnic market" became a marketing priority. The economic growth of Brazil, Russia, India, and China (the BRICs) not only created huge new markets for the industry but also highlighted the wider range of skin tones, hair textures, and facial features which characterize humanity.

The impact of this new wave of globalization was complex. The spread of megabrands, the globalization of celebrity culture, and the aspirational appeal of New York and Paris to a new generation of consumers in the BRICs represented further homogenization. Certain beauty ideals, especially for women, are widely diffused worldwide. Yet there has also been a resurgence of pride in local beauty identities. Globalization was no longer a one-way street. Companies competed to learn the ancient knowledge of Chinese and India and to buy local brands from these countries as potential assets to globalize. In pursuit of profitable opportunities and in recognition of a changing world, beauty firms actively spread different, not homogenized, beauty ideals among different countries. As a result, they were at the epicenter of the contradictions in the contemporary global world, which is simultaneously flat and spiky.

It remains in dispute when, or whether, the beauty ideals of Shanghai, Mumbai, Moscow, or Rio de Janeiro will be seen to be as globally relevant as those of Paris and New York. Country of origin still matters in brands, and the world remains decidedly spiky in this regard. What is apparent, though, is the changing role of country of origin in brand identities, as psychographic segmentation based on attitudes towards such matters as the environment, social responsibility, and the use of science take center stage.

Meanwhile, firms continue to drive a democratization of beauty, reaching ever-growing numbers of people ranging from inhabitants of remote villages in

China and Russia to pre-teens and seniors in Manhattan, and most of humanity in between. It remains, however, a democracy where incomes determine options. The growing sophistication in the application of scientific research to beauty suggested that the story of the growing accessibility of beauty products might soon need to be retold. After decades of claiming that products were based on extensive scientific research, by the first decade of the twenty-first century there was the real prospect of "beauty drugs" of one kind or another that could delay or remove wrinkled skin, or restore or remove hair as desired, as well as ever more advanced cosmetic surgery to change and redesign faces. A plausible future scenario would see the consumers in rich countries gaining access to tools which significantly delay the physical signs of aging into their eighties, while those less wealthy would continue to wrinkle with age.

Cycles of legitimacy

The third lens used to examine the history of the beauty industry has concerned its legitimacy. Beauty was not an industry which, like tobacco, posed major health risks, although some pre-industrial products and, later, certain hair dyes and other products did. However, it was traditionally suspect for moral and religious reasons. The founding entrepreneurs of the nineteenth century worked long and hard to turn their marginal activities on the fringes of moral respectability into a legitimate industry. This involved making products that were much safer than in the past, and especially associating their use with aspiration rather then degradation. The founding of industry associations and institutes of beauty were important components of the legitimization of beauty.

As the industry grew in stature and respectability, the question of legitimacy centered on the choices it offered to consumers. Insofar as the industry reflected societies' contemporary assumptions, it reflected all the imperfections of those societies as well. It could align itself with the ideologies of Nazi Germany. It took the prejudice about skin color in Indian society and translated it into brands. Beauty companies were rarely founded as radical agents of change to societal norms. Occasionally, and motivated usually by the perennial need to find new customers, strategies were ahead of such norms. During the 1960s, for example, Avon's marketing towards black consumers and involvement with inner-city communities were probably ahead of most American consumer goods firms.

During the 1960s and 1970s there was growing criticism of the industry for offering consumers choices that were constrained by bigoted assumptions about ethnicity, class, age, and gender. Reduced to its basics, the industry's marketing seemed preoccupied with, in the words of Anita Roddick, manipulating the emotions of "women desperate to cling to their fading youth." It used heavy advertising, extensive market research, and expensive packaging to sell products at prices which were far above the cost of the ingredients, making claims which at best could be described as hyperbole. As large corporations usually headed by men became pre-eminent, the industry's apparent role in retaining female submission within patriarchal societies seemed ever more evident to its critics.

Legitimacy is so hard to disentangle because the industry assumed a paradoxical position as both enslaving and modernizing for women. It was enslaving because it celebrated norms of femininity that were difficult for most women to achieve, and restrictive by privileging Western and age-bound constructions of female beauty. The parading of swimsuit-clad young women in beauty pageants and the globalization of blonde and blue-eyed Barbie dolls provided evidence of an all-too-visible preoccupation with young, nubile female bodies. Yet it is unlikely that generations of female consumers believed in some simplistic way assertions that they would look like film stars overnight by using such brands. Helen Landsdowne Resor, Elly Heuss-Knapp, and Shirley Polykoff were strong-willed female writers of advertising copy for the industry, who cannot plausibly be regarded as drones of a patriarchal conspiracy against their gender.

The industry was also modernizing because women gained agency and autonomy as consumers, transforming them from dependents on men to independent persons who made their own choices on what to buy and how to appear. As Western beauty products reached developing countries, they were frequently received as modernizers and progressive forces for women. Arguably, as women entered the workforce, they did better in the job market by using beauty products, such was the apparent strength of the "beauty premium." At the same time, female entrepreneurs were able to build businesses, including some of the largest in the industry, and tens of thousands more became quasi-entrepreneurs as direct sellers.

By the 1970s the industry's role in promoting John Kenneth Galbraith's "unreal needs" was increasingly discussed, as health scares about the safety of chemical ingredients, changing societal attitudes towards ethnicity, and surging feminist criticism combined to cause growing skepticism about the industry. During this decade changes were set in motion which would, over the following decades, shift some fundamental aspects of the industry's assumptions about race, gender, and ingredients. Changes often began with firms which were smaller and more marginal, such as The Body Shop and Natura. Larger firms joined and drove trends once the market appeal was seen as proved.

The extent to which the beauty industry today has regained legitimacy depends on the criteria being employed. It remains, as it always has been, primarily an industry based on aspiration. It continues to spend lavishly on advertising and packaging. The use of attractive young models rather than typically bodied people in advertising remains the norm, despite the spreading acknowledgement that a face and body of someone aged over 40 can still be considered attractive. Yet the growing recognition of the diversity of beauty suggests also a new level of maturity. Insofar as companies have sought to provide more "real stories" and to sell products of "real quality," there has been a gain in legitimacy.

Offering individuals a choice about their appearance and scent is, in the last resort, a positive activity. Enabling people to feel better about themselves when they apply a moisturizer in the morning, or making them feel sexy before a date by wearing a particular scent, or giving someone the choice whether to have blonde or black hair, enriches the daily lives of people. It gives each of us the opportunity to appreciate our own body as an aesthetic object, a work of art. It may even enable us to capture some of the "beauty premium" awarded to attractive people. It certainly gives individuals the choice to look and feel different in a world which, if remaining spiky, has decidedly flat and homogenous features. Insofar as the beauty industry can devote fewer resources to telling us what to do and limiting our choices, and be more open to exploring the rich diversity of human beings in the choices and options which it offers, its legitimacy will be assured.

Appendix 1

The Global Beauty Market Over Time

1.1 World Production of the Beauty Industry, 1914–1989 ($m)

	1914	1938	1950	1966	1976	1989
US	17	148	560	2,500	5,670	16,700
France	19[1]	87	62	430	1,372	5,862
Germany	-	-	62	350	1,268	3,987
UK	-	26	58	290	581	2,025[3]
Spain	-	-	-	60	364	-
Sweden	4	11	14	30	66	132
Japan	-	16[2]	25	317	1,957	8,978
China	-	-	-	-	117	531
Brazil	-	-	28	-	372	-
World	72[e]	470[e]	1,026	5,200	15,000[e]	60,000
World (in 2008 dollars)	1,600	7,182	9,183	34,490	56,718[e]	104,180

Note: Most figures exclude toilet soap.

[e]Estimated.

[1]1912.

[2]1939.

[3]1988.

Sources: 1914: for US, "Perfumery and Cosmetics," *US Census of Manufactures: General Totals for the United States by Geographic Divisions, States and Industries*, Department of Commerce, Bureau of the Census (Washington, DC: Government Printing Office, 1916); for France, Eugénie Briot, "La chimie des élégances: La parfumerie parisienne au XIXe siècle, naissance d'une industrie du luxe," unpubl. doctoral diss., Conservatoire National des Arts et Métiers, Centre d'Histoire des Techniques et de l'Environnement, 2008, p. 108; for Sweden, CfN 1093.05, *Den svenska tvål- och tvättmedelsindustrien*, Report on the Swedish soap and detergent industry (c.1946), Centre for Business History, Stockholm; world production estimated at double combined production of US and France.

1938: for US, "Perfumes, Cosmetics, and Other Toilet Preparations," *Sixteenth Census of the United States: 1940—Census of Business Volume V—Distribution of Manufacturers' Sales 1939*, Department of Commerce, Bureau of the Census (Washington, DC: United States Government Printing Office, 1942); for France, Crédit Lyonnais archive (hereafter CL), DEEF 57198/1, "Monographie—Parfumerie" (October 1945); for UK, "British Cosmetic Sales," *Drug and Cosmetic Industry* 57 (October 1945); for Sweden, Statens Officiella Statistik (SOS), Central Bureau of Statistics,

Stockholm, Sweden; for Japan: *Keshohinkogyo 120 Nen no Ayumi* (*The Course of 120 Years of the [Japanese] Cosmetics Industry*) (Tokyo: Japan Cosmetic Industry Association, 1995); world production estimated at double combined production of US and France.

1950: for US, France, Germany, UK, Spain, Brazil, and world total, Geoffrey Jones, "Blonde and Blue-eyed? Globalizing Beauty, c.1945–c.1980," *Economic History Review* 61 (2008), p. 131, which is based on Unilever data which exclude Japan. Unilever's estimate of the world total (which also excludes Communist countries) is increased by the Japanese figure; for Sweden, Statens Officiella Statistik (SOS), Central Bureau of Statistics, Stockholm; for Japan, *Keshohinkogyo*.

1966: for US, *US Industrial Outlook for 1968* (Washington, DC: United States Department of Commerce, Business and Defense Services Administration, 1968), pp. 137–8; for France, Germany, UK, Spain, Sweden, and world total, S. A. Mann, *Cosmetics Industry of Europe 1968* (Park Ridge, NJ: Noyes Development Corporation, 1968); for Japan, *Keshohinkogyo*.

1976: for US, UK, and Brazil, and estimated world total, Jones, "Blonde and blue-eyed," p. 131; for France, Germany, Spain, and Sweden, *European Marketing Data and Statistics 1978/79*, vol. 15 (London: Euromonitor Publications, 1979), p. 106; for Japan, *Keshohinkogyo*; for China, Fang Wenhui, *Keshohinkogyo no Hikakukeieishi* (*Comparative Business History of the Cosmetic Industry*) (Tokyo: Nihon Keizai Hyouron-sha, 1999), p. 190.

1989: for US, France, and UK, *L'industrie mondiale de la parfumerie et cosmétologie*, Eurostaf, Collection "analyse de secteurs," 2e trimestre 1991; for Germany, cosmetics trade newsletter *Kosmetik Report*, no. 11, April 25, 1994; for Sweden, *Industri 1989: 2*, pp. 81–2, Sveriges Officiella Statistik, Central Bureau of Statistics, Stockholm; for China, Wenhui, *Keshouhinkogyou*; for Japan, *Keshohinkogyo*; for world total, Catherine Brady, "Cosmetics: Consolidation Characterizes a Moderately Paced Market," *Chemical Week*, November 15, 1989, p. 20.

1.2 World Retail Sales of Beauty Products ($bn)

	1989	2008
US	25.5	52.0
France	5.8	16.2
Germany	6.0	16.9
UK	4.7	15.7
Sweden	0.6	2.0
Russia		12.4
Japan	20.9[1]	33.7
South Korea		5.9
China	2.5[1]	17.7
India		5.5
Brazil		28.8
Mexico		8.2
Venezuela		3.1
World		333

[1] 1994.

Sources: 1989: for US, Donald A. Davis, "Tight Market, Trim Profits Accelerate Pressure for Merger and Divestment," *Drug and Cosmetic Industry*, July 1990, p. 7; for France, Germany, UK, and Sweden, *European Marketing Data and Statistics 1991* (London: Euromonitor Publications, 1991), Table 1411, pp. 338–9; for Japan and China, these are 1994 figures from Geoffrey Jones, Akiko Kanno, and Masako Egawa, "Making China Beautiful: Shiseido and the China Market," Harvard Business School Case no. 9–805–003 (July 3, 2008).

2008: Global Market Information Database (GMID), industry statistics.

Appendix 2

World's Largest Beauty Companies by Revenues, 1929–2008

2.1 Selected Large Beauty Firms, 1929 ($m)

Firm	Nationality	Beauty revenues	Total revenues	Main product categories
Coty	US	60	60	F, C
Colgate-Palmolive	US	40[e]	100	T, O
Lever Brothers	UK	33[e]	334	T
Procter & Gamble	US	10[e]	193	T
Andrew Jergens	US	10	10	T
L'Oréal	France	4	4	H
Pond's	US	3	3	S
California Perfume Company	US	2.9	2.9	C, T, F
Armand[1]	US	2.5	2.5	C
Roger et Gallet	France	2.3	2.3	F, C
Beiersdorf	Germany	2[e]	3.4	S
Elizabeth Arden	US	2	2	S, C
Helena Rubinstein	US	2	2	S, C
Kao [2]	Japan	2	2	T
Bristol-Myers[3]	US	1.5[e]	6.1	T, O
E. R. Squibb[3]	US	1[e]	13.2	F
American Home Products[3]	US	1[e]	11.9	O
Shiseido	Japan	0.9	0.9	S, C

[e]Estimated.
C = color cosmetics; F = fragrances; H = hair care; O = oral hygiene; S = skin care; T = toiletries including bath and body and shaving cream.

[1]1927.
[2]1930.
[3]1928.

2.2 The World's 30 Largest Beauty Companies in 1950 ($m)

Firm	Nationality	Beauty revenues	Total revenues	International revenues (%)	Main product categories
Colgate-Palmolive	US	58[e]	312	32	T, O
Unilever	UK/Neth	48	2,240	80	T, O, H, C
Avon	US	31	31	6	C, T, F
Shulton	US	23	25	-	T
Pond's[1]	US	22	22	40	S
Coty[2]	US	21	21	12	F, C
Revlon	US	19	19	10	C
Andrew Jergens[3]	US	17	17	-	T, C
Johnson & Johnson	US	16	162	-	T, BC
Gillette	US	16[e]	99	20[e]	H, T
Max Factor[4]	US	15	15	25[e]	C
Bristol-Myers	US	13	52	10	T, O, H
Helena Rubinstein	US	13	13	-	S, C
Procter & Gamble	US	13	633	15[e]	T
Lehn & Fink	US	12	16	8	O, T
Elizabeth Arden	US	12	12	-	S, C
L'Oréal	France	11	11	10	H, T
Chesebrough	US	11	11	-	S
Beecham	UK	11[5]	47	42	O, H
Helene Curtis	US	9	10	-	H
Warner-Hudnut	US	9[e]	47	43	C
Charles of the Ritz	US	6	6	-	F, C
Noxzema Chemical	US	6	6	-	S
Lambert	US	6[e]	25	9	T, O
Northam Warren[6]	US	6[e]	6[e]	-	T, C
Yardley	UK	5	5	-	F, T. C
Bourjois[7]	France	4[e]	4[e]	-	F, C
Nestlé-LeMur[8]	US	4	4	-	C, H
Shiseido	Japan	3	3	0	C, T
Vick Chemical	US	3	43	10[e]	C, T
Wella	Germany	3	3	2	H
Beiersdorf[4]	Germany	3	7	-	S, O
Kao Soap	Japan	3	3	-	T

[e]Estimated.

BC = baby care; C = color cosmetics; F = fragrances; H = hair care; O = oral hygiene; S = skin care; T = toiletries including bath and body and shaving cream.

[1]1948.
[2]Combined sales of Coty Inc. and Coty International, which were then separate companies. Coty Inc. sales were $18 million in 1950. Coty International sales were $4.7 million in 1956; assuming a 10 per cent per annum growth rate between 1950 and 1956, sales were $2.6 million in 1950.
[3]Andrew Jergens revenues were $29.5 million in 1956; estimate for 1950 assumes a 10 per cent per annum growth rate.
[4] 1949.
[5]Sales are for Britain only; there were significant sales in the US.
[6]Estimate based on sales of $3 million in 1941 and $10 million in 1960.
[7]Bourjois sales were $8 million in 1956; estimate for 1950 assumes a 10 per cent per annum growth rate.
[8]1953.

2.3 The World's 30 Largest Beauty Companies in 1977 ($m)

	Nationality	Beauty revenues	Total revenues	International revenues (%)	Main product categories
Avon	US	1,356	1,648	41	C, S, T, F
Colgate-Palmolive	US	1,300[e]	3,875	55	T, O, C, S
Shiseido	Japan	870	916	5	S, C, T
Revlon	US	810	1,143	28	S, C, S
L'Oréal	France	803	923	53	H, S, C, F, T
Bristol-Myers	US	749	2,233	31	O, H, T
Unilever	UK/Neths	665	16,007	71	T, H, O, C
Procter & Gamble	US	630	7,284	27	T, O, H
Chesebrough-Pond's	US	492	808	28	S, C, F
Wella	Germany	432	543	78	H
Johnson & Johnson	US	416[e1]	2,914	41	C, T, BC
Gillette	US	413	1,587	55	T, S, C
Schwarzkopf	Germany	379	379	36	H
Norton Simon	US	352	1,808	17	C, F
American Cyanamid	US	321	2,413	33	H, F
Sanofi	France	316[2]	691[3]	-	S, C, T
Lion	Japan	260	636	-	O, T, H
Kao	Japan	230[e]	698	-	T, H, S
Beecham	UK	230[e4]	1,261	68	T, C, S
Beiersdorf	Germany	230	571	50	S, T
Fabergé	US	228	233	24	F, C
Kanebo	Japan	219	1,345	15	C, T
Pfizer	US	200[5]	2,032	63	F, C, T
Estée Lauder	US	200	200	-	S, F, C
Hoechst	Germany	200[e]	10,038	-	C, S, F
Moët-Hennessy	France	188[6]	-	-	F, C
BAT	UK	184	10,871	86	F, C, S
Henkel	Germany	163	2,593	51	H, T, S, F
Pamerco (including Chanel, Bourjois)	France	160[e7]	160[e7]	-	F, C, S
Eli Lilly	US	152[8]	1,550[8]	28	F, C, S

[e]Estimated.

BC = baby care; C = color cosmetics; F = fragrances; H = hair care; O = oral hygiene; S = skin care; T = toiletries including bath and body and shaving cream.

[1]Johnson & Johnson consumer segmented had sales of $1,268 million, which included baby care, feminine hygiene, toiletries, first aid, and drugs.
[2]1980.
[3]1979.
[4]Consumer Products sales were $772 million, of which an estimated 30% were personal care.
[5]Personal Care Division sales of $227 million included not only Coty but dietary foods and plant care.
[6]1980.
[7]1980.
[8]1978.

2.4 The World's 30 Largest Beauty Companies in 1989 ($m)

	Nationality	Beauty revenues	Total revenues	International revenues (%)	Main product categories
Unilever	UK/Neth	3,699	34,434	85[e]	T, H, O, S, C, F
L'Oréal[1]	France	3,698	4,259	63	H, F, S, C, T
Shiseido[2]	Japan	2,758	3,147	8	S, C, F, H, T
Revlon	US	2,445	2,942	33	C, F, S
Procter & Gamble	US	2,300[e]	21,398	38	T, H, C
Avon	US	2,200	3,300	52	C, F, S, H
Johnson & Johnson	US	2,000[e3]	9,757	50	H, T, BC
Pola	Japan	1,800[e]	2,000	2[e]	S, T, H, C
Colgate-Palmolive	US	1,900	5,039	64	O, T, S
Estée Lauder	US	1,700	1,700	45[e]	S, C, F, H
Beecham	UK	1,500[e]	4,415	82	T, O, C, S, F
Kao	Japan	1,280	4,144	-	T, S, H
Bristol Myers Squibb	US	1,300[e]	9,189	30	H, T
Wella	Germany	1,126	1,281	74	H, F, S
Sanofi	France	1,157[4]	2,695	58	F, S, C
Gillette	US	1,036	3,819	65	T, S, O, C, H
Kanebo	Japan	971	3,635	5	S, T, H
Beiersdorf	Germany	836	2,016	62	S, T, C
LVMH	France	700	3,077	81[5]	C, S, F
Lion	Japan	716[e6]	2,182	-	O, S, T, H
Helene Curtis	US	736	736	21	H, T
Chanel	Switzerland	705	705	-	F, C, S
American Cyanamid	US	610	4,825	39	T, F
Muehlens	Germany	500[e]	500[e]	-	F, T, H, S
Schwarzkopf	Germany	499	499	52	H
Schering-Plough	US	450[e7]	3,158	37	C
Henkel	Germany	436	6,188	73	H, T, S, O, F
Pfizer	US	400[e8]	5,672	45	C, F, T
Mary Kay	US	400	450	-	C, S
Yves Saint Laurent Beauté	France	399	479	82	F, C, S

[e]Estimated.
BC = baby care; C = color cosmetics; F = fragrances; H = hair care; O = oral hygiene; S = skin care; T = toiletries including bath and body and shaving cream.
[1]Figures do not include the sales for Cosmair in the United States ($1.2 billion revenues in 1992).
[2]April 1989–March 1990.
[3]Estimated as half of consumer segment sales of $3.9 billion.
[4]Includes sales of Sanofi Beauté and the associated companies Yves Rocher and Nina Ricci.
[5]1990.
[6]"Beauty and Healthcare" sales, including beauty products, tooth brushes, and feminine care, was $795 million.
[7]Toiletries sales calculated as one-third of proprietary and toiletries product sales ($468 million) and added to cosmetics sales ($297 million).
[8]Calculated as two-thirds of total consumer products sales (consumer segment consists of consumer health care, Coty, and oral care segments).

2.5 The World's 30 Largest Beauty Companies in 2008 ($bn)

	Nationality	Beauty revenues	Total corporate revenues	Revenues outside home region (%)	Main product categories
Procter & Gamble	US	26,000[e1]	83,503	56	H, T, O, C, S, F
L'Oréal	France	24,089	25,831	55	H, F, S, C, BC
Unilever	UK/Neth	16,762	59,672	68	T, H, O, S, C
Colgate-Palmolive	US	9,658	15,330	81	O,T, BC
Estée Lauder	US	7,911	7,911	59	S, C, F, H
Avon	US	7,604	10,690	77	S, C, F, H, T, BC
Beiersdorf	Germany	7,547	8,793	31[2]	S, T, C, H, O, F, BC
Johnson & Johnson	US	7,200	63,747	49	BC, H, T, S, O
Shiseido	Japan	7,011	7,220	20	S, F, C, T, H
Kao	Japan	6,267	13,160	15	T, S, H, C
Henkel	Germany	4,441	20,808	46	H, T, S, O
Chanel	Switzerland	4,430	4,430	-	F, C, S
LVMH	France	4,223	25,317	62[2]	F, C, S
Coty	US	4,000	4,000	68	F, C, S, T
Alliance Boots	Switzerland	3,084	30,750[3]	-	S, C, T, O, F, H
Natura	Brazil	2,680	2,680	6	S, T, C, F, H, BC
Mary Kay	US	2,600	2,600	39[4]	S, C, F, T
Yves Rocher	France	2,340	2,987	23	S, C, F, T
Limited Brands	US	2,060	9,043	7	F, T, C
Amway	US	1,900	7,100[4]	80	C, S, T, H
AmorePacific	Korea	1,840	1,840	45	S, T, F, C, H, O
Oriflame	Sweden	1,761	1,957	92[5]	S, C, T, F
Kosé	Japan	1,719	1,743	-	S, H, T, C, F
Puig Beauty & Fashion Group	Spain	1,520	1,520	29[6]	F, T, S, C
Clarins	France	1,400	1,400	44	S, C, T, F
Alberto-Culver	US	1,359	1,443	40	H, S, T
Revlon	US	1,347	1,347	42	S, C, F, H
Elizabeth Arden	US	1,340	1,340	40	S, F, C
Pierre Fabre	France	1,260	2,577	47[7]	S, T, H, O, C
GlaxoSmithKline	UK	1,080[8]	36,528	66[2]	O

[e]Estimated.
BC = baby care; C = color cosmetics; F = fragrances; H = hair care; O = oral hygiene; S = skin care; T = toiletries including bath and body and shaving cream.

[1]Procter & Gamble breaks down revenues by global segment. Beauty was $19,515m. In addition, face and shave products are included in the grooming total of $8,254m, and oral hygiene is included in the health care total of $14,478m. GMID ranks firms by retail value of global brands. By this ranking, P & G is given as $42bn, L'Oréal $34.8bn, and Unilever $23.7bn.
[2]2008, proportion of total sales outside of Europe (including Eastern Europe).
[3]April 2008–March 2009.
[4]2007.
[5]Proportion of sales outside Western Europe and Africa.
[6]2007, proportion of sales outside Europe (including Eastern Europe).
[7] 2007, proportion of sales outside France.
[8]Beauty sales estimated as 60 per cent; of oral healthcare sales.

Sources: company annual reports; 10Ks; company histories; Global Market Information Database (GMID); *Women's Wear Daily*; Orbis. Foreign currencies are converted to $US at the exchange rate prevailing in that year.

Appendix 3

Principal Mergers, Acquisitions, and Divestments in the Beauty Industry since 1955

Date	Acquirer	Acquired	Price ($m)	Divested
1955	Chesebrough	Pond's	n.a.	acquired 1987
1959	Bristol-Myers	Clairol	22.5	2000
1963	Pfizer	Coty	18.6	1992
1963	American Cyanamid	Breck	19.6	1990
1965	L'Oréal	Lancôme	-	c.
1966	Sterling Drug	Lehn & Fink	66	1988
1967	Plough	Maybelline	102	1989
1967	Beecham	Lancaster	8	1990
1967	BAT	Yardley	80	1984
1970	American Cyanamid	Shulton	100	1990
1970	Eli Lilly	Elizabeth Arden	37	1987
1970	American Brands	Andrew Jergens	107	1988
1971	ITT	Rimmel	23	1978
1971	Squibb	Charles of the Ritz	210	1986
1973	Norton Simon	Max Factor	480	1983
1974	Colgate-Palmolive	Helena Rubinstein	219	1980
1980	Schering-Plough	Rimmel	-	1989
1979	Beecham	Jovan	85	1990
1984	Beecham	British American Cosmetics	168	1990
1985	Procter & Gamble	Richardson-Vicks	1,240	c.
1987	Unilever	Chesebrough-Pond's	3,100	c.
1986	Yves Saint Laurent	Charles of the Ritz	630	acquired 1987
1987	Fabergé	Elizabeth Arden	700	1989
1987	Moët-Hennessy	Louis Vuitton	n.a.	c.
1987	Revlon	Yves Saint Laurent	150	1993
1987	Revlon	Max Factor	300	1991
1988	Kao	Andrew Jergens	300	c.
1989	Unilever	Rimmel/Chicogo	120	1996
1989	Unilever	Calvin Klein	376	2005
1989	Unilever	Fabergé/Elizabeth Arden	1,663	2001
1989	Procter & Gamble	Noxell	1,300	c.

1989	Procter & Gamble	Shulton	330	c.
1991	Procter & Gamble	Max Factor/Betrix	1,140	c.
1990	Wasserstein Perella	Maybelline	300	1996
1990	Wasserstein Perella	Yardley Lenthéric	196	1998
1990	Benckiser	Astor Lancaster	355	1996[1]
1992	Benckiser	Coty	440	1996[1]
1992	Colgate-Palmolive	Mennen	670	c.
1993	L'Oréal	Redken	200[e]	c.
1993	Sanofi	Yves Saint Laurent	636	1999
1994	Bristol-Myers Squibb	Matrix	400[e]	2000
1994	LVMH	Guerlain	356[2]	c.
1995	Henkel	Schwarzkopf	700[e]	c
1996	Benckiser	Rimmel	-	1996[1]
1996	L'Oréal	Maybelline	508	c.
1996	Unilever	Helene Curtis	915	c.
1996	LVMH	DFS	-	c.
1997	Hindustan Lever	Lakme[3]	-	c.
1997	Estée Lauder	Aveda	300	c.
1998	L'Oréal	Soft Sheen	120	c.
1999	Gucci Group	Sanofi Beauté[4]	952	2008
2000	L'Oréal	Matrix	500[e]	c.
2000	L'Oréal	Shu Uemura[5]	-	c.
2001	FFI Fragrances	Elizabeth Arden	225	c.
2001	Procter & Gamble	Clairol	4,950	c.
2003	Procter & Gamble	Wella	5,100	c.
2004	Henkel	Dial	2,900	c.
2005	Procter & Gamble	Gillette	55,000	c.
2005	Coty	Calvin Klein	800	c.
2005	Kao	Molton Brown	298	c.
2006	L'Oréal	The Body Shop	1,100	c.
2006	Kao	Kanebo	3,700	c.
2006	Boots	Alliance UniChem	n.a.	c.
2007	Beiersdorf	C-Bons[6]	3,000	c.
2008	Johnson & Johnson	Beijing Dabao	300[e]	c.
2007	Coty	DLI	800	c.
2008	L'Oréal	YSL Beauté	1,680	c.
2009	Unilever	TIGI	411	c.
2009	Procter & Gamble	Zirh	-	c.

c. = continues.
[e]Estimated.

[1]In 1996 these were placed in a new company, Coty, which was spun off from Benckiser.
[2]The price paid for 51.2 per cent of the family company which owned 85.8 per cent of Guerlain. LVMH had acquired the remainder of Guerlain in 1987.
[3]50 per cent of Lakmé was acquired from Tata. In 1998 the remaining 50 per cent was acquired for $76m.
[4]Sanofi Beauté included Yves Saint Laurent beauty brands, and was renamed YSL Beauté at the time of acquisition by the Gucci Group.
[5]L'Oréal acquired 35 per cent at this time, and majority control three years later.
[6]Beiersdorf acquired 85 per cent of C-Bons.

Bibliography

Primary sources

This book draws extensively on the historical archives of companies involved in the beauty industry which are held both in public repositories and by the companies themselves. In the United States, the Hagley Museum and Library, Wilmington, Delaware, holds the historical records of Avon (AVON); the Thomas J. Dodd Research Center, University of Connecticut Archives, Storrs, houses the archives of J. B. Williams (UConn); the John W. Hartman Center for Sales, Advertising and Marketing History, Duke University, Durham, North Carolina, holds the J. Walter Thompson Archives (JWT); and the Tobacco Control Archives, University of California, San Francisco, holds records on British American Tobacco and its beauty affiliates. The Baker Library at the Harvard Business School contains an extensive collection of trade cards and other advertising ephemera related to the beauty industry. The Schlesinger Library, Radcliffe Institute, Harvard University, holds the Hazel Bishop Papers.

In Germany, the archives of J. G. Mouson & Co. are held at the Institut für Stadtgeschichte, Karmeliterkloster, Frankfurt; the records of Muehlens are held at the Rheinisch Westfälisches Wirtschafts Archiv (RWWA), Cologne; the records of Hoechst are held at HistoCom Industriepark Höchst, Frankfurt. In Britain, the History of Advertising Trust, Norwich, holds the archives of both J. Walter Thompson and Ogilvy & Mather (HAT); the National Archives, Kew, holds archives concerning the British government's relations with the beauty industry. In Sweden, the Centre for Business History/Centrum för Näringslivshistoria, Stockholm, holds the records of Barnängens Tekniska Fabrikers AB, as well as the firm data sheets collected by Erik Dahmén between 1919 and 1946 (CfN). In France, the Centre des archives économiques et financières (CAEF), Savigny-le-Temple, holds the archives of the French ministry of finance and the state treasury. The Chambre de commerce et d'industrie de Paris (CCIP), in Paris, holds the archived cases of the Centre de perfectionnement aux affaires (CPA).

A number of archival collections retained by companies were consulted. In the United States, P & G Corporate Archives, Cincinnati, Ohio, holds the historical archives of P & G and many of the companies it has acquired, including Clairol, Max Factor, and Noxell (P & G). The archives of Gillette in Boston were also consulted. The Coty Archive, New York, provided historical information and photographs. In France, the L'Oréal archives were consulted for internal documents, newsletters, and photographic collections. The archives of Crédit Lyonnais contain extensive historical information on the French beauty industry (CL). In Germany, the historical archives of Wella, Darmstadt, Henkel, Düsseldorf, and Beiersdorf, Hamburg, were consulted. The Unilever Archives in London and Port Sunlight, in Britain, and Rotterdam, in the Netherlands, was used for a previous study by the author, and they contain valuable historical information about the beauty industry.

Extensive use was made of the leading trade journals in the industry. The most important journal is *Women's Wear Daily*, which was surveyed between 1930 and the present. In addition, the following trade journals and newspapers were consulted: *Advertising Age, Cosmetics and Perfumery, Cosmetic World, Drug and Cosmetic Industry, Drug Markets, Drug Store News, The Economist, Financial Times, Frankfurter Allgemeine Zeitung, Global Cosmetic Industry, Handelsblatt, New York Times, Printers' Ink, Product Management, Sales Management, Soap and Chemical Specialties*, and the *Wall Street Journal*. For the contemporary period, the website of Cosmetics Design Europe, <www.cosmeticsdesign-europe.com>, was a valuable source of news and data.

Interviews were conducted between 2004 and 2009 with practitioners in the industry. These provided invaluable background information for this book and related Harvard Business School cases. The list of interviewees is too lengthy to give in full, but special acknowledgement is due to Jean-Paul Agon, Bernd Beetz, Alessandro Carlucci, Philip Clough, Antonio Luiz da Cunha Seabra, Béatrice Dautresme, Carsten Fischer, Patricia Frydman-Maarek, Yoshihara Fukuhara, Jean-François Grollier, Peter Harf, Robert af Jochnick, George Korres, Lena Philippou Korres, Géraud-Marie Lacassagne, Guilherme Leal, Celeste Lee, Marc Menesguen, Eric Morgan, Steve Mormoris, Jean Mortier, Youçef Nabi, Lindsay Owen-Jones, Pedro Passos, Ketan Patel, Patricia Pineau, Patrick Rabain, Nicolas Rosselli, Odile Roujol, Tadakatsu Saito, Michele Scannavini, Hans Peter Schwarzkopf, Lori Singer, Geoff Skingsley, Satoshi Suzuki, the late Shu Uemura, Emma Walmsley, and Catherine Walsh.

Select secondary sources
This list contains the most important secondary sources used in this book. The notes for individual chapters contain full references.

Abescat, Bruno, *La Saga des Bettencourt* (Paris: Plon, 2002).

—— and Stavridès, Yves, "Derrière l'empire Chanel . . . La fabuleuse histoire des Wertheimer," *L'Express*, April 7–August 8, 2005, <www.lexpress.fr/actualite/economie/la-fabuleuse-histoire-des-wertheimer_485301.html>, accessed October 14, 2009.

Allen, Margaret, *Selling Dreams* (New York: Simon and Schuster, 1981).

Angeloglou, Maggie, *A History of Make-up* (New York: Macmillan, 1970).

Arnault, Bernard, *La passion créative: Entretiens avec Yves Messarovitch* (Paris: Plon, 2000).

Ashenburg, Katherine, *The Dirt on Clean: An Unsanitized History* (New York: North Point Press, 2007).

Ashikari, Mikiko, "The Memory of the Women's White Faces: Japaneseness and the Ideal Image of Women," *Japan Forum* 15 (2003), pp. 55–79.

Banet-Weiser, Sarah, *The Most Beautiful Girl in the World* (Berkeley: University of California Press, 1999).

Banner, Lois W., *American Beauty* (Chicago: University of Chicago Press, 1983).

Barille, Elizabeth, and Tahara, Keiichi, *Coty: Parfumeur and Visionary* (Paris: Éditions Assouline, 1995).

Basten, Fred E., *Max Factor: The Man Who Changed the Faces of the World* (New York: Arcade, 2008).

Beiersdorf AG, *100 Jahre Beiersdorf, 1882–1982* (Hamburg: Beiersdorf AG, 1982).

—— *Nivea: Evolution of a World-famous Brand* (Hamburg: Beiersdorf AG, 2001).

Bergeron, Louis, *Les industries du luxe en France* (Paris: Éditions Odile Jacob, 1998).

Blaszczyk, Regina Lee, *American Consumer Society 1865–2005* (Wheeling, Ill.: Harlan Davidson, 2009).

—— *Imagining Consumers: Design and Innovation from Wedgwood to Corning* (Baltimore: Johns Hopkins University Press, 2000).

—— (ed.), *Producing Fashion: Commerce, Culture and Consumers* (Philadelphia: University of Pennsylvania Press, 2009).

Briot, Eugénie, "La chimie des élégances: La parfumerie parisienne au XIXe siècle, naissance d'une industrie du luxe," unpubl. doctoral diss., Conservatoire National des Arts et Métiers, Centre d'Histoire des Techniques et de l'Environnement, 2008.

Burke, Timothy, *Lifebuoy Men, Lux Women* (Durham, NC: Duke University Press, 1996).

Burr, Chandler, *The Perfect Scent: A Year Inside the Perfume Industry in Paris and New York* (New York: Henry Holt and Company, 2008).

Bushman, Richard L., and Bushman, Claudia L., "The Early History of Cleanliness in America," *Journal of American History* 74 (1988), pp. 1213–38.

Caldwell, Helen Marie, "The Development and Democratization of the American Perfume Market 1920–1975," unpubl. doctoral diss., University of Connecticut, 1995.

Chessel, Marie-Emmanuelle, "Une méthode publicitaire américaine? Cadum dans la France de l'entre-deux-guerres," *Entreprises et Histoire* 11 (1996), pp. 61–76.

Classen, Constance, Howes, David, and Synnott, Anthony, *Aroma: The Cultural History of Smell* (New York: Routledge, 1994).

Colard, Grégoire, *Le charme secret d'une maison parfumée* (Paris: Éditions J. C. Lattès, 1984).

Corbin, Alain, *The Foul and the Fragrant: Odor and the French Social Imagination* (Cambridge, Mass.: Harvard University Press, 1986).

Corson, Richard, *Fashions in Makeup, From Ancient to Modern Times* (London: Peter Owen, 2003).

Courtin, Jacques, *Une réussite en beauté* (Paris: J. C. Lattès, 2006).

Cox, Caroline, *Good Hair Days: A History of British Hairstyling* (London: Quartet, 1999).

Dade, Penny, *All Made Up: 100 Years of Cosmetics Advertising* (London: Middlesex University Press, 2007).

Dalle, François, *L'aventure L'Oréal* (Paris: Éditions Odile Jacob, 2001).

DeJean, Joan, *The Essence of Style: How the French Invented High Fashion, Fine Food, Chic Cafes, Style, Sophistication and Glamour* (New York: Free Press, 2005).

Dyer, Davis, Dalzell, Frederick, and Olegario, Rowena, *Rising Tide: Lessons from 165 Years of Brand Building at Procter & Gamble* (Boston, Mass.: Harvard Business School Press, 2004).

Estrin, Norman F. (ed.), *The Cosmetic Industry: Scientific and Regulatory Foundations* (New York: Marcel Dekker, 1984).

Etcoff, Nancy, *Survival of the Prettiest* (New York: Anchor Books, 2000).

Feldenkirchen, Wilfried, and Hilger, Susanne, *Menschen und Marken: 125 Jahre Henkel 1876–2001* (Düsseldorf: Henkel KGaA, 2001).

Feydeau, Elisabeth de, "De l'hygiène au rêve: L'industrie française du parfum (1830–1939)," unpubl. doctoral diss., University of Lille, 1997.

Foreman-Peck, James, *Smith & Nephew in the Health Care Industry* (Aldershot: Edward Elgar, 1995).

Gill, Tiffany M., "Civic Beauty: Beauty Culturists and the Politics of African-American Female Entrepreneurship, 1900–1965," *Enterprise & Society* 5 (2004), pp. 583–93.

Grazia, Victoria de, *Irresistible Empire: America's Advance through Twentieth-century Europe* (Cambridge, Mass.: Harvard University Press, 2005).

Guenther, Irene, *Nazi Chic? Fashioning Women in the Third Reich* (Oxford: Berg, 2004).

Gundle, Stephen, *Glamour: A History* (Oxford: Oxford University Press, 2008).

Gunn, Fenja, *The Artificial Face: A History of Cosmetics* (New York: Hippocene Books, 1973).

Hamermesh, Daniel S., and Biddle, Jeff E., "Beauty and the Labor Market," *American Economic Review* 84 (1994), pp. 1174–94.

Herz, Rachel, *The Scent of Desire* (New York: William Morrow, 2007).

Hilger, Susanne, "Reluctant Americanization? The Reaction of Henkel to the Influences and Competition from the United States," in Akira Kudo, Matthias Kipping, and Harm G. Schröter (eds), *German and Japanese Business in the Boom Years* (London: Routledge, 2004).

Högberg, Arne, *Skönhetens entreprenör: Knut Wulff berättar om sitt liv* (Malmö: Corona Förlag, 2004).

Houy, Yvonne Barbara, " 'Of Course the German Woman Should be Modern': The Modernization of Women's Appearance during National Socialism," unpubl. doctoral diss., Cornell University, 2002.

Hoy, Suellen, *Chasing Dirt: The American Pursuit of Cleanliness* (New York and Oxford: Oxford University Press, 1995).

Israel, Lee, *Estée Lauder: Beyond the Magic* (New York: Macmillan, 1985).

Jones, Geoffrey, "Blonde and Blue-eyed? Globalizing Beauty, c.1945-c.1980," *Economic History Review* 61 (2008), pp. 125–54.

—— *Renewing Unilever: Transformation and Tradition* (Oxford: Oxford University Press, 2005).

—— Kanno, Akiko, and Egawa, Masako, "Making China Beautiful: Shiseido and the China Market," Harvard Business School Case no. 9-805-003 (July 3, 2008).

—— and Kiron, David, "Bernd Beetz: Creating the New Coty," Harvard Business School Case no. 9-808-133 (December 8, 2008).

—— ——Dessain, Vincent, and Sjöman, Anders, "L'Oréal and the Globalization of American Beauty," Harvard Business School Case no. 9-805-086 (February 2, 2006).

—— and Reisen de Pinho, Ricardo, "Natura: Global Beauty Made in Brazil," Harvard Business School Case, no. 9-807-029 (August 29, 2007).

Kapferer, J. N., and Bastien, V., *The Luxury Strategy* (London: Kogan Page, 2009).

Kaum, Ekkehard, *Oscar Troplowitz: Forscher, Unternehmer, Bürger* (Hamburg: Verlag Günther Wesche, 1982).

Koehn, Nancy F., *Brand New* (Boston, Mass.: Harvard Business School Press, 2001).

Körner, Erich, *Zauber der Frisur: 5000 Jahre Haarkosmetik und Mode* (Darmstadt: Wella AG, 1964).

Kruse, Hellmut, *Wagen und Winnen: Ein hanseatisches Kaufmannsleben im 20. Jahrhundert* (Hamburg: Die Hanse, 2006).

Lafley, A. G., and Charan, Ram, *The Game Changer: How You Can Drive Revenue and Profit Growth with Innovation* (New York: Crown Business, 2008).

Laird, Pamela Walker, *Advertising Progress: American Business and the Rise of Consumer Marketing* (Baltimore: Johns Hopkins University Press, 1998).

Lanoë, Catherine, *La poudre et le fard: Une histoire des cosmétiques de la renaissance aux lumières* (Seyssel, France: Éditions Champ Vallon, 2008).

Lauder, Estée, *Estée: A Success Story* (New York: Random House, 1985).

Lavin, Leonard H., *Winners Make It Happen: Reflections of a Self-Made Man* (Chicago: Bonus Books, 2003).

Le Guérer, Annick, *Le Parfum: Des origines à nos jours* (Paris: Éditions Odile Jacob, 2005).

Manko, Katina Lee, "A Depression-proof Business Strategy: The Californian Perfume Company's Motivational Literature," in Philip Scranton (ed.), *Beauty and Business* (New York: Routledge, 2001), pp. 142–68.

—— "'Ding Dong! Avon Calling!': Gender, Business and Door-to-Door Selling, 1890–1955," unpubl. doctoral diss., University of Delaware, 2001.

Martin, Morag Sarah, "Consuming Beauty: The Commerce of Cosmetics in France 1750–1800," unpubl. doctoral diss., University of California, Irvine, 1999.

Martin-Hattemberg, Jean-Marie, *Caron* (Toulouse: Éditions Milan, 2000).

McClintock, Anne, *Imperial Leather: Race, Gender and Sexuality in the Colonial Context* (New York: Routledge, 1995).

McKibben, Gordon, *Cutting Edge: Gillette's Journey to Global Leadership* (Boston, Mass.: Harvard Business School Press, 1998).

Miskell, Peter, "Cavity Protection or Cosmetic Perfection? Innovation and Marketing of Toothpaste Brands in the United States and Western Europe, 1955–1989," *Business History Review* 78 (2004), pp. 29–60.

Modern Girl around the World Research Group, The (eds), *The Modern Girl around the World: Consumption, Modernity, and Globalization* (Durham, NC: Duke University Press, 2008).

Morris, Edwin T., *Fragrance: The Story of Perfume from Cleopatra to Chanel* (New York: Charles Scribner, 1984).

Mulvey, Kate, and Richards, Melissa, *Decades of Beauty: The Changing Image of Women 1890s–1990s* (New York: Octopus, 1998).

Oh, Chang Hoon, and Rugman, Alan M., "Regional Sales of Multinationals in the World Cosmetics Industry," *European Management Journal* 24 (2006), pp. 163–73.

Pallingston, Jessica, *Lipstick: A Celebration of the World's Favorite Cosmetic* (New York: St. Martin's Press, 1999).

Peiss, Kathy, "Educating the Eye of the Beholder: American Cosmetics Abroad," *Daedalus* 131 (Fall 2002), pp. 101–9.

—— *Hope in a Jar* (New York: Henry Holt, 1998).

Perlmutter, Dawn, "Miss America: Whose Ideal?," in Peg Zeglin Brand (ed.), *Beauty Matters* (Bloomington: Indiana University Press, 2000), pp. 155–68.

Poiger, Uta G., "Beauty, Business and German International Relations," *Werkstatt-Geschichte* 16: 45 (2007), pp. 53–71.

Puig, Núria, "The Search for Identity: Spanish Perfume in the International Market," *Business History* 45 (2003), pp. 90–118.

Reichert, Tom, *The Erotic History of Advertising* (New York: Prometheus, 2003).

Rimmel, Eugène, *The Book of Perfumes* (London: Chapman & Hall, 1865; repr. Chestnut Hill, Mass.: Elibron Classics, 2004).

Roddick, Anita, *Body and Soul. Profits with Principles: The Amazing Success Story of Anita Roddick and The Body Shop* (New York: Crown Publishers, 1991).

—— *Business as Unusual* (Chichester: Anita Roddick Books, 2005).

Rubinfien, Louisa Daria, "Commodity to National Brand: Manufacturers, Merchants, and the Development of the Consumer Market in Interwar Japan," unpubl. doctoral diss., Harvard University, 1995.

Schröter, Harm, "Erfolgsfaktor Marketing: Der Strukturwandel von der Reklame zur Unternehmenssteuerung," in Wilfried Feldenkirchen, Frauke Schönert-Röhlk, and Günther Schulz (eds), *Wirtschaft, Gesellschaft, Unternehmen: Festschrift für Hans Pohl zum 60. Geburtstag*, vol. 2 (Stuttgart: Franz Steiner Verlag, 1995), pp. 1099–127.

Scott, Linda, *Fresh Lipstick: Redressing Fashion and Feminism* (New York: Palgrave Macmillan, 2005).

Segrave, Kerry, *Sun Tanning in 20th Century America* (Jefferson, NC: McFarland, 2005).

Sicard-Picchiottino, Ghislaine, *François Coty: Un industriel corse sous la IIIe République* (Ajaccio: Albiana, 2006).

Sivulka, Juliann, *Stronger than Dirt* (New York: Humanity Books, 2001).

Söderberg, Johan, "Controversial Consumption in Sweden, 1914–1945," *Scandinavian Economic History Review* 48:3 (2000), pp. 5–21.

—— *Röda Lappar och shinglat hår: Konsumtionen av kosmetika i Sverige, 1900–1960* (Stockholm: Ekonomisk-historiska institutionen, 2001).

Stamelman, Richard, *Perfume: Joy, Obsession, Scandal, Sin. A Cultural History of Fragrance from 1750 to the Present* (New York: Rizzoli, 2006).

Stevenson, Karen, "Hairy Business: Organizing the Gendered Self," in Ruth Holliday and John Hassard (eds), *Contested Bodies* (London and New York: Routledge, 2001), pp. 137–52.

Stranger, Howard R., "From Factory to Family: The Creation of a Corporate Culture in the Larkin Company of Buffalo, New York," *Business History Review* 74:3 (Autumn 2000), pp. 407–33.

Strasser, Susan, *Satisfaction Guaranteed: The Making of the American Mass Market* (New York: Pantheon, 1989).

Tedlow, Richard, *Giants of Enterprise: Seven Business Innovators and the Empires They Built* (New York: HarperCollins, 2001).

Thomas, Dana, *Deluxe: How Luxury Lost its Luster* (New York: Penguin, 2007).

Thomas, E. Wynne, *The House of Yardley 1770–1953* (London: Sylvan Press, 1953).

Vail, Gilbert, *A History of Cosmetics in America* (New York: Toilet Goods Association, 1947).

Vigarello, G., *Concepts of Cleanliness: Changing Attitudes in France since the Middle Ages* (Cambridge: Cambridge University Press, 1988).

Vilaithong, Villa, "A Cultural History of Hygiene Advertising in Thailand, 1940s–early 1980s," unpubl. doctoral diss., Australian National University, 2006.

Walker, Juliet E. K., *The History of Black Business in America: Capitalism, Race, Entrepreneurship* (New York: Twayne, 1998).

Walker, Susannah, *Style and Status: Selling Beauty to African American Women, 1920–1975* (Lexington, Ky: University Press of Kentucky, 2007).

Wall, Florence E., "Historical Development of the Cosmetics Industry," in M. S. Balsam and Edward Sagarin (eds), *Cosmetics: Science and Technology*, 2nd edn, vol. 3 (New York: John Wiley, 1974), pp. 37–161.

Willett, Julie A., *Permanent Waves* (New York: New York University Press, 2000).

Williams, Neville, *Powder and Paint: A History of the Englishwoman's Toilet Elizabeth I–Elizabeth II* (Longmans: London, 1957).

Wilson, Charles, *The History of Unilever*, 2 vols (London: Cassell, 1954).

Wolf, Naomi, *The Beauty Myth: How Images of Beauty Are Used Against Women* (New York: Harper Perennial, 1992).

Woodhead, Lindy, *War Paint* (Hoboken, NJ: John Wiley, 2004).

Zdatny, Steve, *Fashion, Work, and Politics in Modern France* (New York: Palgrave Macmillan, 2006).

—— (ed.), *Hairstyles and Fashion* (New York: Berg, 1999).

Zweiniger-Bargielowska, Ina, "The Body and Consumer Culture," in Ina Zweiniger-Bargielowska (ed.), *Women in Twentieth-century Britain* (London: Pearson Educational, 2001), pp. 183–97.

—— "The Culture of the Abdomen: Obesity and Reducing in Britain, circa 1900–1939," *Journal of British Studies* 44:2 (April 2005), pp. 239–73.

Index

The letter n indicates an endnote. Page numbers in *Italics* indicate illustrations.

entrepreneurship (*cont.*)
  brand managers and 308
  cognition 5, 351–2
  color cosmetics 65
  and creativity 19, 187–8, 353, 355, 357
  direct selling 159, 232
  duty-free retail 210
  Europe 98
  female 2, 30, 45, 51–2, 58–60, 103–6, 118, 125, 133, 154, 159, 163–4, 201–2, 261, 283–5, 291, 328, 332, 338, 353, 364
  fragrances 21, 23, 25, 36–7
  France 116–17
  Germany 123
  hairdressing 46, 47, 48, 119, 170
  immigrant 37, 75, 166, 289, 352
  Japan 85, 86, 87, 120–1
  Jewish 32, 36–7, 59, 66
  and legitimacy 65, 89, 353
  and natural beauty 280–6, 333
  "outsider" status 18, 37, 66, 108, 352
  pharmacies 116
  post-war 156
  skin creams 52–3
  Sweden 179, 180–2
  United States 98
environment 279–80, 286, 291, 362
Erace concealer 153
Erdt, Hans Rudi 57–8
eroticism 126–7, 245, 246
    see also advertising: sex and sexual imagery in
Esmark 255
espionage 157
essential oils 15, 16, 17, 20, 21–2, 161, 164, 247, 284

Estée Lauder 165, 206, 256, 293, 294, 316, 317, 321, 330, 332, 333, 334, 338, 370, 371, 372, 374 *see also* Lauder, Estée
ethics 63, 64, 65, 124, 159, 214, 284, 330, 358, 364 *see also* consumer activism; religion
ethnicity 50–1, 99, 111, 179, 225–8, 287–90, 294, 311, 312, 359–63
Eucerit ointment base 57
Eudermine 61
Eugénie, Empress 20, 45
Euphoria Blossom 325
Eve of Roma 259
Evening in Paris 106, 206
exclusivity 25, 310 *see also* brands: luxury
exoticization 22, 27, 36, 37, 126, 189, 201, 330–1, 351, 354 *see also* orientalism
exporting 17, 29, 34, 35, 36–7, 54, 58, 62, 77, 83–4, 88, 114, 122, 124, 126, 127, 128, 134, 135, 136, 161, 162, 201, 203–5, 206, 210, 216, 220, 221, 225, 230, 331, 360
eyes
  cosmetics 153, 154, 186, 221
    eye shadow 64, 65, 102, 103, 189
  eyebrows 7, 60, 61, 65
  eyelashes 335
    mascara 19, 102, 190, 221
  shape 61, 361

FFI Fragrances 374
Fa 259, 261
Fabergé 249, 264, 318, 370, 373
Faberlic 339
face
  creams 1, 54, 58, 60, 100, 112, 185, 190
    "cold creams" 52, 100
  facial paper, powdered 335

toiletries (*cont.*)
China 201
development of 78–80, 88
herbal-based 328
India 225–8
Japan 216, 221–2
male market 113
mass-market 100, 116, 184, 203,
211, 254
Tokyo 61, 87, 121, 185, 187, 188–9,
210, 310
Tomiro, Nagase 88
Tom's of Maine 283
Toni hair-care 154, 259
tooth blackening (Japan) 60, 360
tooth powder 79, 87
toothbrushes 79, 87
toothpaste 100
advertising 111, 160
China 134, 201
German 54–5
Germany 123
India 226
Indonesia 216
Japan 61, 87–8, 260
Latin America 132
markets 79–80, 190, 203, 212, 213, 215
packaging 358
see also under brand names
toxic shock syndrome 280
trade 33–7, 87, 122
fairs 87
journals 9 n2, 117, 118
names 25, 51
organizations 241, 266 n2
tariff barriers 35, 83–4, 106, 107, 109,
122, 132, 138, 201, 211, 215, 319,
323, 326

see also exporting
trademarks 18, 21, 48, 50, 58, 72, 122, 123,
124, 220, 223
transport 88, 357
travel 33, 125, 202, 225, 352
see also retail: travel
tribalization 300, 301, 317, 341
Troplowitz, Oscar 54–5, 55, 57, 61,
123, 179, 351
Tsubaki 308–9, 314
tulle 48
Tüllemoid 48
Tupperware 159
Turkey 6–7, 212, 219
Turnbo Malone, Annie 51–2, 111, 353, 355
Tussey 109
Twiggy 183, 293
Two Gorgeous Girls 62
Tylenol pain reliever 244

USSR *see* Soviet Union
Uemura, Shu 187–8, 315, 352, 354 *see also*
Shu Uemura
Unilever 3, 100, 129, 130, 132, 170, 177,
184, 202–3, 209, 211, 212, 213–14,
222–3, 225, 241, 249, 253, 256,
259, 261, 262, 264, 265, 289, 308,
313, 317–18, 319–20, 322, 323,
326, 334, 354, 356, 369, 370, 371,
373, 374
see also Hindustan Lever
United Africa Company 266 n1
United Drug 116
United Kingdom *see* Britain
United States
expenditure 3
exports 34
fragrances 136, 163–5, 167